Land and Liberalism

Irish land in the 1880s was a site of ideological conflict, with resonances for liberal politics far beyond Ireland itself. The Irish Land War – internationalised partly through the influence of Henry George, the American social reformer and political economist – came at a decisive juncture in Anglo-American political thought and provided many radicals across the North Atlantic with a vision of a more just and morally coherent political economy. Looking at the discourses and practices of these agrarian radicals, alongside developments in liberal political thought, Andrew Phemister shows how they utilised the land question to articulate a natural and universal right to life that highlighted the contradictions between liberty and property. In response to this popular agrarian movement, liberal thinkers discarded many older individualistic assumptions, and their radical democratic implications, in the name of protecting social order, property, and economic progress. *Land and Liberalism* thus vividly demonstrates the centrality of Henry George and the Irish Land War to the transformation of liberal thought.

ANDREW PHEMISTER is a Research Associate at Newcastle University. He has previously held postdoctoral positions in History at NUI Galway, the University of Oxford, and Edinburgh's Institute for Advanced Studies in the Humanities.

Land and Liberalism

Henry George and the Irish Land War

Andrew Phemister

Newcastle University

CAMBRIDGE
UNIVERSITY PRESS

CAMBRIDGE
UNIVERSITY PRESS

Shaftesbury Road, Cambridge CB2 8EA, United Kingdom

One Liberty Plaza, 20th Floor, New York, NY 10006, USA

477 Williamstown Road, Port Melbourne, VIC 3207, Australia

314–321, 3rd Floor, Plot 3, Splendor Forum, Jasola District Centre, New Delhi – 110025, India

103 Penang Road, #05–06/07, Visioncrest Commercial, Singapore 238467

Cambridge University Press is part of Cambridge University Press & Assessment, a department of the University of Cambridge.

We share the University's mission to contribute to society through the pursuit of education, learning and research at the highest international levels of excellence.

www.cambridge.org
Information on this title: www.cambridge.org/9781009202893

DOI: 10.1017/9781009202909

First published 2023

A catalogue record for this publication is available from the British Library.

Library of Congress Cataloging-in-Publication Data
Names: Phemister, Andrew, author.
Title: Land and liberalism : Henry George and the Irish land war / Andrew Phemister.
Description: Cambridge, United Kingdom ; New York, NY : Cambridge University Press, 2023. | Includes bibliographical references and index.
Identifiers: LCCN 2022033776 | ISBN 9781009202893 (hardback) | ISBN 9781009202909 (ebook)
Subjects: LCSH: George, Henry, 1839–1897. | Land tenure – Ireland – History – 19th century. | Land use – Ireland – History – 19th century. | Land reform – Ireland – History – 19th century.
Classification: LCC HD625 .P46 2023 | DDC 333.3/1415–dc23/eng/20220825
LC record available at https://lccn.loc.gov/2022033776

ISBN 978-1-009-20289-3 Hardback

For Sarah,
and Norah,
and Brodie,
and Jamie.

Contents

Acknowledgements

I have been extremely fortunate to have benefited from the support and encouragement of a great many kind, thoughtful, and generous people during the long gestation of this work. Foremost among them is Enda Delaney, who supervised both my undergraduate and doctoral dissertations at Edinburgh. I am deeply grateful for his unstinting assistance and the consistent belief he has shown in my research. Without his scholarly guidance, expertise, and support, this book would not exist. This work is also indebted to the advice and judicious criticism of Ewen Cameron, whose extensive knowledge of the land question shaped its direction. At Cambridge, where I first started working on Henry George and Ireland, I was extremely lucky to learn a great deal from Eugenio Biagini. His scholarship on Victorian liberalism and his generous, collegial intellect were formative influences. Earlier iterations of this research were meticulously and valuably deconstructed by Niall Whelehan, David Silkenat, and David Sim, all of whom provided helpful criticism. Alvin Jackson, Owen Dudley Edwards, and Andrew Newby have also offered sage advice at important junctures. At Edinburgh, I was privileged to have been part of a supportive community of talented young historians of Ireland (and beyond), including Sophie Cooper, Tommy Dolan, Roseanna Doughty, Catherine Bateson, Joe Curran, and Bobbie Nolan. Further afield, friendships and fascinating conversations shared with colleagues have been, as they are for many, among the most enriching aspects of academic life. Time spent with Pete Hession, Cathal Smith, Patrick Doyle, Rose Luminiello, Sean Donnelly, Alison Garden, Maurice Casey, and many others unnamed reliably reenergised an often tired and confused mind. A special thanks must also go to my school history teachers, Stephen Brady and Graeme Wright, for kindling an interest that I've yet to shake off.

This book is the product of several years of research and therefore also of a number of different institutions. The staff and fellows at the University of Edinburgh's Institute for Advanced Studies in the Humanities provided a friendly and stimulating environment for developing some aspects of this work. At Oxford, I found a similarly engaging atmosphere at Hertford College, and I am indebted to both Ian McBride and Marc Mulholland for their help and support. In Galway, although my time was constrained by the exigencies of the pandemic, I was very fortunate to encounter Dan Carey and John Cunningham, both of whom were extremely hospitable and charitable with their time, energy, and expertise. The research was made possible by various funders, including the School of History, Classics and Archaeology at the University of Edinburgh; the British Association for Irish Studies; the Royal Historical Society; Edinburgh's Institute for Advanced Studies in the Humanities; the Irish government; and the Irish Research Council. I am grateful to my editor, Liz Friend-Smith, for her guidance and patience and also to the librarians and archivists at all the institutions and repositories I visited, especially at the Archives of the Catholic University of America and the Archives of the Archdiocese of New York, for their invaluable assistance.

Academia can be a precarious pursuit, and in that regard, none of this would have been possible without the love, support, and reassurance of my family. My mum, a dedicated and brilliant professor of philosophy, raised me on her own and has been a constant source of encouragement. Whatever talent and insight I can bring to the study of history, I owe to her Socratic parenting. With resolute support, my dad has provided perspective and the wisdom to recognise the importance of other things in life. Finally, and most importantly, I am grateful to my wife Sarah, whose sharp intellect, kindness, and humour have inspired and sustained me throughout, and our children, Norah, Brodie, and Jamie. Their infectious enthusiasm and endless curiosity have taught me far more than I could ever hope to learn by reading books.

Introduction

'The old *laissez-faire* Liberalism is dead', declared the progressive liberal thinker J. A. Hobson in 1909. 'Its early demise', he continued, 'might indeed have been predicted from the time when Cobden recognised the necessity of "freeing" the land'.[1] Attempts to 'free the land', Hobson observed, had involved public control and interventions that brought 'in its wake a long series of further enlargements of State activity'.[2] By the early twentieth century, from Hobson's elevated vantage point, the debates over the land question that had dominated the 1880s were simply the stirrings of a more expansive social liberalism. In retrospective analysis by Fabian socialists, too, the arguments over land in the early 1880s, 'while not distinctly socialist', had been the primary driving force of the 'new current of thought', which later crystallised 'into a popular socialist movement'.[3] In his influential early history of socialism, Thomas Kirkup identified the doctrines of Henry George, the American social reformer, combined with the Irish Land War itself, as 'really the beginning of a radical change in English economics'.[4] Yet within a generation, the question of the right to land had gone from being the primary and most fundamental plank of many socialist platforms to a political anachronism, and George himself recast from an inadvertent founding father to an awkward footnote in the histories of democratic socialism and progressive liberalism.[5] Claims of a

[1] J. A. Hobson, *The Crisis of Liberalism: New Issues of Democracy* (London: P. S. King & Son, 1909), 3.

[2] Hobson, *The Crisis of Liberalism*, 3.

[3] Thomas Kirkup, *A History of Socialism* [1892], 4th ed. (London: Adam and Charles Black, 1909), 328; Sidney Webb, and Beatrice Webb, *The History of Trade Unionism* [1894], 2nd ed. (London: Longmans, Green and Co., 1896), 361; Sidney Webb, *Socialism in England* (London: Swan Sonnenschein, 1890), 21.

[4] Kirkup, *A History of Socialism*, 328.

[5] Henry Fawcett, *State Socialism and the Nationalisation of the Land* (London: Macmillan, 1883), 3; F. M. L. Thompson, 'Changing Perceptions of Land Tenure in Britain, 1750–1914', in Donald Winch, and Patrick O'Brien (eds.), *The Political Economy of British Historical Experience* (Oxford: Oxford University Press, 2002), 134; Malcolm Chase, *The People's Farm: English Radical Agrarianism, 1775–1840* (Oxford: Oxford University Press, 1988), 188–189; Daniel T. Rodgers, *Atlantic Crossings: Social Politics in a Progressive Age* (Cambridge, MA: Harvard

popular right to land came to be seen as simply a 'particular brand of deviation' from capitalism, or even, as Marx himself had argued, 'The Capitalists' last ditch'.[6] Similarly, in Ireland itself, the mass agrarian movement that had seemed poised to overleap national boundaries and undermine oligarchical power in 'the grandest battle ever fought for the rights of human beings' would later contract into a narrower national struggle.[7]

This is a story about the role of land in the dramatic reorientations in liberal political thought during the late-nineteenth century. It takes as its primary focus the experiences of the most notorious protagonist within the most notable field of conflict in this encounter over the land question: Henry George and Ireland. It is a story of how, in an era most often associated with the growth of the urban environment, a resurgent agrarianism briefly reclaimed centre stage. While late-Victorians often attributed political disagreement to an intractable conflict between individualism and collectivism, the land issue provided a confounding and disorientating challenge to such assumptions.[8] Hobson's linear narrative that painted the international struggle over land as the economically naïve kernel of an incipient progressive liberalism was a misconceived revision; an assumption it was only possible to make by ignoring the very questions of popular power and natural right which had really been the animating forces behind the land struggle.

***

Built in 1871 at the Laird shipyards in Birkenhead, the steamship *Spain* operated on the National Line between Liverpool, Queenstown in County Cork, and New York, connecting Britain and Ireland to continental North America with a journey time of around a week and a half. With accommodation for 120 first-class and 1,400 third-class passengers, the ship was part of a vast fleet that served on North Atlantic routes, drawing Europe and North America into an ever-closer nexus. The huge transfer of people, and the ideas and commodities they carried, was reshaping the relationship between these countries, creating shared political concerns and economic demands, all while solidifying

University Press, 1998), 90; Roy Douglas, 'God Gave the Land to the People', in A. J. A. Morris (ed.), *Edwardian Radicalism, 1900–1914: Some Aspects of British Radicalism* (London: Routledge and Kegan Paul, 1974), 148–161.

6 Theodore W. Adorno, and Max Horkheimer, *Dialectic of Enlightenment* [1944] (London: Verso, 1997), 132; Henry Mayers Hyndman, *The Record of an Adventurous Life* (London: Macmillan, 1911), 281.

7 Matthew Maguire, 'Address Adopted at the Workingmen's "No Rent Rally"', New York, 30 January 1882, *Irish Nation*, 2 February 1882; Edward T. O'Donnell, '"Henry George and the New Political Forces": Ethnic Nationalism, Labor Radicalism and Politics in Gilded Age New York City' (PhD dissertation, Columbia University, 1995), 165.

8 Michael Taylor, 'Introduction', in Michael Taylor (ed.), *Herbert Spencer and the Limits of the State: The Late Nineteenth-Century Debate between Individualism and Collectivism* (Bristol: Thoemmes Press, 1996).

the structures of transatlantic capitalism. In August 1876, the steamship *Spain* had carried the Baptist minister, abolitionist, and former slave Thomas Lewis Johnson from New York to Liverpool, and eventually to a new life on the south coast of England.[9] In July 1877, the ship carried a twenty-six-year-old mother, Margaret Madden, and her infant daughter Lizzie across in the other direction, where they would travel onwards to be reunited with her husband Matthew in East Boston; just one family among the hundreds of thousands who would make this particular journey.[10]

On 15 October 1881, the *Spain* sailed again for Liverpool from New York, and on board on this occasion was Henry George, his wife Annie, and their daughters Jennie and Anna.[11] George was travelling under the auspices of the *Irish World and American Industrial Liberator*, as an international correspondent for Irish-America's leading newspaper. It was a propitious moment for the self-anointed social philosopher to make the journey to Ireland. George's book, *Progress and Poverty*, which had been published over a year earlier, would soon elevate him to worldwide renown as the prophetic voice of a social revolution; one committed to the collective reclamation of earth's natural resources. In Ireland, where the ongoing revolt against landlordism was entering its third year, George not only saw fertile ground for his ideas, but a springboard for a transformational moment of world-historical proportions. 'What brings this question into peculiar prominence in Ireland', George explained to readers of the *Irish World*, 'is merely that certain conditions there prevail which [...] compel people to see a relation between want and landownership which they do not see in other countries, though it no less truly exists'.[12]

George was not alone in seeing the Irish Land War as a portentous and epochal conflict. In many radical imaginations, and indeed the nightmares of conservative observers, the Irish fight against land monopoly was the start of something much more fundamental. George's claim that the Land War was 'greater than either the French or American Revolutions' was typical of his extravagant sermonising, but the sentiment was endorsed by many others who believed they were witnessing the final keystone that would fulfil the emancipatory promise of those late-eighteenth-century political transformations.[13] Heavily reliant on a discourse of natural right, and reaffirming the interdependency between landownership and democratic-republican citizenship, the Land War expressed these popular radical aspirations at a moment when an increasingly positivist and

[9] Thomas L. Johnson, *Twenty-Eight Years a Slave, or the Story of My Life in Three Continents* (Bournemouth: W. Mate & Sons, 1909).
[10] 1880 US Federal Census: Boston, Suffolk County, Massachusetts, Enumeration district 576, 38; steamship *Spain* manifest, From Liverpool and Queenstown to New York, 9 July 1877.
[11] Charles Albro Barker, *Henry George* (New York: Oxford University Press, 1955), 339–340.
[12] Henry George, *Irish World*, 1 May 1880. [13] Henry George, *Irish World*, 9 July 1881.

sociologically minded liberalism appeared to have identified such archaic ambitions as nothing more than dangerous ideological relics.[14] In this way, through its political rhetoric and social practices, the Land War became a proxy conflict, conjoining the small farmer and the labour radical against what they perceived as both the centralising technocratic tendencies and the constricting possessiveness of late-Victorian liberalism. For supporters of Henry George, just as for many other radicals in Ireland and beyond, the Land War offered the brief hope of realising the fractured republican trinity of 'liberty, equality, and fraternity'.[15]

It was not to be. George left Ireland in the summer of 1882, disappointed and deflated by the political compromises of the Land League coalition, but by no means defeated. As his work gained increasing notoriety, his political prominence grew on the other side of the Atlantic. George would become a leading intellectual light among labour radicals in the United States and beyond, a hero for figures as diverse as Leo Tolstoy, José Martí, and Keir Hardie, and his prominence as an ideological totem reached its pinnacle during his 1886 mayoral campaign in New York City, where he stood as an independent labour candidate. *Progress and Poverty*, George's magnum opus, remained the most influential non-fiction book among British Labour Party politicians into the early twentieth century.[16] His unifying role during this early highpoint of the transatlantic labour movement is an indication of the critically overlooked question of land in reshaping political discourse during this ideologically tumultuous period.

[14] Stefan Collini, *Liberalism and Sociology: L. T. Hobhouse and Political Argument in England, 1880–1914* (Cambridge: Cambridge University Press, 1979); Daniel T. Rodgers, *Atlantic Crossings: Social Politics in a Progressive Age* (Cambridge, MA: Harvard University Press, 1998); Dorothy Ross, 'Socialism and American Liberalism: Academic Social Thought in the 1880s', *Perspectives in American History* 11 (1978): 7–79; Mary O. Furner, 'The Republican Tradition and the New Liberalism: Social Investigation, State Building, and Social Learning in the Gilded Age', in Michael J. Lacey, and Mary O. Furner (eds.), *The State and Social Investigation in Britain and the United States* (Cambridge: Cambridge University Press, 1993); Sandra den Otter, *British Idealism and Social Explanation: A Study in Late Victorian Thought* (Oxford: Oxford University Press, 1996); Robert Adcock, *Liberalism and the Emergence of American Political Science: A Transatlantic Tale* (Oxford: Oxford University Press, 2014).

[15] *Freeman's Journal* 16 January 1883; On the international spread of the land issue, see Andrew G. Newby, *Ireland, Radicalism and the Scottish Highlands, c. 1870–1912* (Edinburgh: Edinburgh University Press, 2007); Ewen A. Cameron, 'Communication or Separation? Reactions to Irish Land Agitation and Legislation in the Highlands of Scotland c.1870–1910', *The English Historical Review* 120, no. 487 (2005): 633–666; John D. Wood, 'Transatlantic Land Reform: America and the Crofters' Revolt, 1878–1888', *The Scottish Historical Review* 63, no. 175 (1984): 79–104; Ely M. Janis, *A Greater Ireland: The Land League and Transatlantic Nationalism in Gilded Age America* (Madison, WI: University of Wisconsin Press, 2015); Peter d'A. Jones, 'Henry George and British Socialism', *American Journal of Economics and Sociology* 47, no. 4 (1988): 473–491; Anthony Taylor, 'Richard Cobden, J. E. Thorold Rogers and Henry George', in Matthew Cragoe, and Paul Readman (eds.), *The Land Question in Britain, 1750–1950* (Basingstoke: Palgrave, 2010).

[16] 'The Labour Party and the Books That Helped to Make It', *The Review of Reviews* 33, no. 198 (June 1906), 571.

Taking up the mantle of E. P. Thompson's famous fight against the 'condescension of posterity', the historian of Chartism Malcolm Chase once noted that labour historians' attention tended to be drawn towards 'those elements and personalities' that appeared to presage the concerns of the modern movement, ignoring other untaken, abandoned, or obstructed intellectual avenues. 'From this perspective', he continued, 'the land question can seem irrelevant, and working class absorption in it even mildly embarrassing'.[17] This general historiographical disinterest has helped to shape assumptions that nineteenth-century arguments over the right to land were intellectual cul-de-sacs.[18] Yet even in the midst of the rapid industrialisation of the 1880s, the land issue had still not been eclipsed and, if anything, became more pronounced as labour radicals on both sides of the Atlantic found that urban poverty simply reinforced 'the connection between alienation from the land and the rigors of the wages system'.[19]

This work is an attempt to rectify this imbalance and to allow both the Irish Land War and Henry George to reclaim the position of importance accorded them by contemporaries.[20] It places them at the centre of the intellectual transfiguration of liberal political thought across the Gilded Age Atlantic World. The moral and material advantages conferred by the possession of land had long been central to most theories of political legitimacy and sovereignty. So too was the issue of land ownership tied at the root to political conflicts over the nature and origins of economic value. The perception, common among many political economists until the middle of the century, that land should be viewed as a distinct form of property, opened the intellectual space for communitarian conclusions about its possession to maturate. It was here that George's campaign, and the Land War itself, found their ideological niche. Both suggested individualised but non-possessive rights to nature which were limited by a broader 'common good' but grounded upon a natural 'right to life'. This was an articulation of natural rights framed within a wider cosmology of a harmonious moral universe. In this way, the practical and discursive demand for a right to land traversed the uneasy bifurcation of individualism or collectivism that dominated

17 Chase, *The People's Farm*, 4.

18 Alex Gourevitch, *From Slavery to the Cooperative Commonwealth: Labor and Republican Liberty in the Nineteenth Century* (Cambridge: Cambridge University Press, 2015), 95, 145.

19 David Montgomery, *Citizen Worker: The Experience of Workers in the United States with Democracy and the Free Market during the Nineteenth Century* (Cambridge: Cambridge University Press, 1994), 112.

20 Eric Foner, 'Class, Ethnicity, and Radicalism in the Gilded Age: The Land League and Irish America', in Eric Foner, *Politics and Ideology in the Age of the Civil War* (New York: Oxford University Press, 1981), 180; Sean Wilentz, 'Industrialising America and the Irish: Towards the New Departure', *Labor History* 29, no. 4 (1979): 587; David N. Doyle, 'Unestablished Irishmen: New Immigrants and Industrial America, 1870–1910', in Dirk Hoerder (ed.), *American Labor and Immigration History, 1877–1920s: Recent European Research* (Urbana: University of Illinois Press, 1983), 193.

concurrent debates in political economy. George's famous claim that his land plan demonstrated that '*laissez-faire* (in its full true meaning) opens the way to a realization of the noble dreams of socialism' came to seem, by the early twentieth century, like an impenetrable paradox.[21] But not before it animated a movement of remarkable popular appeal and righteous moral ambition.

The notion of paradox runs deeply through this topic. Historians of the Irish Land War have often dwelt on the apparent contradiction of a mass movement demanding 'Land for the People' leading inexorably to a more engrained system of private land ownership through its claims for more secure possession of the soil.[22] It was a tension which many contemporary observers alluded to as well.[23] If Henry George's historiographical ambiguity can be attributed, as Daniel T. Rodgers has suggested, to his liminal place on the political spectrum, a place 'where left and right can no longer easily be distinguished', the same can be said of the Land War itself.[24] Was it a signal moment of radically egalitarian possibilities, a petty-bourgeois land-grab whereby 'one class of Irish capitalists waged economic war against another class of Irish capitalists', or the birthplace of socially liberal state interventionism?[25]

It was only appropriate that Ireland should be the primary site of this incongruity. The country occupied a liminal place in the transatlantic world – variously colonised and coloniser, enlightened and primitive, according to ideological

[21] Henry George, *Progress and Poverty: An Inquiry into the Cause of Industrial Depressions, and of Increase of Want with Increase of Wealth. The Remedy* [1879], 10th ed. (New York: D. Appleton and Co., 1882), xi.

[22] Oliver MacDonagh, *States of Mind: Two Centuries of Anglo-Irish Conflict, 1780–1980* (London: Pimlico, 1983), 51; Gearóid Ó Tuathaigh, 'Irish Land Questions in the State of the Union', in Fergus Campbell, and Tony Varley (eds.), *Land Questions in Modern Ireland* (Manchester: Manchester University Press, 2013), 17.

[23] William Edward Hartpole Lecky, *Democracy and Liberty*, vol. II [1896] (London: Longmans, Green, and Co., 1913), 228; Robert Wallace, 'The Philosophy of Liberalism', *The Nineteenth Century: A Monthly Review* 9, no. 48 (1881): 320.

[24] Rodgers, *Atlantic Crossings*, 90.

[25] R. V. Comerford, *The Fenians in Context: Irish Politics & Society 1848–82* (Dublin: Wolfhound Press, 1985), 234; see also, Samuel Clark, *The Social Origins of the Irish Land War* (Princeton: Princeton University Press, 1979); Paul Bew, *Land and the National Question in Ireland, 1858–82* (Atlantic Highlands, NJ: Humanities Press, 1979); F. S. L. Lyons, *Charles Stewart Parnell* (Dublin: Gill and Macmillan, 1977); Donald E. Jordan, Jr., *Land and Popular Politics in Ireland: County Mayo from the Plantation to the Land War* (Cambridge: Cambridge University Press, 1994); Philip Bull, *Land, Politics and Nationalism: A Study of the Irish Land Question* (Dublin: Gill and Macmillan, 1996); Barbara L. Solow, *The Land Question and the Irish Economy, 1870–1903* (Cambridge, MA: Harvard University Press, 1971); T. W. Moody, *Davitt and the Irish Revolution, 1846–82* (Oxford: Oxford University Press, 1982); P. J. Drudy (ed.), *Ireland: Land, Politics and People* (Cambridge: Cambridge University Press, 1982); Samuel Clark, and James S. Donnelly, Jr. (eds.), *Irish Peasants: Violence and Political Unrest, 1780–1914* (Madison: University of Wisconsin Press, 1983); Andrew W. Orridge, 'Who Supported the Land War? An Aggregate Data Analysis of Irish Agrarian Discontent, 1879–1882', *Economic and Social Review* 12 (1980–81): 203–233.

preference – a multivalence which allowed utopian and oppositional political ideas about land to be projected on to and incubated within the country.[26] An agricultural fringe to the British metropole, Ireland was also a central node in transatlantic networks through its vast and powerful diaspora. Viewed in this way, Ireland was both the known and the unknown in the Atlantic world: its geographical proximity to Britain placed it at the frontier of capitalist modernity; its religion, language, and culture provided a contrasting perspective which formed a dialogue with these new capitalist social forms.[27] Ireland was able, in Joe Cleary's words, to perform as a 'sublime periphery to the European mainstream', and therefore its effect on contemporary political thought was a consequence of its position of 'overlap and coexistence between two incommensurable realities'.[28] It was precisely this situational anomaly that provided the potency for Irish critiques of British power and of liberal capitalism.

The question of land, too, had long shaped the distinctiveness of Irish political economy. Throughout the nineteenth century, radicals in Britain and the United States had looked to Ireland as an example of the worst effects of landed oligarchy.[29] No event could have more forcefully and catastrophically reinforced this concern than the Famine, which, if it did not immediately undermine, fatally destabilised the absolutist commitment to the notion that markets and morals always aligned. Due to their proximity to the worst excesses of mid-century *laissez-faire* in the case of the Great Famine, many Irish economists were much more ambivalent about the moral authority of the market than their counterparts nearer the imperial capital.[30] Ireland's predominantly rural complexion and its

[26] Deirdre Ní Chuanchâin, *Utopianism in Eighteenth-Century Ireland* (Cork: Cork University Press, 2016).

[27] Mark Bevir, and Frank Trentmann, 'Critique within Capitalism: Historiographical Problems, Theoretical Perspectives', in Mark Bevir, and Frank Trentmann (eds.), *Critiques of Capital in Modern Britain and America: Transatlantic Exchanges 1800 to the Present Day* (Basingstoke: Palgrave Macmillan, 2002), 1.

[28] Joe Cleary, 'Ireland and Modernity', in Joe Cleary, and Claire Connolly (eds.), *The Cambridge Companion to Modern Irish Culture* (Cambridge: Cambridge University Press, 2005), 9; Frederic Jameson, 'Modernism and Imperialism', in Terry Eagleton, Fredric Jameson, and Edward W. Said (eds.), *Nationalism, Colonialism and Literature* (Minneapolis, MN: University of Minnesota Press, 1990), 59.

[29] Thomas Hodgskin, *The Natural and Artificial Right of Property Contrasted* (London: B. Steil, 1832), 44–45; Wendell Phillips, *Daniel O'Connell: The Irish Patriot*, 6 (Archives of Irish America, 047, New York University); Jamie L. Bronstein, 'Land Reform and Political Traditions in Nineteenth Century Britain and the United States', in Mark Bevir, and Frank Trentmann (eds.), *Critiques of Capital in Modern Britain and America: Transatlantic Exchanges 1800 to the Present Day* (Basingstoke: Palgrave Macmillan, 2002), 33–34.

[30] R. D. C. Black, *Economic Thought and the Irish Question, 1817–1870* (Cambridge: Cambridge University Press, 1960); Peter Gray, 'Irish Social Thought and the Relief of Poverty', *Transactions of the Royal Historical Society* 20 (2010): 1–23; Boyd Hilton, *The Age of Atonement: The Influence of Evangelicalism on Social and Economic Thought, 1785–1865* (Oxford: Oxford University Press, 1986); Thomas A. Boylan and Timothy P. Foley, *Political Economy and Colonial Ireland: The Propagation and Ideological Function of Economic*

semi-colonial relationship with Britain added vivid emphasis to the contention that land ownership was central to realising personal, political, and economic liberty. Critically, not only had the question of Irish nationality and independence been tied up with the ownership of Irish soil, but the millions of sons and daughters of Ireland that coursed though America's cities, the blood in its industrial veins, ensured that Irish land would become an international issue. It was not surprising then that during the economic and political crises of the 1880s, when rapid technological advance was accompanied by both economic convulsions and social disquiet, Ireland assumed a prominent position in both international geopolitics and political thought.

However, this centrality has not often been fully appreciated. For a long time, historians of nineteenth-century Ireland have largely rejected the admittedly grandiose view of the Land War put forward by its radical and international supporters and its most anxious critics, noting that the partial and incremental victories it won were hardly suggestive of such high-minded claims.[31] Others have viewed the political language used during the Land War as obfuscation, a way to disguise what was really 'an exclusive form of historical regression, based on the economic expectation of an anti-urban, small tenant class intent on promoting the glorification of their own status'.[32] Domestic perspectives on the conflict have dominated, making it harder to observe how the ideological issues thrown up by the Land War were contested in a wider context. As a consequence of this, the ideas articulated by the Irish Land League and its supporters have often been seen as secondary to its actual ambitions; a rhetorical veneer on a bourgeois nationalist revolt.[33] In returning the focus to the ideas which orientated and directed the conflict, this work is an attempt to pay serious attention to Irish intellectual history, which has, at least in regard to the nineteenth and twentieth centuries, been comparatively neglected.[34]

Discourse in the Nineteenth Century (London: Routledge, 1992); Thomas Boylan, Renee Prendergast, and John D. Turner (eds.), *A History of Irish Economic Thought* (Abingdon: Routledge, 2011).

31 R. V. Comerford, 'The Politics of Distress, 1877–82', in W. E. Vaughan (ed.), *A New History of Ireland, vol. VI* (Oxford: Oxford University Press, 1989), 47.

32 Padraig G. Lane, 'Poor Crayturs: The West's Agricultural Labourers in the Nineteenth Century', in Carla King, and Conor McNamara (eds.), *The West of Ireland: New Perspectives on the Nineteenth Century* (Dublin: History Press Ireland, 2011), 46.

33 For instance, Thomas N. Brown, *Irish American Nationalism, 1870–1890* (Philadelphia: J. B. Lippincott, 1966), 53–54; Comerford, 'The Politics of Distress'. Tom Garvin, 'Republicanism and Democracy in Ireland', *Studies: An Irish Quarterly Review* 102, no. 406 (2013): 181–189.

34 The case for greater attention has been made by Colin Reid, 'Democracy, Sovereignty and Unionist Political Thought during the Revolutionary Period in Ireland, c. 1912–22', *Transactions of the Royal Historical Society*, 27 (2017): 211–232; Richard Bourke, 'Languages of Conflict and the Northern Irish Troubles', *Journal of Modern History* 83, no. 3 (2011): 544–578; Iseult Honohan, 'Introduction: Putting Irish Republicanism in a Wider Context', in Iseult Honohan (ed.), *Republicanism in Ireland: Confronting Theories and Traditions* (Manchester: Manchester University Press, 2008), 1–20.

When it comes to questions of land and democracy in particular, the spectre of 'republicanism' hangs uncomfortably over the historiography. This complex term acquires darker hues in an Irish context, and historians have been generally resistant to applying the label to distinctive modes of thought in order to avoid conflating Irish republicanism with the history of republican political thought, thereby allowing it to stagnate as a simple synonym for nationalism.[35] As Fearghal McGarry and James McConnel have reflected, the assumption remains 'that the real importance of Fenianism lay in its attitude rather than its ideas'.[36] Excavating these dormant intellectual histories is a guiding ambition of this book.

More than any other issue, the land question opens the most promising avenues for this. For one thing, it was deeply implicated in broad and far-reaching questions of political economy, individual personality, theology and morality, community and nationality, and citizenship and democracy. At the same time, it was also a more mundane and prosaic issue, one that directly shaped daily lives, and which fostered particular social practices. In this way, the land question can provide a connecting thread between popular attitudes and political thought, sewing together the concerns of social historians and those of intellectual historians. It opens up the possibility of a properly social history of ideas, recognising 'that complex systems of ideas and knowledge also lodge within every sociological division of society', even if there remain significant challenges in decoding and elaborating political claims that are not distilled in careful prose, but formed and articulated through social action and practice.[37] This present study involves reading social practices themselves as emergent non-textual articulations of political ideas and connecting them to more familiar textual analyses of political theory with the ambition of constructing a workable intellectual history from below that can best represent the complex interplay between linguistic and material influence.[38]

[35] Margaret O'Callaghan, 'Reconsidering the Republican Tradition in Nineteenth Century Ireland', in Iseult Honohan (ed.) *Republicanism in Ireland: Confronting Theories and Traditions* (Manchester: Manchester University Press, 2008), 31–44.

[36] Fearghal McGarry, and James McConnel, 'Introduction', in Fearghal McGarry, and James McConnel (eds.), *The Black Hand of Republicanism: Fenianism in Modern Ireland* (Dublin: Irish Academic Press, 2008), xiv.

[37] Daniel T. Rodgers, 'Paths in the Social History of Ideas', in Joel Isaac, James T. Kloppenberg, Michael O'Brien, and Jennifer Ratner-Rosenhagen (eds.), *The Worlds of American Intellectual History* (New York: Oxford University Press, 2017), 310.

[38] E. P. Thompson, 'The Poverty of Theory or an Orrey of Errors', in E. P. Thompson (ed.), *The Poverty of Theory and Other Essays* (London: Merlin Press, 1978), 3; Eric Hobsbawm, 'History from Below – Some Reflections', in Frederick Krantz (ed.), *History from Below: Studies in Popular Protest and Popular Ideology in Honour of George Rudé* (Montréal: Concordia University Press, 1985), 64. Mark Bevir, *The Logic of the History of Ideas* (Cambridge: Cambridge University Press, 1999), 312.

The land question undoubtedly opens an important window into the non-textual social world, enabling popular attitudes about the distinctiveness of property in land to be observed and interpreted as political thought. In this way, praxiographic analysis can provide a complimentary corrective to a contextual and discursive analysis.[39] A specific ontology of value tended to emerge from beliefs about the distinctness of land, itself a result of proximity to and reliance upon agriculture, and upon which a number of corollary assumptions often rested. These epistemic structures of agrarian life laid significant moral value on natural processes such as fertility and labour, as well notions of holistic harmony, and although these beliefs translated into political commitments in myriad ways, they dovetailed closely with typical republican commitments. Malcolm Chase has described this as an 'ethos of a pre-industrial natural order' which was 'borne of continuing proximity (spatial and psychological) to the land'.[40] Within this ideological context, land unavoidably socialised and restricted the question of possession, preventing rights claims from slipping into an acquisitive individualism. This was the fertile ideological ground that allowed George's ideas to take root.

The structure of this book is thematic rather than chronological and adopts a number of different methodological approaches. George's own intellectual background, alongside the wider context of the 1880s, is examined more fully in Chapter 1, which takes as its title the sarcastic yet revealing moniker of 'our American Aristotle', bestowed on George by a Catholic cleric.[41] Thinking of the North Atlantic as a semi-integrated whole during this period, as is argued in this first chapter, clarifies Ireland's centrality in this chaotic decade, as well as the remarkable influence of the United States, and Irish-America in particular, on Irish political life. It also facilitates a contextual analysis of George's most famous work, *Progress and Poverty*. Chapter 2 examines the role of land in the history of political thought, specifically with regard to the concepts of value, productivity, natural harmony and independence, and how, via the notion of the body as a universal materialist foundation, these have been conceptualised in the history of land reform agitation, both in Ireland and beyond. With these contexts established, the next chapter provides an account of the course and development of the Land War itself, and how the ideas discussed in Chapter 2

39 See Christian Bueger, 'Pathways to Practice: Praxiography and International Politics', *European Political Science Review* 6, no. 3 (2014): 383–406; Theodore R. Schatzki, 'Introduction', in Theodore R. Schatzki, Karin Knorr Cetina, and Eike von Savigny (eds.), *The Practice Turn in Contemporary Theory* (London: Routledge, 2001), 10–23; Inanna Hamati-Ataya, 'The Sociology of Knowledge as Postphilosophical Epistemology: Out of IR's "Socially Constructed" Idealism', *International Studies Review* 20 (2018): 3–29.

40 Chase, *The People's Farm*, 15.

41 Rev Henry A. Brann, *Henry George and His Land Theories* (New York: The Catholic Publication Society, 1887), 10.

were articulated by the Land League and its supporters, both explicitly in the rhetorical claims made on public platforms and implicitly in the tactical strategies employed.

No other institution wielded comparable transnational power over such a large body of the Irish diaspora than the Catholic Church, yet it was riven with internal divisions over the questions of land and labour during the 1880s, and its grip on Irish popular opinion was increasingly strained and contingent. In Chapter 4, the relationship of the Church to questions of land reform is discussed, particularly its role in sustaining radical critiques of liberal modernity and capitalism. Chapter 5 tracks the impact of George and the Land War on some of the central ideological currents of the period, revealing how the transatlantic Land War came to occupy its fractious place in liberal political thinking. This chapter suggests the importance of George's radical campaigns and the Irish land agitation in accelerating acceptance of the more technocratic sightlines of new liberalism and economic marginalism. Pressed by the destabilising threat of demands for access to land grounded in natural rights, liberal political thinkers discarded the last vestiges of the tradition's democratic-republican heritage in favour of a statist and ostensibly 'value-free' perspective enunciated in a language of scientific authority.

It is these themes which provide the oppositional backdrop to the final chapter, in which George's remarkable popularity among Irish-Americans is used as a lens through which to review the cultural force of 'Irishness' as a potent subaltern category. Here the intersections of class and culture that shaped the distinctive form of Irish-American social radicalism are examined by looking at the enmeshed nationalist, pan-Celticist, anarchist, socialist, agrarian, journalistic, commercial, charitable, and ethno-religious networks that constituted Irish-American associational culture, and the political and poetic discourses they utilised. If the new social liberalism had proposed a solution to the discordance between individualism and collectivism that favoured rational order, control, and scientific expertise as the tools to achieve freedom, it was one that failed to achieve much of a foothold in the Irish diaspora, where a focus on land engendered what many critics saw as a naïvely optimistic and outdated radicalism, orientated around the idea of natural harmony; that the removal of injurious and corrupt laws would wither the false distinction between individualism and collectivism.

The collapse, as a political platform, of the popular democratic republicanism evinced by George and the Land League represented an uneasy rupture between the cultures of liberalism and liberal political thought itself. The apparently interminable complexity of novel forms of urban-industrial life towards the end of the nineteenth century was accompanied by an equivalent sense of social and moral disjuncture, and a feeling that older 'common sense' assumptions were no longer useful, or even counterproductive.

Perhaps no group was so well placed to articulate this sense of disconnection and alienation as the Irish, at home and abroad, who in their physical displacement faced and reacted to the dominant force of capitalist rationality in a variety of ways.[42] Also trapped awkwardly between the constraining forces of classical and progressive liberalism was an older republican formation and, underlying it, the question of land. This productive tension propelled the Irish Land War and Henry George to international significance, reshaping liberal political thought across the Atlantic. The erasure of land as the preeminent site of political power and personal independence was marked by the collapse of natural nights from political discourse. The old radical banner of 'Land and Liberty', which had never been a dyad but rather a unitary vision, slipped out of view.

Towards the end of his life in the early 1870s, the great liberal thinker John Stuart Mill had become increasingly preoccupied with the question of land. Moving away from the narrower notions political freedom that had marked some of his earlier work, Mill came to see the collective possession of land as the fulcrum from which his vision of an emancipated liberalism, or even socialism, could be achieved. Mill, like others before him, had come to see that the monopolisation of land was perhaps the most important driving force for the political ills of centralisation and the dependency of poverty that he condemned, auguring the signal importance of the land question to the economic conflict and demographic transformation of the following two decades. Mill died in 1873, not long before the Irish Land War was to add dramatic expression and political force to the problem. Although their working lives did not properly overlap, George and Mill did briefly correspond in 1869 – with both men agreeing that the right to land was the most important question of contemporary political economy.[43] Such a judgement reflects the core argument advanced in this book: that Irish land in the 1880s was a site of philosophical conflict with resonances for liberal political thought far beyond Ireland itself.

[42] Jurgen Habermas, *The Philosophical Discourses of Modernity* (Oxford: Polity, 1989), 83.

[43] John Stuart Mill to Henry George, 23 October 1869 (Henry George Papers, Series I: A, Box 2, New York Public Library).

1 'Our American Aristotle'
Henry George's Gilded Age

> For we are living in a grand and wonderful time – a time when old ideas, traditions and customs have broken loose from their moorings and are hopelessly adrift on the great shoreless, boundless sea of human thought.[1]

Fuelled by rapid economic growth across the Atlantic world, ideological uncertainty was the motif of the age. New challenges radiated from the realms of technology and philosophy that shook previously firm convictions and moral foundations, and with this onrushing tide came both an unrestrained devotion to a new future and a crisis of confidence in the certainties of the past. A near boundless optimism in human and mechanical potential competed with, and was sometimes bound to, a seething anger at present injustice. 'It is as if we were somehow being endow'd with a vast and more and more thoroughly-appointed body, and then left with little or no soul' was how Walt Whitman expressed the disquieting changes.[2] From one vantage, such appraisals simply represented the ubiquitous tectonic friction that has characterised many experiences of modernity, but the speed and dynamism of economic transformation across the North Atlantic world gave a particular ferocity to the intellectual shockwaves. As one observer overconfidently claimed, 'at no time in the history of the world has there been such a rapid – I might say revolutionary – advance of opinion'.[3] For some, this offered hope that 'a great change was imminent', but others were dismayed to find themselves in 'an age when revolutionary ideas are in the air, and when all traditional and customary conceptions as to the nature of property have been disturbed, and have lost their solidity and definiteness'.[4]

[1] Mary Elizabeth Lease, 'Speech to the Women's Christian Temperance Movement' [1890], in Howard Zinn, and Anthony Arnove (eds.), *Voices of a People's History of the United States* (New York: Seven Stories, 2004), 226.

[2] Walt Whitman, *Specimen Days & Collect* (Philadelphia: Rees Welsh, 1882), 211.

[3] 'What Morality Have We Left', *The North American Review*, 132, no. 294 (1881): 497.

[4] *Irish World*, 9 July 1881; Standish O'Grady, *The Crisis in Ireland* (Dublin: E. Ponsonby, 1882), 25.

This restive sensibility could find an equally hospitable environment on both sides of the Atlantic during what was undoubtedly a global Gilded Age. Due to the extensive growth of transatlantic commerce, expanding print networks, immense migration, and the concomitant solidification of the political structures of capitalism, western Europe and North America in particular were increasingly tied together in a regional economy.[5] This context ensured that the Irish Land War was an international event; both its causes and consequences were not confined to Ireland. It was precipitated as much by the effect of economic globalisation, particularly by the pressures of international competition from the United States, as by a succession of poor harvests and fuelled by the transfer of both money and ideas from America, Britain, and further afield. It succeeded in mobilising a vast tranche of the Irish diaspora, not only in the cause of their homeland but also as part of a more ambitious vision. Yet the Land War was only the most visible and hotly contested theatre in the wider war over the right to natural resources and the possession of political power. Land and labour campaigns across the North Atlantic, from northern France to western Ireland, Pennsylvania to County Durham, involving Californian workingmen, agricultural labourers from the British midlands, Irish tenants, brewers in New York, farmers in the American Midwest, Scottish crofters, and Scouse dockers, erupted during the 1870s and 1880s, all sharing a common interest in how access to natural resources could provide a basis for common emancipation. This fact alone enjoins us to take seriously the transnational currents of thought that nourished these campaigns.

The immediate precipitants for many of these movements, including the Irish Land War, were the recurrent economic crises of the 1870s, particularly in the later part of the decade in Britain and Ireland.[6] Inevitably, the far-reaching economic ripples caused by such commercial interdependence were accompanied by a heightened awareness of a burgeoning 'globalisation'. With their thick networks of diasporic communities, the Irish were front and centre in this process, and as the Land War demonstrated, well placed to grasp all its potentials and pitfalls.[7] Cognisance of this new interconnectedness was also key to Henry George's appeal, and he regularly encouraged audiences to consider the issue,

5 Rodgers, *Atlantic Crossings*, 4, 33; Robert Kelley, *The Transatlantic Persuasion: The Liberal-Democratic Mind in the Age of Gladstone* (New York: Alfred A. Knopf, 1969).

6 J. A. Hobson, 'Preface', in John Allet Hobson (ed.), *Co-operative Labour upon the Land, and Other Papers; The Report of a Conference upon 'Land, Co-operation and the Unemployed', Held at Holborn Town Hall in October, 1894* (London: Swan Sonnenshein & Co., 1895), vii.

7 Janis, *A Greater Ireland*; Timothy J. Meagher, 'From the World to the Village and the Beginning to the End and After: Research Opportunities in Irish American History', *Journal of American Ethnic History* 28, no. 4 (2009): 118–135; Kerby Miller, *Ireland and Irish America: Culture, Class, and Transatlantic Migration* (Dublin: Field Day, 2008); Enda Delaney, 'Directions in Historiography, Our Island Story? Towards a Transnational History of Late Modern Ireland', *Irish Historical Studies* 37, no. 148 (2011): 83–105.

reminding them, 'A war on another continent produces famine in Lancashire; a change of fashion and Coventry operatives are only saved from starvation by public alms; a bank breaks in New York and in all the large American cities soup houses must be opened'.[8] Although the economic crises of the 1870s catalysed the agrarian and industrial conflict of the 1880s, in his first example, George gestured towards one of two monumental and era-defining events during the middle of the nineteenth century, each one transnational catastrophes, which loomed largest over the social world he inhabited. These watershed moments had caused a caesura with the past and given birth to new political and economic environments in the late nineteenth-century Atlantic world.

In myriad ways, the legacies of both the Irish Famine and the US Civil War remained keenly visible. Not only did both events reshape economic structures and ideas of ownership but also, in their wake, destabilised many political and economic assumptions that remained contested into the 1880s. Together, both events helped to undermine the unrestrained confidence in the moral authority of the market and to force a reassessment of the relationship between property and political freedom. Paving the way for the economic uncertainty of the 1870s and 1880s, the two crises remained intellectual touchstones and points of reference for reformers and radicals a generation later.[9] References to the Civil War and the abolition of slavery featured heavily in Henry George's work, and indeed, like many other radical republicans and former abolitionists who later adopted the Land League's cause with enthusiasm, George decried the failure to redistribute land to freed slaves as an injustice almost as great as slavery itself.[10] The Famine, too, had a profound effect by delegitimising the arrogant providentialism and economic dogmatism of mid-century *laissez-faire*, the notion that political economy was a universal science, even if the progress of the countervailing historicism was gradual and uneven.[11] As Frederick Engels

8 Henry George, 'Land and Labor', speech given to Knights of Labor, Binghamton, NY, 12 April 1883 (HGP, Series II, Box 13, NYPL); Henry George, 'The Irish Question from an American Standpoint', 1886 (HGP, Series II, Box 13, NYPL).

9 On the intellectual legacies of the Civil War, see Eric Foner, *Politics and Ideology in the Age of the Civil War* (New York: Oxford University Press, 1981); Eric Foner, *Reconstruction: America's Unfinished Revolution* [1988], rev. ed. (New York: HarperCollins, 2015); Leslie Butler, *Critical Americans: Victorian Intellectuals and Transatlantic Liberal Reform* (Chapel Hill: University of North Carolina Press, 2007); Adam Rowe, 'The New Creed of the Nation: Charles Eliot Norton, E. L. Godkin, and the Meaning of Freedom in the Civil War Era', *Journal of American Studies* 54, no. 4 (2020): 671–705; Susan-Mary Grant, and Peter J. Parish (eds.), *Legacy of Disunion: The Enduring Significance of the American Civil War* (Baton Rouge: Louisiana State University Press, 2003).

10 Henry George, 'Land and Labor', speech given to Knights of Labor, Binghamton, NY, 12 April 1883 (HGP, Series II, Box 13, NYPL); O'Donnell, 'Henry George and the "New Political Forces"', 85.

11 Peter Gray, *Famine, Land and Politics: British Government and Irish Society, 1843–50* (Dublin: Irish Academic Press, 1999).

remarked in his notes on the history of Ireland, 'The existence of five million Irish is in itself a smack in the eye to all the laws of political economy'.[12]

In the aftermath of the Civil War, the United States witnessed a dramatic period of economic growth, enabled by technological developments such as an expanding railway and telegraph network. Every indicator of industrial output and finance mushroomed as rapid urbanisation changed the social and political landscape of America. In their wake, these developments brought crises of overproduction, followed by violently unpredictably cycles of boom and bust and chronic insecurity for many workers.[13] Inevitably industrial unrest followed, particularly from the summer of 1877 onwards, which brought the spectre of European revolutions to the door of American industrialists, leading to tighter government controls over trade union activity.[14] The extensive labour activity that marked the subsequent two decades cast a pallid hue over the optimistic vision of untrammelled American progress that had previously dominated. As the 1880s dawned, there was, according to one observer, a 'very general foreboding of evil [...] which evinces almost universal doubt and fear as to our future conditions'.[15]

This disquiet was not limited to fears of social revolution among the political and economic elites. The social structure of the country had been reassembled within a generation, with significant consequences for conceptions of political independence and economic fairness. The United States had moved from a society predominantly of independent producers, and slaves and slaveholders in the South, to one where the majority of working men and women were wage labourers. While the ideal of the 'self-made man' and the natural inventiveness of the American character persisted, it became harder to justify when the connection between economic success and individual labour was much less evident.[16]

The development and spread of the limited liability corporation perhaps best embodied this change, an innovation that underpinned the commercial growth of the period and marked a significant shift in the transition from a market-based

[12] Frederick Engels, 'History of Ireland', in Karl Marx, and Frederick Engels (eds.), *Ireland and the Irish Question* (Moscow: Progress Publishers, 1971), 191.

[13] David Montgomery, *Beyond Equality: Labor and the Radical Republicans, 1862–1872* (Urbana: University of Illinois Press, 1981), 3; Alan Trachtenberg, *The Incorporation of America: Culture and Society in the Gilded Age* (New York: Hill and Wang, 1982), 39; Willard Wolfe, *From Radicalism to Socialism: Men and Ideas in the Formation of Fabian Socialist Doctrines, 1881–1889* (New Haven: Yale University Press, 1975), 68.

[14] Foner, *Reconstruction*, 585.

[15] George D. Wolff, 'Catholicity and Protestantism in Relation to Our Future as a People', *American Catholic Quarterly Review* 4 (1879): 143–144.

[16] Trachtenberg, *The Incorporation of America*, 67.

proprietary economy to one dominated by large capital concentrations.[17] While those with utilitarian predilections welcomed the development, radicals saw also the corrupting potential of this moral 'unmooring'.[18] New York's *Irish World* lamented not only the vast size, power, and unaccountability of these corporations but regarded limited liability as a moral dodge, designed 'to shield theft from criminality and crime from punishment'.[19] Others saw in these developments the Faustian bargain of progress. Frank H. Horton, editor of *The Era* in New York, considered 'combination and concentration' to be necessary for growth but also 'deleterious to morals and manners'. In a caution to the hubris of the age, he concluded, 'One hardly knows what he is antagonizing, when he controls the exaggeration of these forces, [...we may be] following and sustaining a pernicious philosophy'.[20]

Commercial integration and technological complexity stratified the economic sphere as material wealth, and with it, the means for education and advancement congealed in fewer and fewer hands. But small manufacturers, farmers, artisans, and independent proprietors did not immediately lose their central place in popular conceptions of economic freedom and republican democracy, and the growth of wage labour was widely mourned, particularly by many labour radicals who saw 'wage slavery' as suffocating a broader conception of human value and existence.[21] Speaking about the choices facing the country on the eve of the 1880 presidential election, Henry George reflected on these pressing problems. He expressed his unease with the 'independent mechanic [...] turning into the factory hand; the small shopkeeper into a clerk; the wagoner into a brakesman; the editor into a literary operative; the farmer [...] into the agricultural labourer, who owns nothing but his blankets', and inveighed against the consequent destruction of 'that personal independence of the masses which is at the root of all the civic virtues'.[22]

In Britain and America, the image of the independent autodidactic artisan, intellectually 'head and shoulders in advance of the capitalist' in his combination of physical and intellectual labour, remained a potent vision, but changing work patterns, alongside suburbanisation, compounded the growing wealth gap and devalued such labour, undermining the traditional foundations of radical

17 Montgomery, *Beyond Equality*, 8; Richard Schneirov, 'Thoughts on Periodizing the Gilded Age: Capital Accumulation, Society, and Politics, 1873–1898', *The Journal of the Gilded Age and Progressive Era* 5, no. 3 (2006): 197; Trachtenberg, *The Incorporation of America*, 83–84.
18 Jeffrey Sklansky, *The Soul's Economy: Market Society and Selfhood in American Thought, 1820–1920* (Chapel Hill: University of North Carolina Press, 2002), 8–9.
19 *Irish World*, 30 November 1878.
20 Frank H. Horton to Henry George, 9 July 1880 (HGP, Series I: A, Box 2, NYPL).
21 Montgomery, *Beyond Equality*, 25.
22 Henry George, 'Garfield or Hancock', 1880 (HGP, Series II, Box 12, NYPL).

politics.[23] The old 'artisanal conception of activity, a visible, limited, and directed relationship to nature' was giving way, separating employment from other spheres of life, and constricting definitions of political engagement to the ballot alone.[24] While progressive economists and liberals often embraced the positive authority of a 'natural aristocracy' of merit, dismissing the ideal of a 'democracy of the local assembly' as a relic from a bygone age, entirely unsuited to the complexity of modern governmental administration, George's political vision offered a more optimistic assessment of popular politics.[25] Freed from the drudgery and exploitation of industrial life, and elevated by the security and responsibility of self-possession provided by the land, common education and self-improvement would naturally lead to an egalitarian democracy. Once no longer reduced to 'mere feeders of machines', many radicals believed that people would have the chance to fully develop their human capabilities and, with time for mental improvement, 'might be as wise as Plato'.[26]

In Ireland itself, although retaining much of its rural demography in contrast to the urbanisation that marked Britain and America, significant changes to patterns of land ownership took place in the wake of the Famine, which were eliciting similar concerns about social and economic stratification. In the south and southwest, many larger farmers had successfully capitalised and consolidated their farms and transitioned from tillage to pastoral farming in order to take advantage of rising prices for beef and butter.[27] This process was accompanied by rural depopulation in these areas, as the land could no longer support as many people. In contrast, areas such as West Cork, Galway, and Mayo still retained a significant proportion of small farmers; yet, even here, the expansion of administrative and transport technologies drew many into new networks of commerce and credit.[28] The tensions between these different patterns of land

[23] *Irish World*, 30 November 1878; Gareth Stedman Jones, *Languages of Class: Studies in English Working Class History, 1832–1982* (Cambridge: Cambridge University Press, 1983), 228.

[24] Stedman Jones, *Languages of Class*, 217.

[25] Ross, 'Socialism and American Liberalism', 73; Woodrow Wilson, 'A Lecture on Democracy' [1891], in Arthur S. Link (ed.), *The Papers of Woodrow Wilson*, vol. VII (Princeton: Princeton University Press, 1968), 347.

[26] Henry George, *Social Problems* [1883] (New York: Doubleday and McClure Co., 1898), 140; Henry George, 'Lecture Notes for Glasgow', 17 March 1882 (HGP, Series II, Box 12, NYPL); Unsigned letter to Henry George, Philadelphia, 16 September 1871 (HGP, Series I: A, Box 2, NYPL); Leon Fink, *Workingmen's Democracy: The Knights of Labor and American Politics* (Urbana: University of Illinois Press, 1983), 9–11.

[27] Donnacha Seán Lucey, *Land, Popular Politics and Agrarian Violence in Ireland: The Case of County Kerry, 1872–86* (Dublin: University College Dublin Press, 2011), 9.

[28] Andrew Shields, '"Serving the Farmer": The Tenant Right Movement in the West, 1848–57', in Carla King, and Conor McNamara (eds.), *The West of Ireland* (Dublin: The History Press, 2011), 69; R. V. Comerford, 'Ireland 1850–70: Post-famine and Mid-Victorian', in W. E. Vaughan (ed.), *A New History of Ireland, Volume V: Ireland under the Union, 1801–70* (Oxford: Oxford University Press, 1989), 372–395. See also, J. J. Lee, *The Modernisation of Irish Society, 1848–1918* (Dublin: Gill and Macmillan, 1973).

use, and the conflicting social forms and conceptions of political economy that emerged from them, would shape the course of the Land War. In Ireland as elsewhere, new modes of production and exchange were directly threatening to long familiar notions of political freedom and social value.

Many other developments were factors in this change, such as the expansion of advertising and mass production, and a shift, as many historians have noted, from a focus on production to consumption – a transition evident in economic, political, and philosophical thought.[29] In the radical mind, this was part of a subversive reorientation away from naturalised notions of right and self-preservation upon which they had built their demands that humans should be treated as ends rather than means, and towards a more organic conception of the social whole. Once conceptions of value were liberated from their direct connection to production, with use value and exchange value subsumed within the enveloping concept of marginal utility, many feared that property in general would also be freed from such moral encumbrances, with its claims to profit and acquisition resting much more comfortably on the malleable justification of utility. This was also a problem of political power. For while the older radical ideal located democracy as emerging inescapably from the inalienable right of the individual to self-preservation, seeing individuals as possessors of rights and autonomy that they could exercise, a consequentialist politics did not require popular participation to justify its humanitarian authority – no right to participation grew naturally through the land from the bedrock of the right to life. The implications of this line of thought troubled many radicals, even as they perceived the material benefits that such an approach might deliver.

Such was the transnational intellectual context of the Irish Land War. As demands for popular power shifted towards demands for popular welfare, and the ideal of democracy was tempered by the attenuating role of progressive state administration, the Land War appeared to offer resistance based on the older radical vision – an opportunity to fight back, reclaim the Paineite hope of uniting liberty with equality, and finally establish the harmonious cooperative commonwealth. Patrick Ford, Galway-born editor of the New York *Irish World*, captured this narrowing conception of democracy in his demand for 'something more than the semblance of the thing called "Liberty" – something more than the hollow privilege of casting a vote for one of two caucus-made politicians'.[30] In a public letter to William Gladstone, he offered his competing

[29] Raymond Williams, 'Advertising: The Magic System', in Raymond Williams (ed.), *Culture and Materialism: Selected Essays* (London: Verso, 1980), 177; George, *Progress and Poverty*, 24; Ross, 'Socialism and American Liberalism', 57; Lawrence Glickman, *A Living Wage: American Workers and the Making of Consumer Society* (Ithaca, NY: Cornell University Press, 1997).

[30] Patrick Ford, *The Criminal History of the British Empire* [1881] (New York: The Irish World, 1915), 63.

definition of republican freedom as 'lands, and homes, and happy firesides, and schools, and popular intelligence [. . .] uncontaminated by statecraft. This is the *Irish World*'s idea of Freedom'.[31]

Yet, at the same time, the extensive economic and social changes wrought across the Atlantic by industrial capitalism also fostered an acquiescence to new conditions that made the radical vision seem archaic and hopelessly naïve. Centralised technologies, embedded in the management of the state, increasingly formed an 'immovable horizon' for many labour activists.[32] Into the 1890s and beyond, growing trades unionism in the form of the American Federation of Labor (AFL), as well as middle-class progressivism, was constructed upon a defensive (or in the latter case, optimistic) acceptance of the new realities rather than a concerted opposition. Following the ideological transition from power to welfare, the AFL maintained that 'the way out of the wage system is higher wages'.[33] To the Georgists and republican radicals who had sought deliverance in a transnational land war, such an approach was supine quietism, 'in its essence selfish and one-sided', that recognised and perpetuated wage slavery instead of trying to destroy it. Their answer was simple: instead of '*improving* the condition of the wage serfs', all that was needed was to 'establish Man in his *inalienable* RIGHTS'.[34]

Henry George in the History of Political Thought

At the epicentre of this was Henry George. His first major book, *Progress and Poverty*, which argued for land nationalisation through full taxation of ground rents, became the best-selling work of political economy in the nineteenth century, making its author an international name.[35] Variously a reformer, amateur political economist, and social philosopher, George remains a strikingly understudied figure, given his stature and prominence during the final decades of the nineteenth century. Perhaps this is most evident in regard to his relationship with Ireland, where interest in the domestic aspects of the Land War has drawn focus away from the international dimension in which George was pivotal, simultaneously obscuring the centrality of the international Irish working class to his success.[36] More broadly, there are a number of reasons for the historical amnesia that afflicts George. Although he was the most intellectually

[31] Ford, *The Criminal History*, 63; 'True Economy', *Irish World*, 4 January 1879.

[32] Stedman Jones, *Languages of Class*, 237; Gabriel Kolko, *The Triumph of Conservatism: A Reinterpretation of American History, 1900–1916* (New York: The Free Press, 1963), 279.

[33] Schneirov, 'Thoughts on Periodizing the Gilded Age', 214.

[34] *Irish World*, 12 July 1879; 27 December 1879. [35] Sklansky, *The Soul's Economy*, 115.

[36] Fintan Lane, *The Origins of Modern Irish Socialism, 1881–1896* (Cork: Cork University Press, 1997), 65; Doyle, 'Unestablished Irishmen'; Sean Wilentz, 'Industrializing America and the Irish: Towards the New Departure', *Labor History* 20, no. 4 (1979): 587.

influential actor in the transatlantic radical world of the 1880s, George very quickly became a taxonomically obtrusive figure: not clearly of the right or the left.[37] His unrepentant individualism and effusive religiosity has made him an uncomfortable fit in either histories of socialism or progressive liberalism. His cause, that of land reform, similarly cut across familiar class and party political affiliations, and as early as the first few decades of the twentieth century appeared inadequate, and often simply irrelevant, to meet the challenges of industrial modernity.[38]

It would be a mistake to assume that his ideas were an ideological hangover from a previous age and his popularity a historical curiosity of little wider interest. This was the approach taken by many of George's contemporary critics in economics and social science, who mocked his ignorance of current developments in their fields. Their condescension has generally lingered on in the academic literature on George and, with some notable exceptions, ensured his exclusion from the canon of political thinkers. Lacking sustained engagement with other economists or philosophers, he could not be directly fitted into any pre-existing genealogical tradition – he appeared more like a mouthpiece for popular discontent; a reaction rather than a cause. As a result, while George is unavoidably present in most studies of the period, detailed academic analyses of his life and work are far from abundant.[39] But it is precisely his immense international popularity, and indeed the absence in his work of dialogue with other economic theorists, that allows his ideas to be seen as an expression of popular moral and economic perspectives. George provides a window into a history of political thought from below, an escape from the textual limitations imposed by a focus on political languages as themselves constitutive of political thought, an invaluable connecting thread between social practices and political ideas.[40]

George tapped into long-standing continuities in transatlantic radical thought and became a representative of a persistent set of political demands and their allied ethical and metaphysical presumptions. For this alone, his ideas should

[37] Rodgers, *Atlantic Crossings*, 90.

[38] Bronstein, *Land Reform and Working-Class Experience*, 4; Thompson, 'Changing Perceptions of Land Tenure in Britain'; Chase, *The People's Farm*, 188–189; Douglas, 'God Gave the Land to the People'; F. M. L. Thompson, 'Epilogue: The Strange Death of the English Land Question', in M. Cragoe, and P. Readman (eds.), *The Land Question in Britain* (London: Palgrave Macmillan, 2010), 257–270.

[39] Charles Albro Barker's comprehensive 1955 study remains the primary biographical text on George. See also, Edward T. O'Donnell, *Henry George and the Crisis of Inequality: Progress and Poverty in the Gilded Age* (New York: Columbia University Press, 2015).

[40] Samuel Moyn, 'Imaginary Intellectual History', in Samuel Moyn, and Darrin M. McMahon (eds.), *Rethinking Modern European Intellectual History* (New York: Oxford University Press, 2014), 112–130; Quentin Skinner, *Visions of Politics: Volume 1, Regarding Method* (Cambridge: Cambridge University Press, 2002), 177; J. G. A. Pocock, 'The Concept of a Language and the *Metier d'Historien*: Some Considerations on Practice', in Anthony Pagden (ed.), *Languages of Political Theory in Early Modern Europe* (Cambridge: Cambridge University Press, 1987), 19–38.

be accorded significant attention. He was not an original thinker and, although deeply invested in making his own mark on the world, was delighted rather than disappointed to discover the long history of land plans that mirrored his own.[41] George's work shows him to be a conceptual magpie, picking up second-hand aphorisms and established metaphors to structure his ideas and arguments. From William Paley, he lifted (and slightly modified) a familiar parable of 100 pigeons, in which 99 collected corn as one sat atop the pile.[42] He was fond of John Stuart Mill's description of a feast in which all the seats had been taken by the rich man who arrived early, itself an image of biblical origins, and made effective use of Patrick Dove's thought experiment about the value of an enclosed and untouched acre in central London from his 1854 *Elements of Political Science*.[43] This tendency only bolstered his image as a purveyor of popular moral common sense and was an important facet of his popularity.

But George was no intellectual philistine. He thought deeply about the question of land and about the social and political structures that would maintain his ideal moral commonwealth. It was not only his popularity but also the tight logic and careful argumentation of his central thesis that made him appear so dangerous (especially to those who remained committed to some conception of natural right). He recognised a causative historical role for ideas, even as his plan rested on decidedly materialist foundations. 'Thought must precede action and govern action', he wrote, framing his attack on Malthus and social Darwinism, 'so those who establish theories are, at least within the domain of action, the precursors and pathfinders of the practical men'.[44] On both counts then, George deserves to be taken seriously: as a popular ideological avatar and as an articulator of complex and meaningful political thought. He was an intellectual broker, spanning elite and demotic divisions by virtue of his prominence and erudition. His popular appeal was inescapably bound to his use of a commonly intelligible and culturally relevant political language; his work evidence that political languages are tangible and participatory processes involving the acceptance, support, or dissention of their wider audiences.[45]

A sense of liminality and ambiguity emanates from George's work, something replicated too in subsequent interpretations of his ideas, and it is precisely

41 Henry George to Patrick Ford, 9 March 1882 (HGP, Series I: A, Box 3, NYPL).

42 George, *Progress and Poverty*, 347.

43 George, *Progress and Poverty*, 344; Lecky, *Democracy and Liberty*, vol. II, 232; Patrick Edward Dove, *The Elements of Political Science* (Edinburgh: Johnstone and Hunter, 1854), 283.

44 Henry George, 'Lecture Notes and Text: "Malthusian Theory"' (HGP, Series II, Box 12, NYPL).

45 Raymond Williams, 'Ideas of Nature', in *Culture and Materialism: Selected Essays* (London: Verso, 1980), 67–68; see Kerby Miller's use of the concept of 'culture broker': Miller, *Ireland and Irish America*, 275; Rogers, 'Paths in the Social History of Ideas', 315.

this feature that provides a unique vantage on the remarkable intellectual transformations of the 1880s. The particular fluidity of political languages in the decade marks it out as one where existing terminology was being adapted and contested to adequately comprehend a new social reality.[46] In different ways across the Anglophone world, languages of republican radicalism, liberalism, paternalism, socialism, imperialism, and their myriad modifications were in flux. In negotiating this complexity, George's ideas appear to strain against established boundaries and classifications of political opinion, and for some have indeed appeared to be 'thoroughly ambiguous', caught between two incommensurable ideological poles.[47]

A socialist who lauded individual enterprise, a proponent of capitalism who fought against capital, and a land reformer concerned with the urban environment, George can appear a confounding figure. His plans for the effective nationalisation of the land were grounded in deeply individualist premises, but would have involved extensive state intervention. With a revitalised agrarianism, he embraced a vision of urban modernity, but also possessed an unshakable longing for a simpler and more wholesome existence. Writing to his sister in 1861, he expressed what would be a common refrain in his early life, a frustration with 'the fierce struggle of our civilised life', wishing instead for 'the promised Millennium, when each one will be free to follow his best and noblest impulses'.[48] The distaste, verging on anger, George expressed at social decadence, greed and excess in the face of poverty spoke of his strongly egalitarian instincts, which belied subsequent and simplistic libertarian interpretations of his work.[49] Anna George de Mille later recalled her father's belief that 'the law of God does not allow the heaping up of riches by honest means'.[50] Right from the earliest point of his political career, George spoke in the language of radicalism, of hostility to the deep injustice and soul-sapping weight of economic oppression, which, he observed in 1865, were crushing 'the poor man beneath the wheel of the capitalist's carriage'.[51]

[46] Stedman Jones, *Languages of Class*, 21.

[47] For Wolfe, these conflicting pressures are economic individualism and Christian charity: Wolfe, *From Radicalism to Socialism*, 87; For Sklansky, George's 'productive tension' is between retrogression and modernisation, and also social organicism and autonomous individualism: Sklansky, *The Soul's Economy*, 113, 135.

[48] Henry George to his sister, San Francisco, 15th September 1861 (HGP, Series I: A, Box 1, NYPL).

[49] See, Raymond Geiger, *The Philosophy of Henry George* (New York: Macmillan, 1933), in particular Chapter 5, 'George and Socialism', 227–284, and, critical of this tendency, Edward Pessen, *Most Uncommon Jacksonians: The Radical Leaders of the Early Labor Movement* (Albany: State University of New York Press, 1967), 178.

[50] Anna George de Mille to Fr Thomas Dawson [n.d.] (HGP, Series I: D, Box 11, NYPL).

[51] George, cited in Barker, *Henry George*, 66.

In this regard, his political authenticity cannot be faulted. But it would also be a mistake to view this multiplicity as evidence of simple contradiction in his thought, particularly in the light of his immense popular support. Indeed, what are apparently confounding contradictions offer instead a clarifying perspective on the contested understandings of liberalism in the period. One assessment of his intellectual contribution bestowed on George the laudable title of 'the most authentic late-Victorian successor of John Stuart Mill', and there is much evidence to support such a valediction.[52] Yet George remained largely opposed by self-proclaimed liberals of various stripes, and of course, through his involvement with the Irish Land War, catalysed labour and socialist movements on both sides of the Atlantic. 'The spread among the town artisans of [George's] conception of rent', according to Sidney and Beatrice Webb, had both 'transformed the economic views of the Trade Union world' and shifted 'the lines of party politics'.[53] It was George's intellectual contribution that had drawn together radicals and socialists, and it was his adherents that formed the nuclei of subsequent labour societies.[54] Despite this, George himself was soon abandoned. He was, according to the American economist Richard T. Ely, only 'an entering wedge' for socialism and had apparently quickly outlived his usefulness.[55] 'A preacher of Communism', who 'wants to stop half-way'.[56] His rapid abandonment by socialists, directly enacted in the early histories of socialism, shows him to be an awkward fit in this historical narrative too. Thomas Kirkup, for instance, whose 1887 *An Inquiry into Socialism* was a development of his entries on the topic in the *Encyclopaedia Britannica*, and which provided the prototype for many subsequent socialist genealogies, also credited George as the catalyst for contemporary socialism, but only 'indirectly', since his ideas 'were not distinctly socialist'.[57] Although he moved primarily in socialist and radical liberal circles, his intense and unshakable individualism gradually isolated him from many of these networks as his political vision, along with its undergirding individualist metaphysics, became cast as inescapably regressive.

The Foundations of 'Progress and Poverty'

Born in 1839, Henry George finished formal schooling at the relatively early age of 13 and, after a stint in the merchant navy, left his native Philadelphia for

[52] Wolfe, *From Radicalism to Socialism*, 87.
[53] Webb and Webb, *The History of Trade Unionism*, 362.
[54] Webb, *Socialism in England*, 21–22.
[55] Richard T. Ely, *Recent American Socialism* (Baltimore, MD: N. Murray, Johns Hopkins University, 1885), 18; 'A Capitalist', *Rational Communism: The Present and Future Republic of North America* (New York: The Social Science Publishing Co., 1885), 464.
[56] J. Bleecker Miller, *Trade Organizations in Politics, Also, Progress and Robbery, an Answer to Henry George* (New York: Baker & Taylor, 1887), 174.
[57] Kirkup, *A History of Socialism*, 328.

California. He did not fight in the Civil War, but lived an itinerant life in early adulthood, often working, but enduring frequent periods of unemployment.[58] Lacking formal education, George was self-taught; his intellectual development forged in public libraries and literary societies in Philadelphia and San Francisco. Such auto-didacticism was not uncommon prior to the professionalisation of the social sciences at the end of the century so that George's lack of credentialed education was not a significant hindrance to his first forays into economic and political thought.[59] Amateur interjections in political economy still appeared unexceptional while the distinction between elite and popular thought remained somewhat blurred, although this would notably change over the course of his career.[60] It appears as though George read little economics during his formative years, focussing on literature, poetry, history, and biography – subjects that would serve him well in popularising his ideas.[61] The celebrated neo-classical economist Alfred Marshall famously dismissed George as 'by nature a poet' rather than a serious economic thinker, but George's poetic inclinations enabled him to express an appealing moral clarity that could escape his critics' narrow economistic reasoning.[62] The recollection of his damascene moment – his conversion to the panacea of equitable distribution of land – on a road in California demonstrated George's spirituality, as well as his tendency for bombast and righteous indignation.[63] Consequently, although these were ingredients in his success, the critical perception of George as a self-anointed saviour and demagogue was a label easily applied to him by his critics, who were unnerved by both the spiritual and the populist dimensions of his work and oratory.[64]

Displaying a restless intellectual curiosity from an early age, George's formative years were marked by the anxiousness of an ambitious but unfocussed young man eager to make an impact on the world. To satisfy this feeling, George joined the merchant navy in search of the excitement of a peripatetic life. In April 1855, he departed on the clipper *Hindoo*, sailing to Australia and India. His correspondence with friends and family back home reveal both the devout religiosity of his home life and his persistent curiosity with political

58 Sklansky, *The Soul's Economy*, 105; Barker, *Henry George*, 51.
59 Rodgers, *Atlantic Crossings*, 26.
60 Emma Rothschild, 'Political Economy', in Gareth Stedman Jones, and Gregory Claeys (eds.), *The Cambridge History of Nineteenth-Century Political Thought* (Cambridge: Cambridge University Press, 2011), 749.
61 Barker, *Henry George*, 45, 137.
62 Alfred Marshall, 'Three Lectures on Progress and Poverty' [1883–4], *The Journal of Law and Economics* 12, no. 1 (1969): 186.
63 Barker, *Henry George*, 136.
64 George Campbell, Duke of Argyll, 'The Prophet of San Francisco', in *Property in Land: A Passage-at-Arms between the Duke of Argyll and Henry George* (New York: Funk & Wagnalls, 1884), 7–42.

developments back in America and across the world.[65] After returning from his travels, George aimed to set out again once more, this time for the west coast in search of his fortune: 'I am still of the same determination in regard to going west', he wrote, and soon set about investigating wages and employment opportunities in the Pacific states.[66] While sometimes admonished by his family for spending too much time enjoying himself and losing sight of his ambitions, George was still keen to work hard. Nevertheless, he complained, his restless intellect had made him the 'jack of three different trades, and I am afraid, master of none'.[67]

Once in California, George's fascination with political life continued unabated, and he became frustrated at the paucity of civic discussion and engagement there.[68] 'Even the news of the "bloody Harper's Ferry rebellion"', he complained to his mother, 'couldn't get up the smallest kind of excitement, except among the political papers'.[69] Stirred by the turmoil of the developing Civil War, George, as a committed abolitionist, contemplated joining the Union army but eventually decided it would be fruitless to do so in the west.[70] Instead, George started working for the *San Francisco Monitor*, and it was here that he first engaged with Irish conditions and political issues.[71]

In 1869, he became the temporary editor of the *Monitor*, which was the regional Irish Catholic paper. It was at this juncture that George took his first forays into the topic of land, even though some of his ideas had been percolating during the preceding decade. It is more than coincidental that George's firm and strident commitment to the idea of a natural right to land, and his nascent ideas for reform, developed in tandem with his interest in Irish conditions.[72] His expression of natural law principles fit comfortably at the newspaper, and his editorials on Irish land in the early 1870s set much of the tone and shape of his later work. But it was not just Irish conditions that helped to form his ideas. In so many ways, the rapid and unrestrained development of California at the time, lacking firmly established social structures and cultural hierarchies, helped George to reach his particular conclusions. With great numbers of people, like George himself, heading west in search of wealth, land speculation

65 Charles Walton to Henry George, 10 May 1855 (HGP, Series I: A, Box 1, NYPL).
66 Henry George to unspecified, 3 April 1857 (HGP, Series I: A, Box 1, NYPL).
67 Henry George to unspecified, 3 April 1857 (HGP, Series I: A, Box 1, NYPL); Jefferies to Henry George, 19 May 1858 (HGP, Series I: A, Box 1, NYPL).
68 Henry George to Sir George Grey, 3 July 1880 (HGP, Series I: A, Box 2, NYPL).
69 Henry George to Catherine George, November 1859 (HGP, Series I: A, Box 1, NYPL).
70 Henry George to his brother, 19 August 1861 (HGP, Series I: A, Box 1, NYPL).
71 O'Donnell, 'Henry George and the "New Political Forces"', 40.
72 James J. Greene, 'The Impact of Henry George's Theories on American Catholics' (PhD dissertation, University of Notre Dame, 1956), 75; O'Donnell, 'Henry George and the "New Political Forces"', 52; Barker, *Henry George*, 126–127.

soon became rife.[73] Older Mexican Catholic traditions of public ownership of town land were soon in conflict with the acquisitive ambitions of newer arrivals to the area.[74] With speculators devouring land beside the unfolding railway network, economic expansion was cannibalising itself along with the livelihoods of many. George had his own personal experiences with the suffocating forces of monopoly too in his legal battles with the Western Union telegraph company, which saw his fledgling journalistic enterprise crushed by the forces of capital.[75]

Political graft and corruption accompanied the uncontrolled expansion as the heady search for profit encircled Californian land. The expansion of San Francisco brought spectacular riches to speculators while public needs were ignored.[76] George's moral sense was outraged at all this, and he soon found a valuable niche as a crusading journalist, exposing fraud and venality, a worthy public service that quickly drew him into the political world. Here he argued for an end to the 'monopoly of land and water' and attacked 'the shameful state of things which compels men to beg who are willing to work'.[77] Trips to the east coast had reminded George of the stark disparity evident there between luxurious wealth and harrowing poverty, and he was determined to resist such developments in his new home. The particular cultural and ethnic composition of California also gave added tension and prominence to labour issues there, where Irish workers often rallied round the cause of Chinese exclusion in pursuit of better conditions for themselves, a world that George was briefly drawn into as well before he rejected its nativist xenophobia.[78]

Critics often reached a similar conclusion about the centrality of Californian conditions to George's ideas.[79] Even those somewhat sympathetic to George could equivocate that while his plans to nationalise the land might be suitable for areas of 'new' settlement like the American west, they were infeasible in countries where private property was more established.[80] There can be no doubt that George and his work were distinctively

73 O'Donnell, *Henry George and the Crisis of Inequality*, 20–21.

74 Paul W. Gates, 'Pre-Henry George Land Warfare in California', *California Historical Society Quarterly* 46, no. 2 (1967): 121–148; Barker, *Henry George*, 87–90.

75 O'Donnell, 'Henry George and the "New Political Forces"', 40.

76 Sklansky, *The Soul's Economy*, 115; Rodgers, *Atlantic Crossings*, 48.

77 Henry George, 'To the Voters of San Francisco', clipping from unnamed newspaper, 3 May 1878 (HGP, Series I: A, Box 2, NYPL).

78 Edward Connolly [People's Reform and Anti-Chinese Party of San Francisco] to Henry George, 25 August 1877 (HGP, Series I: A, Box 2, NYPL).

79 Arnold Toynbee, *'Progress and Poverty,' A Criticism of Mr. Henry George, Being Two Lectures Delivered in St. Andrew's Hall, Newman Street, London, by the Late Arnold Toynbee* (London: Kegan Paul, Trench & Co., 1883), 8.

80 The 'main idea of the book would be very beneficial in the allotment of land in new colonies', but would be too disruptive elsewhere suggested a reviewer from the University of Edinburgh. Unnamed to Henry George, 8 January 1880 (HGP, Series I:A, Box 2, NYPL).

forged on the American frontier. California represented the termination of the economic and imaginative possibilities offered by the expansive continental landmass, and as the state grew, the supposed character forming and immaterial qualities of the land became myths of the past rather than the present. Anticipating Frederick Jackson Turner, George also recognised that the availability of land had caused Americans to attribute 'to themselves and their institutions what is really due to conditions now rapidly passing away' and that this would make republican government more difficult.[81] Nevertheless, this certainly did not make George's concerns narrowly Californian. The idea of new and 'unoccupied' land had shaped European and American political thought for several centuries, providing a place for utopian dreams to be enacted, an escape from the confines of social hierarchy and economic exploitation, and a natural resource that fed a hunger for profit and power. When the aristocratic Liberty and Property Defence League in Britain could straightforwardly assert that colonial expansion was proof that land was not finite and could be increased, it was clear that the end of the 'frontier', such as it was conceived, was not a Californian issue, but one that concerned political imaginations far beyond.[82]

Altogether, these influences permeated George's thinking during the 1870s, but would only achieve a clear enunciation by the end of the decade. Setbacks in his journalistic enterprises provided George with the time, from 1877, to work closely on ideas he had first expressed in 1871 in *Our Land and Land Policy*, primarily that access to land 'cannot be alienated' and is 'a right as sacred, as indefeasible as [the] right to life itself'.[83] In his magnum opus, published just weeks before the start of the 1880s, George made the moral and economic case for equal access to land (and the wealth of the natural world more broadly), relying heavily on a foundation of natural rights. Put in its simplest form, George proposed to make the state the national landlord by appropriating all rents 'to the common benefit'.[84] He made it clear, however, that 'the complete recognition of common rights to land need in no way interfere with the complete recognition of individual right to improvements or produce'.[85] The basis for his scheme was that 'private property in land has no warrant in justice, but stands condemned as the denial of natural right – a subversion of the law of nature', and his plan, later known as the 'Single-Tax', was simply

[81] Henry George, *The Irish Land Question: What It Involves, and How Alone It Can Be Settled. An Appeal to the Land Leagues* (London: Cameron & Ferguson, 1881), 57; Henry George, 'Garfield or Hancock', 1880 (HGP, Series II, Box 12, NYPL).

[82] Liberty and Property Defence League, *Land* (London: Parliamentary Committee of the Liberty and Property Defence League, 1885), 18.

[83] Henry George, 'Our Land and Land Policy' [1871], in *Our Land and Land Policy: Speeches, Lectures and Miscellaneous Writings* (New York: Doubleday and McClure Co., 1901), 85.

[84] George, *Progress and Poverty*, 359. [85] George, *Progress and Poverty*, 359

to 'appropriate rent by taxation'.[86] This would not require an increase in the machinery of the state and even leave current landlords in 'possession of what they are please to call *their* land'.[87] Nevertheless, George believed – and the 10 sections, 45 chapters, and over 500 pages of analysis in *Progress and Poverty* made the case – that this effective nationalisation of the value of land would 'raise wages, increase the earnings of capital, extirpate pauperism, abolish poverty, give remunerative employment to whoever wishes it, afford free scope to human powers, lessen crime, elevate morals, and taste, and intelligence, purify government and carry civilization to yet nobler heights'.[88]

His analysis covered economics, anthropology, modern and ancient history, politics, ethics, and comparative linguistics, but, as he made clear in his preface to the fourth edition of *Progress and Poverty*, 'no previous reading is necessary to the understanding of the argument, [its central tenets] are facts of common observation and common knowledge, which every reader can verify for himself'.[89] His scheme bore resemblances to those that had earlier been made by radical theorists such as Thomas Paine, Thomas Spence, and William Ogilvie in the eighteenth century and advocated by Chartists and labour associations in the nineteenth century. For his own part, George absolutely denied any familiarity with these earlier schemes of land nationalisation. His explanation for this was simple and articulated effectively his vision of a moral order emanating from the natural world – it was a mistake 'to think that men must draw from one another to see the same truths or to fall into the same errors. Truth is, in fact, a relation of things which has to be seen independently because it exists independently'.[90]

Reaction, Evaluation, and Critique

On 20 September 1879, Philip Van Patten, head of the perilously fragmenting Socialist Labor Party, wrote to Terence V. Powderly, his counterpart at the Knights of Labor, lamenting the disparate concerns and ambitions of America's labour radicals. 'If only we could rally a gigantic independent Labor Party', he wrote, 'with Labor measures first [and] leaving out all radical socialistic planks which are not expedient to advocate yet, but of course retaining the proper spirit and tendency, we could make the country shake in 1880!'.[91] Another friend of Powderly wrote to him around this time also disheartened that 'the clouds in the labor sky are just as dark as they ever were'.[92] Edward Stevens of

86 George, *Progress and Poverty*, 362, 264.
87 George, *Progress and Poverty*, 364.
88 George, *Progress and Poverty*, 364.
89 George, *Progress and Poverty*, 1.
90 George, cited in Barker, *Henry George*, 137.
91 Philip Van Patten to Terence V. Powderly, 20 September 1879 (Powderly Papers, Series 1: Box 2, Catholic University of America).
92 G. S. Boyle to Terence V. Powderly, 13 September 1879 (PP, Series 1: Box 2, CUA).

Chicago complained similarly at the very end of the 1870s that 'there is a great dearth of labor writers who can present ideas, clear and sharply defined. Some are so full of abstract theories that to the masses they are incomprehensible, while the others are either so dry or crude that they fail to accomplish the work they really desire'.[93] Little did any of these men know that a book was about to be released that would supply a new impetus, cohesion, and clarity for so many labour radicals. *Progress and Poverty* was published at the tail end of 1879, and George worked tirelessly to find reviewers and critics who could bring the book to public attention.

For the first half of 1880, the book did not cause much of a stir, but as the year progressed, it began to reach a wider audience. This was partly due to George's efforts, as well as the publicity given to the book by the *Irish World*. By the beginning of 1881, George was confident enough to confide to a friend that 'the future of the book is, I think, secure' and bragged that 'as far as I can learn no book on political economy has even yet been published in the United States, or (to my astonishment in England either) that has ever yet sold a 1,000 copies in the first year'.[94] In July, the wealthy philanthropist and former abolitionist Francis G. Shaw, in huge admiration for George's work, ordered 1,000 copies of the book to be placed in libraries across the United States, and by the summer of 1882, George's publishers were struggling to keep up with the overwhelming demand.[95] The next year, 1883, saw 80,000 copies sold in Britain alone, and it had gone through over a hundred editions in the United States.[96] Its incredible success made the book 'second only to the Bible in nineteenth-century readership and its author the most influential American economist worldwide'.[97] The opinion of George's own publisher was equally striking. It was his belief that 'never before, probably has a single book so influenced the public mind in so short a time'.[98]

The *Irish World* initially greeted the book with an unimpressive review. 'He evidently means well', sighed the reviewer, who found his scheme 'laborious' although welcomed the book as 'an indication that public thought is at last veering into the right direction'.[99] The writer suggested that instead of George's calculations, 'to just make one simple sweeping change'; a more familiar agrarian suggestion 'that individual property in land shall not be

93 Edward Stevens to Terence V. Powderly, 20 November 1879 (PP, Series 1: Box 2, CUA).
94 Henry George to Edward Robeson Taylor, 4 January 1881 (HGP, Series I: A, Box 3, NYPL).
95 Francis G. Shaw to Henry George, 18 July 1881 (HGP, Series I: A, Box 3, NYPL).
96 'Anarchic Socialism', *New Englander*, 7, no. 178 (January 1884): 125; W. H. Mallock, *Property and Progress, or a Brief Inquiry into Contemporary Social Agitation in England* (New York: G. P. Putnam's Sons, 1884), 4.
97 Sklansky, *The Soul's Economy*, 115.
98 J. C. Durant to Henry George, London, n.d. (HGP, Series I: A, Box 3, NYPL).
99 *Irish World*, 3 January 1880.

recognized in the courts of this country beyond what is sufficient for the cultivation and support of a family'.[100] Quickly, however, the paper was to adopt George with enthusiasm, recommending in May that a copy of *Progress and Poverty* 'should be in the hands of every reader'.[101] Through association with its editor, Patrick Ford, George began to write regularly for the *Irish World*.[102] He was also introduced to Michael Davitt when the Irish Land League leader and labour radical arrived in New York in the autumn of 1880. The two men soon recognised their ideological affinities, with George writing a year later that Davitt's 'idea of the ultimate solution of the question went as far as mine does'.[103] It was at this initial meeting, George claimed, that Davitt had 'pledge[d] the Land League to push' *Progress and Poverty*.[104] He soon gained popularity within New York's Irish communities, manifested in invitations to speak at Land League branches on the eastern seaboard because of his 'hearty interest in the Land League'.[105]

Further afield, George was delighted with the responses to his work, with the book making, to his mind, all the right friends and enemies. Yale's William Graham Sumner, one of America's most prominent classical liberal and social Darwinist academics, naturally attacked the work.[106] As did Alfred Marshall, the Cambridge economist, and Arnold Toynbee of Oxford, both in sustained fashion. Professor Bonamy Price, too, was 'entirely opposed' to *Progress and Poverty*. A student of Price showed George's book to the Oxford economist and recollected to George in a letter that, 'he neither convinced me that your views were entirely utopian, nor did he ever return me your book'.[107] Despite their scathing and dismissive evaluations, the prominence of these critics was evidence of George's already extensive reputation, as well as helping to develop it further. George's publisher was delighted by these hostile reviews, noting that in garnering attention for the work they 'have done us an immense amount of good'.[108]

More positive responses came from expected sources. George was thrilled when the naturalist and land nationaliser Alfred Russel Wallace endorsed the book, declaring it 'the most remarkable and important work of the present century'.[109] The first continental European review came from

[100] *Irish World*, 3 January 1880. [101] *Irish World*, 1 May 1880.

[102] On Ford, see James P. Rodechko, *Patrick Ford and His Search for America: A Case Study of Irish-American Journalism, 1870–1913* [1968] (New York: Arno Press, 1976).

[103] Henry George, *Irish World*, 10 December 1881.

[104] Henry George to Edward Robeson Taylor, 20 November 1880 (HGP, Series I: A, Box 2, NYPL).

[105] James A. Murphy, Sec. South Boston Land League, to Henry George, 3 February 1881 (HGP, Series I: A, Box 3, NYPL).

[106] Barker, *Henry George*, 332.

[107] F. MacMillan to Henry George, 3 October 1882 (HGP, Series I: A, Box 3, NYPL).

[108] J. C. Durant to Henry George, n.d. (HGP, Series I: A, Box 3, NYPL).

[109] Henry George to Edward Robeson Taylor, 7 September 1881 (HGP, Series I: A, Box 3, NYPL); Alfred R. Wallace to Henry George, 3 June 1882; Alfred R. Wallace to Henry George, 7 June 1882 (HGP, Series I: A, Box 3, NYPL).

the Belgian political economist Émile de Laveleye, a glowing commendation in the Parisian *Revue Scientifique* which 'endorse[d] substantially the whole programme', to George's great satisfaction.[110] Laveleye, a proponent of historical anthropology with a Christian socialist ideological bent, was best known for his work *Primitive Property* and his attacks on Herbert Spencer's social philosophy, and acted as a conduit for George's work in Europe.[111] The Belgian was hostile to positivist liberalism, although he found reliance on the idea of 'natural rights' to be similarly spurious, preferring instead a concept of 'rational right'.[112] The two men shared ongoing work and ideas, as Laveleye connected George to friends and associates in the world of 'rational socialism', a non-Marxian heterodox Franco-Hispanic current of socialism that drew heavily from Proudhonism and Louis Blanc.[113] In these and other radical networks, George soon found that his ideas had a natural constituency and an older radical genealogy, and George made use of these discoveries to buttress his own argument and support his plan.[114]

The first wave of reviews and critiques were inevitably accompanied by a familiar problem for George. As early as 1871, when he had shared some of his embryonic theories with a friend back in Philadelphia, George had been confronted with the challenge of misunderstanding and misrepresentation. At that time, his correspondent had gently cautioned him that although his plan had much to commend it, 'the mass of mankind are not sufficiently enlightened to understand its workings', and, despite praise from his supporters for the clarity of his exposition, critical interpretations continued to prey upon its ambiguities.[115] It was an issue raised by one English supporter,

110 Henry George to Edward Robeson Taylor, 19 February 1880 (HGP, Series I: A, Box 2, NYPL).

111 Émile de Laveleye, *Primitive Property* (London: Macmillan and Co., 1878). Laveleye's work was influential for Henry Summer Maine, as well as Irish radicals interested in ideas about ownership of land in other places and contexts. See A. M. Sullivan, 'Ireland's Great Grievance: Land Tenure in Ireland and Other Countries', *American Catholic Quarterly Review* 6 (1881): 62.

112 Émile de Laveleye, 'The State versus the Man: A Criticism of Herbert Spencer', *The Eclectic Magazine of Foreign Literature* 41, no. 6 (1885): 733–734.

113 This included economist Émile Justin Menier and political theorist Agathon de Potter of Brussels, whose work had 'very much pleased and impressed' George. Recounted in a letter from Henry George to John Swinton, 29 April 1880 (HGP, Series I: A, Box 2, NYPL); Menier was a relative unknown who published a treatise called *L'Avenir Economique*, and Agathon de Potter, the son of famous historian and socialist Louis de Potter, was a Belgian philosopher and sociologist. He published *Economie Sociale* in 1874 and *Le Socialisme Libertaire ou Anarchisme Individualiste et le Socialisme Rationnel* in 1891. See Gregory Claeys, 'Non-Marxian Socialism, 1815–1914', in Stedman Jones Gareth, and Gregory Claeys (eds.), *The Cambridge History of Nineteenth-Century Political Thought* (Cambridge: Cambridge University Press, 2011), 548.

114 Henry George, lecture notes for Cambridge, 10 March 1884 (HGP, Series II, Box 12, NYPL).

115 Unsigned letter to Henry George, 16 September 1871 (HGP, Series I: A, Box 2, NYPL).

who felt that George did not make 'sufficiently clear' that his plan did not intend to 'interfere with house property'.[116] In the writer's experience, 'I find that people to whom your doctrines are mentioned, fly away with the impression, that their houses are in danger'. George was again warned about this in 1882 by his friend and advocate Fr Thomas Dawson who cautioned the American that 'I find by experience that the expression "Private property in land" is misunderstood, and keeps people from going deeply into what you have written. This may be unreasonable and even stupid, but it is the fact. People think that you condemn the private use of land'.[117] George's exasperated response that 'people will misunderstand until they take the trouble to understand' betrayed an unerring confidence in his ideas and stubborn refusal to compromise – something that would hinder his support in Ireland.

Many formal critiques that appeared in contemporary periodicals (and shortly thereafter as books and pamphlets) exhibited a similar degree of misunderstanding, which tended to be accompanied by brusque dismissal and the assumption 'that a passing sneer will dispose of him'.[118] The Duke of Argyll badly missed the mark when he wrote that George, 'like all Communists', regarded the state 'as a great abstract Personality, in which all power is to be centred', but he at least considered George worthy of sustained condemnation.[119] The Fabian writer Sydney Olivier, although not overly sympathetic to George himself, complained in 1882 that he was 'anxious to see, what I have never yet seen', a careful refutation of George that relied on 'some other argument than the pooh-pooh one, which is all one is generally treated to'.[120] Notwithstanding the interventions mentioned earlier, academic economists were generally reluctant to engage in public debate because to do so would leave their status as experts open to popular evaluation, threatening their newly professionalised authority which increasingly relied, not on shaping public opinion, but influence over government policy.[121] For those who were drawn into public criticism of George, attacking his lack of economic training and his failure to properly engage with contemporary economic theory provided the most direct and self-congratulatory approach. 'The whole literature of "economics" is a denial of

[116] W. Duignan to Henry George, 25 September 1882 (HGP, Series I: A, Box 3, NYPL).
[117] Fr Thomas Dawson to Henry George, 21 September 1882 (HGP, Series I: A, Box 3, NYPL).
[118] Mallock, *Property and Progress*, 1.
[119] Argyll, 'The Prophet of San Francisco', in *Property in Land*, 22.
[120] Sydney Olivier to Graham Wallas, 15 November 1882, in Margaret Olivier (ed.), *Sydney Olivier: Letters and Selected Writings* (London: George Allen & Unwin, 1948), 54.
[121] Furner, 'The Republican Tradition and the New Liberalism', 173; Robert L. Church, 'Economists as Experts: The Rise of an Academic Profession in America, 1870–1917' in Lawrence Stone (ed.), *The University in Society, Volume II: Europe, Scotland, and the United States from the 16th to the 20th Century* (Princeton: Princeton University Press, 1974), 573, 589.

George's dictum that it is the simplest of the sciences', cautioned Professor Carl Plehn of the University of California; it only appears so 'to the unscientific'.[122]

Yet the explosive popularity of George's work demanded critical recognition, and the first major wave of published refutations by economists, social scientists, politicians, and political thinkers crested between 1882 and 1884. A tone of resigned obligation permeated many of these responses to George's work. It was necessary because 'leading statesmen' could 'no longer keep quiet on the subject'.[123] Henry Fawcett, M.P. and Professor of Political Economy, noted that 'it has rarely happened that a book dealing with social and economic questions has been more widely read than Mr George's work. It therefore becomes more important carefully to examine the proposals there advocated'.[124] For conservatives, the need to respond to George's work was in some senses even more urgent, concerned as they were that this book was 'at the moment selling by thousands in the alleys and back streets of England, and is being audibly welcomed there as a glorious gospel of justice'.[125] Perhaps most worryingly, at least to the Tory novelist William Hurrell Mallock, writing in the pages of the *Quarterly Review*, George's ideas were 'well calculated to turn the head of an artisan [...] It is not the poor, it is not the seditious only, who have thus been affected by Mr George's doctrines'.[126]

In light of this precipitous danger, attacks on George's work proliferated. Perhaps the dominant rhetorical stance taken in opposition was to condemn his scheme as naïve, archaic, and utopian, adopted with varying degrees of sympathy or hostility by social liberal, classical liberal, and conservative writers. *Progress and Poverty* was evidence in this regard that 'we must abandon the belief in the discovery [...] of a panacea for all social evils'.[127] For Arnold Toynbee, George's 'delusive panacea' was both politically dangerous and woefully insufficient to meet the demands of economic equality it promised.[128] His plans were inexpedient, but they also represented a naivety about the harmonious cooperation of individuals in society. There was no such thing as a natural economic harmony that could be unearthed by removing

122 Carl Plehn in T. H. Benton De Witt (ed.), *A Correspondence between an Amateur and a Professor of Political Economy* (Philadelphia: J. B. Lippincott, 1898), 18, 17.

123 Samuel Smith, *The Nationalisation of the Land* (London: Kegan Paul, Trench & Co., 1884), 3; Jesse Collings, 'Occupying Ownership', *Fortnightly Review* 35, no. 206 (February 1884): 257.

124 Fawcett, *State Socialism*, 4; John Rae, *Contemporary Socialism* (New York: Charles Scribner's Sons, 1884), 385.

125 Mallock, *Property and Progress*, 4.

126 Mallock, *Property and Progress*, 5; The popularity of George among 'the artizans of our great towns' was a particularly concerning facet of his support. Smith, *The Nationalisation of the Land*, 3.

127 George Basil Dixwell, *'Progress and Poverty.' A Review of the Doctrines of Henry George* (Cambridge: John Wilson and Son, 1882), 45.

128 Toynbee, *'Progress and Poverty'*, 8.

private property in land, Toynbee told his audience at St. Andrew's Hall in London, and economists had long since stopped believing in such false hopes, understanding instead that individual self-interest was akin to 'a great physical force, [...] the laws of which must be studied in order that it may be controlled'.[129] It was only through increased and more enlightened administration that such economic problems could be solved.

While social liberals like Toynbee did not deny the necessity of improving the social and economic conditions currently existing, they shared with many conservative writers a rejection of George's most fundamental claim – that poverty was increasing with industrial complexity and concentrating wealth.[130] John Rae, editor of the *Contemporary Review*, saw this as a fallacious assumption, describing it as 'the enigma of the apparently receding train'; a matter of perception rather than fact.[131] Recourse to apparently irrefutable statistical fact, at least in the minds of critics, showing the gradually improving social and economic condition of the poor, proved to be a lynchpin for dismissals of proposals for reform, and one applied liberally to George. 'It is much desired' opined one writer, that George's supporters would start to 'apply themselves closely to the study [...] of the statistical facts and the statistical analysis'.[132] This criticism got to the nub of the issue: whether such social questions should be addressed in terms of popular power and right, or calculations of purchasing power and economic welfare. John Rae's criticism of George, that for the American 'the poverty of the labourer consists in the greater wealth of the landlord', rang true in so far as great disparities of wealth were not only morally iniquitous to George, but threatened the functioning of a popular democracy and the individual moral development that naturally attended it.[133]

Taken together, George's naïve view of the harmoniousness of the natural and social world, his lack of attention to contemporary economic theory, and apparent obliviousness to the myriad benefits of economic and industrial development led critics to see George as irredeemably archaic and indeed anti-modern. George's plan appeared retrograde, conjuring up a facile approach to political economy belonging to an earlier age. This line of attack was common to conservative, liberal, and socialist critics alike.[134] The Irish historian W. E. H. Lecky, a conservative Whig, remarked that 'few things are more curious to observe in the extreme radical speculation of our times than the revival of beliefs which had been supposed to have been long since finally exploded – the aspirations to customs belonging to early and rudimentary

[129] Toynbee, *'Progress and Poverty'*, 22. [130] Toynbee, *'Progress and Poverty'*, 28.
[131] Rae, *Contemporary Socialism*, 386; Smith, *The Nationalisation of the Land*, 15.
[132] 'Review of Property and Progress, or Facts against Fallacies', *London Quarterly Review*, 2, no. 124 (July 1884): 384.
[133] Rae, *Contemporary Socialism*, 397. [134] Smith, *The Nationalisation of the Land*, 6–7.

stages of society'.[135] The idea of common ownership of the soil, he observed, was common to 'barbarous or semi-barbarous stages of national development' and typical of 'archaic types of thought and custom'.[136] 'Jefferson had already anticipated these writers', sneered Lecky, and had long been proven wrong by the course of history.[137]

In other respects, however, Lecky's analysis was an example of the more prosaic and familiar conservative criticisms of George: The 'great popularity and influence' of *Progress and Poverty* was due primarily to the author's 'eminent literary skill' rather than the ideas contained therein;[138] labour and capital had been so long intertwined with land that the idea of separating them was both impossible and morally unjustifiable;[139] and finally, that to deny the absolute and complete ownership of land by an individual was to negate all forms of possession, leaving the French, Lecky thought, with as much right to the land of England as the English.[140] Naturally, sitting comfortably and barely hidden beneath most of these uninspired defences of the status quo was a haughty moralism, one that regularly compelled conservative critics to remind their readers that poverty was ultimately a personal moral failure. The economists Alfred Marshall and George Basil Dixwell both easily slipped from disinterested financial analysis to a discussion of moral weakness, suggesting that lack of thrift rather than land monopoly was the primary cause of poverty and that 'much vice, crime, ignorance, and brutality [are] the cause of poverty, instead of being caused by poverty, as Mr George assumes'.[141] An extended critique of *Progress and Poverty* in the *Edinburgh Review* offered similar advice. Not only was the book 'dangerous reading' for the 'half-educated and ill informed', a 'public mischief' composed of a 'deleterious compound of anarchical principles and spurious political economy', but it ignored the fact that 'indolence, improvidence, physical disease, inherited weakness of mind or body, vicious dispositions and all manner of evil passions, are the chief factors of this conglomeration of misery'.[142]

[135] Lecky, *Democracy and Liberty*, vol. II, 224.

[136] Lecky, *Democracy and Liberty*, vol. II, 224, 228.

[137] W. E. H. Lecky, *Democracy and Liberty,* vol. I [1896] (New York: Longmans, Green, and Co., 1903), 216–217; George's reliance on the founding documents of the United States attracted derision among elite British critics. 'Mr. George and His Books', *The Saturday Review of Politics, Literature, Science, and Art,* 57, no. 1,474 (26 January 1884): 97.

[138] Lecky, *Democracy and Liberty*, vol. II, 353; Argyll, 'The Prophet of San Francisco', in *Property in Land*, 10.

[139] Lecky, *Democracy and Liberty*, vol. II, 354; Guilford L. Molesworth, *Land as Property* (E & F. N. Spon, London, 1885), 12.

[140] Lecky, *Democracy and Liberty*, vol. II, 354.

[141] Dixwell, '*Progress and Poverty*', 7; Marshall, 'Three Lectures on *Progress and Poverty*', 217–226.

[142] *Edinburgh Review* 157, no. 321 (1883): 288, 266–267.

In this regard, at least, criticisms of George mirrored similar effusions directed against other socialist thinkers. In other ways, however, *Progress and Poverty* presented a more unique set of intellectual challenges. The title of George's magnum opus revealed the book's heredity; its animating paradox echoing the much older and more fundamental tension between what Istvan Hont has described as 'the traditional egalitarian intuitions of Western moral thought and the guiding assumption of modern political economy'.[143] Where the birth of modern liberalism may be traced to a presumptive accommodation of economic inequality with political equality, George rejected the necessity of such a comfortable compromise, all while retaining an unerring belief in the established liberal freedoms of possession, speech, and association. As a consequence, he proved a more complex adversary for liberal thinkers who, in general, found his moral claims about land ownership difficult to refute on their own terms. Instead, within liberal circles, a critical opinion coalesced around the inexpediency of his plans, rather than any moral inequity. The Liberal M.P. for Liverpool, Samuel Smith, penned a critique of George's ideas for the *Contemporary Review*, subsequently republished in book form. Smith conceded that the history of popular alienation from the land was 'cruel and unjust', but that 'modern civilisation is the web woven of the warp and woof of conqueror and conquered' and it would be best if such claims were left undisturbed.[144] For Smith, it was simply a matter of practicality, and he adroitly directed his historicist argument to utilitarian conclusions: political reform should have no recourse to grand historical or moral claims, but be limited to contemporary need. As for George's arguments for a natural right to land, Smith was in this way able to brush them away alongside the historical detritus. It would simply be inexpedient to the security of property needed for capital accumulation to nationalise the land: 'I could not conceive anything more destructive of the social welfare of any old and peaceful country than to tear up the foundation of all property by disputing existing titles to the soil.'[145]

That George's plan was simultaneously too radical in its disruption of the status quo and too limited and conservative in its potential consequences was a criticism offered by Gladstonian, progressive and even radical liberal rebuttals. As part of Joseph Chamberlain's influential Radical Programme, for instance, the municipal reformer Jesse Collings, who advocated small-holdings and allotments for rural labourers, categorised George's plan as one of 'certain remedies, not only drastic, but alarming, in their scope and magnitude', that would 'be applied for the sake of a problematical gain'.[146] Pressed

[143] Istvan Hont, *Jealousy of Trade: International Competition and the Nation-State in Historical Perspective* (Cambridge, MA: Harvard University Press, 2005), 92, 389.

[144] Smith, *The Nationalisation of the Land*, 10. [145] Smith, *The Nationalisation of the Land*, 12.

[146] 'The Radical Programme', *Fortnightly Review* 34, no. 201 (September 1883): 444.

away from claims of natural or universal right by George's arguments, these very diverse liberal positions converged on the response that such ills as resulted from land ownership could be obviated simply by improved state management and regulation, albeit to vastly different degrees. For Smith, the harms erroneously attributed to the general principle of absolute ownership of the soil or private possession were merely the effects of bad owners and therefore should not be rectified by the application of a universal enactment based on any moral claim, but instead by the piecemeal intervention of the state, taking expedient measures in order 'to sweeten the lot of our labouring poor [...and] impose any restrictions on landed property that may be shown to be necessary'.[147] Collings similarly, despite sharing many of George's broader ambitions and inclinations, thought it far more straightforward to simply 'confer upon the State larger powers in these matters than she now possesses', making it 'the right and duty of the State to fix within certain broad limits the extent, and to control the conditions, of private ownership'.[148] In this way, George's vision of a popular resumption of natural rights (which would be itself the bedrock of popular democratic authority) was submerged by the liberal response; an ambition for the reclamation of power drowned out by calls for amelioration.

One of the more remarkable aspects to this was the degree to which the shift from the ground of rights to that of utility enabled a significant convergence between conservative and liberal thinkers. Insofar as George's moral claims were addressed, and of course these were absolutely the bedrock of his thesis, there was a striking degree of conformity of opinion across the political spectrum. Among the most prominent and astute rejoinders came from conservative ranks, that of the aforementioned William Hurrell Mallock, whose collected *Quarterly Review* articles were published in 1884.[149] As one reviewer noted observantly, despite Mallock's avowed Toryism 'there is no principle, nor any detail of argumentative illustration, contained in the articles which might not well have been written by as thorough-going a Liberal as Mr Fawcett'.[150] The ideas of Henry George, he continued, 'are no less opposed to the principles of political economists who may be called "Liberals" in politics than to those of the "Conservative" economists'.[151]

[147] Smith, *The Nationalisation of the Land*, 33.

[148] 'The Radical Programme', 445; Collings' plan was in actuality a much more complex local authority purchase scheme in which more tenants would become owner-occupiers, something akin to Irish peasant proprietary, but with the government possessing full rights of resumption. Collings, 'Occupying Ownership', 256–266.

[149] Mallock's book, alongside John Rae's *Contemporary Socialism*, had significant transatlantic influence. Bleecker Miller, *Trade Organization in Politics*, 167.

[150] 'Review of Property and Progress, or Facts against Fallacies', 383.

[151] 'Review of Property and Progress, or Facts against Fallacies', 383.

Initially, Mallock followed what would soon become a well-worn line of attack on George. He began by praising George's intellect and erudition, alongside his laudable sympathy for the poor and downtrodden, before rejecting his anti-Malthusian assumptions. As Mallock intoned: 'what ought to be, is not always what is'.[152] Next, he dismantled the claim that agricultural rents were sufficient to cause the poverty George described, before arguing that the real cause of George's popularity was the 'logical hocus-pocus' he performed on his readers.[153] Nevertheless, Mallock then proceeded to pay close attention to George's ideas, noting quite accurately that although historical argumentation was often used in support of land nationalisation, the histories of actual dispossession were irrelevant to George, since his ideas rested solely on the 'principle of natural and universal justice'; his view of land-owning, Mallock observed, 'is very much like the view which other people take of slave-owning'.[154] Mallock acknowledged what most other critics tended to either miss or ignore: that George's ideas, like the claims of the Land League for 'the land for the people', were grounded in an assertion of a natural right to life, existence, and self-preservation.

This key observation enabled Mallock to be explicit about the necessity of an argument against George based on social utility alone, for 'it is impossible to answer these questions by any appeal to the natural rights of man'.[155] This produced, for Mallock, an argument with strikingly similar structures to that of Toynbee, Smith, and even Collings. No natural right to life was denied by the monopolisation of land as long as others, excluded from access to it, could mostly manage to stay alive. Were the owners of land to *actively* deny existence, then this could be forbidden in law, but 'our point is, that the law has no call to forbid them, because it does not appear that such monstrous evictions are probable'.[156] Mallock's claim, much like that contained within other liberal critiques, was the quintessentially liberal argument that it was not domination, but actual interference itself, that was to be condemned; not private property, but simply its blatant abuses. He wrote:

> When the Duke of Westminster shows any desire to expel all the Belgravians, when the Duke of Bedford proposes to turn Covent-Garden into a game preserve, and when it comes to be the ambition of English landlords generally, not to get their rents, but to get rid of their tenantry, then we may be certain that English land-laws will be altered; and we should ourselves be the first to admit they ought to be.[157]

The unacknowledged resonances with the Irish context in the above passage were striking, but perhaps more importantly it represented one of the most

[152] Mallock, *Property and Progress*, 11–12; Rae, *Contemporary Socialism*, 410.
[153] Mallock, *Property and Progress*, 81. [154] Mallock, *Property and Progress*, 107.
[155] Mallock, *Property and Progress*, 125. [156] Mallock, *Property and Progress*, 114.
[157] Mallock, *Property and Progress*, 114.

astute conservative critics being drawn, by force of George's claims, to explicitly reject the narrowly contractual arguments regarding property and land that had often dominated conservative and classical liberal responses to the Irish Land War, in order to defend existing proprietorial structures.[158] As we will see, jettisoning familiar classical liberal arguments regarding property would be a common response to both George and the Land League. Mallock disregarded the idea that private property is ever such that 'its possessor can be allowed to use in any way he pleases'.[159] On the contrary, he explained in a Gladstonian fashion, 'the law, under certain circumstances, should compel a landlord to let his land, just as it compels a cabman to take a passenger in his cab, and perhaps compel him to let it on certain fixed conditions'.[160] Naturally, the 'certain conditions' that Mallock imagined were different from Collings, Toynbee, or Smith, but, in need of a refutation of George's claim that a right to the natural world was implied by a right to life, Mallock also found the firmest ground on a social conception of property rights.

If Mallock's widely read and much-admired critique of George brought out some important intellectual commonalities between the varying strands of liberal and conservative thought, two interconnected propositions can be identified therein that united nearly all of George's detractors from across the political spectrum: a rejection of the distinctiveness of land as property and a suspicion of claims to natural right. Both socialist and conservative opponents believed that George's claims regarding land amounted to an inadequate and inconsistent intermediate position. 'If property in land be not lawful', decreed one critic, 'then it is impossible logically to avoid the conclusion that *all other property is theft*'.[161] A priest, writing in the *Irish World*, made a similar deduction, albeit one that hinted at some form of distinction, arguing that the right to land and to other property 'blend into each other' making the difference between the two 'nugatory'.[162] 'There is no reason', wrote one American business leader, 'for the division between personal and real property, on the ground that the former is the product of man and the latter created by God'.[163] 'Property in one is as sacred as in the other.'[164] Similarly for Henry Hyndman, leader of the English Social Democratic Federation (SDF), the question of rent,

158 Tom Boylan, and Tadhg Foley, 'John Elliot Cairnes: Land, *Laissez-faire* and Ireland', in Thomas Boylan, Renee Prendergast, and John D. Turner (eds.), *A History of Irish Economic Thought* (Abingdon: Routledge, 2011), 160–161.
159 Mallock, *Property and Progress*, 116.
160 Mallock, *Property and Progress*, 117.
161 Molesworth, *Land as Property*, 12; Argyll, 'The Prophet of San Francisco', in *Property in Land*, 25.
162 Fr Januarius de Concillio, *Irish World*, 23 April 1881.
163 Bleecker Miller, *Trade Organization in Politics*, 158.
164 Bleecker Miller, *Trade Organization in Politics*, 164.

which was so fundamental for George and the Irish Land League, was simply a matter of capital and interest, since 'the land is only one of the means of production and [...] is useless without the others'.[165]

Traces of uncertainty and ambiguity can nevertheless be found in the work of some writers on this issue. So for Samuel Smith, while he could 'conceive no equitable reason why this form of wealth [i.e. land] should not have the protection of the law like all other kinds', some specific contexts provoked equivocation.[166] It was to the moral language of natural rights that Smith turned to in making his concession 'that property in land ought not to be as absolute as property in chattels', since 'the owner of land has no moral right to destroy its value'. 'I think it is contrary to natural law', he continued, 'that vast tracts of barren land in the Highlands should be shut up against the harmless tourist, because a deer-stalker does not wish his game to be disturbed'.[167] The complications introduced into his logic by this particular sentiment did not occupy Smith for long, but it is significant that it was not the language of expediency, but that of natural law, to which he turned in expressing it.

This linguistic prevarication on the issue of natural rights was not uncommon among political theorists and economists dealing with the land question; a consequence of the uneven transition away from such conceptual foundations. Nevertheless, radical reliance on this rhetoric continued unabated when it came to the land. There was a mutual dependence between what Mallock mocked as 'these high discussions as to natural justice and inalienable rights', and the assertion of a common claim to the soil.[168] Although the implicit challenge posed to private property by such language had been increasingly recognised by the propertied classes at least since the mid-eighteenth century, it had proved difficult to properly expunge these rhetorical formulations from political discourse, especially in the United States where the founding documents had given them a durable resonance.[169] British periodicals were especially scathing about George's use of this American political language, one commenting that 'the "natural, equal, and inalienable rights of men," which Mr George recognizes, mean simply the natural and unalterable level of savagery'.[170]

[165] Henry George, and H. M. Hyndman, 'Socialism and Rent-Appropriation', *The Nineteenth Century: A Monthly Review* 17, no. 96 (February 1885): 374.
[166] Smith, *The Nationalisation of the Land*, 13.
[167] Smith, *The Nationalisation of the Land*, 32–33. [168] Mallock, *Property and Progress*, 126.
[169] Daniel T. Rogers, *Contested Truths: Keywords in American Politics since Independence* (Cambridge, MA: Harvard University Press, 1987), 128–129.
[170] 'Mr. George and His Books', *The Saturday Review of Politics, Literature, Science, and Art* 57, no. 1,474 (26 January 1884): 97.

Others had found George's reliance on 'Divine Purpose and Final Causes exceedingly incongruous in such a treatise' on political economy, yet it was only within such a conceptual universe that his claims were fully intelligible.[171] George's dialogue with Hyndman exemplified this, since for all the English Marxist argued that capitalists, rather than landlords, were the primary expropriating class, George returned that it was 'only necessary to argue from the facts of nature, which are the same to-day as they have always been. Give men land, and they can produce capital. Deprive them of land, and they cease to exist'.[172] While Hyndman took exception to George's reliance on 'natural rights', it was only on these grounds, rooted ultimately in the right to life, and to the necessity of land to both existence and production, that George's political economy took flight. It was simple: 'people are suffering and are starving because the element which is indispensable to existence, and to which all have naturally equal rights, has been monopolised by some.'[173]

The idea of a natural right to land was not yet a parochial or unsophisticated claim among transatlantic radicals during the early 1880s, although it soon would be. For most of the decade, as Henry Fawcett noted, the nationalisation of the land was the foundational core and intellectual ballast that supported all other commitments.[174] It had a significant popular resonance too, far beyond the ranks of declared socialists. This sense that it chimed with common perceptions of justice, that 'a number of persons, who are by no means Socialists, appear to entertain some vague suspicion that it may be true', was a deep concern to many opponents, just as such 'striking consensus of moral perceptions' was, for George, evidence of the Divine justice of common property in land.[175] The ruptures and disagreements in British and American labour movements that were soon to follow, between Hyndman's SDF and William Morris' Socialist League, or between the Knights of Labor, the Socialist Labor Party, and the AFL, merely highlighted the divergent moral cosmologies between an ascendant scientism and an older radical tradition grounded in a more holistic conception of land and labour. In the early 1880s, George could be adequately, if broadly, described as a Christian socialist, admiring Marxism's bold critique and sharing political platforms with other socialists, although dreaming of his own vision of a cooperative commonwealth as 'true socialism'; his scheme

171 Sydney Olivier to Graham Wallas, 15 November 1882, in Margaret Olivier (ed.), *Sydney Olivier*, 55.

172 George and Hyndman, 'Socialism and Rent-Appropriation', 373.

173 George and Hyndman, 'Socialism and Rent-Appropriation', 377.

174 Fawcett, *State Socialism*, 3.

175 Mallock, *Property and Progress*, 126; Henry George, 'The "Reduction to Iniquity"', in George Campbell, and Henry George (eds.), *Property in Land: A Passage-at-Arms between the Duke of Argyll and Henry George* (New York: Funk & Wagnalls, 1884), 47.

of rent taxation being a means rather than an end, and conceding the potential propitiousness of a broader system of nationalisation in the future.[176] By the 1890s, however, this categorisation was no longer tenable.

George was not simply a mouthpiece of political atavism, however, but articulated a powerful challenge to established property rights, all while reaffirming an optimistic vision of collective sociability built on an 'ineradicable [...] moral sense' and the natural rights of the individual.[177] Critically, these two central lines of attack on George's ideas – towards the distinctiveness of land and the idea of a natural right to life – were also rhetorically and praxiographically central to the Land War in Ireland. Their political force was magnified by the ferocity of the conflict and created significant challenges for liberal thinkers to content with. Joined together, the right to life and the distinctness of land set a check on property, limiting ambitions of wealth accumulation within the boundaries of natural fertility and human necessity, while a naturalised individualism provided a moral justification for participatory democracy that stood over and above the state's claim to technocratic authority. Consequently, the reaction against George, animated by, and inseparable from the Land War itself, highlighted some of the patrician inheritance of social liberal thought, as well as helping to drive conservatives into the more malleable and adaptable embrace of the state in order to preserve property on the basis of utility.

[176] Barker, *Henry George*, 201; see also John Plowright, 'Political Economy and Christian Polity: The Influence of Henry George in England Reassessed', *Victorian Studies* 30, no. 2 (1987): 235–252; Peter D'Alroy Jones, *The Christian Socialist Revival, 1877–1914: Religion, Class, and Social Conscience in Late-Victorian England* (Princeton: Princeton University Press, 1968).

[177] Henry George to John Swinton, 2 June 1878 (HGP, Series I: A, Box 2, NYPL); George, 'The "Reduction to Iniquity"', 46; see also Sklansky, *The Soul's Economy*, 106; Avery Offer, *Property and Politics, 1870–1914: Landowners, Law, Ideology and Urban Development in England* (Cambridge: Cambridge University Press, 1981), 185.

2 Agrarianism and Political Thought

Being both the locus of economic and political power and the essential prerequisite of human life and habitation, land has long been a critically unstable element in political thought. With significant social, spiritual, and political dimensions extending far beyond any narrowly economic functions, the right to use land, and to exclude others from using it, has been central to the organisation of political life.[1] Classical conceptions of republican sovereignty had assumed the necessity of land for economic and therefore political independence, providing the space for the rational judgement required by public deliberation. Long before Thomas Jefferson's prediction that it would take the United States over a thousand years to colonise the continent of North America, a false prophesy upon which the foundations of the republic were built, land was the primary economic and political battleground; a source of power, independence, and security upon which democratic and collectivist ideals, from the Levellers to the Chartists, could be constructed.

In conjunction with these political and economic functions, the natural world has also been the setting and scaffolding for all human existence. Perceptions and beliefs about justice, fairness, and obligation; conceptions of value, significance, and purpose; ideas, social customs, behaviours, and modes of thought, indeed the whole moral and metaphysical universe which humans occupy, have been shaped by land, in its broadest sense.[2] The natural world, of which human bodies are physically a part, has always been the primary materialist lens through which human perceptions are formed.[3] As such, this chapter aims to tie together two particular threads. On the one hand, it offers a history of land in political thought, highlighting the tensions that the subject regularly drew out. It will trace the conceptual strands

1 Pierre Charbonnier, *Affluence and Freedom: An Environmental History of Political Ideas* (Cambridge: Polity Press, 2021), 49.
2 Karl Polanyi, *The Great Transformation: The Political and Economic Origins of Our Time* [1944] (Boston: Beacon Press, 1957), 178.
3 Alasdair MacIntyre, *Dependent Rational Animals* (London: Duckworth, 1999), 8; Terry Eagleton, *After Theory* (London: Penguin, 2004).

that knitted together many land and labour radicals, including George and the Irish Land League, within a shared, albeit often rigorously contested, ideological heritage. On the other, it suggests how these ideas had their own materialist roots in agrarian life, emerging from particular value structures that grew from a close dependence on the natural world. This peasant political theory, as it might be termed, will be developed more fully in Chapter 3, but it suggests that social practices, themselves products of a material environment, can be understood as nurturing specific political ideals. Connected to a more familiar textual and discursive analysis, this approach aims to provide a firmer footing for the extensive reach of the specific political commitments in question by anchoring them in a materiality beneath the tides and currents of thought.[4]

Land, Bodies, and Purpose

'People don't appreciate what land is', George was prone to lament.[5] Occupying the focal point of his theory and his philosophy, 'the question of all questions, the most fundamental and important', much of George's time and effort was spent discussing the difference between land, as 'the mother of the universe', and other forms of property.[6] 'Land is not merely one of the means of production', he explained, 'but the natural factor in all production, the field and material upon which alone human labour can be exerted'.[7] But George's conception of the natural world extended further than questions of economic value, significant as this was. It was grounded in a holistic harmoniousness that located human beings firmly within nature, and where it was possible to extend outwards universalising prescriptions based on the purposiveness of the human body in the natural world. In this, George was not undertaking a particularly original intellectual endeavour, resonant as these views were with long-standing natural law presumptions. Nevertheless, it is worth dwelling on both the structure and implications of George's arguments on this issue, as they can help to identify the key metaphysical divergences between what could be termed his 'corporeal' republicanism and the nascent liberal idealism that formed the basis of the ideological conflict.

The earth was inevitably a naturally harmonious system for George, since it was a closed one. 'For that man cannot exhaust or lessen the powers of nature follows from the indestructibility of matter and the persistence of force', he explained.

[4] Hamati-Ataya, 'The Sociology of Knowledge', 11.
[5] Henry George, Lecture notes for Shoreditch Hall, 31 March 1884, 'Lecture notes, Britain [1880s]' (HGP, Series II, Box 12, NYPL).
[6] Henry George, 'Unidentified Lectures [1881]' (HGP, Series II, Box 12, NYPL); Henry George, *Irish World*, 9 July 1881.
[7] George and Hyndman, 'Socialism and Rent-Appropriation', 374.

Human activity, no matter how economically productive, 'could not make this rolling sphere one atom heavier or one atom lighter, could not add to or diminish by one iota the sum of the force whose everlasting circling produces all motion and sustains all life'.[8] Within this holistic system, humans were inescapably rooted, their own bodies part of the natural matter of the world and similarly bound by its natural laws. 'Truly the earth is our mother. This very flesh and blood is but borrowed from the soil [...] we are children of the soil as truly as the blade of grass or the flower of the field'.[9] It was not just soil, however; it was all matter, 'the whole material universe'. He explained that once 'you grasp this idea you see the connection between the land question and the labor question – they are the same thing'.[10]

It was upon this basis that he constructed his universalised, non-historicist right to land grounded in the human body. All 'material creation is [humanity's] inheritance', George argued, but it was humans' 'physical construction' that provided their 'title deed'.[11] In other words, George argued, moral claims to right and value were unavoidable deductions from people's bodily constitution, and applicable to all humans. The human body provided the basis for George's refutation of the Duke of Argyll's criticisms, with both companion pieces published initially in *Nineteenth Century* and subsequently reissued in book form as a particularly constructive elucidation of his ideas. What is the difference, he asked the aristocrat, between the baby of a landowner and that of a workhouse inmate? 'Put the bodies of a duke and a peasant on a dissecting table, and bring, if you can, the surgeon who, by laying bare the brain or examining the viscera, can tell which is duke and which is peasant'.[12]

The natural world, of which human bodies were a part, provided moral guidance. There was, as George saw it, 'intent in Nature' that could be observed. Conformity to such intent was 'natural, wise, and righteous', and contravention of it 'unnatural, foolish, and iniquitous'.[13] Within this obviously Aristotelian schema, human flourishing, as dictated by the capabilities of the human body, was the highest good, and one which political economy should enable rather than stunt. Giving fullest freedom to his own powers of expression, George assailed the Duke by turning the aristocrat's detailed descriptions of how adaptations among animal species were perfectly fitted for their natural habitats against him: 'Will he let me ask him to look in the same way at the human beings around him?' George replied. Describing monstrous scenes of human immiseration, the American inquired, 'if the hook of the bat be intended to

[8] George, *Progress and Poverty*, 118.

[9] George, 'Garfield or Hancock', 1880 (HGP, Series II, Box 12, NYPL).

[10] Henry George, 'Lecture to the Ladies Prisoner Aid Society', 1882 (HGP, Series II, Box 13, NYPL).

[11] Henry George, *Irish World,* 10 January 1880.

[12] George, 'The "Reduction to Iniquity"', 55.

[13] George, 'The "Reduction to Iniquity"', 54–55.

climb by and the wing of the bird be intended to fly by, with what intent have human creatures been given capabilities of body and mind which under conditions that exist in such countries as Great Britain only a few of them can use and enjoy?'[14] George's concern was not only economic hardship, but the trail of moral and mental decay, the corruption of human potentialities, which accompanied it.[15] Given the inherent harmoniousness of the natural world observable around him, he concluded, it could only be the imposition of false, artificial, and unnatural laws that impeded human flourishing. 'The moment we consider in the largest way what kind of animal man is', George explained, 'we see in the most important of social adjustments [private property in land] a violation of Nature's intent sufficient to account for want and misery and aborted development'.[16]

Such a diagnosis and prescription was typical of many radical critiques, especially when directed towards the question of land, and notions of natural harmony and justice were vital to this moral cosmology, and to the Land War in particular. Michael Davitt, the Fenian and Land League leader, argued in identical terms that if man 'revels not in the possession of all the Nature has so beauteously placed within reach of his industry, he has but to blame modern society for having placed a law between him and the enjoyment of his natural rights'.[17] A focus on the moral purposiveness of the body in nature had further important implications, however. One of these was its universalism, which offered radicals a means of escape from the constricting focus on utility and context which historicism brought in its wake.[18] The 'striking consensus of moral perceptions' across time and space, that George perceived, was due to this shared material basis of bodies and land.[19] Although social and economic relations varied, George argued that because land remained 'the only indispensable requisite for existence' it determined a particular ontology of value and moral schema that was only gradually obscured 'by the complexities of the civilized state, the warpings of selfish interests, and the false direction which the speculations of the learned have taken'.[20] 'The first and universal perception of mankind' was that land was not to be considered as other forms of property, an observation that grew naturally from the universal awareness of human

[14] George, 'The "Reduction to Iniquity"', 53–54.

[15] Henry George, 'The Crime of Poverty' [1885], in *Our Land and Land Policy: Speeches, Lectures and Miscellaneous Writings* (New York: Doubleday and McClure, 1901).

[16] George, 'The "Reduction to Iniquity"', 54.

[17] Michael Davitt, 'Random Thoughts on the Irish Land War', in Carla King (ed.), *Jottings in Solitary* (Dublin: University College Dublin Press, 2003), 187.

[18] George G. Iggers, 'Historicism: The History and Meaning of the Term', *Journal of the History of Ideas* 56, no. 1 (1995): 133.

[19] George, 'The "Reduction to Iniquity"', 47.

[20] George and Hyndman, 'Socialism and Rent-Appropriation', 376; George, *Progress and Poverty*, 199.

bodies in nature. The distinction between land and other forms of property, George claimed, 'has been everywhere recognized by the first perceptions of men. It was recognized in the Mosaic Code, [...], by the feudal system, by the Brehon Laws. It is recognized to this day by all primitive peoples, and traces of it yet remain in our customs and laws and in such traditions and feelings as yet persist among the Irish people'.[21]

These pre-modern imaginative contexts were important ideological redoubts for much late-nineteenth-century socialist thought, although they were particularly reflective of its radical and republican inheritances.[22] Focussing on the needs of the human body as part of a natural whole had marked early Marxian concepts of alienation, but also tended to draw out familiarly republican themes.[23] This can be seen, for instance, in Thomas Kirkup's 'decentralist' Christian socialism. Kirkup was an archetypical working-class socialist. From a Northumbrian shepherding family, his intellectual talents, evident at his village school in the Borders, brought him to the University of Edinburgh, and then to a career in writing and publishing which established him as the foremost voice in the early historiography of socialism. Although sympathetic to Marxism, Kirkup was critical of overly 'scientific' approaches which chafed against popular attitudes: particularly on questions of religion and family life.[24] For Kirkup, the human body showed that there was a natural limit to need, 'after all, a man, however huge his capacity, can only eat and drink to a limited extent'. Everything beyond this was 'vanity, labour and sorrow, cupidity and rapacity'. Once such economic gluttony took hold on a social level it produced morally distending effects not only on the wealthy, but on the constitution of the state itself, leading to, Kirkup declared in typically republican language, 'parasitism, luxury, extravagance and vice, to the demoralisation of society, to civil disturbance, and to the ruin of states'.[25]

The focus on the moral purposiveness of the body in nature, a corporeal republicanism, secured a conception of individual rights that stood beyond the reach or authority of the state, yet remained limited by the damaging effects of excess, as well as the necessities of other persons. The ownership of property in land, therefore, was not to be accumulative. This radical formulation rooted collective emancipation in the individualist 'precept of self-preservation', and

[21] Henry George, *Irish World,* 1 May 1880.

[22] Mark Bevir, 'British Socialism and American Romanticism', in Mark Bevir, and Frank Trentmann (eds.), *Critiques of Capital* in Modern Britain and America: Transatlantic Exchanges 1800 to the Present Day (Basingstoke: Palgrave Macmillan, 2002), 76.

[23] Karl Marx, 'Estranged Labour', First Manuscript XXIV, *Economic and Philosophic Manuscripts of 1844.*

[24] Noel Thompson, 'Thomas Kirkup', *Oxford Dictionary of National Biography*, October 2018.

[25] Thomas Kirkup, *An Inquiry into Socialism* [1887], 2nd ed. (London: Longmans, Green, and Co., 1888), 156–157.

its conception of property rights was suffused with natural law presumptions and 'the value-laden, purposive nature of Aristotelianism', as well as Christian naturalism.[26] It is clear that the recognition of land's distinctiveness as a form of property, precisely because of its critical importance to human life, brought in its wake particular moral commitments that tethered possessive rights within the structures of natural law.[27] Not only is this loose syllogism visible through analysis of political language, but crucially it can be read backwards, and used to reconstruct popular political beliefs.[28] Implicit claims regarding land, evident in agrarian social practices, can be understood as presupposing inherent political philosophies and interpreted as emergent non-textual articulations of political ideas, opening up an immanent political theory of Irish land in the late-nineteenth-century Atlantic world.

Raymond Williams once described rural life as fostering a 'retrospective radicalism' that projected the harmony of the natural world onto social life.[29] This agrarian epistemology took nature to be normative and structured a sociology around it. Natural processes, such as fertility or labour, were elevated as the morally commendable foundation of social value, and harmony was centred as a guiding principle. Depending on the precise political contexts, these presumptions have produced a variety of practical demands, but work in comparative historical anthropology has long shown that there are specific epistemic structures that germinate in agrarian social relations and practices.[30]

[26] Hodgskin, *The Natural and Artificial Right*, 46; Hannah Dawson, 'The Normativity of Nature in Locke and Pufendorf', *Historical Journal* 63, no. 3 (2020): 553; B. Andrew Lustig, 'Natural Law, Property, and Justice: The General Justification of Property in John Locke', *The Journal of Religious Ethics* 19, no. 1 (1991): 119–149; Building on James Tully's reinterpretation of Locke's theories of property (see James Tully, *A Discourse on Property: John Locke and His Adversaries* (Cambridge: Cambridge University Press, 1980), 131–154 in particular), scholars have traced how such 'radical Lockeanism' influenced producerist labour traditions across the nineteenth-century Atlantic world: see Richard J. Ellis, 'Radical Lockeanism in American Political Culture', *The Western Political Quarterly* 45, no. 4 (1992): 825–849.

[27] Brian Tierney, *The Idea of Natural Rights* (Grand Rapids, MI: William B. Eerdmans, 1997), 186.

[28] 'The ontological nature of property (common use) requires that man maintain both an inner freedom and external equality in the private possession and use of things', Anthony Parel, 'Aquinas' Theory of Property', in Anthony Parel, and Thomas Flanagan (eds.), *Theories of Property: Aristotle to the Present* (Waterloo: Wilfred Laurier Press, 1979), 106.

[29] Raymond Williams, *The Country and the City* (London: Chatto & Windus, 1973), 37.

[30] Global historical and anthropological work on peasant political theory draws out many of these same themes: John Gledhill, 'Agrarian Social Movements and Forms of Consciousness', *Bulletin of Latin American Research* 7, no. 2 (1988): 257–276; Joel S. Kahn, 'Peasant Ideologies in the Third World', *Annual Review of Anthropology* 14 (1985): 49–74; Eric Hobsbawm, 'Peasant Land Occupations', *Past & Present* 62 (1974): 120–152; John D. Wood, 'Transatlantic Land Reform: America and the Crofters' Revolt, 1878–1888', *The Scottish Historical Review* 63, no. 175 (1984): 79–104; John William Knott, 'Land, Kinship and Identity: The Cultural Roots of Agrarian Agitation in Eighteenth- and Nineteenth-Century Ireland', *Journal of Peasant Studies* 12, no. 1 (1984): 93–108; James C. Scott, *The Moral Economy of the Peasant: Peasant Rebellion and Subsistence in Southeast Asia* (New Haven: Yale University Press, 1975), vii, elucidated a 'subsistence ethic' which informed 'conceptions of social justice, of rights and obligations, of reciprocity'.

Interpreted in this way, agrarian modes of practice can cohere into a peasant political theory. In lives shaped by the rhythms and requirements of the natural world, as well as the 'commonly intelligible morality' formed in stable, small-scale communities, this moral cosmology had its own internal coherence; a practical rationality that resisted liberal critique.[31] How this translated into definable political ideals was always uneven and fractious, but certain embryonic features can be discerned.[32] Direct dependence on natural fertility and human labour for survival both naturalised harmony and harmonised nature, crystallising resistance to Malthusian perspectives, and opposition towards the 'un-naturalness' of non-productive commercial enterprises such as usury: in the words of one labour radical, the 'monstrous fallacy' that 'gambling, theft, and speculation could supply human want'.[33] Within this ideological context, land unavoidably socialised and restricted the question of possession, preventing rights claims from slipping into an acquisitive individualism.

By understanding political theory as embedded in a social reality, it is possible to see that the Irish in the United States were not accidental interlopers in a pre-existing tradition of republican radicalism, or that they gradually abandoned their Catholic inheritance as part of an integration into a peculiarly American (and Protestant) reform tradition.[34] Instead, there were deep commonalities between Irish agrarian practices, such as boycotting, and radical republican political thought. An insistence on the distinctiveness

[31] Kelvin Knight, 'Revolutionary Aristotelianism', in Paul Blackledge, and Kelvin Knight (eds.), *Virtue and Politics: Alasdair MacIntyre's Revolutionary Aristotelianism* (Notre Dame, IN: University of Notre Dame Press, 2011), 23. Conversely, liberalism has often framed urban life as an escape from the suffering inflicted by nature. See Karl Widerquist and Grant S. McCall, *Prehistoric Myths in Modern Political Philosophy* (Edinburgh: Edinburgh University Press, 2017), in particular Chapter 6, 'The Hobbesian Hypothesis in Nineteenth-Century Political Thought'; Annabel Brett, *Liberty, Right and Nature: Individual Rights in Later Scholastic Thought* (Cambridge: Cambridge University Press, 1997), 205.

[32] This has been most clearly examined in relation to practices of resistance. See, for instance: James C. Scott, *Weapons of the Weak: Everyday Forms of Peasant Resistance* (New Haven: Yale University Press, 1986); Eric Hobsbawm, *Primitive Rebels: Studies in Archaic Forms of Social Movement in the Nineteenth and Twentieth Centuries* (Manchester: Manchester University Press, 1959); E. P. Thompson, *Customs in Common: Studies in Traditional Popular Culture* (Pontypool: The Merlin Press, 1991); E. P. Thompson, 'Rough Music Reconsidered', *Folklore* 103, no. 1 (1992): 3–26; Brian Casey (ed.), *Defying the Law of the Land: Agrarian Radicals in Irish History* (Dublin: The History Press Ireland, 2013); James Kelly, *Food Rioting in Ireland in the Eighteenth and Nineteenth Centuries: The 'Moral Economy' and the Irish Crowd* (Dublin: Four Courts Press, 2017).

[33] J. K. Ingalls, *Land and Labor; Their Relations in Nature – How Violated by Monopoly* (Princeton, MA: Co-operative Publishing Co., 1877), 7, 3; See also, Louis Dumont, 'Agriculture and the Birth of Classical Economics: The *Docteur* Quesnay', in Eric Hobsbawm (ed.), *Peasants in History: Essays in Honour of Daniel Thorner* (Calcutta: Oxford University Press, 1980); Jean-Luc Chappey and Julien Vincent, 'A Republican Ecology? Citizenship, Nature and the French Revolution (1795–1799), *Past & Present* 243 (2019): 109–140; Michael Merrill, 'Cash Is Good to Eat: Self-Sufficiency and Exchange in the Rural Economy of the United States', *Radical History Review* 16 (1977): 42–71.

[34] Janis, *A Greater Ireland*, 128; Foner, 'Class, Ethnicity, and Radicalism', 151.

of land is evident both in discourse and in practical action. Both eschewed abstracted moral theorising and calculation in favour of 'natural' or 'common-sense' claims founded in human sensibilities, avoiding, what George called, 'the abstract speculations where thought so easily loses and wastes itself'.[35] Both embodied or valorised stable and self-sustaining harmonious social systems and were unable to accommodate pluralist moral visions.[36] Both implicitly understood freedom as a social value, only comprehensible through a commonly constructed rationality.[37] Ultimately, land lay at the bottom of this convergence: materially producing the conditions for a normative naturalism and intellectually providing resistance to a 'disembodied' liberal idealism.

Republicanism, Harmony, and Natural Right

The guiding principles of George's radicalism and the agrarian social practices of the Land War – natural harmony of humans in nature, fertility and labour as the origins of value, and the right to life and self-preservation – had long been central to republican political thought. Drawing heavily from a combination of Aristotelian philosophy and Thomist theology, which considered the fulfilment of natural purposes to be the highest good, republican political thought tended towards the integration of politics and ethics, rejecting the idea that moral claims could be abstracted from social life and presupposing that moral development was only possible in social contexts.[38] Aristotle's *Politics* was first translated into Latin by thirteenth-century Dominicans and subsequently formed the 'archetypical definition of participatory republican society'.[39] His *Nicomachean Ethics*, which placed human development, the fullest exercise of human potentialities, as the highest moral purpose, provided the mechanism by which such a polity could be achieved.[40] In connecting an ethical theory of human flourishing to a political theory that aimed at the fulfilment

[35] Henry George, 'Moses' (HGP, Series II, Box 13, NYPL); *Irish World*, 16 November 1878.

[36] See, for instance, Jean-Jacques Rousseau, 'Of Civil Religion' [1762], in Jean-Jacques Rousseau (ed.), *The Social Contract and Other Later Political Writings* (Cambridge: Cambridge University Press, 1997), 142–151.

[37] See, for instance, the linguistic reverberations of this linkage in Peter McQuillan, *Native and Natural: Aspects of the Concepts of Right and Freedom in Irish* (Cork: Cork University Press, 2004), 228.

[38] Alan Cromartie, 'Harringtonian Virtue: Harrington, Machiavelli, and the Method of the Moment', *The Historical Journal* 41, no. 4 (1998): 1006.

[39] K. Steven Vincent, *Pierre-Joseph Proudhon and the Rise of French Republican Socialism* (New York: Oxford University Press, 1984), 36. Aristotle, *The Politics and The Constitution of Athens*, Stephen Everson (ed.), (Cambridge: Cambridge University Press, 1996).

[40] Lesley Brown, 'Introduction', in Aristotle, *The Nicomachean Ethics* (Oxford: Oxford University Press, 2009), xvii.

of such flourishing, Aristotle's framework provided a totalising schema that naturalised social organisation.

Antipathy towards all forms of domination has marked republican thought, but only within the context that personal independence was itself a political condition rather than an apolitical one.[41] One consequence of this proposition has been the necessity for an underlying naturally harmonious social order in which the good of the individual could align with that of the commonwealth. If politics was ethics in action, then the idea of a pre-social individual, unencumbered by collective commitments, remained a morally vacant concept.[42] As such, the concept of harmony was itself constitutive of republican politics, underpinning the formation of a necessary social rationality and morality through communication and shared social practices. This was usually assumed to be of Divine origin, but nevertheless there was a presumptive alignment between human development and the fulfilment of social roles. As Jefferson explained, 'Man was destined for society. His morality, therefore, was to be formed to this object'.[43]

This view of social morality, and the necessity of political engagement to human flourishing, tended to generate an ambivalent perception of personal wealth.[44] In viewing the political freedom to exercise public virtue as determined by economic independence, republicanism has often resulted in an exclusionary politics, but in its more democratic formulations, it also provoked a greater attention towards the political dangers and moral consequences of economic inequality. The ideological world which George and his fellow republican radicals inhabited was deeply imbued with such inferences, taking it for granted that political freedom and individual freedom, intertwined as they were, could be curtailed to the point of meaninglessness by economic dependence. The worry that 'enormous private wealth is inconsistent with the spirit of republicanism' dominated the radicalism of the nineteenth-century Atlantic world.[45] John Francis Bray, one of a number of land

41 Quentin Skinner, *Liberty before Liberalism* (Cambridge: Cambridge University Press, 1998), 60; Honohan, 'Introduction', 3.

42 Michael Sandel, *Liberalism and the Limits of Justice* (Cambridge: Cambridge University Press, 1982), 180.

43 Thomas Jefferson to Peter Carr, 10 August 1787, in Adrienne Koch, and William Peden (eds.), *The Life and Selected Writings of Thomas Jefferson* (New York: Random House, 1944), 430.

44 For example, Jean Jacques Rousseau, 'Discourse on Political Economy' [1755], in Victor Gourevitch (ed.), *The Social Contract and Other Later Political Writings* (Cambridge: Cambridge University Press, 1997), 20; Aristotle, *Nicomachean Ethics*, Book 1:5 (Oxford: Oxford University Press, 2009), 7.

45 John Francis Bray, *Labour's Wrongs and Labour's Remedy; or, The Age of Might and the Age of Reason* (Leeds: David Green, 1839), 206; *Irish World*, 4 December 1880; *Irish World*, 27 December 1879; George W. Bell, *Peasant Proprietary for Ireland: A Communication from Captain George W. Bell, Lawyer and Journalist, Ottawa, Illinois, U.S.A., to Thomas Sexton, Esq., M.P.* (Dublin: Irish National Land League, 1881), 20.

and labour radicals whose political career spanned from the Chartist agitation of the 1830s and 1840s to the Land War in the 1880s, remarked in 1839 that the United States would slide into 'an oligarchy before the end of the present century' unless wealth was tied to labour: 'Such has invariably been the ultimate fate of all republics, in ancient and modern times; and such ever must be their fate while one man is rich and another is poor – while one man works and another does nothing.'[46]

The evident intersections with Catholic natural law thinking will be examined more fully in Chapter 4, but both shared in common a commitment to an underlying natural harmony in the moral universe that produced a concomitant suspicion of the atomising and disaggregating tendencies of commerce. Indeed, radical republican conceptions of economic value drew heavily from these religious roots. The scholastic doctrines of the medieval church had condemned the sinfulness of the accumulation of wealth, drawing heavily on Aristotle's notion of 'barrenness', which elevated biological fertility as morally commendable and defined money as a non-reproductive element in exchange.[47] The corresponding moral discomfort with the idea of profit without labour proved remarkably durable, persisting in both theological circles and in popular opposition to middlemen and traders, moneylenders, and graziers.[48] The connection of productivity with biological fertility was, however, also indebted to agrarian epistemologies independently of directly Aristotelian or Thomist influences. This positive association of productivity and biological fertility was the foundation of popular republican economic attitudes throughout the long nineteenth century.[49] It lay behind the declaration of Sidney H. Morse, the *Irish World* correspondent and individualist anarchist, that he was 'a capitalist who denies the right of capital to self-increase', and the claim of Rev David Humphrys, the curate of Clonoulty, Co. Tipperary during the Land War, that agriculture was 'the foundation of all other industries'.[50] Biological fertility enabled republican radicals to extol the workman and denigrate the merchant and the banker, to attack luxury and conspicuous consumption, and to challenge the moral authority of the market.[51]

46 Bray, *Labour's Wrongs and Labour's Remedy*, 20.

47 Jacob Viner, *Religious Thought and Economic Society: Four Chapters of an Unfinished Work* (Durham, NC: Duke University Press, 1978), 61; Joel Kaye, *Economy and Nature in the Fourteenth Century: Money, Market Exchange, and the Emergence of Scientific Thought* (Cambridge: Cambridge University Press, 1998), 86–87.

48 Gregory Claeys, *Machinery, Money and the Millennium: From Moral Economy to Socialism, 1815–1860* (Princeton: Princeton University Press, 1987), 5–9.

49 Sklansky, *The Soul's Economy*, 19.

50 'Phillip' [Sidney H. Morse], *Irish World*, 14 December 1878; Rev David Humphrys, *The Justice of the Land League* (London: Kegan Paul, 1881), 14.

51 Ellis, 'Radical Lockeanism', 828; 'belief in the unrestrained fertility of the soil was a feature of the agrarian response' during Chartism, Chase, *The People's Farm*, 8.

Notions of natural harmony and an ontology of value that prioritised the moral worth of labour and fertility were significant ideological markers precisely because they were so deeply contested by the 1880s. For radicals, the language of biological naturalism and fertility provided the means to explain their contemporary malaise, the unnatural situation whereby 'dead wealth asserts its power over living wealth; the banker over the producer; the bondholder over the taxpayer'.[52] Labour was a living force that produced all wealth, but only through reproductive engagement with the natural world.[53] These disagreements about the essential order or chaos of the universe were shaped by attitudes and beliefs about nature; what it constituted and how it was structured. Competing socio-scientific theories of the operation of the natural world, as either harmonious symbiosis or as a brutal struggle for survival, gave credence to respective views on how human society should be organised, and attitudes towards 'Nature' both in its physical and philosophical sense provided a key test of political allegiance and sympathy.[54] Did society require the dedicated and informed expertise of a political elite to temper the naturally chaotic, precarious, and pitiless consequences of unrestrained human inclinations, or was the state 'simply asked to undo, by peaceful and equitable means, the confiscation' it had previously enacted, ushering in a 'new system in harmony with the Laws of God and Nature'.[55]

This metaphysic of natural harmony, an undergirding belief that the universe was an 'ordered whole', was something that George and many other transatlantic radicals shared with their eighteenth-century predecessors. George dedicated his 1886 *Protection or Free Trade* to 'Quesnay, Turgot, Mirabeau, Condorcet', in recognition of his ideological affinity with the agrarian physiocracy of eighteenth-century French republicanism.[56] The harmonious unity of the economic whole, so prominent in François Quesnay's work, was also hugely influential for Adam Smith, with the latter's natural law assumptions mediated through the work of his own predecessor Francis Hutcheson.[57] Smith's vision of economic harmony remained securely bound to a counterbalancing moral philosophy that

52 *Irish World*, 30 November 1878.

53 G. Y. Malcolm and Robert Blissert to Henry George, 8 December 1882 (HGP, Series I: A, Box 3, NYPL).

54 Williams, 'Ideas of Nature', 70.

55 James J. Clancy, *The Land League Manual* (New York: Thomas Kelly, 1881), 5; *Irish World*, 27 December 1879.

56 Dumont, 'Agriculture and the Birth of Classical Economics', 273; Hiram Caton, 'The Preindustrial Economics of Adam Smith', *The Journal of Economic History* 45, no. 4 (1985): 833; Chappey and Vincent, 'A Republican Ecology?', 135, 137.

57 Donald R. Stabile, 'Adam Smith and the Natural Wage: Sympathy, Subsistence and Social Distance', *Review of Social Economy* 55, no. 3 (1997): 296. See also A. S. Skinner, 'Pufendorf, Hutcheson and Adam Smith: Some Principles of Political Economy', *Scottish Journal of Political Economy* 42, no. 2 (1995): 165–182; Emma Rothschild, 'Adam Smith and Conservative Economics', *Economic History Review* 45, no. 1 (1992): 74–96.

would be posthumously eliminated during the nineteenth century under the twin influences of Malthusianism and Benthamism.[58]

In his infamous *Essay on the Principle of Population*, Rev Thomas Malthus had rejected a positive harmoniousness in the natural world. While a faith in the coherence and synchronicity of the universe were allowed to remain, he had alighted on a new idea of nature; a theodicy absent of any recourse to higher principle and better able to incorporate discord and injustice into its operation. In blaming the limitations of nature and overpopulation for the growth of poverty, Malthus had theorised that human and animal life had a persistent and unavoidable tendency to outstrip subsistence, leading to persistent and unavoidable poverty. The implication was that poverty could not be attributed to institutions or social and economic structures, but rather, through nature, the poor were condemned to their situation; 'the unhappy persons who in the great lottery of life have drawn a blank'.[59] In the absence of any natural justice, only the careful calculus of utility offered a means of judging the most propitious course of action and of mitigating the suffering inflicted by a cold, austere nature.

These Malthusian arguments had calcified into simple economic common sense by the 1880s, and while the details were disputed and refined over the course of the century, they formed the intellectual bedrock of most economic opposition to the radical claims made by George and the Land League.[60] Adam Smith's natural harmonies had become embarrassingly anachronistic to most economists, who would have shared John Kells Ingram's opinion that the famous economist had been 'secretly led' by his '*a priori* theological ideas' about the existence of an ordered universe in which there was a natural harmony of men and in nature.[61] 'What he regarded as the system of nature', explained the economist T. E. Cliffe Leslie, 'was a descendant of the System of Nature as conceived by the ancients'.[62] When the progressive liberal economic historian Arnold Toynbee took aim at George, for instance, he did so by comparing the American to Adam Smith, as a believer 'in what economists no longer believe

58 Hont, *Jealousy of Trade*, 401; Donald Winch, 'Adam Smith: Scottish Moral Philosopher as Political Economist', *The Historical Journal* 35, no. 1 (1992): 91–113; James T. Kloppenberg, 'The Virtues of Liberalism: Christianity, Republicanism, and Ethics in Early American Political Discourse', *The Journal of American History* 74, no. 1 (1987): 19; Richard F. Teichgraeber, 'Adam Smith and Tradition; the Wealth of Nations before Malthus', in Stefan Collini, Richard Whatmore, and Brian Young (eds.), *Economy, Polity, and Society: British Intellectual History 1750–1950* (Cambridge: Cambridge University Press, 2000), 85–104; Rothschild, 'Political Economy', 758.

59 Thomas Malthus, *An Essay on the Principle of Population; or, A View of Its Past and Present Effects on Human Happiness; with an Inquiry into Our Prospects Respecting the Future Removal or Mitigation of the Evils Which It Occasions [1798]*, 6th ed. (London: John Murray, 1826), 34.

60 For instance Mallock, *Property and Progress*, 11–12; Rae, *Contemporary Socialism*, 410.

61 John Kells Ingram, *A History of Political Economy* (London: A & C Black, 1888), 106.

62 T. E. Cliffe Leslie, 'The Political Economy of Adam Smith', *The Fortnightly Review* 8, no. 47 (1870): 550.

in, [...] economic harmonies, [...that] individual interests will harmonise with common interests'.[63] George embraced such flattering comparisons. For him, 'the laws of the universe are harmonious', and, absent mendacious interference, would extinguish suffering.[64] Attacking Herbert Spencer's Malthusian metaphysics, George denied the possibility of a theory of justice that did not rely on an 'appointed order' rooted in nature.[65] The inherent goodness of the natural world meant that a system of economic subjugation 'could never sustain itself in being but through special laws'.[66]

In such a context, it is hardly surprising that Malthus was a perennial object of radical contempt. Anti-Malthusian tirades had been a hallmark of transatlantic radicalism throughout the nineteenth century, from American labour radicals like Thomas Skidmore and Stephen Simpson, to Francis Place and William Thompson in Britain and Ireland.[67] For the Chartist land reformer Allen Davenport, Malthus was the 'rebel of Nature'.[68] Critically, Malthus had denuded land of its significance in providing for life, since the inability to acquire sustenance was the mechanism for restraining population. This was a deep and significant incision to the umbilical connection between land and natural rights. No person, claimed Malthus in 1803, has anything like a 'claim of *right* to the smallest portion of food'. Reversing St Basil's analogy of the wealthy occupying a space made to be sufficient for all, Malthus declared: 'At Nature's mighty feast there is no vacant cover for him. She tells him to be gone, and will quickly execute her own orders'.[69] Without a beneficent conception of the natural world and the inherent harmoniousness of nature, conceptions as deeply embedded in Irish republicanism as they were in labour radicalism, land could offer no solace or shelter from the merciless fight for survival. As such, nearly all schemes of land communalisation through the long nineteenth century were marked by their foundational belief in a benevolent natural harmony, that 'collision or antagonism' was not 'part of the plan of Nature'.[70] As the *Irish*

[63] Toynbee, *'Progress and Poverty'*, 22.

[64] George, *Progress and Poverty*, 296; Henry George, *Irish World*, 1 May 1880.

[65] Henry George, *A Perplexed Philosopher* [1892] (London: Vacher and Sons, 1937), 122.

[66] Ingalls, *Land and Labor*, 3; see also Bevir, 'British Socialism and American Romanticism', 91; Eugenio Biagini, *British Democracy and Irish Nationalism, 1876–1906* (Cambridge: Cambridge University Press, 2007), 110–111; K. Steven Vincent, 'Visions of a Stateless Society', in Gareth Stedman Jones, and Gregory Claeys (eds.), *Nineteenth-Century Political Thought*, 449.

[67] Pessen, *Most Uncommon Jacksonians*, 131, 140; Rodgers, *Contested Truths*, 129.

[68] Allen Davenport, 'Agrarian Equality', *Republican* 10, no. 13 (1 October 1824), 410, citied in Chase, *The People's Farm*, 184.

[69] Malthus, *An Essay on the Principle of Population; or, A View of Its Past and Present Effects on Human Happiness*, 2nd ed. (London: J. Johnson, 1803), 531. This quote was only in the second edition in 1803, but gained notoriety though William Hazlitt, *A Reply to the Essay on Population by the Rev. T. R. Malthus* (London: Longman, Hurst, Rees and Orme, 1807), 290.

[70] J. R. Buchanan, 'Nationalization of the Land as First Presented' [1847, 1 Cincinnati *Herald of Truth*], repr. in *Arena* 3 (1892): 401.

World explained, 'as God, operating through Nature, has shown Himself to be All-Bountiful, it is clear that the one and only obstacle standing in the way of these blessings is the false system of political economy now at work'.[71]

George's view of Malthusianism was typically hostile. To his mind, it was clear that the success and longevity of Malthus' heresy resulted from him telling 'what the most powerful class in the times in which he lived was not only willing to hear but anxious to hear'.[72] This 'blasphemous doctrine', which robbed human life of 'dignity and responsibility', was 'invented for the defense of a landlord aristocracy'.[73] Spreading like a sinister ideological infection, it had 'stilled the sensibilities of naturally humane men', anaesthetising their innate moral senses.[74] As George explained, this political economy mapped onto a pre-existing discord over the bounteousness of nature and was embraced eagerly by 'a powerful class, in whom an intense fear of any questioning of the existing state of things had been generated by the outburst of the French Revolution'.[75] In contemporary society, George noted that this pessimistic naturalism found its scientific consummation in Darwin's theory of evolution, a 'tendency of modern thought' that provided 'fresh and strong support' for Malthusianism.[76] Indeed, through his forced marriage to Malthus, Darwin bequeathed an analogue for the social world that buttressed cold calculations of economic utility with a triumphalist scientism, further pressing notions of natural right out of the realms of political discourse. Complaining that German socialists had accepted Malthusianism as a given, George exclaimed that 'with Atheism Malthusianism seems to me to thoroughly harmonize; but with Republicanism, no!'[77]

In relieving land of its divine obligation to provide sustenance, Malthusianism had provided one potential route out of the ambiguities that land created for notions of private property. Such ambiguities were long-standing, to say the least. Since Aquinas, who had proclaimed that the natural world had initially been divinely bestowed to all humans in common for their sustenance and survival, the institution of private property in land had rested on the uneasy

[71] *Irish World*, 16 November 1878; see also Matthew Harris, Letter to the *Irishman*, Ballinasloe, 19 June 1880 (Heffernan Papers, MS 21,910, National Library of Ireland); John Swinton to Henry George, 30 October 1879 (HGP, Series I: A, Box 2, NYPL).

[72] Henry George, 'Lecture Notes and Text 'Malthusian Theory' [1880s]' (HGP, Series II, Box 12, NYPL).

[73] Henry George, *Irish World*, 23 April 1881.

[74] Henry George, 'Lecture Notes and Text 'Malthusian Theory' [1880s]' (HGP, Series II, Box 12, NYPL).

[75] George, *Progress and Poverty*, 87–88.

[76] Henry George, 'Lecture Notes and Text 'Malthusian Theory' [1880s]' (HGP, Series II, Box 12, NYPL); Donald Winch, 'Darwin Fallen among Political Economists', *Proceedings of the American Philosophical Society* 145, no. 4 (2001): 415–437.

[77] Henry George, 'Lecture Notes and Text 'Malthusian Theory' [1880s]' (HGP, Series II, Box 12, NYPL).

foundation of human rather than natural law.[78] As such, the right to life and self-preservation took absolute priority and precedence over any right to private property, which was not itself natural nor divinely prescribed. As Aquinas had written:

Now, according to the natural order instituted by divine providence, material goods are provided for the satisfaction of human needs. Therefore the division and appropriation of property, which proceeds from human law, must not hinder the satisfaction of man's necessity from such goods. Equally, whatever a man has in superabundance is owed, of natural right, to the poor for their sustenance.[79]

Consequently, all justifications of individual possession had to provide some type of conjectural claim rooted in utility or moral necessity, to explain how it facilitated human survival. Aquinas's hierarchy of laws placed Natural Law, intrinsically just and implanted in the mind, above the human law of private property, leaving private property to be 'defended only on the ground that the alternative is less desirable'.[80] If natural law sought to provide a final purpose for all created matter, then absolute possession was hamstrung by its subordination to the 'final end' of human survival and development.[81] It was a central moral constraint on notions of private property that land radicals had long recognised and indeed often voiced their complaints that 'the advocate of land monopoly has never met the question on the broad basis of human rights'.[82] Malthus' discordant and hostile natural world had later helped to sever the connection between land and a natural right to life. In doing so, the constraints on rights languages that had limited their possessive and absolutist aspects within natural law presumptions about final purposes were increasingly lifted.

Yet Malthus himself was but one, albeit critical, figure in this long decoupling of rights discourse from its natural law foundations. Significantly, the connection between land and a natural right to life had always been an inherently political one, and the arguments concerned not only the question of property, but the basis and justification for political authority. Naturalised rights to existence, through the physical land on which they could solely be realised, tended to delegitimise the authority of the state to preserve order, or claims

[78] Hont, *Jealousy of Trade*, 421; Viner, *Religious Thought and Economic Society*, 67; Peter Singer, 'Famine, Affluence and Morality', in Peter Laslett, and James Fishkin (eds.), *Philosophy, Politics and Society* (Oxford: Oxford University Press, 1979), 31.

[79] Aquinas, *Summa Theologica*, II-II, Question 66, Article 7.

[80] Quentin Skinner, *The Foundations of Modern Political Thought*: Volume II, *The Age of Reformation* (Cambridge: Cambridge University Press, 1979), 153, 148; Alfred O'Rahilly, 'St Thomas's Theory of Property', *Studies: An Irish Quarterly Review* 9, no. 35 (1920): 341.

[81] For a detailed examination of this aspect of the topic in particular, see Miriam Ann Cunningham, 'A Thomistic Appraisal of the Philosophy of Henry George' (MA dissertation, Catholic University of America, 1950), 42.

[82] Ingalls, *Land and Labor*, 3.

of divine right like those made by monarchical absolutists.[83] It was on this basis that scholastic thinkers in the sixteenth and seventeenth centuries, such as Francisco Suarez and Cardinal Bellarmine, refuted the idea that the political order, and its possession of the natural world, held Divine authority itself and rejected Machiavellian claims that stable political rule was a sufficient justification for absolute authority or possession.[84] It was no coincidence that Catholic and republican critics of social liberalism in the late nineteenth century would return to these arguments specifically in order to equate the claims of technocratic authority made by the state with the divine authority of seventeenth-century monarchs, as well as to reject the Godliness of the social order that grounded the providentalist assumptions of Victorian evangelicalism.[85]

One key figure in dismantling this older holistic Aristotelian cosmology was Thomas Hobbes, whose vision of a discordant and dangerous natural world provided the basis on which state authority was seen to supersede rather than incorporate any pre-existing or natural rights. Disconnecting individual rights from a wider system of moral purposes and 'the teleology of human life', Hobbes' political structure assumed a necessary imposition on the chaos of human nature, as individual claims of right were entirely subordinated to, rather than enmeshed within, the authority of the state.[86] It was against this position that radical rights theorists of the seventeenth century took their stand, often drawing collectivist conclusions from the individualist premise of the inalienable right to self-preservation. From English Levellers to Spanish Dominicans, natural rights were commonly conceived of not as 'disposable property' to be exchanged at will, but remained encoded within a harmonious moral universe.[87] Just as an individual did not possess the right to enslave or kill themselves, argued the Leveller Richard Overton, neither could they willingly alienate themselves from the land on which their survival depended.[88] Here again, the question of land pressed natural rights arguments into deeply radical and communitarian conclusions hostile to private property.

[83] Robert Filmer, in Peter Laslett (ed.), *Patriarcha and Other Political Works of Sir Robert Filmer* (Oxford: Basil Blackwell, 1949), 13, 17; Alfred O'Rahilly, 'The Source of English and American Democracy', *Studies: An Irish Quarterly Review* 8, no. 31 (1919): 206.

[84] Skinner, *The Foundations of Modern Political Thought*, 138–153; Alfred O'Rahilly, 'The Catholic Origin of Democracy', *Studies: An Irish Quarterly Review* 8, no. 29 (1919): 1–18; O'Rahilly, 'St Thomas's Theory of Property', 341.

[85] Skinner, *The Foundations of Modern Political Thought*, 167; see, for instance, Merwin-Marie Snell, 'The Catholic Social-Reform Movement', *American Journal of Sociology* 5, no. 1 (1899): 16–50.

[86] Brett, *Liberty, Right and Nature*, 235.

[87] Knud Haakonssen, and Michael J. Seidler, 'Natural Law: Law, Rights and Duties', in Richard Whatmore, and Brian Young (ed.), *A Companion to Intellectual History* (Newark: Wiley, 2015), 426–452.

[88] Richard Overton, 'An Appeale from the Degenerate Representative Body [1647]', in Don M. Wolfe (ed.), *Leveller Manifestoes of the Puritan Revolution* (New York: Thomas Nelson, 1944), 162. See also Richard Tuck, *Natural Rights Theories: Their Origin and Development* (Cambridge: Cambridge University Press, 1979), 48–49, 149.

This moral schema found a hospitable intellectual habitat in both the Thomist and the Scottish 'commonsense' traditions, where a positive view of the naturally social human survived, and indeed the republican and proto-democratic implications of this way of thinking occasionally pushed through.[89] Long after Robert Filmer, the royalist defender of the divine right of kings, attacked a nefarious conflagration of Jesuits and Presbyterians for using the natural right to life to promote the anarchy of the multitude, radical conclusions about the possession of land continued to flow from beliefs about the harmony of the natural and human world.[90] Was the political community a consenting expression of the natural sociability of humans and the harmony of the natural world, or a necessary imposition on their greed, violence, and rapacity and an escape from nature's unforgiving brutality? Was the allocation of natural resources simply a matter of political stability, or did humans have pre-existing claims rooted in their purposive natures? Since the only stable conception of a natural right to land was rooted in self-preservation and the role of land to facilitate it, the absolutist or possessive aspects of such rights were constrained by natural law presumptions about final purposes.

As a consequence of this, the question of land inevitably drove many political thinkers away from naturalised notions of right and towards justifications of private property and political authority on the basis on utility, protection, or civil necessity. William Blackstone, the eighteenth-century English jurist whose codification of English common law was hugely influential in the early American republic and remained a point of reference during the nineteenth century, provided a useful example in this regard.[91] Blackstone's work exhibited a microcosm of the instability and ambiguity of the natural law defence of private land. Examining the development of feudal tenures, he was drawn inexorably into a positivist defence of private property.[92] As he explained, the reason why 'we seem afraid to look back to the means by which [landed

[89] Paul Sigmund, *Natural Law in Political Thought* (Cambridge, MA: Winthrop, 1971); Brian Tierney, 'Natural Law and Natural Rights: Old Problems and Recent Approaches', *The Review of Politics* 64, no. 3 (2002): 401, 404.

[90] Robert Filmer, *Patriarcha*, 53–54; O'Rahilly, 'The Source of English and American Democracy', 206.

[91] Donald S. Lutz, 'The Relative Influence of European Writers on Late Eighteenth-Century American Political Thought', *The American Political Science Review* 78, no. 1 (1984): 193; Gregory Claeys, 'The Origins of the Rights of Labor: Republicanism, Commerce, and the Construction of Modern Social Theory in Britain, 1796–1805, *The Journal of Modern History* 66, no. 2 (1994): 283; Also referenced by Edmund F. Dunne, *Ireland: Rights, Wrongs and Remedies: An Address Delivered before the Fort Wayne, Indiana, U.S.A. Branch of the National Land League of Ireland, on St. Patrick's Day, 1881* (Chicago: S. W. Roth, 1881), 24–25 (Pamphlets, 103, Box 34, P.001.1804, Philadelphia Archdiocese Historical Research Center); William Blackstone, *Nature of Laws in General,* cited by, A. M. Sullivan, 'Ireland's Great Grievance: Land Tenure in Ireland and Other Countries', *American Catholic Quarterly Review* 6 (1881): 51; James Fintan Lalor, in L. Fogarty (ed.), *James Fintan Lalor: Patriot & Political Essasyist, 1807–1849* (Dublin: Talbot Press, 1919), 99.

[92] Michael Lobban, 'Blackstone and the Science of Law', *The Historical Journal* 30, no. 2 (1987): 312.

property] was acquired' was because 'accurately and strictly speaking, there is no foundation in nature or in natural law, why a set of words upon parchment should convey the dominion of land'. Blackstone warned his learned readers, however, that such questions would be 'troublesome in common life. It is well if the mass of mankind will obey the laws when made, without scrutinizing too nicely into the reasons of making them'.[93]

Yet for radicals, the scrutinising continued, as did the attempt to defend the emancipatory potential of natural rights in the teeth of an enveloping utilitarian positivism. Attacking Benthamism for its presumptuous rationalism, the English radical Thomas Hodgskin, writing in the 1830s, declared that even Filmer's divine right of kings was 'benevolence, compared to the monstrous assertion that "all right is factitious, and only exists by the will of the law-maker"'.[94] Hodgskin believed that the abandonment of concepts of natural right had been driven by the 'legislating classes of society' to protect their property. It was in Ireland particularly, he noted, that land laws, shorn of their adherence to natural rights, were used to degrade a peasant population by refusing their right to live on the land. 'Perish the people, but let the law live' was his summation of the situation.[95] Significantly, Hodgskin argued that the basis for a natural right to land was 'the precept of self-preservation', something he described in materialist and bodily terms as 'the dictate of the holy and delightful impulse by which we cherish our happy animal existence'.[96] It was this principle, he argued, that was being reorientated away from the individual and towards the state – 'transferred to the institutions of barbarous men' in order to secure for legislators 'the produce of those who cultivate the soil'.[97] As such, while utilitarian legislators may claim to act in accordance with a principle of communal self-preservation, the subject population are, Hodgskin claimed, 'continually called on to preserve the institutions of the legislator by violating the principle [self-preservation] from which the analogy is derived'.[98]

Resentment against this reorientation, against the loss of the natural right to self-preservation in order to defend property, animated the radical vision through most of the nineteenth century and reinforced the presumption that property in land was entirely distinct from moveable and manufactured possessions.[99]

93 William Blackstone, in Robert Malcolm Kerr (ed.), *The Commentaries on the Laws of England Vol. II, of the Rights of Things* [1765] (London: John Murray, 1876), 1–2.

94 Hodgskin, *The Natural and Artificial Right*, 21. His quote is from James Mill's entry on 'Jurisprudence' in the Encyclopaedia Britannica.

95 Hodgskin, *The Natural and Artificial Right*, 130; 44–45.

96 Hodgskin, *The Natural and Artificial Right*, 46.

97 Hodgskin, *The Natural and Artificial Right*, 46.

98 Hodgskin, *The Natural and Artificial Right*, 46.

99 John Gast, *Calumny Defeated, or a Complete Vindication of the Conduct of the Working Shipwrights', during the Late Disputes with Their Employers* (London: J. Delahoy, 1802), 9; see, E. P. Thompson, *The Making of the English Working Class* [1963] (London: Penguin, 1981), 774.

Relying on a harmonious view of man in society and the natural world, labour radicals and democrats from the late eighteenth to the end of the nineteenth century, men like John Thelwall, author of *The Rights of Nature*, allied land with the individualist proposition of self-preservation to draw out radical conclusions.[100] This was the basis of both George and the Land League's approach to the land question. The right to self-preservation rejected the sanctification of contractual obligations, or the claims of reform made in the name of utility or expediency, since, as George explained, 'all the people could not give away the right of the humblest child'.[101] The ownership of land remained a question of natural right. 'What is the origin of this possession?' queried the constitution of an American Land League branch, concluding that it could rest on no other foundation than to ensure 'the tillers of the soil' retained in full 'the fruits of their labors'.[102]

George, as a tribune of popular opinion rather than an original thinker, helped merely to open up this deep vein of contradiction, latent in European and American political thought, over questions of possession and political authority that were grounded in competing visions of natural harmony and justice. Among the most significant figures upon whom George relied in making his arguments was Thomas Jefferson, who provided an impeachable authority as, what the *Irish World* described as, 'the truest embodiment of the animating principle of the American Revolution'.[103] In reframing Locke's famous dictum of the right to 'life, liberty and property' as the right to 'life, liberty, and the pursuit of happiness', Jefferson had confronted the Aquinian dilemma by affirming that the rights of the human were superior to the rights of property.[104] Property laws could be 'so far extended as to violate natural right', Jefferson had explained, because the 'fundamental right to labour the earth' was inextinguishable in a way that mere possession was not.[105] An innate moral sense, divinely 'given to all human beings', 'as much a part of man as his arm or leg', provided the basis on which to construct this potentially egalitarian vision of property ownership.[106] Regardless that Jefferson was by no means a land

[100] John Thelwall, *The Rights of Nature, against the Usurpations of Establishments* (London: H. D. Symonds, 1796), 18; see also, Claeys, 'The Origins of the Rights of Labor', 266–267.

[101] Henry George, 'Lecture Notes for Wick 1884' (HGP, Series II, Box 12, NYPL).

[102] 'Constitution of the Middletown, N.Y. Branch of the Irish National Land League of the United States, adopted, 6 March 1881', 3 (103, Box 34, P008.883, PAHRC).

[103] *Irish World*, 8 February 1879.

[104] David M. Post, 'Jeffersonian Revisions of Locke: Education, Property-Rights, and Liberty', *Journal of the History of Ideas* 47, no. 1 (1986): 147–157.

[105] Jefferson to James Madison, 28 October 1795, in Joyce Appleby, and Terence Ball (eds.), *Jefferson: Political Writings* (Cambridge: Cambridge University Press, 1999), 107.

[106] Thomas Jefferson to Peter Carr, Paris, 10 August 1787, in Adrienne Koch, and William Peden (eds.), *The Life and Selected Writings of Thomas Jefferson*, 430–431; Jefferson to Francis W. Gilmer, 7 June 1816, in Joyce Appleby, and Terence Ball (eds.), *Jefferson*, 143; 'So true, so ineradicable is the moral sense, that where selfishness or passion would outrage it, the intellectual faculties are always called upon to supply excuse', Henry George, 'The "Reduction to Iniquity"', 47.

nationaliser, George explained to an audience at the Brooklyn Revenue Reform Club in 1883 that this was the essence of his political thought, 'though the times in which he lived might not have been the time for their full development'.[107]

Other intellectual predecessors of George, such as Thomas Spence, offered more explicit schemes to reorganise the distribution of land in harmony with natural rights. It was not until 1882, however, when the English Marxist Henry Hyndman unearthed an old lecture from the bowels of the British Museum, that George became acquainted with Spence's ideas.[108] Yet Spence, a Newcastle school teacher and contemporary of Jefferson, had a long trajectory of influence, particularly on Chartist radicalism in the early nineteenth century.[109] Cynical about the corrupting influence of commerce, in which 'all bounds must be thrown down and every thing must be vendible', Spence rejected any moral defence of land ownership on the familiar basis of the necessity of land to human life: for 'there is no living but on land and its productions, consequently, what we cannot live without we have the same property in as our lives'.[110] For Spence, the possession of land and political power were inseparable. His scheme, therefore, was one of decentralisation, in which every parish would democratically manage their own lands, making each one 'a little polished Athens'.[111]

Among the most striking of George's intellectual ancestors was Thomas Paine, whose 1797 pamphlet *Agrarian Justice* argued for a separation between 'natural' and 'artificial' property.[112] Like George's later complaint that 'the tramp comes with the locomotive', Paine too had been animated by the depressing contrast between wealth and want, writing that 'on one side the spectator is dazzled by splendid appearances; on the other he is shocked by extremes of wretchedness'.[113] The similarities between the two proposals extended to their solutions, since both Paine and George were aware that a redistribution of the common inheritance of land could not be straightforwardly achieved by simple physical expropriation and reallocation, and favoured a land tax with, in Paine's

107 Henry George, 'Wanted: A Democratic Party', speech to the Brooklyn Revenue Reform Club, 12 March 1883 (HGP, Series II, Box 13, NYPL).

108 Henry George to Patrick Ford, 9 March 1882 (HGP, Series I: A, Box 3, NYPL).

109 T. M. Parssinen, 'Thomas Spence and the Origins of English Land Nationalization', *Journal of the History of Ideas* 34, no. 1 (1973): 135–141; Thomas R. Knox, 'Thomas Spence: The Trumpet of Jubilee', *Past & Present* 76 (1977): 75–98.

110 Thomas Spence, repr. in Henry M. Hyndman (ed.), *The Nationalization of the Land in 1775 and 1882* (London: E. W. Allen, 1882), 10.

111 Thomas Spence, quoted in Malcolm Chase, 'From Millennium to Anniversary: The Concept of Jubilee in Late Eighteenth and Nineteenth-Century England', *Past & Present* 129 (1990): 139.

112 Robert Lamb, 'Liberty, Equality, and the Boundaries of Ownership: Thomas Paine's Theory of Property Rights', *The Review of Politics* 72, no. 3 (2010): 510.

113 George, *Progress and Poverty*, 7; Thomas Paine, 'Agrarian Justice' [1797], in Max Beer (ed.), *The Pioneers of Land Reform: Thomas Spence, William Ogilvie, Thomas Paine* (London: G. Bell, 1920), 181.

case, a universal individual endowment. More importantly, and like nearly all schemes for radical land reform, Paine's arguments demonstrated the inescapable reliance on the natural law position that God had created the earth to provide for human survival. While Paine attempted to provide secular foundations for the claims of the materially disenfranchised to a share in 'natural' property, he could not escape the necessity of divine origination to justify land as the common inheritance of humanity: 'It is wrong to say that God made *Rich* and *Poor*; he made only *Male* and *Female*; and he gave them the earth for their inheritance.'[114]

This ineradicable connection between natural law arguments and land reform persisted throughout the nineteenth century, even if sometimes partially obscured, such as in the work of Edinburgh landowner Patrick Dove, but usually detectable in some form. Dove, whose 1850 volume, *The Theory of Human Progression*, received a favourable, albeit limited, reception among scholars and politically interested parties, relied heavily on the Scottish commonsense tradition to constrain an otherwise utilitarian argument through an '*a priori* principle of justice'.[115] Despite Dove's commitment to a teleology of scientific and human progress, he could not avoid the principle that 'creation is the only means by which an individual right to property can be generated' and that the initial creation of the earth had been divine.[116] Again, the confrontation of the land question with considerations of natural justice destabilised notions of property and drove possessive rights back into the restraining embrace of the natural law tradition. In Dove's case forcing an otherwise straightforwardly utilitarian mid-century liberal, committed to free trade, scientific progress and a Whiggish teleology of liberty, to develop a radical scheme of property redistribution.[117]

There is of course a much more notable example of such an intellectual journey. A towering figure in mid-nineteenth-century politics and philosophy, John Stuart Mill was the most significant economic influence on George. Mill's *Principles of Political Economy* represented George's first academic introduction to the subject, and his work on land tenure reform in the early 1870s had a visible impact on George's ideas.[118] In his correspondence with the ageing Mill, George flattered the famous philosopher and economist as 'that highest

114 Paine, *Agrarian Justice* [1797], 179–180; see also Gregory Claeys, *Thomas Paine: Social and Political Thought* (Abingdon: Routledge, 1989), 199–206.

115 Alexander Harvey, 'The Book and the Author', in Patrick Edward Dove, *The Theory of Human Progression* [1850], Julia A. Kellogg (ed.) (New York: Blanchard, 1910), ii; Dove, *The Theory of Human Progression*, 38; Dove was a student and devotee of Victor Cousin, a French philosopher in the Scottish commonsense tradition. See Edward H. Madden, 'Victor Cousin and the Commonsense Tradition', *History of Philosophy Quarterly* 1, no. 1 (1984): 94; George Elder Davie, 'Victor Cousin and the Scottish Philosophers', *Journal of Scottish Philosophy* 7, no. 2 (2009): 193–214.

116 Dove, *The Theory of Human Progression*, 63, 121.

117 Dove, *The Theory of Human Progression*, 20, 23, 26, 91.

118 Barker, *Henry George*, 122; Henry George, *Irish World*, 9 July 1881.

of all characters – the "great, good man"'.[119] George's respect for the esteemed scholar was evident in the letter but also in his work in general, and he was very proud to have received a reply from Avignon, where Mill resided in his later years. Indeed, given Mill's political commitments in later life, which contributed greatly to his deeply contested legacy, it is fair to consider George one of the most faithful torchbearers of Mill's political and economic principles.[120]

Appropriately, of course, Mill's 'conversion' to socialism in later life had itself taken root in the question of land.[121] It was here specifically that Mill discarded the most astringent elements of his Benthamite inheritance in favour of an 'appeal to the communitarian legacy of the natural law tradition'.[122] Mill's focus on the distinctiveness of land as property in its elemental necessity to human life again drove an individualist metaphysic to a communal conclusion.[123] On the question of property and possession of the natural world, Mill drew directly upon the purposiveness of land in its provision for human sustenance through cultivation or habitation. 'Now, when we know the reason of a thing, we know what ought to be its limits', he explained. 'The limits of the reason ought to be the limits of the thing. The thing itself should stop where the reason stops'.[124] Under this familiar schema, the rights to land could not be given up or contracted away, for even if the initial occupation or distribution of land had been equitable, there was, Mill argued, 'an apparent wrong to posterity, to at least all those subsequently born who do not inherit a share'.[125] Critically, too, Mill insisted on the distinctiveness of land as property, since 'the land is not of man's creation', it was instead 'the original inheritance of the whole species', 'a mere gift of nature' which 'belonged as much to all others'.[126]

Like other radical republican thinkers, Mill's commitment to a form of land communalisation was informed by a broader moral vision of social

119 Henry George to John Stuart Mill, 22 August 1869 (HGP, Series I: A, Box 2, NYPL).
120 Wolfe, *From Radicalism to Socialism*, 61–63.
121 John Stuart Mill, *Autobiography* [1873] (New York: P. F. Collier and Sons, 1919), 149.
122 Ursula Vogel, 'The Land-Question: A Liberal Theory of Communal Property', *History Workshop* 27 (1989): 117; see also Alasdair MacIntyre, *After Virtue: A Study in Moral Theory* (London: Duckworth, 1981), 63; Rothschild, 'Political Economy', 759; A. W. Coats, 'The Historicist Reaction in English Political Economy, 1870–90', *Economica* 21 (1954): 143–153.
123 John Gray, 'John Stuart Mill on the Theory of Property', in Anthony Parel, and Thomas Flanagan (eds.), *Theories of Property: Aristotle to the Present* (Waterloo: Wilfred Laurier Press, 1979), 274.
124 John Stuart Mill, '*Tract on the Right of Property in Land*, Land Tenure Reform Association' [1873], in Hugh S. R. Elliot (ed.), *The Letters of John Stuart Mill*, vol. II (London: Longmans, Green, and Co., 1910), 388.
125 Mill, *Tract on the Right of Property in Land*.
126 John Stuart Mill, quoted in Clancy, *The Land League Manual*, 16; Mill, *Tract on the Right of Property in Land*, 387; John Stuart Mill to C. E. Norton, 24 September 1868, in Elliot, *The Letters*, 123; John Stuart Mill, 'Advice to Land Reformers', *The Examiner*, 4 January 1873; Wolfe, *From Radicalism to Socialism*, 59.

interdependence and individual flourishing.[127] Echoing familiar republican and natural law discourses, Mill lauded the moral qualities, the 'sturdy independence', of a small, owner-occupier class as a political ballast for ensuring individual freedom could be bound securely with greater equality within a polity orientated towards the common good.[128] Mill's primary concern, just as it would be for George, was to enable the development of human capacities by ensuring that people were not 'enslaved or made dependent [...] by force of poverty'.[129] His prioritisation of moral and political concerns over more narrowly economic ones, and indeed his propensity to understand political economy as inseparable from social and ethical evaluations, mirrored a similar sensibility evident in George's work.[130] Both men envisioned a future socialist polity as a desirable moral utopia, but saw it as something that could only grow organically through greater social interdependence, lest individual freedoms be subsumed and destroyed.[131] Linguisitically too, Mill's keen moral vision and incisive imagery, evident in his scorn for landowners whose wealth, 'produced by other people's labour and enterprise [falls] into their mouths while they sleep', found a later reiteration in George's writing.[132]

Mill's work, at least in the abridged form of quotes, also provided a valuable resource for Land Leaguers seeking to add weight to their position. His active and empathetic understanding of the Irish situation combined with his intellectual authority had made him a useful irritant, his sympathies proudly wielded to demonstrate the probity of land reform or nationalisation, the difference between the two frequently left ambiguous by intent.[133] Yet by the 1880s, Mill's eminence had waned significantly, and his legacy itself was a

[127] Gregory Claeys, *Mill and Paternalism* (Cambridge: Cambridge University Press, 2013), 171; See also Eugenio F. Biagini, 'Liberalism and Direct Democracy: John Stuart Mill and the Model of Ancient Athens', in Eugenio F. Biagini (ed.), *Citizenship and Community: Liberals, Radicals, and Collective Identities in the British Isles, 1865–1931* (Cambridge: Cambridge University Press, 1996), 21–44.

[128] John Stuart Mill, *Chapters and Speeches on the Irish Land Question* (London: Longmans, Green, Reader, and Dyer, 1870), 2.

[129] John Stuart Mill, 'Chapters on Socialism' [1869], in Jonathan Riley (ed.), *Principles of Political Economy* [1848] (Oxford: Oxford University Press, 1994), 377.

[130] A. W. Coats, 'The Classical Economists and the Labourer', in A. W. Coats (ed.), *The Classical Economists and Economic Policy* (London: Methuen and Co., 1971), 13; Gareth Stedman Jones, 'Religion and the Origins of Socialism', in Ira Katznelson, and Gareth Stedman Jones (eds.), *Religion and the Political Imagination* (Cambridge: Cambridge University Press, 2010), 171–189; Wolfe, *From Radicalism to Socialism,* 32.

[131] George, *Progress and Poverty*, 288–289; Wolfe, *From Radicalism to Socialism*, 27.

[132] John Stuart Mill, 'Should Public Bodies Be Required to Sell Their Lands', *The Examiner*, 11 January 1873.

[133] Clancy, *The Land League Manual*, 12–13; E. D. Steele, 'J. S. Mill and the Irish Question: The Principles of Political Economy, 1848–1865', *The Historical Journal* 13, no. 2 (1970): 216–236; Bruce L. Kinzer, 'J. S. Mill and Irish Land: A Reassessment', *The Historical Journal* 27, no. 1 (1984): 111–127.

matter of debate. For many erstwhile admirers, his later interest in land reform, as well as his underlying moralism, was a sour coda to his great achievements in economic theory (although even they were being rapidly rendered obsolete).[134] Discussing Mill's land reform plans, Henry Fawcett acknowledged that Mill's 'high authority' made his ideas at least 'deserving of most careful consideration', but concluded, despite his reverence, that they could 'neither be defended on grounds of justice nor expediency'.[135]

Mill's ideas, by the 1880s, were fundamentally at odds with the central assumptions that informed liberal politics and economic theory. His commitment to the distinctiveness of land as property and propagation of the idea of the 'unearned increment' – this was the increase in the value of land not due to the exertions of its owner – made him a subject of condemnation for both liberal idealists and neo-classical economists towards the end of the century. Joseph Shield Nicholson, Professor of Political Economy at Edinburgh, considered him 'largely to blame for the present clamour for the land for the people and the appropriation of the unearned increment'.[136] From the less critical perspective of the Fabians, Mill's unearned increment had 'gradually prepared the public mind for Socialist proposals', but despite this his political philosophy remained irretrievably individualist.[137] For free trade liberals, conversely, his socialistic views on land were inexcusable. Louis Mallet, a founding member of the Cobden Club, complained to the noted economic historian J. E. Thorold Rogers that 'all who have any faith in the great principle of Free Exchange should take their stand against Mill's false science'. While the great mid-century apostle of free trade Richard Cobden had worked hard to dismantle the obdurate and obsolete division between land and moveable property, Mallet protested, 'Mill begins by reasserting the distinction in its most naked form'.[138] It was this critical distinction, however, that moulded an individualist metaphysic into a collectivist politics, restraining, as Mill had desired, possessiveness with purposiveness.

Land in Irish Political Economy

The land question had long given a distinctive texture to Irish political economy. 'Wherever a number of men are gathered together in Ireland', reported

[134] Henry Sidgwick, 'Philosophy and Science', *The Academy* IV, no. 77 (1873): 293; David Stack, 'The Death of John Stuart Mill', *The Historical Journal* 54, no. 1 (2011): 167–190; See also Jocelyn Paul Betts, 'John Stuart Mill, Victorian Liberalism, and the Failure of Co-operative Production', *The Historical Journal* 59, no. 1 (2016): 153–174; Jeff Lipkes, *Politics, Religion and Classical Political Economy in Britain: John Stuart Mill and His Followers* (Basingstoke: Palgrave, 1999).

[135] Fawcett, *State Socialism*, 10.

[136] Joseph Shield Nicholson, 'A Plea for Orthodox Political Economy', *National Review* VI (1885), 557.

[137] Webb, *Socialism in England*, 19.

[138] Louis Mallet to J. E. Thorold Rogers, 5 November 1873, cited in Anthony Howe, *Free Trade and Liberal England, 1846–1946* (Oxford: Oxford University Press, 1998), 125.

the *Irish World* towards the end of 1878, 'that solid, significant monosyllable LAND is the first word that presents itself'.[139] While the Land War clearly represented an unusually elevated interest in the land question, the perpetual dominance of agrarian issues in an overwhelmingly rural country had fostered, over the course of the nineteenth century, an intellectual distance from orthodox, purportedly English, political economy. In the early 1800s, the pioneering Cork-born socialist William Thompson had attributed such hard-headed economic 'laws' emerging from English academic institutions to the physical distance between their privileged theoreticians and the moral truths that emerged from material reality. Such political economy could only be a false science for Thompson if it conflicted with universal morality.[140] This friction between an 'English' and an 'Irish' political economy persisted through the nineteenth century. Observing the 'physical and moral degradation' evident in English cities in the 1880s, Irish writer William Dillon attributed the suffering to the English idea that 'the greatest possible wealth' was the purpose to which 'every other consideration ought to be sacrificed'.[141]

The Famine, too, and its catastrophic effects on mid-century Ireland had a more immediate and profound effect on the study of political economy in Ireland than on its English counterpart, reinforcing the appearance of divergence between the two approaches. Because of their proximity to the Famine and its aftermath, Irish economists developed a more firmly historicist methodology earlier than their English peers and were quicker to abandon providentialist and narrowly utilitarian schema.[142] The Famine had played a central role in crystallising the historicist view that, as Isaac Butt explained, 'political economy does not, and cannot, lay down any general rules of action applicable to all circumstances'.[143] While this helped Irish political economists to reject the evangelical belief in the 'redemptive function of commerce' earlier than most, the focus on land also meant that the constraining positivism that succeeded it elsewhere had less traction and appeal.[144] After mercifully unhitching

[139] 'Land and Thought', *Irish World*, 30 November 1878.

[140] Terry Eagleton, 'The Radicalism of William Thompson', *The Irish Review* 26 (2000): 80–88; Fintan Lane, 'William Thompson, Bankruptcy and the West Cork Estate, 1808–34, *Irish Historical Studies* 39, no. 153 (2014): 24–39.

[141] William Dillon, *The Dismal Science: A Criticism on Modern English Political Economy* (Dublin: M. H. Gill & Son, 1882), 18.

[142] Peter Gray, 'Irish Social Thought and the Relief of Poverty', *Transactions of the Royal Historical Society* 20 (2010): 2; Hilton, *The Age of Atonement*, 111; Boylan and Foley, *Political Economy and Colonial Ireland*, 151; on a similar process in Scotland, see Allan W. MacColl, *Land, Faith and the Crofting Community: Christianity and Social Criticism in the Highlands of Scotland, 1843–93* (Edinburgh: Edinburgh University Press, 2006), 213.

[143] Isaac Butt, *Land Tenure in Ireland: A Plea for the Celtic Race* (Dublin: John Falconer, 1866), 61.

[144] Hilton, *The Age of Atonement*, 31; Clive Dewey, 'Celtic Agrarian Legislation and the Celtic Revival: Historicist Implications of Gladstone's Irish and Scottish Land Acts, 1870–1886', *Past & Present* 64 (1974): 37.

them from the juggernaut of economic progress, the imprimatur of external moral laws was subsequently cast off by many economists as an archaic irrelevance. Yet in Ireland, historicist thought did not appear to lead so inexorably to positivist conclusions. Although Irish political economists were in the vanguard of the developing historicism in the 1860s, its imprint in Ireland did not bear the same moral absenteeism, as ideas of 'natural justice and right' rooted in agrarian questions were less likely to be abandoned entirely.[145]

The occupier of the Whately Chair of Political Economy at Trinity College Dublin during the Famine was William Neilson Hancock, whose work demonstrated this process in microcosm. As founder of the *Statistical and Social Inquiry Society of Ireland*, Hancock played an important role in development of Irish economics, writing prolifically during the middle of the nineteenth century. Hancock's early historicism was shaped by those two seismic mid-century events, the Famine and the US Civil War, which drew him away from viewing justice as embedded in the functions of the market.[146] Despite this, Hancock did not turn to economic positivism, and he remained committed to an external notion of social morality that, he thought, should play a pivotal role in any economic system. Observing the disjuncture between moral and economic rectitude, Hancock argued that generous relief should be an entitlement by 'right' for workers, who themselves were blamelessly suffering from economic crises.[147] Hancock's commitment to Smithean political economy was predicated on his particular affinity for Smith's emphasis on role of the public sphere in keeping the self-interest of capitalists in check. As early as 1862, he confidently asserted the importance of disentangling private vices from public virtues, stating 'that the tendency of capitalists, when unrestrained by a vigilant public opinion, is that ascribed to them by Adam Smith, the greatest of political economists, of sacrificing the public interest to their own'. The solution was a 'strong and enlightened moral public opinion', a public sphere animated by the ideal of civic duty over atomised self-interest.[148]

This distinct separation of economics and morals as two related but independent systems offered refuge from the claims of economic positivism. It was a shelter utilised by a number of Irish economists during the later part of the century, often prompted primarily by the question of land. But this also brought out familiar tensions and contradictions, the same problems over the issue of natural right that had pestered earlier thinkers. Thomas Edward Cliffe Leslie, for instance, historicist Professor of Political Economy at Belfast, favoured

[145] Butt, *Land Tenure in Ireland*, 81.

[146] W. N. Hancock, *The Difference between English and Irish Poor Law as to the Treatment of Women and Unemployed Workmen* (Dublin: R. D. Webb and Son, 1862), 18.

[147] Hancock, *The Difference between English and Irish Poor Law*, 18.

[148] W. N. Hancock, *The Journeyman Bakers' Case* (London: Emily Faithful, 1862), 11–12.

smaller proprietorship and more widespread access to land, but recoiled from proposals that might jeopardise 'all and any property in land'.[149] He based his arguments for smaller agricultural holdings firmly on the basis of increased productivity.[150] While it would be socially desirable to ensure an egalitarian access to the natural world, in his view, this could not be allowed to threaten property more broadly, especially since it would be a 'scandalous injustice' not to compensate owners of land.[151]

Yet Cliffe Leslie was clear that land was not like other property; there was a 'fundamental distinction between property in land, and all other kinds of property'.[152] Land was unique because, as Cliffe Leslie admitted, 'it is the sphere, not of agriculture alone, but of every form of human industry, and even human existence'.[153] This position did not lead him to suppose a collective right to benefit from this, but rather that such possession should fall under the auspices of state management. Avoiding naturalistic claims and relying on a historical argument that private property in land had always been subordinate 'to the interests of the State; the land itself belong[ing] by law to the State', Cliffe Leslie's arguments for greater security to tenants relied primarily on the absence of the landlords' claim to the contrary: that nobody could claim absolute control over the soil 'either upon legal or economical grounds'.[154]

Identifying the misuses of Adam Smith's work, and fallacies propagated in his name to support an unrestrained *laissez-faire*, Cliffe Leslie blamed the Scottish philosopher's 'classical conception of Nature [which] supposed simplicity, harmony, order, and equality in the moral as in the physical world'.[155] Influenced by Henry Maine's *Ancient Law*, and its critique of such naturalistic assumptions, Cliffe Leslie argued that this inclination towards a beneficent conception of nature, such as a belief in natural liberty or natural equality, had facilitated an unrepentantly callous economism that had devastated countless lives. 'The mischief done in political economy by this assumption respecting the beneficent constitution of nature, and therefore of all human inclinations and desires, has been incalculable', he declared.[156] No moral value could be deduced from the natural world; there could be no intent observed. Malthus, therefore, far from being the heretical voice undermining the possibilities of natural harmony,

149 Thomas Edward Cliffe Leslie to Henry George, 26 November 1879 (HGP, Series I: A, Box 2, NYPL).

150 T. E. Cliffe Leslie, 'Political Economy and the Tenure of Land', *The Fortnightly Review* 5, no. 26 (1 June 1866): 227.

151 Thomas Edward Cliffe Leslie to Henry George, 26 September 1880 (HGP, Series I: A, Box 2, NYPL). This would frequently be a stumbling block, since very few political economists were willing to countenance economic expropriation, even by means of a full value tax.

152 Cliffe Leslie, 'Political Economy', 221.

153 Cliffe Leslie, 'Political Economy', 223.

154 Cliffe Leslie, 'Political Economy', 221, 228.

155 Cliffe Leslie, 'The Political Economy of Adam Smith', 553.

156 Cliffe Leslie, 'The Political Economy of Adam Smith', 554.

was for Cliffe Leslie the inaugurator of the inductive science of economics, interested in 'the real, as contrasted with an ideal, order of things'.[157] From the perspective of republican radicals like George, Cliffe Leslie's ire, though well intentioned, was entirely misplaced. As they saw it, Cliffe Leslie's view of the distinctiveness of land rested on no moral foundations and was ultimately at the mercy of economic expediency and subordinate to the needs of a state. Left only with the negative argument that land need not be considered the absolute possession of the legal owner, not the positive argument that all should possess a share by right, the claim of land's distinctiveness was left to wither, since all contractual relations and property rights were ultimately dependent on their political expediency to functioning of an orderly state.

Perhaps most revealing in this regard was the work of John Elliot Cairnes. Another Irish economist adrift from metropolitan orthodoxy, Cairnes' historicist political economy also subordinated property rights in land to question of general welfare, accepting to a degree the notion that agriculture differed from other industries.[158] He recognised economic laws as indications of human behaviour only 'in given circumstances', and as entirely separate from morality; economic laws did not entail 'a realization of the principles of abstract justice' and operated 'essentially out of the moral sphere'.[159] This, however, led him into some familiar problems. While he admitted that ethical concerns should shape economic designs because 'our existing system of industry is not such as entitles us to claim for it [...] the character of satisfying the requirements of moral justice', he was unable find a firm moral footing upon which to base such judgements. Cairnes was drawn towards but ultimately recoiled from a notion of natural right, arguing instead that the producer had a greater claim than the landowner to the products of the soil on the basis that such a judgment was closer to 'the elementary ideas of justice' that were 'the main propelling force of human progress'.[160] Keen to subordinate economic considerations to an external moral frame of reference, yet reluctant to embrace a solid foundation for this, Cairnes' argument for the expediency of progress contained a subtle circularity.

Cairnes, much like George and Mill, held that the unimproved value of land was a commodity distinct from others by dint of the fact that 'no man made the land'. But he was also aware that this position suggested a natural right to land.

[157] Cliffe Leslie, 'The Political Economy of Adam Smith', 551.

[158] Charles Hickson, 'The Classical Economist Perspective on Landed-Property Reform', in Thomas Boylan, Renee Prendergast, and John D. Turner (eds.), *A History of Irish Economic Thought* (Abingdon: Routledge, 2011), 149; Thomas Boylan, Renee Prendergast, and John D. Turner, 'Introduction', in Thomas Boylan, Renee Prendergast, and John D. Turner (eds.), *A History of Irish Economic Thought* (Abingdon: Routledge, 2011), 8.

[159] John Elliot Cairnes, *Some Leading Principles of Political Economy* (New York: Harper and Brothers, 1878), 185, 268–269.

[160] John Elliot Cairnes, quoted in Boylan and Foley, 'John Elliot Cairnes', 168.

Cairnes took great care to dismiss 'so-called "natural rights"', footnoting his argument on this topic: 'To guard against misapprehension, it may be as well to state that I do not recognize in this argument any proof of a "natural right" to property in anything, even that which our hands have just made.' But this was a slightly disingenuous dodge because Cairnes did hold that it was possible to distinguish between the products due to the 'exertions' of labour and those 'to which he has no more right than anyone else'.[161] Although the basis of this distinction was not explicitly rooted in a 'naturalised' notion of right, but simply one vested in economic utility, Cairnes continued to use it to contrast with the naturalistic non-man-made conception of land, even though such rights to landed property could also be as easily rooted in arguments for economic utility. His historical arguments regarding property in land implicitly framed access to land as a necessity for life, but he resisted the conclusions of natural right that could be drawn from this, falling back not only on a more limited and negative argument that sidestepped the question of necessity for existence, but one that could be applied to all forms of property, implicitly rendering his focus on the distinction between land and moveables superfluous.[162]

Writing in the *Fortnightly Review* in 1870, Cairnes began with his argument that land was an atypical form of property because its value was dependent on natural and social conditions rather than human labour. Property in land, he explained, 'consists largely in value which no human industry employed on the land has created. The ordinary economic considerations, therefore, which apply to, and justify property in other forms of wealth, do not apply here'.[163] Yet, as Cairnes had explained elsewhere, those 'considerations' which justified other property were simply that it was 'efficacious as a stimulus to industry' to recognise a right of ownership for the producer in a thing they have produced.[164] Moveable property in this respect was not possessed on the basis of labour, but on the basis that such rights were inducements to further labour, and this on the basis that further labour would increase progress and prosperity. Yet Cairnes often glossed over this distinction. Despite Cairnes' use of typically naturalistic republican language when making his claim that restricting landlords' rights to property would secure 'the labourer in the fruit of his toil', such fruits, just like the land itself, were held, according to his own analysis, only on the basis of economic prudence.[165] It was an awkward balancing act for Cairnes, struggling to reconcile his moral inclinations on the Irish land question – his strong aversion to landlords pocketing the unearned increment –

[161] John Elliot Cairnes, *Essays in Political Economy: Theoretical and Applied* (London: Macmillan, 1873), 191, 210.

[162] John Elliot Cairnes, 'Political Economy and Land', *The Fortnightly Review* 7, no. 37 (1870): 48–49.

[163] Cairnes, 'Political Economy and Land', 45.

[164] Cairnes, 'Political Economy and Land', 42.

[165] Cairnes, 'Political Economy and Land', 45.

with his utilitarian commitments.[166] Allowing landlords to keep economic rent, even though it 'cannot properly be said to owe its existence to either labourer, capitalist, or landlord', rested for the economist only on 'the considerations of practical utility'.[167] Recognising the hollowness of his position, Cairnes' conceded that 'the feeling appealed to may, if you like, be a coarse one, but it is at any rate efficacious' as it 'furnishes society with the necessary material basis for civilized progress'.[168]

Cairnes' insistence on the uniqueness of land, especially when his argument could proceed without it, was puzzling to some observers. Henry Maine, critiquing Cairnes' work in the *Pall Mall Gazette*, did not understand why Cairnes devoted 'so much space to the question of the comparative sacredness of the title to moveable and of that to immoveable property'.[169] Maine admitted that there were some interesting observations to be made in regard to the notion of the unearned increment that Cairnes was discussing, but that since the question of Irish land was one of contract rather than property and was a problem that could be solved by special regulation of such, there need not be any discussion of the origins and foundations of property. Maine saw that taking the discussion into the realms of property, rather than looking at the problem as a question of the 'powers which the law of any particularly country allows to be exercised by persons over things', could inadvertently draw out very radical and naturalistic conclusions regarding possession that would only fuel destabilising socialistic schemes. Such speculations into the foundations of property were, just as Blackstone had warned, not only 'idle' but also 'exceedingly dangerous', since they rested on custom and economic expediency and should not be disentangled. Indeed, he was bemused by Cairnes' circuitous use of labour to justify possession, a potentially incendiary proposition, especially since it was not actually labour, but ultimately economic probity, upon which Cairnes balanced his proposals. As Maine condescended, 'we confess we should prefer a shorter method' that would reach the same proposals without placing so much weight on the value of labour to justify possession, a notion which carried such a high risk of radicalism.[170] Indeed, seeing the dangers to existing notions of property inherently pressed by the Irish land question, Maine concluded that 'the more special, and the less general and abstract' the solution to it, the better.

As for so many others, the land question had forced Cairnes into a choice between natural rights and utility, although it was one he was unwilling to make firmly. Cairnes' disjointed and unstable position marked him as one of

[166] Cairnes, *Essays in Political Economy*, 193, 198; Black, *Economic Thought and the Irish Question*, 54.
[167] Cairnes, *Essays in Political Economy*, 197; Cairnes, 'Political Economy and Land', 53.
[168] Cairnes, *Some Leading Principles*, 269–270, 272.
[169] Henry Maine, 'Political Economy and Land', *Pall Mall Gazette* 6 January 1870.
[170] Henry Maine, 'Political Economy and Land', *Pall Mall Gazette* 6 January 1870.

the last of the classical economists.[171] His struggle, like that of Cliffe Leslie, to accommodate a conviction that land was distinct without relying on naturalised notions of right or value was central to his 'vacillation of view' that John Kells Ingram, perhaps the most positivist of Irish political economists, and most in tune with the organic sociology of Spencer and the functionalism of the new liberalism, condemned in the 1880s as 'intrinsically unsound'.[172] Where Maine and Cairnes found agreement, however, was on the value of historically and culturally informed economic knowledge. Although this historicist approach could be put to a variety of contrasting and conflicting purposes, a growing interest from the 1860s in customs, folkways, and historically legitimated cultural claims led a generation of legislators and political thinkers to express the hope that these new insights could lead to a more benign and effective management of the Irish situation.[173] It also offered a means by which the historical mythologising that saturated many radical demands could be dissolved. With this particular ambition in mind, it was during the 1860s that William Neilson Hancock became known for his work preparing the ancient Irish Brehon Laws, an early Irish legal code, for publication alongside commentaries.[174]

The Brehon Laws had provided generations of Irish nationalists with historical support for their claims regarding Irish land. Fenian journalist James Clancy's *Ireland: As She Is*, later republished as part of his *Land League Manual*, contained a potted history of the Laws that was typical of the genre: 'Land was owned in common by each clan', Clancy explained, and allotted by need to the constituent families 'according to the number of children they possessed'. Drawing comparisons with the Israelites to establish a legitimating biblical precedence, the reader was told that in Ireland, prior to the English occupation, 'no man could own the land, save the man who cultivated it, and he only so much as his domestic responsibility entitled him to'.[175] The Young Irelander David Power Conyngham similarly described a legal system in which it was 'held that the land was for the benefit of the people'. He sought to emphasise Irish distinctiveness in the matter of both land holding and the political independence that resulted from it by informing his readers that 'on

171 Thomas Sowell, *Classical Economics Reconsidered* (Princeton: Princeton University Press, 1974), 14.

172 Ingram, *A History of Political Economy*, 151; See also G. K. Peatling, 'Who Fears to Speak of Politics? John Kells Ingram and Hypothetical Nationalism', *Irish Historical Studies* 31, no. 122 (1998): 207, 214.

173 E. D. Steele, *Irish Land and British Politics: Tenant-Right and Nationality, 1865–1870* (Cambridge: Cambridge University Press, 1974), 105; Dewey, 'Celtic Agrarian Legislation and the Celtic Revival', 43.

174 William Neilson Hancock (ed.), *Ancient Laws of Ireland. Senchus Mor: Introduction to Senchus Mor, and Achgabail; or Law of Distress, as Contained in the Harleian Manuscripts*, vol. I (Dublin: Alexander Thomas, 1865).

175 James J. Clancy, *Ireland: As She Is, as She Has Been, and as She Ought to Be* (New York: Thomas Kelly, 1877), 30.

the Continent and in England the feudal system held sway, and it debased the people by keeping them dependent on the nobles who held the land. The Brehon Code held sway in Ireland until after the English invasion'.[176] In this way, the laws were taken to explain a cultural preference for localism and an ingrained historical commitment to interpersonal loyalty over abstract 'national' identity.[177] They formed part of a powerful narrative in Irish political life, which, like republican thought more broadly, expressed the centrality of land to both the production of economic and social value, and the security of personal independence and political power.

A subsequent editor of this multivolume translation, writing on the eve of the Land War, expressed the forlorn hope that his work would be 'sufficient to put an end, once and for ever' to the assertion, 'which seems to have become an axiom adopted by all authors on Irish history and antiquities, and which has also gained considerable political notoriety', that the ancient Irish possessed no concept of 'exclusive ownership in land' until influenced by English law.[178] However, although the specifics were often mangled in popular renderings, Alexander George Richey made clear the Brehon Laws did put much more stringent restrictions on exclusive ownership and limited freedom of alienation through a variety of means. As Richey explained in his commentaries, 'the "alienation" applied to the ownership of land, such as we are dealing with, must be understood as alienation in accordance with the local custom, and so far as it was thereby permitted, is not to be confounded with the unrestricted rights of disposal, which we now associate with absolute ownership'. The work also established an imagined development of land tenure from familial to collective, with Richey demonstrating the progressive development towards 'an organization of households and a community, or land held by a community (coibne), instead of land held by an individual as head of an house'.[179] Certainly his hope that the radical uses of the Brehon Laws would be restricted by his efforts would go unrealised. Into the 1920s and beyond Irish nationalists were still using them to demonstrate the 'security of liberty and property' in a pre-anglicised Ireland.[180]

Naturally, George, just like other land radicals, also quickly embraced this historically grounded idea of communal land ownership. He found the concept of Irish 'tribal tenure in law' useful to highlight the historicity of his

176 David Power Conyngham, *Ireland Past and Present: Embracing a Complete History of the Land Question from the Earliest Period to the Present Time* (New York: James Sheehy, 1884), 26.

177 Clancy, *The Land League Manual*, 209–210.

178 Alexander George Richey (ed.), *Ancient Laws of Ireland: Din Tectugad, and Certain Other Selected Brehon Law Tracts*, vol. IV (Dublin: A Thom & Co., 1879), cxxxix–cxl.

179 Richey (ed.), *Ancient Laws of Ireland*, vol. IV, cviii–cxiv, lxxxii.

180 Edward McSweeny, 'Ireland Is an American Question', 41 (Archives of Irish America Pamphlet Collection, AIA.47, NYU); see, for instance, Laurence Ginnell, *The Brehon Laws: A Legal Handbook* (London: T. Fisher Unwin, 1894).

proposals, providing them with an aura of immutable and transcendent truth. In his own inimitable way George recalled, with some decorative élan, that 'what the English call your "new fangled and Yankee inventions", are truths that I have heard over and over again from the likes of old men who could not speak a word of English when I sat by the peat fires of Connaught cabins'.[181] The radical argument did not have to choose between a historicist and universalist presumption, however; the Irish had merely retained more successfully a historic awareness of a universal truth, making their attitudes to land closer to the 'main stream of human existence and human feeling and opinion' than the English, just as Mill had declared.[182] Although a valuable intellectual construction, providing precedent of communal ownership and usufruct, Irish arguments for historical possession of the soil were in this way subsumed within a discourse of natural rights.

This folding of a historical argument into a natural rights claim for the land was a familiar one in Ireland. The imaginative creation of the Irish nation, undertaken by nationalists throughout the nineteenth century, often vigorously eschewed an abstracted Enlightenment universalism, but was simultaneously comfortable with the construction of a normative naturalism in which the 'British System' performed the role of unnatural aberration.[183] Even for decidedly romantic and particularist nationalists, men like Thomas Davis and John Mitchel, the land question had been both the economic engine and the emotional heart of the demand for Irish nationhood, and it was here where arguments of natural right were hardest to ignore. But while the long tradition of land reform in Ireland had been dominated by advocates for a more delicate and piecemeal reordering of proprietorial relations – men such as William Sharman Crawford, William Conner, Charles Gavin Duffy, and Isaac Butt – who largely focussed their efforts towards tenurial stability and financial security for farmers, it is indicative that the most significant mid-century precursor for the Land League was Young Irelander James Fintan Lalor.[184]

[181] Henry George, 'Letter in Defense of Michael Davitt and the Irish Land League' (HGP, Series II, Box 12, NYPL).

[182] John Stuart Mill, HC Deb. 17 May 1866, vol. 183, c. 1088; Also quoted by Clancy, *The Land League Manual*, 15; and T. M. Healy, *Why There Is an Irish Land Question and an Irish Land League* (Boston: Kiley, 1881), 53.

[183] Niamh Lynch, 'Defining Irish Nationalist Anti-Imperialism: Thomas Davis and John Mitchel', *Éire-Ireland* 42, no. 1 (2007): 95; John Mitchel to Fr Kenyon, in William Dillon, *Life of John Mitchel*, vol. II (London: Kegan Paul, Trench and Co., 1888), 106; Colin Kidd, 'Gaelic Antiquity and National Identity in Enlightenment Ireland and Scotland', *English Historical Review* 109, no. 434 (1994): 1197–1214; David Dwan, *The Great Community: Culture and Nationalism in Ireland* (Dublin: Field Day, 2008).

[184] James P. Bruce, *Ireland's Hope: The 'Peculiar Theories' of James Fintan Lalor* (Wilmington: Vernon Press, 2020), 125; Isaac Butt, *The Irish People and the Irish land: A Letter to Lord Lifford* (Dublin: John Falconer, 1867), 5.

Born in 1807 in Queen's County (Laois) to prosperous tenant farmers, Lalor's political education was provided by the Tithe War of the 1830s and, in particular, the Famine. Appalled at the zeal with which British legislators sought to extirpate small holders as a matter of economic faith, with no 'voice to protect against the principle, the feasibility, the consequences' of such a policy, Lalor directed his attention to the development of a 'social economy', an economic system that secured social rights as preeminent over property.[185] He determined that the only means by which such a stable and contented republican society could be developed was by fostering a solid agricultural base. 'Create the husbandman', wrote Lalor, asserting the moral foundationalism of agriculture, 'and you create the mechanic, the artisan, the manufacturer, the merchant. Thus you will work on the ordinance of God, in the order and with the powers of nature'.[186]

It was through the primacy of natural law that Lalor explained and defended his ideas. Agriculture was the first and most significant occupation because it was 'first in the order of nature'; living and working one's own land was 'as God and nature intended', and 'no law of nature' forbid the starving man to steal bread – indeed, as Lalor made clear, it was demanded by 'the great necessity of self-defence' and 'self-protection', which was 'the first law of nature, the first duty of man'.[187] Lalor connected the discourses of eighteenth-century republicanism with the later radical tradition, not just in placing the right to land as central to 'the vigour and vitality of all other rights', but as the basis for an active and disinterested public sphere.[188] A truly free country would be 'based on a peasantry rooted like rocks in the soil of the land'.[189] He echoed Paine (and many others) in arguing for the inalienability of land, that 'no generation of living men can bind a generation that is not yet born, or can sell or squander the rights of man', and came to similar conclusions that rents should be paid 'to themselves, the people, for public purposes'.[190]

Lalor's influence was extensive not only through contemporary nationalists like John Mitchel but also on Michael Davitt and, latterly, James Connolly.[191] Like both of these subsequent Irish radicals, Lalor found that the signal importance of land in Ireland's long and fraught relationship with British rule

185 James Fintan Lalor, 'Tenants' Right and Landlord's Law' [1847], in Marta Ramón (ed.) '*The Faith of a Felon' and Other Writings* (Dublin: University College Dublin Press, 2012), 86.

186 Lalor, in L. Fogarty (ed.), *James Fintan Lalor*, 22.

187 Lalor, in L. Fogarty (ed.), *James Fintan Lalor*, 22, 66, 129, 85.

188 Lalor, 'Tenants' Right and Landlord's Law'', 104.

189 Lalor, in L. Fogarty (ed.), *James Fintan Lalor*, 59.

190 Lalor, 'Tenants' Right and Landlord's Law'', 140, 134.

191 In 1900 Connolly declared the Socialist Party of Ireland 'the only political party in Ireland which fully accepts Fintan Lalor's teaching', James Connolly, 'Introduction', in James Fintan Lalor, *The Rights of Ireland and The Faith of a Felon* (Dublin: Socialist Party of Ireland, 1900), ii.

allowed romantic nationalist arguments to fit seamlessly alongside naturalised or universalist ones. Ireland could be both particularly oppressed by British misrule and an exemplar of a more pervasive economic domination involving the violation of natural laws. Lalor's democratic republicanism, presaging the Land League's connection of land with democratic sovereignty – that the 'people' were 'the first landowners and lords paramount as well as the lawmakers of this island' – was a self-conscious attempt to 'take up the mission of the United Irishmen'.[192] He was a conduit for a transatlantic radical republicanism that was indelibly bound to Ireland through its history and agrarian complexion; a country where the inherent tensions of private property in land that had been laid out by Aquinas, and which posed tectonic problems for liberal ideals, were plainly and unavoidably manifest in daily life and political struggle. But it was the Land War that would drive this most fundamental political question of land on to the international stage.

[192] Fintan Lalor, in L. Fogarty (ed.), *James Fintan Lalor*, 43–44; Fintan Lalor, 'Tenants' Right and Landlord's Law'', 97.

3 The Land War and the Land League

> You whose interests are bound up with theirs, you suffer from the effects of the very same cause. Up, then, men of Dublin, and with liberty and labour as your watchword, strike for the emancipation of enslaved humanity (cheers).
>
> The resolution was carried.[1]

By the mid-1870s, Ireland's cultural and economic life remained inseparable from the land. Despite some urban growth, Ireland was still predominantly rural. The 1881 census recorded only 24 per cent of the population living in towns over 2,000, with that percentage varying between only 7.6 per cent in Connacht and 38.3 per cent in Leinster. Urban life, outside of Dublin and Belfast, was largely an extension of rural life, sharing similar concerns and remaining socially and economically dependent on agriculture.[2] Since the Famine in the 1840s, rising agricultural prices and comparatively stable rents had created some burgeoning prosperity, especially in the south and east of the country.[3] The upheaval of the 1840s had also had a significant, albeit unevenly spread, demographic impact, reducing the numbers of smaller farmers and labourers and leaving, especially in the south and east, a more accentuated class structure dominated by larger farmers, graziers, and labourers. Beyond the west of Ireland, where severe poverty marked the lives of small farmers, agricultural tenants occupied a position of relative privilege when compared to urban and rural labourers.[4] In the south-west especially, the post-Famine era saw an increasing commercialisation of agriculture.[5] However, these socio-economic developments were not smooth or even. For all the changes wrought by the Famine, by 1870 landlords owning 1,000 acres or

[1] Thomas Brennan, speaking at a Land and Labour Meeting in Phoenix Park, Dublin, *Freeman's Journal*, 15 March 1880.

[2] Gerard Moran, 'The Land War, Urban Destitution and Town Tenant Protest, 1879–1882', *Saothar: Journal of Irish Labour Studies* 20 (1995): 17; W. E. Vaughan, 'Ireland c.1870', in W. E. Vaughan (ed.), *A New History of Ireland*, vol. V, 781.

[3] Vaughan, 'Ireland c.1870', 756–758. [4] Vaughan, 'Ireland c.1870', 781, 754.

[5] Lucey, *Land, Popular Politics and Agrarian Violence*, 8.

more possessed 81 per cent of Irish land, and economic security remained contingent and precarious.[6]

The Land War was directly precipitated by a partial crop failure that soon threatened to turn into widespread distress. There was a collapse of the potato crop in 1877, with significant credit extended by shopkeepers bridging the gap, but the subsequent failure in 1879 left even this means of survival overstretched. The potato harvest in 1879 was less than half the yield of the previous year and forebode tough times ahead; indeed by 1880, evictions increased dramatically as a result.[7] Bishop Thomas Nulty of Meath could not remember having seen 'such depression in trade and such universal poverty among the farming and grazing classes in this Diocese'.[8] Crucially, as the Bishop made clear, the distress was not confined only to those who subsisted directly off the land but threatened 'respectable' farmers and graziers too. Dairies in Cork reported a fall in butter production 'in consequence of the scarcity of grass'.[9] Immediately comparisons were drawn with the Famine, and popular memories, once reanimated, shaped much of the approach towards the impending crisis. The resuscitation of these vivid recollections determined many minds that the lessons learned from those years should not be forgotten.[10] The deanery of Tralee sought to remind those with the power to help that 'the present year is the most disastrous [...] since the calamitous famine of '47 and '48'.[11] The nationalist tradition that had understood the Famine as the malignant construction of British misrule found expression at the very first meeting of the Land League in Irishtown, County Mayo, when Michael O'Sullivan reminded his audience that 'we cannot shut our eyes to the lessons of the past', namely that the 'exterminators' needed to be removed.[12] Evocations of the Famine provided emotional momentum for the League: 'Are we going to permit ourselves to be hunted out of the country as in 1848?', asked one Land League speaker.[13]

[6] James S. Donnelly, Jr., *The Land and People of Nineteenth-Century Cork: The Rural Economy and the Land Question* (London: Routledge, 1975), 250; Samuel Clark, 'Strange Bedfellows? The Land League Alliances', in Fergus Campbell, and Tony Varley (eds.), *Land Questions in Modern Ireland* (Manchester: Manchester University Press, 2013), 94–95.

[7] Average of 590 eviction p/a between 1877 and 1879, 1880 saw 10,657, rising to 26,836 in 1882, Daniel Crilly, *Irish Evictions* (London: Irish Press Agency, 1887), 7–8; *Irish World*, 6 May; 13 May 1882.

[8] Thomas Nulty, quoted in Emmet Larkin, *The Roman Catholic Church and the Creation of the Modern Irish State 1878–1886* (Philadelphia: American Philosophical Society, 1975), 16.

[9] *Irish World*, 5 July 1879. [10] Jordan, *Land and Popular Politics*, 204.

[11] *Galway Vindicator*, 8 November 1879. [12] *Connaught Telegraph*, 26 April 1879.

[13] John Cantwell, Athy, 10 October 1880 (S. L. Anderson Papers, MS 11,289, National Library of Ireland). See also, Enda Delaney, and Breandán Mac Suibhne, 'To Assert Even the Animal's Right of Existence', in Enda Delaney, and Breandán Mac Suibhne (eds.), *Ireland's Great Famine and Popular Politics* (New York: Routledge, 2016), 1–9.

Despite the evocations, and there were certainly comparisons to be drawn, the decline of subsistence farming since the Famine had substantively changed the nature of the crisis.[14] The devastation wrought 30 years earlier was not matched by the deprivation of the late 1870s. The extensive reach of credit, extended to farmers by shopkeepers and banks, had created a much more interdependent economy.[15] With many farmers indebted to them, it was local shopkeepers and merchants who had a significant stake in their debtors' survival.[16] Also significant were the international dimensions of the crisis, which were evident from the very beginning. Developing communication with the United States, and with Irish-America in particular, had expanded popular horizons, making it easier for many in Ireland to see their situation in a wider imperial and global context.[17]

Ireland's place in an ever more integrated North Atlantic economy also conditioned the disaster itself. Increasing mechanisation in British agriculture had led to a reduction in seasonal remittances, but it was the pressure of competition from American agriculture that proved to be particularly damaging to the Irish economy.[18] It was a painful irony that it had been the combination of considerable British financial investment and an emigrant Irish workforce that facilitated the expansion of the railways into the American Midwest, opening up an entire continent for beef exports.[19] The growing impact of international capital, and American natural resources, in creating more dynamic but dyspeptic markets was a distinctive aspect of this increasingly integrated economic area. As Irish farmers found their beef and lamb undercut by American produce, there was a developing awareness of the challenges posed by the intemperate climate of international competition. This ensured that the Land War was never a narrowly national issue, but one that also intersected with questions of free trade, protection, and economic territoriality.[20]

14 Liam Kennedy, 'Farmers, Traders, and Agricultural Politics in Pre-Independence Ireland', in Samuel Clark, and James S. Donnelly (eds.), *Irish Peasants: Violence and Political Unrest, 1780–1914* (Madison: University of Wisconsin Press, 1983), 343.

15 W. E. Vaughan, *Landlords and Tenants in Mid-Victorian Ireland* (Oxford: Oxford University Press, 1994), 213.

16 Kennedy, 'Farmers, Traders, and Agricultural Politics'; Samuel Clark, 'The Social Composition of the Land League', *Irish Historical Studies* 17, no. 68 (1971): 455–456.

17 Healy, *Why There Is an Irish Land Question*, 88; 'Proceedings of the First Annual Convention of the Irish National Land League, held at Buffalo, New York, 12 and 13 January 1881' (Richmond: P. Keenan, 1881), 14 (George D. Cahill Papers, Series III, Box. 5, Boston College).

18 Jordan, *Land and Popular Politics*, 203; Gerard Moran, '"Near Famine": The Roman Catholic Church and the Subsistence Crisis of 1879–82', *Studia Hibernica* 32 (2002): 157.

19 Justin Kastner, *Food and Agricultural Security: An Historical, Multidisciplinary Approach* (Santa Barbara: Praeger, 2010), 7.

20 'American and Canadian Food', *Freeman's Journal*, 22 September 1879; Henry George, 'The Irish Question from an American Standpoint', 1886 (HGP, Series II, Box 13, NYPL); Larkin, *The Roman Catholic Church*, 16.

The 'New Departure', a loose alliance between John Devoy's revolutionary nationalists, Michael Davitt's advanced radicalism, and Charles Stuart Parnell's home rulers, signified an important convergence in Irish separatism prior to the Land War. Nevertheless, the real engine of discontent, in the form of agrarian anger, had long been a familiar ally of political nationalism. Since the late-eighteenth century, the land question had frequently been identified as the nursery of national liberation; the space where freedom could be grown.[21] Importantly, Tenants' Defence Associations during the 1870s, in the west of Ireland especially, began sounding a more radical note in their critiques of Irish landlordism. A direct predecessor of the Land League, the Ballinasloe Tenants' Defence Association in County Galway built its success around an appeal to the more radical demands of smaller tenants.[22] Anticipating the League, these included calls for the mobilisation of public opinion, so as to ensure that Irish people did not have to 'take their rule *or their customs* from Britain'.[23] More significantly perhaps was their doctrine: 'that the land was made for the people, and the people for the land; and we strongly deny the right of absolute ownership of the soil'.[24] Here, the connection between land ownership and nationhood was openly examined. Inspired by the Fenian radicalism of Matthew Harris and Michael O'Sullivan, the Ballinasloe group, as well as Harris' relationship with Michael Davitt and James Daly, was the organisational and ideological embryo for the League itself.[25] It was Davitt, most able and willing to draw on the broader radical implications of the Irish republican tradition, who would become the emotional heart of the League.[26]

The first mass meeting of what was to become an international organisation was in Irishtown, County Mayo, on 20 April 1879. The immediate success of the meeting in securing a reduction in rent from the local landlord served as a

[21] Sara L. Maurer, *The Dispossessed State: Narratives of Ownership in 19th-Century Britain and Ireland* (Baltimore, MD: Johns Hopkins University Press, 2012), 118.

[22] Gerard Moran, '"Laying the Seeds for Agrarian Agitation": The Ballinasloe Tenants' Defence Association', in Carla King, and Conor McNamara (eds.), *The West of Ireland: New Perspectives on the Nineteenth Century* (Dublin: History Press Ireland, 2011), 74; Lucey, *Land, Popular Politics and Agrarian Violence*, 23.

[23] *Connaught Telegraph*, 12 May 1877.

[24] *Connaught Telegraph*, 12 May 1877.

[25] Jordan, *Land and Popular Politics*, 213; Bew, *Land and the National Question*, 54; Brian Casey, 'Matt Harris and the Ballinasloe Tenant Defence Association, 1876–9', in Brian Casey (ed.), *Defying the Law of the Land: Agrarian Radicals in Irish History* (Dublin: The History Press Ireland, 2013), 90–99; Gerard Moran, 'Matthew Harris, Fenianism and Land Agitation in the West of Ireland', in Fergus Campbell, and Tony Varley (eds.), *Land Questions in Modern Ireland* (Manchester: Manchester University Press, 2013), 226.

[26] On Davitt, see Carla King, *Michael Davitt* (Dublin: University College Dublin Press, 2009); Fintan Lane, and Andrew G. Newby (eds.), *Michael Davitt: New Perspectives* (Dublin: Irish Academic Press, 2009); Laurence Marley, *Michael Davitt: Freelance Radical and Frondeur* (Dublin: Four Courts Press, 2007); T. W. Moody, *Davitt and Irish Revolution, 1846–82* (Oxford: Oxford University Press, 1981).

catalyst and an example for future activities. James Daly, the Mayo politician, activist, and owner of the *Connaught Telegraph*, played a key role in organising the Irishtown meeting alongside his friend Michael Davitt – even though the radical publisher John Ferguson would attend in Davitt's place.[27] Articulating a republican image of rural Ireland, one that rejected mechanisation, centralisation, and wage labour, Daly was representative of Paul Bew's 'Land League Ideal' – a vision of a pastoral arcadia, with the sins of urban and commercial life expunged entirely.[28] Daly's paper soon became a League organ, publishing local rentals next to their Griffith's valuations, the government's land survey completed in the 1850s and 1860s, in order to highlight the discrepancy between the two.[29] Here was, in hard numerical form, the landlords' 'unearned increment' for all to see. Newspapers inevitably performed an indispensable role in disseminating ideas and information, fostering the collective ambition that the League required. In the United States, the *Irish World* dramatised the public meetings, helping to form the perception of an impending revolution: 'Revolt – It Thunders On' declared the paper, as the League's public meetings got into their stride. 'Last week a thunder-peel from Westport, of Mayo, shook the House of Commons [...] This week it is an earthquake from Milltown, in Galway, that yawns to swallow them.'[30] Back in Ireland, Daly's *Telegraph*, alongside other papers such as Timothy Harrington's *Kerry Sentinel*, acted as mouthpieces for the League, constructing it both organisationally and ideologically. Daly himself 'hailed the Press as a deliverer'.[31]

Almost as a portent for the future of the League, the next meeting was held at Westport, County Mayo, on the North Atlantic coast on 8 June 1879, looking westwards towards its expansion in the United States. While Davitt remained the principle figure behind this second gathering, the Westport meeting was particularly notable for the introduction of Charles Stewart Parnell, and with him a slowly emerging division between the radical and the parliamentary aims of the League. A natural politician, Parnell's 'political sagacity' was highly rated by many supporters and opponents.[32] Viewed as somewhat above the coarser world of Irish nationalism, much of the respect that Parnell enjoyed was due to his elevated social position and his distinctiveness from both Catholic nationalists and his fellow Protestant landowners.[33] This 'un-Irishness' was a

27 Elaine McFarland, *John Ferguson, 1836–1906: Irish Issues in Scottish Politics* (East Linton: Tuckwell Press, 2003), 90–94.
28 Paul Bew, 'The Land League Ideal: Achievements and Contradictions', in P. J. Drudy (ed.), *Ireland: Land, Politics and People* (Cambridge: Cambridge University Press, 1982), 77–92.
29 Gerard Moran, 'James Daly and the Rise and Fall of the Land League in the West of Ireland, 1879–82', *Irish Historical Studies* 29, no. 114 (1994): 193.
30 *Irish World*, 12 July 1879.
31 William O'Brien, *Recollections* (London, Macmillan, 1905), 224.
32 Henry George to Patrick Ford, 10 November 1881 (HGP, Series I: B, NYPL).
33 Donald Jordan, 'John O'Connor Power, Charles Stewart Parnell and the Centralisation of Popular Politics in Ireland', *Irish Historical Studies* 25, no. 97 (1986): 46; On Parnell,

peculiar advantage in his chosen political ventures, particularly in parliamentary politics, as he reaped dividends from what George at least perceived to be an Irish cultural cringe.[34] As a beneficiary of class snobbery, Parnell was able to command respect and attention in a way that the others could not. James Clancy's analysis of Parnell's appeal was not unusual. He wrote of the aristocrat: 'The typical Irishman is impulsive; Parnell, on the contrary, moves with the deliberation of an accomplished chess-player.' The problematic issue of his English ancestry was neutralised by the 'healthy American blood' inherited from his mother.[35]

Parnell argued at the Westport meeting for the suitably elastic proposition that 'a fair rent is a rent a tenant can reasonably pay according to the times', a proximately Ricardian position.[36] In its early stages, the pliability of this policy meant that there was no clear objective for the emergent Land League. The nascent divisions were evident in the obvious differences of opinion at the meeting. Fenian Michael O'Sullivan, a close friend of Matthew Harris, raised the spectre of class when he said: 'The people are beginning to revolt – to feel that if they did not stand up against such inequity, they would be almost as criminal as the landlords and graziers themselves.'[37] For his part, Parnell played down the possibility of intra-nationalist division. He hoped instead that the land issue could offer sufficient unity and purposefulness to secure parliamentary ambitions for a constitutional settlement to the Irish question. Parnell remained at a slight remove from the deep groundswell of popular opinion that saw the land question as 'the source of the poverty, misery, and social strife of this unhappy country'.[38] He initially displayed an innocent curiosity about centrality of the land issue, but soon came to recognise its utility to constitutional nationalism.[39] He was above all else a political animal, with a keen sense of smell when it came to exercising power.

The Land League was institutionalised on 21 October 1879, in Dublin rather than the west, and with only one active farmer, Andrew Kettle, as a member of its executive. Despite this, as the poor harvest of 1879 turned economic hardship into destitution for many, the Land League's ability to respond positively and materially to the crisis saw it gain significant support.[40] From the

see F. S. L. Lyons, *Charles* Stewart *Parnell* (Dublin: Gill and Macmillan, 1977); Paul Bew, *Enigma: A New Life of Charles Stewart Parnell* (Dublin: Gill and Macmillan, 2011).

34 Henry George, *Irish World*, 28 October 1882.

35 Clancy, *The Land League Manual*, 23–24.

36 Quoted in Larkin, *The Roman Catholic Church*, 21; or a 'just rent' at times, *Freeman's Journal*, 4 November 1878.

37 Jordan, *Land and Popular Politics*, 227.

38 Thomas O'Keefe, Ballingarry, 14 November 1880 (MS 11,289, NLI).

39 Larkin, *The Roman Catholic Church*, 22; Henry George to Francis G. Shaw, 30 May 1882; Henry George to Annie George, 4 May 1882 (HGP, Series I: A, Box 3, NYPL).

40 Jordan, *Land and Popular Politics*, 246.

beginning, one of the League's primary purposes was the distribution of financial aid to those in rent arrears and living under threat of eviction, a strategy that cemented a loyalty and affection for the League from many suffering tenants. Letters to the League's central branch demonstrate the depth and breadth of hardship, but also the perception of the League as an arbiter and authority itself. Correspondence detailed not only personal injustices, but provided information on capricious landlords and transgressors of social codes, such as those taking farms or favours from landlords.[41] The League took a role in assisting the families of men imprisoned or impoverished as a result of their radical activity, such as providing financial aid to the wife and four children of Patrick McManus, a small shopkeeper imprisoned in Kilmainham Gaol. John O'Keeffe, a bailiff thrown out of employment for joining the League and refusing 'to serve or execute any legal document whatever for or on behalf of a landlord', was not atypical in receiving financial aid from the organisation.[42]

As these instances make clear, the Land League was much more than a vehicle for political nationalism or a charity for the distribution of funds. It served as a substitute Irish state, collecting money, alleviating hardship, and mitigating the worst effects of the economic crisis. Incorporating a full platform for the economic and political reconstitution of the country and developing its moral authority through social practices encouraging community cohesion, the Land League offered an alternative central governing structure. This allowed the League to present itself as the legitimate voice of Ireland, operating as part of a newly constituted public sphere. The reach of the organisation not only though newspapers but in the form of regular public meetings, local committees, and social practices such as boycotting meant that the League soon became the primary political organisation in the county. Its authority leading William Forster, the Chief Secretary for Ireland to concede that 'in Ireland the Land League is supreme ... I am forced to acknowledge that to a great extent the ordinary law is powerless'.[43]

Rights, Rents, and Proprietorship

As the conflict rumbled on through 1880 and into 1881, the centre of the movement drifted away from the small tenant farmers of the west. Class disparities started to become more evident in both rhetoric and ambition as the interests of the larger southern and eastern farmers became ascendant in what Matthew

[41] Accounts of rents in arrears, Co. Leitrim (LLP, MS 8291, NLI).
[42] Letter dated 23 April 1881 (LLP, MS 8291, NLI).
[43] Cited in Foner, 'Class, Ethnicity and Radicalism', 155; Donald Jordan, 'The Irish National League and the 'Unwritten Law': Rural Protest and Nation-Building in Ireland 1882–1890', *Past & Present* 158 (1998): 146–171.

Harris pointedly described as the 'union of the shark with its prey'.[44] The more radical edge and aggressive anti-landlord tone of tenant right gatherings across Galway and Mayo were notable for their contrast to League meetings in the south and east, where the social and economic distance between farmers and labourers was greater, and the concentration and consolidation of increasingly large farms had made many farmers in these areas wealthy and comfortable with economic expansion.[45] There is no doubt that such geographical and class tensions in the League meant that there was a chasm of difference in ambition between farmers of different economic standing, not to mention the labourers, shopkeepers, artisans, and professionals also connected to the League. Many larger farmers saw the existence of a class of small tenants, and the ambitions for a patchwork of peasant proprietors spread across the country, as equally anachronistic as a class of landed aristocrats.[46]

Nevertheless, the political rhetoric of the League remained predominantly and unrelentingly radical in its vision. While larger farmers may have spied an opportunity for economic growth and expansion, a chance to realise acquisitive ambitions, these were never popularly or collectively expressed, remaining outwith the boundaries of the League's language. The organisation's focus on peasant proprietorship persisted, even as the narrower political achievement of the 'Three F's' (fair rent, fixity of tenure, and free sale) was taken as a shorter-term goal. Peasant proprietorship carried with it a whole assortment of associated republican political benefits which were central to the demands made on Land League platforms, and which effectively tethered the land question to claims for national independence. While the image of the 'farmer who owns the land he tills' was a broad enough frame to encompass larger and smaller farmers, its political connotations went further.[47] Not only did it tie value to labour, this idealised economic demography formed the basis for a functioning democratic public sphere. It was for this reason that the small farmers of northern France and the Low Countries were idealised as practicing farming as a 'noble occupation'.[48] 'These men as happy as princes, resting under the shade of their own vine, independent of everything about

44 Moran, 'James Daly and the Rise and Fall of the Land League', 200.

45 Michael Turner, 'Output and Productivity in Irish Agriculture from the Famine to the Great War', *Irish Economic and Social History* 17 (1990): 76; David Fitzpatrick, 'The Disappearance of the Irish Agricultural Labourer, 1841–1912', *Irish Economic and Social History* 7 (1980): 66–92; Lucey, *Land, Popular Politics and Agrarian Violence*, 9.

46 Anne Kane, 'Theorizing Meaning Construction in Social Movements: Symbolic Structures and Interpretation during the Irish Land War, 1879–1882', *Sociological Theory* 15, no. 3 (1997): 261.

47 A. M. Sullivan, 'Ireland's Great Grievance: Land Tenure in Ireland and Other Countries', *American Catholic Quarterly Review* 6 (1881): 61.

48 Edmondo de Amicis, *Holland and Its People*, cited in Sullivan, 'Ireland's Great Grievance', 63; *La petite Culture* as the *Irish World* called it: 'the people who *till* the land shall, by *that* title, own the land they till', *Irish World*, 30 November 1878.

them', had developed their sense of civic duty and their suitability for sustaining a democratic politics.[49]

While the demand for the 'Three F's' dominated political and parliamentary discussion of the Irish land question, voices on public platforms across the Irish countryside articulated the more profound and far-reaching ideal of peasant proprietorship. In November 1880 at Ballingarry in Limerick, William O'Sullivan, a well-known agrarian radical, M.P., and member of the League's executive, informed the audience that while 'we want at once to try and settle the question of the land by fixing a fair rent', 'we can never be satisfied until the people themselves are the owners of the soil'.[50] Regardless of the immediate political prospects of such a hope, and the relative viability of the more limited 'Three F's', the image of a stable peasant proprietorship formed the ideological nucleus of the League's political vision. At the same meeting, the County Limerick M.P. Edward Synan developed this theme. Drawing on his travels in 'the countries of peasant proprietorship', Synan explained that this direct ownership of the soil by small farmers had 'elevated the people to be independent, free, and noble, not cringing to any master, and not attempting to descend to the level of slaves'.[51] He concluded his observations by telling the assembled locals that 'peasant proprietorships are the columns upon which that independence must ultimately rest. (Cheers.) I think when you have a peasant proprietorship able to think for themselves, able to act for themselves, and able to govern themselves, that you will have a legislature, an independent legislature, again in College Green'.[52]

A tension between these two ambitions, between legislative amelioration in the form of the 'Three F's' and peasant proprietorship (with its associated social, moral, and political benefits), has often been seen to have marked the ambiguity and amorphousness of the League; a factor both in its immense success as well as its quite rapid disintegration. On the League platforms, and in its published political expressions, however, peasant proprietorship absolutely triumphed. A call for the 'Three F's' at Bawnboy in Cavan was met with shouts of 'We want peasant proprietary' from the crowd. A subsequent speaker took the hint: 'The tiller of the soil shall possess the land. Away with fixity of tenure! Such legislation is already exploded. Fixity of tenure means fixity of landlordism and fixity of degradation (Cheers).'[53]

Nevertheless, the 'Three F's' represented the most plausible parliamentary hopes for a solution, or even just a salve, for the Irish land question. Not only did it offer the possibility of financial relief, especially for middling and larger farmers, but it extracted the land question from the realms of natural or absolute

[49] Dean Quirke, P.P. of Cashel, at Tipperary, 31 October 1880 (MS 11,289, NLI).
[50] W. H. O'Sullivan, Ballingarry, 14 November 1880 (MS 11,289, NLI).
[51] Edward Synan, M.P., Ballingarry, 14 November 1880 (MS 11,289, NLI).
[52] Edward Synan, M.P., Ballingarry, 14 November 1880 (MS 11,289, NLI).
[53] Patrick Brady at Bawnboy, Cavan, 30 October 1880 (MS 11,289, NLI).

right and made it a question of expedient governance. Deeply informed by a historicist interpretation of Irish economic conditions, and a liberal paternalist approach that saw careful arbitration of competing interests as offering a way forward, the 'Three F's' provided a degree of protection to landlords from the demands for 'Land for the People'. By mediating the relationship between tenants and landlords, the government could secure them an income even at the loss of their contractual freedom. A prominent supporter of the policy, Thomas Spring-Rice, a sympathetic Irish landlord otherwise known as Lord Monteagle, made this argument explicitly. Arguing that Ireland was 'not yet fit for contract pure and simple', Spring-Rice wrote that the 'Three F's', by securing the payment of rent, were 'specially intended to preserve them [landlords] and keep them in the country'.[54] The fear of the abolition of rent itself energised this as a plausible solution which would not only constrain claims for a 'natural' right to the land, but, by placing rent claims in the grant of the government, sever the relationship between peasant proprietorship and participatory democracy that found its voice on Land League platforms. Speaking on one such platform, James Maguire marvelled with suspicion at this about-face from 'the Conservative journals in England', who had opposed any intervention at all and 'have now come to believe that reform of the land laws is necessary'.[55]

While many landlords recognised that they had much to gain from legislation to ensure fixity of tenure, free sale, and fair rents, the proposals were not without their challenges and complications.[56] Even those who were agreeable to the potential social benefits of a limited degree of land law reform were apt to see the 'Three F's' as a contradiction in terms. An editorial in the *Times* remarked, prior to the introduction of Gladstone's 1881 act, that 'the "three F's" must be separately considered. "Fair rents" stands on a very different basis, both morally and economically, from "fixity of tenure" and "free sale"'.[57] While the other ambitions could be realised contractually, fair rents represented a deeper conceptual challenge. The other two could be 'defined with precision', but 'no satisfactory definition has ever been given', for what might be considered 'fair' in a fair rent.[58] For Lord Lifford, a Donegal landlord,

54 Thomas Spring-Rice [Lord Monteagle], 'The Three F's', *The Contemporary Review* 39 (January 1881): 168.

55 James Maguire at Belleek, 9 November 1880 (MS 11,289, NLI).

56 Timothy W. Guinnane, and Ronald I. Miller, 'Bonds without Bondsmen: Tenant-Right in Nineteenth-Century Ireland', *Journal of Economic History* 56, no. 1 (1996): 113–114; Vaughan, *Landlords and Tenants*, 68, 72.

57 *The Times*, 13 January 1881; Irish landlord and Anglican Canon of Peterborough, Rev Robert Shapland Carew Blacker, reiterated this point in, *Erin: Her Sisters, Her Nurse, and Her Doctors* (London: William Ridgway, 1881) (AIA.047, NYU).

58 A Land Valuer, *Fixity of Tenure at Fair Rents Impracticable as a Final Settlement of the Irish Land Question* (Dublin: M. H. Gill and Son, 1881), 5.

fixity of tenure might sound bad, but 'in reality it obtains already [on some estates and] I do not see much practical evil in it'; similarly for free sale. But the fixing of a fair rent would be subject to both variation and litigation and, if in any way aligned to Griffith's Valuation, would result in only 'about half the rent which the landlord might equitably require for his farm'.[59]

The question of a 'fair' rent was challenging precisely because it forced an articulation of value as distinct from what the market might suggest. To the Whig historian W. E. H. Lecky, and indeed to many others, the only 'real test of a value of thing is what men are prepared to give for it', and it was precisely this definition that was to be circumvented by the arbitration of a 'fair' rent.[60] It was Gladstone's immense skills of statecraft, continued Lecky, which had 'succeeded in persuading Parliament to abstain from giving any definition or any approximation to a definition of a fair rent'.[61] In reality, the challenge of defining a 'fair' value was one that severely tested the rhetorical abilities of parliamentarians. Edward MacNaughten, M.P. for Antrim, presciently warned that 'it would be very difficult to assign an exact meaning to the word "value"'. And so it proved. Philip Callan of Dundalk felt compelled to ask what 'the difference between "value" and "market value"' was, while others suggested amendments to the word value, such as 'genuine' or 'true' to 'exclude the extreme cases of *pretium affectionis* and land hunger', although T. M. Healy objected to this on the grounds that 'it would lead to a great many complications'. Joseph Biggar reminded the House of Commons that 'the real intrinsic value was a thing that no one knew'.[62] 'What relation has a fair rent to value', mused one land valuer, who concluded that in any case it would be impossible to discern a separate 'value' for land that was separate from improvements, rendering the whole exercise a waste of time.[63]

These arguments over 'fair' rent drew the issue inexorably back to the question of the justice of ownership and shone a light on the gradually disintegrating Ricardian definitions of rent as a distinct economic cost. George put the problem with the 'Three F's' succinctly: 'either the land is rightfully the property of the landlords or it is not. If it is, the landlord has the right to say what rent should be paid. If it is not, WHY SHOULD HE BE PAID ANY RENT AT ALL?'[64] The old Ricardian notion of economic rent that Cairnes had relied on, in which rent was 'surplus profit', crumbled in the face of this issue. This older view had assumed that rent was simply that which was left over in the accounting column, after the tenant had taken 'what will satisfy [him] as an

59 Lord Lifford, 'The Irish Land Question', *The Nineteenth Century: A Monthly Review* 8, no. 46 (December 1880): 893–894.

60 Lecky, *Democracy and Liberty*, vol. I, 188.

61 Lecky, *Democracy and Liberty*, vol. I, 188.

62 HC Deb, 13 June 1881, vol. 262, cc. 360–441.

63 A Land Valuer, *Fixity of Tenure at Fair Rents Impracticable*, 6.

64 Henry George, *Irish World*, 1 May 1880.

adequate reward for entering the business of farming'.[65] This normative definition could accommodate both the distinctiveness of land and a contractually derived evaluation of rent or value. The question of a 'fair' rent, however, which did not rely on contract, but instead upon another scale of value, undid this awkward alliance. What could 'fairness' be defined by if not a consensual agreement nor a market valuation? Notions of natural justice or right led awkwardly and inexorably towards the elimination of landlords entirely, ruling them out. In response, many commentators identified this as an issue of 'custom', or of the especial devotion of Irish farmers to their land. When Lord Sherbrooke claimed that landlords and tenants were but 'persons who have entered into contracts with each other, and they are nothing more', a rebuttal to his narrow contractualism highlighted instead the unique 'thoughts, feelings, and expectations of the Irish tenant'.[66] Such responses failed to apprehend, or sometimes deliberately avoided, the universal and theoretical implications of the distinctiveness of land.

Separating rent from interest (i.e. capital) and wages (i.e. labour) in the Ricardian interpretation had always gestured towards a non-economic value system, even if its potentially radical implications had long been muted. Writing in 1851, the perceptive Scottish aristocrat George MakGill had noted just as much, worrying that while the British public had strict notions of property rights when it came to 'moveables', 'a vague opinion seems to prevail that property in land stands upon a wholly different footing', and that such distinctions threatened to delegitimise claims to landed property.[67] For political economists in the 1880s, and most especially the new cadre of marginalists in the academy, Ricardian economics was deeply implicated in perpetuating such outdated assumptions about the distinctiveness of land that resulted in demands for 'confiscation'.[68] Edwin Cannan, the marginalist professor of economics at the London School of Economics, later observed that land nationalisation 'would probably never have been heard of, if the Ricardian economists had not represented rent as a sort of vampire which continually engrosses' itself.[69] For Cambridge's Alfred Marshall, similarly, 'the landlords could only get as much as competition allowed them'.[70]

65 Bonamy Price, quoted in Healy, *Why There Is an Irish Land Question*, 84–85.

66 Lord Sherbrooke, 'Legislation for Ireland', *The Nineteenth Century: A Monthly Review* 8, no. 45 (November 1880): 679; Lifford, 'The Irish Land Question', 888.

67 George MakGill, *Rent No Robbery: An Examination of Some Erroneous Doctrines Regarding Property in Land* (Edinburgh: William Blackwood and Sons, 1851), 6. MakGill's book was conceived in response to Mill's *Principles*.

68 Edwin Cannan, *A History of the Theories of Production and Distribution in English Political Economy from 1776 to 1848* [1893], 2nd ed. (London: P.S. King, 1903), 393.

69 Cannan, *A History of the Theories of Production*, 393.

70 Marshall, 'Three Lectures on *Progress and Poverty*', 224; James J. Shaw, 'The Nationalization of the Land', *Journal of the Social and Statistical Inquiry Society of Ireland* 8, no. 62 (1884): 492–508.

For the Land League, however, the uniqueness of land naturally remained front and centre. It was, in fact, embedded in the social practices of tenant farmers and the political activism of the League itself. Land taken from its occupier engendered much greater social solidarity than livestock taken from its owner.[71] In contravention of the Irish law of distress, which made landlords the principle creditors, both Parnell and Davitt encouraged people to pay shopkeepers and merchants before anything that their landlord might claim. The radical Irish publisher John Ferguson was clear that 'the shopkeeper must unquestionably be paid and there must be no attempt whatever to meddle with his right to be paid'.[72] While the Boston *Pilot*, under the editorship of John Boyle O'Reilly, told readers that 'the distinction between debt and rent in Ireland is so broad and clear that no one can possible confuse the two except through sheer malice', the conservative Dublin *Evening Mail*, for instance, asserted that there was no material distinction between rent and other debts.[73] Among the rights of property, it observed, 'is that of lending the use of it to another person for a money consideration, called rent'.[74] Landlords and tenants were just as any other contracting parties.

The Ricardian ideal that rent was a surplus due to the landlord after the farmer had taken care of himself, so that 'the rent extracted [should not] encroach upon the domain of wages and profits', was pervasive in the Land League.[75] When the Earl of Lucan concluded that 'it is to communism alone [that] the present state of things in [Ireland] is to be attributed' he was observing that many tenants were not destitute and were instead choosing not to pay rents in straitened times.[76] Such observations and complaints that tenants were deciding for themselves 'how much they ought to pay' were frequently made throughout the land struggle of the 1880s.[77] This was certainly in line with advice from the Land League. As Davitt told a meeting in Milltown, Galway, in 1879, if, once having comfortably fed and clothed their families, provided for education and necessities of the home, 'there was sufficient left to pay the rent, I would pay it'.[78] James Daly similarly defined rent as being 'regulated by the amount of margin left the tenant, after deducting the cost of maintenance of himself and family'.[79]

[71] Adam Pole, 'Sheriffs' Sales during the Land War, 1879–82', *Irish Historical Studies* 34, no. 136 (2005): 399.

[72] *Freemans Journal*, 20 October 1880. [73] *Boston Pilot*, 17 January 1880.

[74] *Dublin Evening Mail*, 10 January 1880.

[75] Cairnes, *Essays in Political Economy*, 198; Black, *Economic Thought and the Irish Question*, 54.

[76] Earl of Lucan, quoted in Jordan, *Land and Popular Politics*, 323.

[77] 'Some Further "Notes and Queries" on the Irish Question for the reflective voter from Irish Loyal and Patriotic Union', in *Publications issued during the year 1887* (Dublin: Irish Loyal and Patriotic Union, 1887).

[78] *Connaught Telegraph*, 21 June 1879. [79] *Connaught Telegraph*, 18 December 1886.

This understanding of rent carried with it implications about the purposiveness of land that can be observed in other League activities. The hostility of the agrarian movement in the west towards graziers, for instance, was a reminder of the role of land to provide for human sustenance and community, rather than economic growth. Graziers occupying large tracts of pasture land, selling beef or lamb for the British market, and often well financed or owned by large corporations based in London were an attack on this direct relationship between the land and life, as well as the tillage ideal of sturdy smallholders.[80] The tensions between smaller farmers and graziers that existed within the League as a result were only ever hidden temporarily; both Matt Harris and James Daly suggested specific and defined limits to landholding and regularly condemned the expansion of grazing. Many graziers were not agricultural men but investors profiting from the commercialisation of the post-famine economy, thereby also undermining pre-existing modes of practices, social roles, and community.[81] Opposition to this rural economic and social recalibration was rhetorically revealing. Thomas O'Rourke of the Kerry Tenants Defence Association complained in 1879 of 'a class of well to do nothings ...[that] act as vampires on the life blood of the nation and whose sole ambition is to turn this old and fertile land into a huge bullock walk'.[82] Laden with symbolism, this language suggested a natural productive fertility under attack from an unnatural and inhuman threat – a parasitic element undermining the very existence of the rural society and the social practices and commonly intelligible morality upon which Irish nationalism was constructed.

What is evident from the discourses surrounding the issues of rent, proprietorship, and land use is that the 'Land for the People' was not simply a political but an ontological statement. It expressed much more than an economic demand, but was rooted in a wider moral cosmology: it asserted that land was *created* for the people. These ideas saturated the public political pronouncements of the League in its attacks on monopoly and Malthusianism. Unsurprisingly, it was often local priests who were most capable of tying together these conceptual nodes within the wider frame of natural rights. Rev Cornelius McCarthy, speaking in Newcastle, Co. Limerick, applauded the Land League for effecting 'a moral regeneration amongst the people'. He continued: 'There is no person in the community at present, however humble his capacity,

80 William Leigh Bernard, *The Irish Land Question: Suggestions for the Extended Establishment of a Peasant Proprietary in Ireland* (Dublin: Hodges, Foster & Figgis, 1880), 16; Niall Whelehan, *The Dynamiters: Irish Nationalism and Political Violence in the Wider World, 1867–1900* (Cambridge: Cambridge University Press, 2012), 249; Jordan, *Land and Popular Politics*, 262.

81 Moran, '"Laying the Seeds for Agrarian Agitation"', 84; Lucey, *Land, Popular Politics and Agrarian Violence*, 15; David S. Jones, 'The Cleavage between Graziers and Peasants in the Land Struggle, 1890–1910', in Samuel Clark, and James S. Donnelly (eds.), *Irish Peasants: Violence and Political Unrest, 1780–1914* (Madison: University of Wisconsin Press, 1983), 413.

82 Thomas O'Rourke, quoted in Lucey, *Land, Popular Politics and Agrarian Violence*, 15.

who does not clearly understand, thanks to the teaching of the League, that the Almighty God created the land for the use and benefit of the people.'[83] The land movement was 'a moral platform', grounded in 'truth, justice, and right', others explained.[84] Tenants' resistance was commonly understood as resting on their natural rights, since, as Alexander Sullivan declared: 'Laws against nature have no validity.'[85]

Understood solely in rhetorical terms then, the Land War was a conflict between landlordism and the natural right to self-preservation, since 'according to the laws of any age every man was entitled to live'. Such a right to life was 'the law of God', and therefore 'higher than any law that can be promulgated by any assembly'.[86] Rejecting the divine purpose of land would be a contravention of natural law, and since 'God gave the land to the people that they might earn their bread by the sweat of their brow', the current 'unnatural state of things' could not be allowed to continue.[87] A resolution from a Kildare branch of the League in the spring of 1881 was incontrovertibly clear that 'the people of Ireland have an inalienable right to live in their own country, on the fruits of their labour, and that to confiscate the fruits of labour and to evict them, for the nonpayment of an unjust and exorbitant rent, is a violation of their natural rights'.[88] At Ballingarry, Limerick, a local priest explained to the assembled crowd: 'We hear a great deal about law from platforms of this kind. The law of England in regard to Ireland is a burlesque upon the natural law. (A voice, "Surely.") The first law of nature is self-preservation. (Hear, hear) The positive, the civil law of England has never recognised that divine principle. (A voice, "Never.").'[89]

The assertion of the unique purposiveness of land, grounded in the natural law primacy of the right to life and self-preservation, was the key ideological claim of the League's agitation. It demonstrated a close ideological alignment with the republican radicalism of George and others, even if the specific policy of nationalisation remained a more awkward fit due to Ireland's political relationship with the British state. One of George's supporters, who had been evangelising on his behalf among her neighbours in County Down, stated this problem succinctly: while local farmers liked the 'principles' involved and 'would willingly see their ground rents belong to the state and usable for the community, […] all Irishmen distrust their rulers and would be loath to

[83] Rev Cornelius McCarthy, P.P. of Knockaderry, at Newcastle, Co. Limerick, 7 November 1880 (MS 11,289, NLI).
[84] John Hogan, Tipperary, 31 October 1880 (MS 11,289, NLI); Michael Davitt's 'Land Nationalisation Scheme', Aberdeen *Daily Free Press*, 30 October 1882 (Davitt Papers, MS 9361.679, Trinity College Dublin).
[85] Sullivan, 'Ireland's Great Grievance', 58.
[86] Joseph Walsh, Ballinlough, 27 June 1880 (MS 11,289, NLI).
[87] Patrick Brady at Ballinagleragh, 5 September 1880 (MS 11,289, NLI).
[88] Resolution from Kildare Branch of INLL, 28 May 1881 (Heffernan Papers, MS 21,910, NLI).
[89] Rev Sheehy, Ballingarry, 14 November 1880 (MS 11,289, NLI).

give up their lands to any government which is not in their own hands'.[90] Not only this, but Ireland's rural demography and geo-social stratification between farmers and labourers made it easier to construe the 'unearned increment', which George had accredited to society at large, as 'made not by the landlords, not by the gentry, but [specifically] by the tenant occupiers of Ireland'.[91] Nevertheless, the attacks on 'land monopoly', which often drew on Ireland's place in a broader fight for access to land, as well as the regular condemnations of Malthusianism, of the policy of 'contravening the law of God and depopulating the country', drove home the political centrality to the conflict of a divinely inspired natural right to life.[92]

The uniqueness of land, and therefore the whole range of concomitant political, moral, and economic assumptions, was baked into the Land League's agitation. At a League meeting in Bailieborough, Co. Cavan, the parish priest of nearby Crosserlough gave a rhetorical reply to an imagined landlord that explained the difference: 'I answer you, you cannot dispose of your farm, because your cart of hay was created by man, but the land was created by God.'[93] This basic assumption, carrying with it the weight of the radical tradition, was very concerning to many liberal politicians. It of course repudiated the Cobdenite 'free trade in land' solutions as lacking acknowledgement of the divine purpose and uniqueness of land, but neither did it embrace social liberal solutions for the same reason. William Harcourt, Home Secretary during the Land War, worriedly informed a Glasgow audience that the Irish Land War was enabling a recrudescence of 'anti-social' ideas about property in land which, under the influence of 'misty philosophers' like Mill, had led the Liberal Party astray in the past. Relying on the familiar argument that such claims regarding land were archaic and anachronistic, he assured those listening that the protection of property was as important as the protection of life and expressed his mystification at the division made between land and moveable property, since 'the landowner has just as good a right to a fair rent as you or I have to the coat upon our back'.[94] Harcourt's reference to 'a fair rent' rather than 'their rent' was revealing. Despite the feverish claims that Gladstonian interventions in Irish land undermined the very principle of private property, what they actually rejected, by careful compromise, was any recourse to a 'natural' or absolute right to land.

Gladstone's 1881 Land Act was the perfect example of just such a compromise. On the one hand, it legislated for the 'Three F's', recognising the potentially coercive nature of freedom of contract, as well as introducing a

[90] Mary Hamilton to Henry George, 10 March 1883 (HGP, Series I: A, Box 4, NYPL).
[91] Mr. Jordan at Bawnboy, Cavan, 30 October 1880 (MS 11,289, NLI).
[92] Major D'Arcy at Athlone, Roscommon, 7 November 1880 (MS 11,289, NLI)
[93] Rev Boylan, P. P. Crosserlough, at Bailiborough, 21 October 1880 (MS 11,289, NLI).
[94] William Harcourt, Speech at Glasgow, 25 October 1881, repr. in 'Some Further "Notes and Queries"'.

'quasi-judicial commission' to adjudicate on rent reductions.[95] Such interventions irritated and indeed deeply worried classical liberals who saw it as an attack on the rights of property to be freely exchanged and contracted for.[96] For Lecky, the landlords had been deprived of 'the plainest and most inseparable rights of ownership' and capital scared away from investment in the land.[97] 'This iniquitous Act', raged one critic, had converted an 'indefeasible title' into 'a mere claim to a precarious rent-charge'.[98] On the other hand, however, it subverted a natural right to land. 'It is a temporary makeshift', explained George, 'not based on any clear principle' other than making 'landlordism tolerable' to a wider segment of society.[99] Focussing primarily on the inequity of contracts rather than property itself, and grounded in historicist reasoning, Gladstonian policy managed to circumvent the problems raised by the 'misty philosophers' of the uniqueness of land, and with it the moral and political vision of agrarian radicalism that such ideas had carried in their wake.

Defended by many advocates simply on the grounds of necessity, Gladstone's bill certainly exacerbated class tensions within the League. While larger farmers saw much to like in it, grasping the opportunity for reduced rents and greater security, western smallholders found little immediate benefit.[100] The *Freeman's Journal* admitted that the Act was 'launched in this country with considerable misgiving', and indeed, the radical wing of the League saw it as a 'Whig reactionary movement' and urged farmers not to waste their efforts on 'delusive lawsuits' but 'continue to stand together as one man'.[101] As well as seeing it as a tactical lever designed to prise apart the League's unity, many radicals also discerned the political assumptions lurking within 'Gladstone's land swindle'.[102] The 'whole Bill is tinctured with that stale argument of the "sacred rights of property"', explained Captain George W. Bell, while it forgets 'the sacred rights of man to *live*'.[103] As the League treasurer Patrick Egan observed similarly, not only did the Act fail to 'win back "the land for the people"', but 'a considerable proportion of its provisions go to consolidate and perpetuate the evil'.[104] So while the Act was favourably received by new liberal thinkers like Arnold Toynbee and Thomas Hill Green, who saw it as a template for careful, contextual, and expedient state intervention in all

[95] Comerford, 'The Politics of Distress', 47.
[96] Howe, *Free Trade and Liberal England,* 132.
[97] Lecky, *Democracy and Liberty*, vol. I, 187.
[98] Molesworth, *Land as Property*, 39.
[99] Henry George, *Irish World,* 19 August 1881.
[100] Lucey, *Land, Popular Politics and Agrarian Violence*, 85; Jordan, *Land and Popular Politics*, 311.
[101] *Freeman's Journal*, 25 July 1881; Patrick Egan to T. C. Harrington, 31 July 1881 (Harrington Papers, MS 8583, National Library of Ireland).
[102] James Keane, Kiltulla Branch INLL to J P Quinn, 13 September 1881 (LLP, MS 17,694, NLI).
[103] Bell, *Peasant Proprietary for Ireland*, 17.
[104] Patrick Egan to T. C. Harrington, 31 July 1881 (HP, MS 8583, NLI).

spheres, many agrarian radicals argued that it actually entrenched landlordism more firmly by entangling it with the state and the dictates of expediency, cloaking landed power in technocratic authority. For Thomas Ainge Devyr, a long-standing veteran of radical struggles, Gladstone's 1881 Land Act simply lifted 'the personal odium of cruelty in all its forms – rack-renting, seizing, selling out and evicting out – entirely off the shoulders of the Blasphemers [landlords], and rests it upon that intangible and morally unapproachable thing called "Law"'.[105]

Labourers and the Land League

Complicating the simplified and idealised vision of an agrarian Ireland were landless rural and urban workers. In many respects, the existence of a class of Irish labourers proved to be as much of an intellectual problem for the ideal of self-sufficient owner-occupiers as the presence of large landowners, and the Land League's awkward and ambivalent relationship with labourers tended to reflect this fact. Many landlords recognised immediately that the existence of a large class of landless workers was a useful cudgel against the League, as well as an ideological irritant. The Property Defence Association, a landlord organisation formed to combat the League, sometimes recruited labourers to work directly for landlords, circumventing tenant farmers and driving a wedge between the two groups.[106] Inevitably, there was significant geographical variation in this respect. In the west, the barriers that separated the small tenant farmer and the landless labourer were thin and permeable, with people falling in and out of land tenancy, or engaging in both wage labour and subsistence farming. 'The poor western peasant', observed one contemporary sociological study, 'may be looked on as the connecting link between the "small holder" and the labourer'.[107] Nevertheless, although rural class structures were especially gradated in the west, land possession itself continued to be highly prized, conferring not only a small measure of economic security, but social value and dignity too.[108] Conversely, in the south and east of Ireland, economic stratification had decimated the small farmer class, leaving a large number of labourers,

[105] Thomas Ainge Devyr, *The Odd Book of the Nineteenth Century, or, "Chivalry" in Modern Days, A Personal Record of Reform – Chiefly Land Reform, for the Last Fifty Years* (New York: T. A. Devyr, 1882), 189.

[106] Padraig G. Lane, 'Agricultural Labourers and Rural Violence, 1850–1914', *Studia Hibernica* 27 (1993): 80.

[107] 'A Guardian of the Poor', *The Irish Peasant: A Sociological Study* (London: Swan Sonnenschein, 1892), 103.

[108] Clark, *Social Origins*, 38; Fitzpatrick, 'The Disappearance of the Irish Agricultural Labourer', 68; John W. Boyle, 'A Marginal Figure: The Irish Rural Labourer', in Samuel Clark, and James S. Donnelly (eds.), *Irish Peasants: Violence and Political Unrest, 1780–1914* (Madison: University of Wisconsin Press, 1983), 311–338.

who greatly outnumbered tenant farmers and graziers.[109] It was for this reason that County Cork was the centre of the labourers' political activity and their resistance to the League's prioritisation of the interests of tenant farmers.

Regardless of location, and irrespective of the marginal improvements made during the post-Famine period, the economic condition of agricultural labourers remained desperately poor; their lives still marked by meagre wages, inadequate housing, and irregular employment. In the years preceding the Land War, efforts to alleviate these issues, such as the attempt to unionise Irish labourers by the English National Agricultural Labourers Union, had foundered on the rocks of Irish political difference and national aspiration.[110] The Irish Agricultural Labourers Union, which emerged from these efforts, survived in Ireland until the beginning of the Land War, but although it was subsequently subsumed within the League's wide ranging economic and political ambitions, such an alliance 'did not extinguish the tensions between farmers and labourers'.[111] During one notable confrontation in Shannagarry, Cork, 150 labourers protested and obstructed a Land League meeting in the village. In this part of the country, the hostility was mutual. It was one tenant farmer's considered opinion that all the 'good' labourers had left for the United States, leaving only the trouble-makers behind.[112] At public meetings, complaints were made of the 'insidious attempts made by the landlords to put the agricultural labourers against the tenant farmers', but the League's rhetoric of the 'Land for the People' stirred up radical ambitions among labourers regardless of any cynical attempts made by landlords stoke division.[113] 'The land shall be ours as well as the farmers [...] they have no more right to the land than we have', proclaimed a poster in Wexford.[114]

Pressure from labourers certainly helped to force the League to pay attention to their demands and to, albeit sometimes reluctantly and absentmindedly, include them in their activism. One branch secretary complained to the League executive that 'there is every effort made to turn them [labourers] from us', but concluded that the League could 'keep them in hand' if there was a resolution put forward for them and a pledge to fight for their interests.[115] Not all efforts made on behalf of the labourers were quite as nakedly self-serving,

109 Pamela Horn, 'The Irish Agricultural Labourers' Union in Ireland', *Irish Historical Studies* 17, no. 67 (1971): 345.

110 Horn, 'The Irish Agricultural Labourers' Union', 345.

111 Fintan Lane, 'P. F. Johnson, Nationalism, and Irish Rural Labourers, 1869–82', *Irish Historical Studies* 33, no. 130 (2002): 194.

112 Lane, 'P. F. Johnson', 204–205.

113 Edward Marum, Thurles, Co. Tipperary, 14 November 1880 (MS 11,289, NLI); Padraig G. Lane, 'Agricultural Labourers and Rural Violence', 78.

114 Lane, 'P. F. Johnson', 204.

115 James Gartland, Robertstown Branch INLL to Thomas Sexton, 29 August 1881 (LLP, MS 17,695, NLI).

however. In some parts of the country, especially in the south and east, labourers were a significant presence in the League, making up to a third of some branch membership rolls.[116] Although there was some uncertainty on occasion, League funds were fully available to support labourers on the same terms as tenant farmers, and requests to the League executive for financial aid to support unemployed labourers were fulfilled. In general terms, the efforts made by landlords under the aegis of the Property Defence Association to woo labourers away from the League were unsuccessful.

This was partly due to the influence of several League leaders who possessed genuine concern for Irish labourers. The more radical elements, particularly men like Michael Davitt, Thomas Brennan, and the Presbyterian Minister Rev Harold Rylett, were keen to embrace the labourers' cause. Davitt was especially vocal about the need to address the dire conditions and restore the rights of currently landless workers, even if it was sometimes challenging to get farmers to see the labourers interests as more than incidental to their own.[117] Despite an often uneasy relationship, the labourers were key to the League's power and success. In his journalistic mode, reporting on events in Ireland for the *Irish World*, George correctly observed as much, writing that 'the strength of the Land League does not, and never did, lie in the farmers themselves, but in the circumambient population of which they were but a part'.[118] This was something labourers themselves asserted. At a labourers' National Convention in Dublin, led by the most prominent rural labourers' advocates P. F. Johnson and Peter O'Leary, himself a supporter of land nationalisation, the League was described as 'the most powerful social and political institution ever formed in the British Isles', its success due to 'the support given to it by the labourers of Ireland'.[119]

Despite this qualified mutual support, there was no escaping the uneasy tension between the needs of rural labourers and the Land League's image of a pastoral Ireland populated by small peasant proprietors. Resolutions in support of labourers at League meetings often appeared as an afterthought, as though their inclusion was a small footnote to the central moral purpose of the agitation. Language that expressed sincere allegiance to the labouring men and women of Ireland simultaneously emphasised their distance and distinctiveness from the farming class. 'Members of the League at home are deeply interested' in

116 John Byrne, Rathdangan Branch, to J P Quinn, 19 August 1881 (LLP, MS 17,695, NLI).
117 Patrick J. Campbell, and Peter Kerr, 'Davitt in Carrickmore', *Seanchas Ardmhacha: Journal of the Armagh Diocesan Historical Society* 11, no. 2 (1985): 389; Fintan Lane, 'Michael Davitt and the Irish Working Class', in Fintan Lane, and Andrew G. Newby (eds.), *Michael Davitt: New Perspectives* (Dublin: Irish Academic Press, 2009), 81.
118 Henry George, *Irish World*, 16 September 1882; Boyle, 'A Marginal Figure', 328.
119 *The Pilot*, 5 November 1881; On Peter O'Leary, Lane, *The Origins of Modern Irish Socialism*, 229; Niall Whelehan, *Changing Land: Diaspora Activism and the Irish Land War* (New York: New York University Press, 2021), 15–44.

improving the economic status of the agricultural labour, and 'anxious to do all that lies in their power to improve' their lot, explained League treasurer Patrick Egan, as he attempted to secure lecturing opportunities for Peter O'Leary in the United States.[120] The labourers remained the object of benevolence rather than equals in the fight. Not only were many tenant farmers resistant to the impositions placed on them by the Labourers Cottages and Allotments Act to improve accommodation provision for labourers, but the very existence of rural labourers was often confounding to the League's vision of a rural, republican Ireland.

Despite the very real potential for a more secure and mutually beneficial alliance between labourers and the more radical wing of the League, the partial and incremental legislative victories achieved by the League only served to fracture unity further. The growth of labourers' organisations after the demise of the Land League, and especially towards the end of the 1880s and early 1890s, was testament to their awkward and partial incorporation in the organisation, as well as the increasing dominance of larger farmers and more conservative nationalist elements in the successive National League.[121] In the autumn of 1882, in the wake of the Kilmainham Treaty and the demise of the Land League, George perceived that 'the laborers are waking up to the bitter consciousness that after all they have done and suffered there is nothing even promised for them'.[122] Davitt's best efforts to more fully conceptualise a republican Ireland that included labourers in his plans for an Irish Labour and Industrial Union were ultimately fruitless, wilting in front of Parnell's demands for a renewed focus on constitutional rather than economic reform.

If a more secure alliance with rural labour was a missed opportunity, then the same could be said for urban Irish labour too. Looked at from an international perspective, the transnational Land War was as much a battle for the landless as it was for those who enjoyed some rights of tenancy. New York's *Irish World and American Industrial Liberator* (to give Patrick Ford's crusading paper its full name) never passed up an opportunity to draw out the connections between landlord greed and urban poverty. In Ireland itself, however, the issue was more complex. Albeit a much smaller demographic, urban workers were also labouring under excessive and increasing rents, and many were receptive to the underlying message of the League.[123] There was hope, in the early stages of the Land War, that urban grievances could be incorporated into the national platform. A 'Land and Labour' mass meeting was held in

[120] Patrick Egan to Patrick A. Collins, 29 November 1881 (Patrick A. Collins Papers, Series 1, Box 2, Boston College).

[121] Fintan Lane, 'Benjamin Pelin, the Knights of the Plough and Social Radicalism, 1852–1934', in Brian Casey (ed.), *Defying the Law of the Land: Agrarian Radicals in Irish History* (Dublin: The History Press Ireland, 2013), 180.

[122] Henry George, *Irish World*, 16 September 1882.

[123] Moran, 'The Land War, Urban Destitution', 24.

Dublin's Phoenix Park on 14 March 1880, at which, 'considering the difficulty of interesting the population of a great city in a purely agricultural agitation' (and the weather), the *Freeman's Journal* estimated an 'exceedingly remarkable' 30,000 in attendance (although *The Nation* gave the rather more optimistic judgement of 100,000).[124] The League's leaders watched a procession of Dublin tradesmen before the crowd were informed that, as George would later reiterate, 'land is the source and labour is the creator of all wealth [therefore] monopoly of land is alike contrary to justice and reason', and that 'rent is the direct antagonism of labour'.[125] An impressive cast of the most radical leaders spoke, including Davitt, Egan, John Ferguson, and James Daly. Thomas Brennan also evinced a labour internationalism, asserting that 'in Ireland, as in every other country in the world' there was 'an unholy conspiracy against the rights of labour' and that Dublin's labourers would remain underpaid until they recognised that 'they had a cause in common, not only with the workers of Ireland, but with the workers of the world'.[126]

Such soaring sentiments would turn out to be largely insufficient to effectively unite urban workers and the economically disparate classes of tenant farmers. The self-conception of a rural Ireland, unblemished by wage-work and the depravities of urban life, retained too strong a hold. Yet, at the same time, there was a symbiosis to the land and labour struggles that nurtured each other. It is important to observe that Land League platforms in rural Ireland were not devoid of appeals to international and industrial working men and women. Tenant farmers, as much as urban workers, were reminded of their shared interests with each other. The Land League cause, explained Rev Sheehy of Ballingarry, Limerick, was not confined to county or country, but was 'of the world, it is the cause of democracy – it is the cause of the industrial classes as advocated against the idle few'.[127] It was a matter of immense pride in Ireland that, as the *Freeman's Journal* reported, 'the great movement which had begun among the poor down-trodden peasantry of Mayo had extended itself so well that it already embraced the continents of Europe and America, on the banks of the Mississippi, the Seine, the Tiber, and the foul and filthy Thames'.[128]

George's experiences in Ireland encapsulated this hopeful unity. On his first tour of the country, he spoke at the 'historic Rotunda' at the top of Dublin's Sackville Street. 'An immense audience', 'wild with enthusiasm', attended his first speech in November 1881, at least according to George's own account.[129]

124 *Freeman's Journal*, 15 March 1880; 21 February 1880; *The Nation* 20 March 1880.
125 *Freeman's Journal*, 15 March 1880.
126 *Freeman's Journal*, 15 March 1880.
127 Rev Sheehy, Ballingarry, 14 November 1880 (MS 11,289, NLI).
128 *Freeman's Journal*, 23 November 1880.
129 Henry George to Edward Robeson Taylor, 20 November 1881 (HGP, Series I: A, Box 2, NYPL); Henry George to Patrick Ford, 15 November 1881 (HGP, Series I: B, NYPL).

In early June 1882, he spoke again at the same venue on his return journey from England. The lecture was attended by Anna Parnell, Thomas Sexton, and Alfred Webb among others, and with the hall decorated with American flags, George received 'a great ovation, one that has rarely been accorded to even the most popular Irishman'.[130] Much like Thomas Brennan at the Phoenix Park meeting two years prior, George tried to demonstrate the essential and elementary relationship between labour and land. Attempting to tailor his talk for an urban audience, he looked for 'something as simple and as striking which will show the relation of the operative and industrial classes to the land'.[131] In the speech itself, George offered a comparison between Ireland and revolutionary America, flattering sensibilities by suggesting that Ireland was 'destined to play an important part in the history of the world at this epoch'.[132] Frustrated by the more conservative nationalist leadership for their attempts to reign in the radical implications of the land agitation, George pointed out that the 'Land for the People' had been much discussed, yet still 'there were many men, who did not give to it its full true meaning'.[133]

One of those who did, at least according to George, was Michael Davitt. During his lecture at the Rotunda, George made reference to a recent speech by Michael Davitt in Liverpool, which drew loud applause from the audience. Only days earlier Davitt had sent shockwaves through the movement when, speaking at a venue on St. Anne street in the heart of Irish Liverpool, he announced his own proposals for land nationalisation in Ireland. Long a supporter of George's *Progress and Poverty*, Davitt described his new scheme as 'National Peasant Proprietary', an amalgam of George's single-tax and peasant proprietary. Davitt insisted that this was not a change of track: his ideas were the same as when he and Parnell 'first stood together upon a public platform in Westport'.[134] His aim was simply to avoid what he saw as the inevitable consequence of peasant proprietorship, that it would 'only extend the absolute ownership of land: an ownership which will always be in the market for purchase and re-consolidation into large estates'.[135] Yet he also feared that George's scheme on its own failed to satisfy the Irish desire for direct and rooted possession of land. Davitt was at

130 Henry George, 'Lecture on the Irish Land Question, Dublin Rotunda', 10 June 1882 (HGP, Series II, Box 13, NYPL).
131 Henry George to Francis G. Shaw, 28 April 1882, and Henry George to M.M, 3 May 1882 (HGP, Series I: A, Box 3, NYPL).
132 Henry George, 'Lecture on the Irish Land Question, Dublin Rotunda', 10 June 1882 (HGP, Series II, Box 13, NYPL).
133 Henry George, 'Lecture on the Irish Land Question, Dublin Rotunda', 10 June 1882 (HGP, Series II, Box 13, NYPL).
134 *Liverpool Mercury*, 7 June 1882.
135 Michael Davitt, 'Irish Social Problems', *To-Day* (April 1884), 255; Terence McBride, 'John Ferguson, Michael Davitt and Henry George – Land for the People', *Irish Studies Review* 14, no. 4 (2006): 425.

pains to stress that, under his plans, 'farmers would possess all the security that a peasant proprietary has to offer', while also abolishing landlordism and rent for profit.[136] The institution of a single-tax on land values at around 10 percent would, according to Davitt, 'meet the public expenditure' and leave the farmer with 'absolute security of tenure from the State, subject to the payment of this nominal tax; while the property which his capital and industry would create in the land which he cultivated would be his'.[137]

Davitt's scheme represented his capacious ability to gather and blend ideas, and it remained one of the more intriguing untested syntheses of the period. Like other agrarian radicals, Davitt justified 'the right of all men to participate in the benefits of the soil' by 'the fact that land is a natural agent', and its financial value 'maintained by the aggregation of population and the exercise of industry by a people'.[138] Two elements stand out in Davitt's delineation of his scheme: firstly, the desire to carefully balance farmers' interest in personal possession of their land with the rights of all members of society to a stake in the land – making sure that the land question was fully understood as a labour question as well. Secondly, his emphasis on resisting the encroachment of state power; far from advocating a system of progressive taxation, Davitt sought to 'remove all the taxes that now fall upon the mercantile, commercial, professional, and industrial classes'.[139] His conception of the state was not a liberal interventionist one, it would instead 'simply be the steward of the national property'.[140] Condemning the 'prescriptive rights of an unjustly privileged class', Davitt did not merely seek material elevation, but a political and moral transformation through providing the means 'sufficient to supply themselves with […] independency'.[141] Rather than being avowedly progressive, Davitt aimed 'simply' for the 'resumption of that state of ownership of the soil which obtained amongst all nations anterior to the system of land monopoly which the Government has established for the aggrandisement of a privileged section in society'.[142]

Davitt's plan attracted a great deal of attention. His ambition to create 'a community of industrious people being removed above the fear of want and regulating their lives like rational beings' was dissected in the *Times* and prompted George's publisher to suggest republishing *Progress and Poverty* in quarto form in order to capitalise on the attention.[143] With the Land League in disarray after the Phoenix Park murders and the Kilmainham Treaty, however,

[136] *Liverpool Mercury*, 7 June 1882. [137] *Liverpool Mercury*, 7 June 1882.
[138] *Glasgow Herald*, 7 June 1882. [139] *Liverpool Mercury*, 7 June 1882.
[140] *Liverpool Mercury*, 7 June 1882. [141] *Liverpool Mercury*, 7 June 1882.
[142] *Glasgow Herald*, 7 June 1882.
[143] *Liverpool Mercury*, 7 June 1882; *The Times*, 7 June 1882; Circular by publisher J. C. Durant (1882) (HGP, Series I: A, Box 3, NYPL).

Davitt's brief attempt to press the movement in a more radical direction fell on stony ground. Travelling from Liverpool to the United States via Cork, Davitt must have already sensed a critical storm brewing. He refused to allow George to accompany him on the journey and, once in America, downplayed the significance of his 'personal' plan for the aims of the wider Irish agitation, despite the very public advice of the radical New York priest Fr Edward McGlynn to 'explain not away one tittle of it, but preach the gospel in its purity'.[144] Torn between an expedient acquiescence to moderate nationalist opinion and his own economic and political analysis of Ireland's malaise, Davitt recoiled from any break with Parnell's authority.

Upon his return to Ireland later that summer, Davitt again tried and failed to direct the movement in a more radical direction, proposing a new organisation, the 'National Land and Industrial Union of Ireland', to carry the torch of the now defunct Land League. In an ambitious plan, Davitt laid out a decentralised, democratic structure of parish, district, county, and provincial hierarchies, forming together a functional nation state. His scheme included the establishment of cooperative loan societies and mechanics institutes throughout Ireland, with a focus on developing national industries, fisheries, agricultural improvement, 'the scientific and practical education of the labouring classes', and the encouragement of Irish language and literature. The political power and economic condition of the Irish working class, rural and urban, was recast as inseparable from the land question. His proposal resolved to achieve 'the complete abolition of the present landlord system'; however, the subsequent line, which added 'the substitution of such a one as shall make the land of Ireland the property of the People of Ireland', had been subsequently crossed out. Such minor changes were insufficient, and Davitt's proposal was 'submitted to and strongly disapproved of by Parnell, Aug. 82'.[145] Into the autumn of 1882, the pages of the *Irish World* carried George's pleas for Davitt to make 'a stand against the notion that loyalty to the Irish cause is synonymous with loyalty to Mr. Parnell', and his complaints that 'there has been far too much of the "uncrowned-king" business in the Irish movement ever since it started', but ultimately Davitt's attempts to construct a solid organisational foundation for Irish agrarian radicalism, one that could properly unite the tenant farmer and the labourer, lay in tatters.[146]

144 Henry George to Patrick Ford, 8 June and 13 June 1882 (HGP, Series I: B NYPL); Anon to Patrick A. Collins, 15 June 1882 (PACP, Series I, Box 2, BC); Michael Davitt, *Land Nationalisation; or, National Peasant Proprietary: Michael Davitt's Lectures in Scotland* (Glasgow: Cameron and Ferguson, 1884), 32; O'Donnell, 'Henry George and the "New Political Forces"', 294.

145 'Proposed Scheme of Reform and Organisation' (Davitt Papers, MS 9398, Trinity College Dublin).

146 Henry George, *Irish World*, 28 October 1882; Bew, *Enigma*, 106.

Republican Praxis and the Boycott

The means of protest and rebellion employed by the League reflected the social structures and political ideology of the movement itself. This simple observation is one that runs contrary to many of the assumptions present in both historical and historiographical interpretations of the Land War. During the conflict itself, critics of the agitation often condemned the 'superficial eloquence' of the League in their use of natural rights for radical ends, complaining that this morally extravagant language only masked baser impulses.[147] This sentiment has largely persisted in the historiography, which has often taken the history of Irish republican thought to be intellectually promiscuous and flimsy; essentially a pretentious excuse for militant nationalism.[148] Yet the practices employed by the League, or more accurately by local communities, to resist landlords and land laws, embodied definable political ideas entirely congruent with the League's stated ambitions.

Popular resistance can too easily be explained as manifestations of specific *mentalités* or worldviews, comprehensible only on their own terms and largely immune to political theorising – a complex interplay of cultural and socio-economic forces which shaped lives with little theoretic content. There is no need to assume, however, that unarticulated political ideas are also illegible; that language is the limit of expression or comprehension. Instead, it is possible to see, as Samuel Moyn has argued, that 'principled rationales for and justifications of the social order always matter and indeed inhabit social practice to the core'.[149] It is in this way that the social practices of rural Ireland in general, and the popular activity undertaken during the Land War specifically, can be seen as republican thought in action. If claims for 'natural rights' from League platforms are treated with interpretive generosity as honestly held sentiments, the moral cosmology embedded in agrarian practices like boycotting can be understood to reinforce this political articulation. In fact, given the persistence of such practices of social resistance during the eighteenth and nineteenth centuries, this approach reinforces the proposition that these political ideas emanated from the structures of agrarian life and were indigenous to Ireland independent of any transatlantic radical influence.

Although boycotting was named and formalised during the Land War, the panoply of public protest that came under this designation were extensions of the social shaming and moral pressures that were familiar to many agrarian

[147] 'Editor of the *Citizen and Irish Artisan*', *An Aspect of the Land Question Forgotten! Will the Land League Solution Wipe Out What Remains of Skilled Industry?* (Dublin: Hastings and Co., 1880), 1.

[148] See, for instance, Tom Garvin, 'An Irish Republican Tradition?', in Iseult Honohan (ed.), *Republicanism in Ireland: Confronting Theories and Traditions* (Manchester: Manchester University Press, 2008), 24.

[149] Moyn, 'Imaginary Intellectual History', 121.

societies across the globe.[150] Irish traditions of communal regulation such as were evident in the activities of the Whiteboys from the middle of the eighteenth century followed a rational 'set of codes and penalties', forming, in one contemporary evaluation, 'a vast trades' union for the protection of the Irish peasantry'.[151] In the wake of the Famine, secret oath-bound Ribbon societies became more agrarian in character and, just as the Land League later, relied on a range of 'informal regulatory rituals' including physical threats and moral coercion, from nocturnal raids and animal slaughter to intimidation through sheer force of numbers.[152] The familiar nature of these activities in the Irish countryside, regardless of the degree of organisational structure attributed by different historians, demonstrates the degree to which the League was an outgrowth of entrenched popular attitudes, rather than an external imposition.[153] Already by the early nineteenth century, the use of social pressure to shape individual behaviour was firmly associated with the Irish peasantry in the minds of British officialdom. During the Welsh Rebecca Riots of the 1840s, moral coercion in this form was described not only as 'characteristic of a rude state of society' but deriving from underlying principles that were 'perfectly Irish'.[154]

It was boycotting in particular that captured both public and official attention during the Land War and, as with earlier episodes of rural resistance, it appeared to critics as inseparable from violence against person or property. Despite the strenuous efforts made by the League to distinguish boycotting and other moral force tactics from physical threats, intimidation, and violence, the line between these categories was often difficult to discern. For those involved in trying to stem the 'surging tide of pauper democracy', as boycotting was described, much effort was expended on condemning it as inexorably linked to

150 See, for instance, Thompson, *Customs in Common*, 467–470.

151 Maura Cronin, *Agrarian Protest in Ireland, 1750–1960* (Dundalk: Dundalgen Press, 2012), 13; George Cornewall Lewis, *On Local Disturbances in Ireland, and on the Irish Church Question* (London: B. Fellowes, 1836), 99.

152 Margaret O'Callaghan, *British High Politics and a Nationalist Ireland: Criminality, Land and the Law under Forster and Balfour* (Cork: Cork University Press, 1994), 9; Oliver MacDonagh, 'Ideas and Institutions, 1830–45', in W. E. Vaughan (ed.), *A New History of Ireland,* Volume V: Ireland under the Union, 1801–70 (Oxford: Oxford University Press, 1989), 202; Lucey, *Land, Popular Politics and Agrarian Violence*, 196; on Ribbonism: W. Steuart Trench, *Realities of Irish Life* (London: Longmans, Green, and Co., 1869), 47.

153 Breandán Mac Suibhne, '"Bastard Ribbonsim": The Molly Maguires, the Uneven Failure of Entitlement and the Politics of Post-Famine Adjustment', in Enda Delaney, and Breandán Mac Suibhne (eds.), *Ireland's Great Famine and Popular Politics* (New York: Routledge, 2016), 188; A. C. Murray, 'Agrarian Violence and Nationalism in Nineteenth-Century Ireland: The Myth of Ribbonism', *Irish Economic and Social History* 13 (1986): 56–73;Tom Garvin, 'Defenders, Ribbonmen and Others: Underground Political Networks in Pre-Famine Ireland', *Past & Present* 96 (1982): 133–155.

154 *First Report of the Constabulary Commissioners* [1839], 83–84, cited in Thompson, 'Rough Music Reconsidered', 17.

violent outrages.[155] Hugh Oakley Arnold-Forster, adopted son and private secretary of the Chief Secretary for Ireland, described the boycott as being solely enforceable by 'the bullet of the assassin or the torch of the incendiary'.[156] Physical attacks were often taken to be 'kindred crimes' of boycotting, a form of rhetorical violence which created the right context for assault, murder, or the destruction of property.[157] One writer, denouncing this deviously seditious and novel Irish craze, discerned an intimate and 'necessary connection [...] between boycotting and violent crime'.[158]

The threat of force implicit in the large crowds that assembled at evictions or sheriff sales was undeniably crucial to the operation of boycotting and similar forms of collective action.[159] The moral power of the community was represented in physical form in these situations, often directed against 'landgrabbers', but also others who, directly or indirectly, propped up the institutions of landed property. Evictions and the serving of writs were public events, attended and watched over by members of the community who sometimes intervened in the situation. 'Obstructing the bailiff in the service of writs' was common. The *Irish World* recounted with obvious delight the tale of an ejectment server 'made to eat the precious documents found on his person [before] repeatedly calling on the Supreme being to witness he never would be again caught in the locality of a similar errand'.[160] Fr Thomas Conefrey of Drumlish recalled how, in January 1881, members of his parish had 'prevented five hundred police and a company of Her Majesty's dragoons from serving processes'. 'For four days', he recounted with pride, 'about twenty thousand persons, armed with pitchforks, &c., and marching to the sound of drums, confronted the police and dragoons, and for a time successfully obstructed the serving of processes'.[161]

Evidently, the fear that boycotting and violence begat one another was not entirely unfounded. The relationship between intimidation and moral condemnation was often left ambiguous by intent. Speakers at Land League meetings regularly encouraged those in attendance to 'be true to one another', while

155 'Ireland under Ordinary Law', *Blackwood's Edinburgh Magazine* 129, no. 785 (1881): 280.

156 Hugh Oakeley Arnold-Forster, *The Truth about the Land League, Its Leaders, and Its Teaching* (London: National Press Agency, 1882), 56.

157 T. W. Rolleston, *Boycotting: A Reply to Mr. S. Laing* (Dublin: E. Ponsonby, 1888), 4.

158 Rolleston, *Boycotting,* 5.

159 Pole, 'Sheriffs' Sales during the Land War', 401; Paul E. W. Roberts, 'Caravats and Shanavests: Whiteboyism and Faction Fighting in East Munster, 1802–11', in Samuel Clark, and James S. Donnelly (eds.), *Irish Peasants: Violence and Political Unrest, 1780–1914* (Madison: University of Wisconsin Press, 1983), 69.

160 *Irish World*, 5 July 1879.

161 Rev Thomas Conefrey, 'An Appeal made by the Drumlish and Ballinamuck Farmer's Defence Association', Drumlish, Co. Longford, 17 April 1881 (103, Box 34, P.001.1801, PAHRC). See also, Richard Hawkins, 'Liberals, Land and Coercion in the Summer of 1880: The Influence of the Carraroe Ejectments', *Journal of the Galway Archaeological and Historical Society* 34 (1975): 40–57.

being careful to avoid explicit advocacy of more coercive behaviour. 'There is no use in telling you how a land-grabber should be treated, as you all know that', said one Offaly priest, before looking over at the watching police and adding, 'I believe it would not be safe to tell you'.[162] At Thurles, a speaker warned similarly: 'Let no man betray his neighbour'.[163] There was a close proximity, and indeed a reciprocal relationship, between the threat of violence and non-violent moral force nationalism.[164] The shouts from the crowd at Land League meetings ('shoot him' 'kill them') were part of the performative texture of the proceedings as speakers often interjected, ostensibly cooling tensions, but, by dint of acknowledgement, timing, and redirection, also embracing the power of the physical threat behind the moral campaign. Although Thomas Brennan, for instance, rejected calls for violence, he found it useful to note that when France 'was getting shut of her landlords, [she] did not give them twenty-years' compensation. No; she gave them twenty feet of a rope (Cheers)'.[165]

At the same time, the power and effectiveness of boycotting stemmed, as its advocates recognised, from its distance from violence and physical coercion, from the fact that it involved 'no infraction of the laws, even the unjust laws'.[166] 'The Land Leaguers assert that "Boycotting"', explained the *Freeman's Journal*, 'means simply a voluntary withdrawal from the service of a person who in their view is a danger to his neighbours'.[167] On Land League platforms, local communities were reminded that boycotting was legal and therefore powerfully effective: 'A landlord could not compel a man to work for him, or to buy or sell from him. Black as the pages of the law were, it could not compel him to do this'.[168] The Land League executive, frustrated by what they saw as cynical attempts 'to couple the agitation with acts of violence and other transactions of an illegal nature', went to great lengths to try and distinguish boycotting as a non-violent protest.[169] It was common for speeches to address violence as a traitorous act that undermined Ireland's cause.[170] This explicit rejection of violence was a defining feature of the boycott, providing its radical and destabilising force, even if a nebulous, less perceptible form of subterranean intimidation flowed underneath it by necessity. Consequently, boycotting

162 'Memorandum as to Speeches Advocating Boycotting, at National League Meetings', 25 April 1885 (Balfour Papers, B.P. 13/4 (10), British Library).

163 Rev James Cantwell, Thurles, Co. Tipperary, 14 November 1880 (LLP, MS 11,289, NLI).

164 L. Perry Curtis, Jr., 'Moral and Physical Force: The Language of Violence in Irish Nationalism', *Journal of British Studies* 27, no. 2 (1988): 155.

165 Thomas Brennan, Cardenstown, 23 May 1880, in Arnold-Forster, *The Truth about the Land League*, 14.

166 *Freeman's Journal*, 28 February 1881.

167 *Freeman's Journal*, 11 November 1880.

168 *Freeman's Journal*, 23 November 1880.

169 *Freeman's Journal*, 17 December 1880.

170 Conyngham, *Ireland Past and Present*, 249; Timothy Daniel Sullivan (ed.), *Condemnations of Crime: Compiled from Speeches Delivered at Meetings of the Land League and National League in Ireland, 1879–1887* (London: The Irish Press Agency, 1888).

did provide something of a popular outlet for frustrations that mitigated, as even some critics accepted, the 'wild fury, the unbridled cruelty' of earlier agrarian revolts in Ireland.[171]

Boycotting was a powerful tool because it was part of a broader participatory processes that offered social solidarity and support for those who were disadvantaged in their loyalty to the Land League. The protection and sheltering of evictees was as important as preventing the land being taken on by new tenants.[172] Neither was the League instigative in many cases, and certainly the executive had little power beyond that which the local community acceded to it, able only to issue general advice.[173] The drive to boycott was a decidedly local one, as tenant farmers banded together 'to pledge ourselves not to take any farm from which another man may have been ejected through inability to pay rent [and to] watch over such an ejected family as over our own, and do all we can to have such a family restored to its farm'.[174] Many farms were 'not taken' following an eviction. A Land League branch in Ballintubber, for example, noted proudly that 'since last report, two land-grabbers gave up the lands they had taken lately in this parish'.[175]

Operating in a largely decentralised structure, discussions over internal democracy within league branches also show that while pre-existing local hierarchies were often reflected therein, and sometimes claimed a measure of authority, this was tempered by attempts to formalise internal democratic processes.[176] In any case, boycotting presented its own innate limitations in as much as it required a critical mass of support to operate. Indeed Parnell, who had played a crucial role in delineating the practice in his famous speech at Ennis, later complained that boycotting had quickly taken on a life of its own, telling the House of Commons that boycotting 'would not have been legitimate' in a self-governed country.[177] These anarchic tendencies of boycotting had created a public sphere centred around social obligation; a popular democratic arena that became a '*de facto* system of alternative government' that

[171] 'Home and Foreign Affairs', *Fortnightly Review* 29, no. 169 (1881): 119; Irish Loyal and Patriotic Union, *The Other "Coercion" as Now in Operation* (Dublin: Hodges, Figgis, 1886), 9; 'Ireland under Ordinary Law', 280.

[172] Letter from Cahir, Co. Tipperary branch, 11 October 1880 (LLP, MS 8291, NLI).

[173] Jordan, *Land and Popular Politics*, 289.

[174] Second Resolution of the Drumlish and Ballinamuck Farmers Defence Association, 'An Appeal made by the Drumlish and Ballinamuck Farmer's Defence Association, on behalf of the many poor Farmers of the Parish of Drumlish, who are threatened with Eviction from their homesteads', Drumlish, Co. Longford, 17 April 1881 (103, Box 34, P.001.1801, PAHRC).

[175] Ballantubber, Co. Mayo, Financial return, December 1880 (LLP, MS 8291, NLI); Kenward Philip, *Boycotting: Or Avenging Ireland's Wrongs* (New York: Richard K. Fox, 1881), 13.

[176] 'To remedy this there should be regular ballot papers supplied by your executive. This is the opinion of all branches that I am acquainted with.' Letter from James Gartland, Robertstown Branch INLL to Thomas Sexton, 29 August 1881 (LLP, MS 17,695, NLI).

[177] Charles Stuart Parnell, HC Deb 25 May 1882, vol. 269 c.1620.

even the Land League itself could not fully control.[178] After the League was suppressed, and there existed no organisation with any power to enforce such rules, the boycotting of 'landgrabbers' remained commonplace.[179]

Neither the government nor the majority of Irish landlords saw this as evidence of grassroots political action. Intellectually, emotionally and often geographically distant from events, the official perspective intoned that demagogic forces had agitated a traditionally supine population. Reporting on the events at Lough Mask House from which the appellation 'boycotting' was derived, the *Freeman's Journal* wrote that 'a very extraordinary change has for some time come over the Mayo peasantry. They have got perhaps more than the boldness of freemen'.[180] For critics, boycotting suggested precisely the opposite. 'A good many of the people of Ireland appear to have taken leave of their senses', spluttered an editorial in one paper.[181] A lack of independent or rational thought was presumed to be the only comprehensible explanation, and boycotting simply evidence that the Irish poor were 'too often made the tools of men more crafty and designing than themselves'.[182] The idea that this was a form of communal self-organisation was too difficult to countenance, primarily because accepting the decision to boycott as a meaningfully free choice rendered it almost impervious to liberal condemnation. It was this challenge to liberal politics that propelled boycotting to international significance.

From its inception, at least as a coherent and definable practice during the ostracism of the eponymous 'Captain' Boycott, the tactic spread rapidly throughout Ireland and beyond. Speaking at Ennis, Co. Clare, on 19 September 1880, Charles Stuart Parnell had famously enjoined the rural population to isolate transgressors from their community; leaving them 'severely alone'.[183] Four days later, Charles Cunningham Boycott's own struggle began, as farmhands left his employment and the land agent for Lord Erne soon found himself unable to buy food or harvest his crops. Through Boycott's own initiative, the affair soon garnered national press attention, and the *Times*, making a familiar howl at Irish implacability, declared in response that 'a more frightful picture

178 Philip Bull, 'The Formation of the United Irish League, 1898–1900: The Dynamics of Irish Agrarian Agitation', *Irish Historical Studies* 33, no. 132 (2003): 420.

179 Lucey, *Land, Popular Politics and Agrarian Violence*, 125; James J. Clancy, *Who Are the Conspirators? Or, the True Story of the Boycotting Prosecutions* (London: Irish Press Agency, 1889), 18; R. Barry O'Brien, 'Playing at Coercion', *Nineteenth Century* 123 (May 1887): 648.

180 *Freeman's Journal*, 11 November 1880.

181 *The Graphic: An Illustrated Weekly Newspaper*, 27 November 1880.

182 Irish Attorney General Hugh Law quoting Irish magistrate Baron Dowse, HC Deb, 8 February 1881, vol. 258, c. 415.

183 Gerard Moran, 'The Origins and Development of Boycotting', *Journal of the Galway Archaeological Society* 40 (1985–6): 49–64.

of triumphant anarchy has never been presented in any community pretending to be civilized and subjected to law'.[184] Within days, communities across the country were being encouraged to 'follow the example set to all Ireland by the brave men of Ballinrobe'.[185] It was only a matter of weeks before 'boycotting' was being used in Britain and then, subsequently, the United States, where it soon attained immense proportions as 'the most formidable weapon yet used by the workers'.[186]

In all its geographical contexts, boycotting encompassed a wide array of behaviours, from refusing service or employment and declining to buy or sell, to public condemnation, yelling and jeering, and picketing. The Cork Defence Union, a landlord organisation, detailed various such 'infringements on liberty', including one man, who, after refusing to join the Land League, was 'boycotted' by his wife and daughter who 'deserted his house, leaving him there alone to shift for himself'.[187] Both the spread of the practice, and its variety, were well represented in the notable case of William Bence Jones.[188] Born in Suffolk, and educated at Harrow and Oxford, Bence Jones had been a London lawyer before inheriting his Irish estate in Cork, at which he spent a few months each year.[189] Blessed with an ability to see only his own virtues, Bence Jones was a utilitarian improver who, in his own words, encouraged 'a process of Natural Selection, in which the tenant's own qualities, good or bad, were made the cause of the Survival of the Fittest'.[190] Trusting the natural providence of the market, he rejected the idea of peasant proprietorship as belonging to a 'simpler stage of civilisation'.[191] For him, the Irish problem was primarily 'a moral difficulty', a collective weakness of will and infirmity of mind, of which boycotting was only the most egregious example.[192] Seeing the removal of tenants as equivalent with improvement, he eliminated subdivision, and pitted his tenants against each other in a fight for more land, in order to

[184] *Times*, 18 October 1880.

[185] *The Manchester Guardian*, 16 November 1880; *The Nation* 16 October 1880; Patrick Cahill, Athy 10 October 1880 (MS 11,289, NLI).

[186] Henry M. Hyndman, 'The Chicago Riots and the Class War in the United States', *Time* 14, no. 18 (June 1886): 692; *New York Times*, 6 December 1880; *New York Tribune*, 11 January 1881; *Washington Post*, 29 January 1881; *New York Times*, 26 February 1881; *Massachusetts Ploughman and New England Journal of Agriculture*, 5 March 1881; *Massachusetts Ploughman and New England Journal of Agriculture*, 23 April 1881; *New York Times*, 23 June 1881; *New York Times*, 7 May 1881.

[187] Cork Defence Union, *Boycotting in the County of Cork* (Cork: Purcell, 1886), 18.

[188] John O'Leary, 'Mr. Bence Jones' Story of His Experiences in Ireland', *Contemporary Review* 40 (July 1881): 127.

[189] William Bence Jones, 'Boycotted: Some Experiences in Ireland during Last Winter', *Contemporary Review* 39 (June 1881): 856.

[190] William Bence Jones, *The Life's Work in Ireland of a Landlord Who Tried to Do His Duty* (London: Macmillan, 1880), 85.

[191] Bence Jones, *The Life's Work*, 204.

[192] Bence Jones, *The Life's Work*, 86.

'give a better chance for exertion to the good ones'.[193] In this way, the number of farms on just one of his five farmlands was reduced from 26 to 4.[194] He also remained baffled as to why his tenants were so implacably hostile towards him.

Despite the numerous evictions, Bence Jones was convinced of the wealth of his tenants. As rumours spread, prior to rent day on 7 December, that his tenants would not pay in full, Bence Jones insisted that they were both willing and able to do so but were restrained only by the 'intimidation practiced by the Land League'.[195] In the end, his tenants paid Griffith's valuation for their land, which left Bence Jones with £100; significantly less than the £1,300 he had been accustomed to.[196] His problems did not end here, however. The next week, Bence Jones sent his cattle to be shipped from Cork, but on arrival in the city, several other graziers continued the boycott. They 'went as a body to one of directors of the [shipping] company [...] and asserted that if Mr. Jones' cattle were allowed on board the *Xema* they would not alone cease to have dealings in future with the company'. The steam packet company acquiesced to their requests. Once the drovers who had been employed to take the cattle to be shipped discovered who they belonged to, they also 'declined to have anything more to do with the cattle', and 'the bullocks and sheep commenced wandering first on the quay, and then into Bridge Street and King Street', until they were finally rounded up by police.[197]

After finding their way, by train, to Dublin, Bence Jones' cattle remained largely untouchable. The fate of the animals quickly became a matter of great public interest. Speaking at a League meeting, nationalist M.P. Thomas Sexton informed his audience: 'I have just heard that the cattle of Mr. Bence Jones would not be sold in Cork or Dublin. On last night the Glasgow boat sailed from Dublin with half a cargo, and would not take his cattle, which are now on the quays of Dublin (cheers). One thing is certain that Mr. Bence Jones will not have much profit off his cattle when he gets them to England (cheers).' It was evidence of the immense power and reach of the tactic, and Sexton concluded in encouragement: 'You see what this weapon can do'.[198] Sexton was correct, for the cattle were left unsold even after finally making it to Liverpool, before eventually being taken by a Manchester butcher. Meat labelled 'Bence Jones' Beef' could be found for sale in London, such was the notoriety of the episode.[199]

As well showing the power of tactics of non-interference, and the inherent limitation of a boycott to a specific moral community, the whole affair set the

[193] Bence Jones, *The Life's Work*, 99, 102. [194] O'Leary, 'Mr. Bence Jones' Story', 133.
[195] Bence Jones, *The Life's Work*, xii. [196] Bence Jones, 'Boycotted: Some Experiences', 860.
[197] *Freeman's Journal*, 15 December 1880. [198] *Freeman's Journal*, 17 December 1880.
[199] *Freeman's Journal*, 20 December 1880.

interpretive context for the practice.[200] The British press responded vigorously, aggravated by the involvement of commercial and mercantile interests. This was no longer just social excommunication carried on by small western farmers, but shaped decisions made by the middle classes too, who 'feel that [the police] are useless and will trust nothing to their protection'.[201] Bence Jones' hastily published book on the matter, *A Life's Work in Ireland of a Landlord Who Tried to Do His Duty* (a title which generated much laughter at Land League meetings), was a deliberate attempt to shape policy and to convince 'those Englishmen who are so tender over constitutional rights' how badly Ireland needed government repression.[202] The book would help to form Anglo-American opinion of the boycott in Ireland as a reign of terror inflicted on a weak-willed peasantry in the name of 'red republicanism'.[203] Despite what T. P. O'Connor described as 'a tone of cant and pharisaic self-complacency', the autobiographical narrative received positive attention from the international press, with its author praised as 'a model landlord in any country', bedevilled with 'thankless tenants [...] uniting in a deliberate attempt to ruin him'.[204] Bence Jones' claim that having difficulty selling his cows meant that 'all the rights of property, as hitherto understood, [...] are in the balance', prefigured the subsequent challenges that boycotting would cause over the next two decades for those notionally committed to protecting both property and liberty.[205]

Significantly, Bence Jones identified the root problem as the 'wholesale suppression of independent thought', an absence of free rationality caused by the collective resort to 'intimidation'.[206] On both sides of the Atlantic, this 'new social peril', a 'subtle and mischievous rebellion' as it was called, made powerful use of the hazy and ambiguous area between persuasion, cooperation, coercion, and intimidation to great effect.[207] When the British government brought a prosecution against the leaders of the Land League on the basis of constructive conspiracy, the Irish Attorney-General, Hugh Law, was unable to

200 It also brought forth instances of counter-boycotting, although naturally Bence Jones' celebrated rather than condemned these. Bence Jones, 'Boycotted: Some Experiences', 865.

201 *Pall Mall Gazette*, 17 December 1880.

202 *Freeman's Journal*, 20 December 1880; Bence Jones, *The Life's Work*, xiii.

203 *New York Times*, 31 December 1880.

204 *Freeman's Journal*, 20 December 1880; *New York Times*, 26 December 1880; *New York Tribune*, 22 February 1881.

205 Bence Jones, *The Life's Work*, 159; Haggai Hurvitz, 'American Labor Law and the Doctrine of Entrepreneurial Property Rights: Boycotts, Courts, and the Juridical Reorientation of 1886–1895', *Industrial Relations Law Journal* 8, no. 3 (1986): 312; see, for instance, 'In re Debs': 'courts of equity have of recent years extended the province of remedy by injunction to cover such cases [boycotting], on the ground of protecting the property rights of the employers from irreparable damage', Henry Budd and Ardemus Stewart, *American and English Decisions in Equity: Being Select Cases Decided in the Appellate Courts of America and England*, vol II (Philadelphia: M. Murphy, 1896), 382.

206 Bence Jones, *The Life's Work*, 157–158.

207 *Newcastle Courant*, 10 December 1880.

prove that the public expressions of Parnell, Thomas Sexton, Matthew Harris, and others were evidence of an organised conspiracy to prevent the payment of rent.[208] The *Conspiracy and Protection of Property Act* of 1875, which had legalised some limited trade union activity, served to protect the defendants. Specifically, the Act stated that, 'an agreement or combination by two or more persons [...] shall not be indictable as a conspiracy if such act committed by one person would not be punishable as a crime'.[209] The Irish leaders relied heavily on this legislation, arguing that it was not a crime to 'persuade any number of other men' to do something that itself was not illegal.[210] While the prosecution attempted to prove an agreed conspiracy by noting the similar expressions used by the leaders, many observers noted the remarkable illiberality of this position. The *Washington Post* reflected that it spread 'the meshes of the law wide enough to catch almost any man who has said anything against high rents'.[211] On the stand, Timothy Sullivan affirmed the same argument, making it clear that what was at stake in the trial were fundamental 'liberal principles', to which a successful prosecution would be 'an act of great apostasy' that would 'strike a blow at freedom of speech, [and] at the sacred right of public meeting'.[212]

As such, boycotting made it incumbent on legislators and political thinkers in both Britain and the United States to find a workable definition of 'intimidation' that proscribed boycotting but left room for freedom of thought and action. The question of intimidation was a prominent feature of parliamentary discussion of the proposed coercion bill, the *Protection of Persons and Property (Ireland) Act,* which subsequently imposed such a capacious definition that almost any behaviour could be interpreted as a form of intimidation. Irish nationalist parliamentarians stridently complained that this conception meant that 'an act of intimidation might be performed without a single movement of the body', leaving the Irish population subject to the 'official malevolence' of any police officer.[213] Subsequent debates followed a similar trajectory. In the House of Commons leading up to the 1882 coercion act, discussion over 'the knotty subject of intimidation' occupied three full days with no coherent

208 *Report of the Trial of the Queen, at the prosecution of the Rt. Hon. The Attorney-General, against Charles Stuart Parnell, John Dillon, Joseph Gillis Biggar, Timothy Daniel Sullivan, Thomas Sexton, Patrick Egan, Thomas Brennan, Michael O'Sullivan, Michael P. Boynton, Patrick Joseph Sheridan, Patrick Joseph Gordon, Mathew Harris, John W. Walsh, and John W. Nally, for Conspiracy in inciting tenants not to pay rents contracted for, and deterring tenants from payment of rent* (Dublin: Alex. Thom. & Co., 1881).

209 1875 c.86 (38&39 Vict.) *Conspiracy, and Protection of Property Act*, 1975, Clause 3; see also Lecky, *Democracy and Liberty*, vol. II, 443–451.

210 Justin McCarthy, HC Deb, 15 March 1881, vol. 259, c. 1106; *Freeman's Journal*, 19 January 1881; *Freeman's Journal*, 26 January 1881.

211 *Washington Post*, 3 January 1881; *New York Times*, 31 December 1880.

212 *Freeman's Journal*, 19 January 1881.

213 HC Deb, 14 February 1881, vol 258, c. 796.

resolution.[214] An amendment was sought to ensure that prosecutions could only be brought on the basis of actual allegations of intimidation, but the Home Secretary William Harcourt rejected this proposal on the grounds that 'the people intimidated dare not complain'.[215] Even signed testimony, endorsed by local priests, 'stating that no intimidation had been exercised' would not be accepted, as the government used the concept of intimidation to reframe all collective action as evidence of restricted freedom; all forms of moral or social suasion as essentially coercive.[216] In this way, it became axiomatic that all 'social power [was] exercised by the influence of fear'.[217]

This was clearly a problem for liberal conceptions of freedom. It was evident to some observers that, no matter how much they may detest the boycotters, 'perhaps no law could be so framed as to reach them without imposing harsh restrictions on the innocent'.[218] Certainly, for William Graham Sumner, America's most prominent classical liberal thinker, boycotting presented 'the severest trial to which our institutions have yet been put'.[219] Others, like the Liberal M.P. for Orkney, Samuel Laing, thought that the proper liberal response was simply to limit the law to 'acts of violence'. Although he disliked the practice of the boycott, Laing defended it in principle, recognising that 'you cannot imprison the whole population of a countryside because they refuse to make or to buy another man's hay'.[220] To have a free public sphere, he argued, there must be 'unlimited liberty [...] of moral coercion'.[221] A similar line was taken in the United States by Oliver Wendell Holmes Jr. in a dissenting opinion on a boycotting case at the Massachusetts Supreme Court, when he argued that the practice was consonant with the principles of free competition in the economic and social sphere.[222] But this was largely a minority position, and the weight of legal opinion favoured restraining such collective action by any means necessary.[223] In the end, in both

214 'The Prevention of Crime Bill', *The Saturday Review* 1,389, no. 53 (10 June 1882): 715.

215 HC Deb, 6 June 1882, vol. 270, cc. 300–301.

216 HC Deb, 6 June 1882, vol. 270, c.303; As another averred, 'the fact is that intimidation is so protean in its shape that it is impossible to define it', HC Deb, 6 June 1882, vol. 270, c. 384.

217 'Ireland under Ordinary Law', 278.

218 William A Hammond, 'The Evolution of the Boycott', *The Forum* (June 1886): 269.

219 William Graham Sumner, 'Industrial War', *The Forum* (September 1886): 7.

220 Samuel Laing, *Boycotting* (London: National Press Agency, 1888), 8.

221 Laing, *Boycotting*, 4.

222 Vegelahn V. Guntner et al., 'Supreme Judicial Court of Massachusetts, 27 October 1896', in Henry Budd, and Ardemus Stewart (eds.), *American and English Decisions in Equity: Being Select Cases Decided in the Appellate Courts of America and England*, vol III (Philadelphia: M. Murphy, 1897), 542–543.

223 Michael A. Gordon, 'The Labor Boycott in New York City, 1880–1886', *Labor History* 16, no. 2 (1975): 184–229; Karen Orren, *Belated Feudalism: Labor, the Law, and Liberal Development in the United States* (Cambridge: Cambridge University Press, 1991); E. P. Cheyney, 'Decisions of the Courts in Conspiracy and Boycott Cases', *Political Science Quarterly* 4, no. 2 (June 1889): 3; 'Judge Brown on Boycotting', *The Independent* 39, no. 199

Ireland and America, the only solution was to be found via parliamentary or judicial fiat, in the temporary suspension of rights through coercion or court injunction to break boycotts.[224]

At its core, however, boycotting was much more than simply a thorny legal puzzle, or even a challenge to the structures supporting existing property rights (although both of these were significant consequences of the international spread and mass adoption of the tactic). Ultimately, it represented a theory of social and political action largely at odds with both classical and social liberal politics. Much like the land question to which it was intimately linked, boycotting was metaphysically individualist and politically collectivist in a way that was disconcerting across the political spectrum. It was deeply threatening to older classical liberal conceptions of autonomous individuals possessing free-standing and socially unimpeded rationality.[225] The 'fierce anarchy' of the boycott, as W. E. H. Lecky termed it, was an example of democracy out of control, that threatened the stability and security of propertied civilisation.[226] But it was also worrying to many socialists and progressive liberals, who saw that its underlying assumptions threatened any external authority at all.[227] As was evident in the defences of the type mounted by Sexton, Laing, and Wendell Holmes Jr., boycotting was reliant on the notion that the individual possessed a pre-existing, perhaps even natural, right to disengage with or to ostracise others. At the same time, as a practice it proved that such choices could never be taken without social influence – that all persons were, as the nationalist M.P. Alexander Sullivan explained, subject to 'the "boycotting" of the age in which they lived'.[228] It operated contrary to the developing liberal idealist notion that the state was the sole creator and guardian of all rights,

(10 March 1887): 20; *New York Times*, 20 March 1886; *New York Times*, 28 August 1887; 'Criminal Law conspiracy', *The Albany Law Journal* 36, no. 1 (2 July 1887): 9.

224 *New York Times*, 4 April 1893; James J. Miller, 'Legal and Economic History of the Secondary Boycott', *Labor Law Journal* 12, no. 8 (1961): 751–759; Samuel Yellen, *American Labor Struggles* (New York: S. A. Russell, 1936); Melvyn Dubofsky, 'The Federal Judiciary, Free Labor, and Equal Rights', in Richard Schneirov, Shelton Stromquist, and Nick Salvatore (eds.), *The Pullman Strike and the Crisis of the 1890s* (Urbana: University of Illinois Press, 1999), 159–178.

225 William Graham Sumner, 'State Interference', *The North American Review* 145, no. 369 (August 1887): 109, 117–118; William Graham Sumner, *What Social Classes Owe to Each Other* (New York: Harper and Brothers, 1883), 9, 39, 109; William Graham Sumner, 'Industrial War', *The Forum* (September 1886): 7.

226 Lecky, *Democracy and Liberty*, vol. I, 54; Arthur George Sedgwick, *The Democratic Mistake, Godkin Lectures of 1909, delivered at Harvard University* (New York: Charles Scribner's Sons, 1912), 79; Henry Sumner Maine, *Popular Government: Four Essays* (London: John Murray, 1885), vii. See also Adcock, *Liberalism and the Emergence of American Political Science*, 173–234.

227 Ely, *Recent American Socialism*, 166.

228 Alexander Sullivan, HC Deb, 28 February 1881, vol. 258, c. 1892.

but also accepted as a foundational principle that no action was ever fully self-regarding.[229]

This central challenge that boycotting posed to liberal politics, and indeed what marked it as a distinctly republican political praxis, can be clearly observed in the most common and unifying critique: that it inexorably drew outsiders into a disagreement, forcing them to take a political position, thereby making a moral community coextensive with a political community and threatening the order of the state.[230] Almost immediately after Boycott's boycott, critics identified 'the co-operation of outsiders in their refusal to supply the offender with provisions' as the key feature which made boycotting a 'combination to injure' and a threat to social order.[231] 'Boycotting differs from an ordinary strike', explained the *New York Times*, in that the boycotters 'induce other men totally uninterested in their quarrel' to get involved.[232] It inhibited freedom by 'assail[ing] the rights of uninterested third parties'.[233] There could no longer be 'any neutrality possible for uninterested or peaceably disposed third classes. They must take part with the boycotted, by dealing with him, or with the boycotters, by refusing to deal with the boycotted'.[234] The consequence of this was that those engaged in boycotting were creating 'large local sovereignty', which threatened to 'usurp or to nullify the state's function of punishing or protecting the individual citizen'.[235] The conservative jurist James Fitzjames Stephen echoed these social liberal arguments against the boycott, albeit with more vehemence, when he denounced them as a 'usurpation of the functions of government' that should 'be recognised in their true light as acts of social war, as the modern representatives of the old conception of high treason'.[236] It was a critique that would continue to mark liberal interpretations of the boycott into the twentieth century and beyond.[237]

'Boycottism', as the term was frequently conjugated in the first few years of the 1880s, contained its own latent political theory.[238] As these liberal critiques

[229] It is no surprise that American anarchists, many of whom were already firm supporters and close allies of the Irish cause, embraced boycotting wholeheartedly, proclaiming its 'true republicanism' and calling for its widespread use. *Liberty*, 31 October 1891; *Liberty*, 17 July 1886.

[230] J. A. Hobson, *Towards International Government* (London: George Allen and Unwin, 1916), 92.

[231] *Newcastle Courant*, 10 December 1880.

[232] *New York Times*, 7 November 1885.

[233] 'Two Kinds of Boycotting', *Century Illustrated Magazine* 32, no. 2 (1886): 321; 'Boycott Not a Legal Weapon', *The Albany Law Journal* 56, no. 22 (1897): 390.

[234] 'Two Kinds of Boycotting', 320–321.

[235] 'Two Kinds of Boycotting', 322.

[236] James Fitzjames Stephen, 'On the Suppression of Boycotting', *Nineteenth Century* 20, no. 118 (December 1886): 769.

[237] Leo Wolman, *The Boycott in American Trade Unions* (Baltimore, MD: Johns Hopkins University Press, 1916), 14.

[238] *The Manchester Guardian*, 12 January 1881; *The Scotsman*, 11 January 1881; *New York Times*, 6 December 1880; 'The Government and Ireland', *Blackwood's Edinburgh Magazine* 129, no. 784 (February 1881), 243; It was suggested that the term 'boycottism' had largely died out by 1883, 'Introduction to the Study of the History of Language', *The Athenaeum* 3326 (1891), 120; Walter W. Skeat, *Principles of English Etymology*, 1st Ser. (2nd ed.) (Oxford: Clarendon Press, 1892), 6–7.

implicitly recognised, boycotting required as its basis a commonly intelligible morality that presumed social harmony was attainable through interaction, without the imposition of an external authority. It therefore suggested a particular, and indeed a particularly republican, political rendering. Public disesteem, as republican thinkers had long recognised, could operate as a socially cohesive force, acting beyond traditional hierarchies of order.[239] Boycotting shared with many strands of republicanism a resistance to the notion of disinterested outsiders within a specific polity. The idea that all were, to some degree, interdependent and morally accountable to each other underpinned a functioning boycott, as well as setting limits on its abuses.[240] The involvement of other people, not directly invested in the primary disagreement, had always been a central and inescapable element of the boycott, just as it had been in Bence Jones' tale. It suggested a political typology in which there were no such things as citizens who were also disinterested outsiders, since it was political participation that created citizenship. While liberal critics condemned the impositions placed on independent parties, boycotting, with its republican inflections, necessarily erased the distinction between political actors and neutral citizens; one must be both or neither.

In demanding political participation in order to both create and sustain a moral and political community, boycotting attested that the locus of power in its operative sociology was rooted ultimately in the individual, rather than any hierarchy of power or maintainer of order in the form of a state.[241] As such, a notion of naturalised rights, however inchoate, inhering in the individual, and very directly limited by the social impositions of human existence, was immanent in the practice of boycotting itself. The boycott expressed in practice an older moral cosmology of social and natural harmony, which was usually associated with republican and agrarian radicalism. Viewed in this way, and allied to the extensive use of natural rights claims made by Land Leaguers, boycotting was clearly a non-textual articulation of a republican political philosophy that effectively authenticated their rhetorical assertions. Like the question of property in land to which it was so intimately and inextricably linked, boycotting expressed naturalised individual rights that were only realisable though collective negotiation. Like the question of property in land, it drew a deeply individualist metaphysic to a strikingly communal conclusion.

239 Jefferson to Francis Gilmer, 7 June 1816, in Joyce Appleby, and Terence Ball (eds.), *Jefferson*, 14.

240 Honohan, 'Introduction', 3.

241 Michael Taylor, *Community, Anarchy and Liberty* (Cambridge: Cambridge University Press, 1982), 158–159; Ellen Meiksins Wood, *Peasant, Citizen & Slave: The Foundations of Athenian Democracy* (London: Verso, 1988), 127–129.

4 The Catholic Church and the Land Question

No organisation could rival the Catholic Church in its incomparable influence over the Irish diaspora. Wielding institutional authority with Divine sanction, the Church was a truly transnational leviathan. It performed a central role in popular life, in political discourse, and in theoretical speculation. Connecting the mundane and the provincial to the abstract and the universal, the theological frameworks of the Catholic Church were the means by which many understood their world and their politics, providing an intellectual scaffolding that shaped daily life and political perceptions. The Church was also a vehicle for the transmission of ideas, cultural forms, and social practices to a transnational population.[1] Yet its authority was ultimately a contingent and delicate thing, more contestable than it was concrete.[2] Between the hierarchy and the lay community, there existed a routine and reflexive oscillation of power, in which the Church was gradually flexed and moulded into different ideological positions. Nationalist leaders, labour radicals, and prominent Irish public figures offered only vacillating and equivocal obedience to the Church hierarchy on political questions, even as many remained loyal to their religion, and indeed the institution of the Church itself, as a central feature of Irish Catholic identity.[3]

Few periods offer quite the dramatic example of this process than the Irish Land War. In both Ireland and the United States, the Church hierarchy was riven with conflict over how to approach the land question. At the same time, the popular demand for a right to the land was made in unmistakably religious terms. The problem of how to contain and control the movement sat alongside questions over its moral rectitude for Irish ecclesiastics on both sides of the Atlantic. Not only did the public discourse on land rest on decidedly theological arguments, which exposed clerical statements on the issue to perilous examination

[1] Meagher, 'From the World to the Village', 125.

[2] Thomas J. Shelly, 'Catholic Greenwich Village: Ethnic Geography and Religious Identity in New York City, 1880–1930', *The Catholic Historical Review* 89, no. 1 (2003): 60–84; Jay P. Dolan, *The Immigrant Church: New York's Irish and German Catholics, 1815–1865* (Baltimore, MD: Johns Hopkins University Press, 1975).

[3] James P. Rodechko, 'An Irish-American Journalist and Catholicism: Patrick Ford of the Irish World', *Church History* 39, no. 4 (1970): 529.

and defiant critique, but many priests, rooted in their communities whether in Manhattan or Mayo, also experienced the pull of the land agitation. In articulating their own moral anger in theological terms, priests frequently set the intellectual and rhetorical framework for the debate about property in land. Catholic arguments over the land question soon became in this way inseparable from confrontations over ecclesiastical authority. Indeed, because of the Irish Catholic Church's significant diaspora, and its ambiguous relationship to state power, multiple factors shaped the Church's varied responses to the land question.

Nevertheless, the image of the Catholic Church as a reactionary monolith, arrayed in all its organisational and spiritual might against progressive reform, has been a persistent one, evident both in contemporary critiques and in subsequent analysis. It is certainly true that the institutional structure of the Church was deeply hostile to social upheaval of any kind. In Ireland, Cardinal Paul Cullen's ultramontanism shaped the devotional revolution of the mid-nineteenth century and encouraged a firm stance against the appeal of nationalism. It is true to say that on questions of social morality a pervasive conservatism reigned. Yet a sweeping view of Catholic conservatism, assuming ideological homogeneity among believers, would be highly misleading.[4] Such a view not only misses the remarkable flexibility and multivalence of Catholic theology, collapsing the issue of religious devotion into a binary between an increasingly secularised, commercial, liberal modernity and a regressive and recalcitrant Catholic anti-modernism, but can also end up reproducing implicitly sectarian assumptions about Catholic Irish passivity and political subservience.

In the late-nineteenth century, these commonplace perceptions about Irish unsuitability for participation in democratic self-government, which shaped political opinion in American as much as British cultural life, were rooted not only in a highly racialised discourse about 'Celtic' peoples, but in long-standing prejudices about the Catholic Church. A simplistic view of the Enlightenment as a unitary project of political deconsecration rendered the Catholic Church, with its totalising metaphysics, largely beyond the intellectual bounds of 'enlightened' 'civilisation'.[5] For this reason, Catholicism was seen to be largely resistant to incorporation within a liberal-capitalist polity. It is true that the turning of 'theology into history', a separation of the civil from the clerical and relegation of the divine to the human, which was characteristic of much 'Enlightened' thought, represented an unwelcome incursion for the Church

[4] Patrick Pasture, 'The Role of Religion in Social and Labour History', in Lex Heerma van Voss, and Marcel van der Linden (eds.), *Class and Other Identities: Gender, Religion and Ethnicity in the Writing of European Labour History* (New York: Berghahn Books, 2002), 110, 116–117.

[5] Catholicism was a feudalist hangover for Kirkup, *An Inquiry into Socialism*, 90–91; see also John T. McGreevy, *Catholicism and American Freedom: A History* (New York: Norton, 2003), 91–126; Elizabeth Fenton, *Religious Liberties: Anti-Catholicism and Liberal Democracy in Nineteenth-Century U.S. Literature and Culture* (New York: Oxford University Press, 2011).

to which it was understandably resistant.[6] It is also clear that, by the middle of the nineteenth century, many Catholic thinkers had embossed a profitable dialectic that equated the Enlightenment with a cold and harsh materialism and philosophical positivism, framing Catholicism as its humane and sympathetic mirror image.[7] The 'cynicism of the "Encyclopedists"' had bequeathed a morally hollow, self-destructive society, one that enabled, through its arrogant naivety, both an exploitative capitalism and a godless communism.[8] As one writer explained, the Enlightenment morality of Kant 'deeply lowers the dignity of man' and had created a context in which 'the morality of public life thus becomes the policy of the iron hand'.[9]

But the Catholic Church enjoyed a much more complex relationship with the legacies of 'Enlightened' thought. The intellectual effusion of the late-eighteenth century contained both an enormous plurality of philosophical ambition and significant continuity with earlier traditions. An overly secular-rationalist or anticlerical view of the Enlightenment presents a particular problem in an Irish context, where all confessional persuasions were reshaped by its influences.[10] Ireland's proximity to and interaction with the Scottish Enlightenment, where irreligious critique was much less central than in continental Europe, was also a factor here.[11] The influence of Ulster-born Presbyterian Francis Hutcheson, for instance, was crucial in retaining the notion of an unquestioned (and unquestionable) innate moral sense, which obviated the need for a justification of morality though a detachable rationality of the type Catholic thinkers later bemoaned.[12] Yet unlike in Scotland, as Colin Kidd has shown, where a stadial view of historical progress relegated native 'pre-enlightened' cultures to obscurity, the image of

[6] J. G. A. Pocock, 'Historiography and Enlightenment: A View of Their History', *Modern Intellectual History* 5, no. 1 (2008): 94; John Robertson, *The Enlightenment, the Public Sphere and Political Economy*, C. Th. Dimaras Annual Lecture, 2010 (Athens: National Hellenic Research Foundation, 2011), 122.

[7] Orestes A. Brownson, 'Conversations on Liberalism and the Church' [1869], in Henry F. Brownson (ed.), *The Works of Orestes A. Brownson*, vol. XIII (Detroit: Thorndike Nourse, 1884), 1–86; James Schmidt, 'What Enlightenment Was, What It Still Might Be, and Why Kant May Have Been Right After All', *American Behavioural Scientist* 49, no. 5 (2006): 649, 652.

[8] Rev Victor Cathrein, *The Champions of Agrarian Socialism: A Refutation of Émile de Laveleye and Henry George* (Buffalo: P. Paul and Bro., 1889), 10.

[9] Rev J. Ming, S. J., 'The Pretended Unity of Modern Philosophy', *American Catholic Quarterly Review* 5 (1880): 24–25.

[10] Michael Brown, *The Irish Enlightenment* (Cambridge, MA: Harvard University Press, 2016), 459, 461; David Denby, 'Ireland, Modernization and the 'Enlightenment' Debate', *Irish Review* 31 (2004): 28–39.

[11] Fania Oz-Salzberger, 'The Political Theory of the Scottish Enlightenment', in Alexander Broadie (ed.), *The Cambridge Companion to the Scottish Enlightenment* (Cambridge: Cambridge University Press, 2003), 157.

[12] Lugio Turco, 'Moral Sense and the Foundations of Morals', in Alexander Broadie (ed.), *The Cambridge Companion to the Scottish Enlightenment* (Cambridge: Cambridge University Press, 2003), 140; Stephen Small, *Political Thought in Ireland 1776–1798: Republicanism, Patriotism, and Radicalism* (Oxford: Oxford University Press), 24.

a morally virtuous and culturally sophisticated Gaelic past 'traversed the quicksand of Enlightenment' in Ireland.[13] This bequeathed to Irish radicals and nationalists over the subsequent century a vision of a 'pre-modern' yet 'enlightened' Ireland, where social and political advancement was not tethered to commercial development, and where early Christianity and a native 'Irish' Catholicism could be seen as a vehicle for, rather than an obstruction to, civilisation.[14]

In this way, by the late-nineteenth century, the concepts of 'enlightenment' and its socio-economic cousin 'civilization' served a dual purpose in Irish Catholic political discourse. In parallel, they were used to gesture towards an idealised but unfulfilled or corrupted vestige of enlightened universalism, and one that could be quite comfortably Catholic in its constitution. 'All the Enlightenment of Europe is on your side', proclaimed Rev O'Dwyer at a Land League meeting in Thurles, Co. Tipperary, home of the newly consecrated Cathedral of the Assumption and centre of the Archdiocese of Cashel.[15] The imperial violence of British rule embodied the distortion of 'civilization', and the inadequacy of defining it by the terms of industrial progress or commercial modernity. 'Which is the civilized part of the earth? What, in short, is civilization?' asked Fenian Thomas J. Mooney, writing under the pen name 'Trans-Atlantic' in the *Irish World*. 'Some would pronounce the march of great armies over dead bodies, and the seizure by the conquerors of the chattels and the lands of the murdered *civilization*.'[16] It was Ireland, according to John Ferguson, that had carried 'the torch of civilization over Europe' while 'the British were painted savages'.[17] The question of whether natural justice was 'incompatible with civilization' or the embodiment of 'true civilization' offered a rhetorical flexibility, allowing Irish radicals to segue between universalist and 'Gaelic' or Catholic visions of Irish nationhood and political economy in land.[18] They did not need to choose between an emancipated future or an idealised Christian Gaelic past. Importantly, this discursive freedom successfully de-coupled the assumed connection between a secularising Protestantism, 'Enlightenment' rationalism, and the schemes of social and economic emancipation which they ostensibly ratified.

Assumptions about the inherent and inescapable social and economic conservatism of a monolithic Catholic Church conditioned the view, as evident during the 1880s as in the subsequent historiography, that Irish demands for economic justice were evidence of a declining Catholicity, and perhaps even the adoption of

13 Colin Kidd, 'Gaelic Antiquity and National Identity in Enlightenment Ireland and Scotland', *English Historical Review* 109, no. 434 (1994): 1197, 1213.

14 Thomas Dolan, 'Imprisonment, Islands, Imperialism: Patrician Dimensions of the Irish Imagination' *History of European Ideas* 46, no. 7 (2020): 1027–1046.

15 Rev O'Dwyer at, Thurles, Co. Tipperary, 14 November 1880 (MS 11,289, NLI).

16 'Trans-Atlantic', *Irish World*, 21 December 1878.

17 John Ferguson, *Irish World*, 16 November 1878.

18 Henry George, *Irish World*, 28 August 1882; Michael Davitt, *Freeman's Journal*, 22 September 1879.

Protestant modes of thought. Irish-Americans, thought Philip Bagenal, had been 'emancipated from ecclesiastical control' – a necessary step for incorporation into American society.[19] More conservative American Catholic prelates, caught up in their internal culture war over the Church's integration into public life, and inclined to see any loss of personal authority as a marker of declining Catholicity, feared that Henry George was drawing honest but misguided Catholic workingmen and women into 'Protestant ways of thinking'.[20] One patronising Unitarian remarked similarly that involvement in social reform had offered subjugated Catholics 'glimpses of a world of liberty' to which they may accede if they cast off their medieval religion.[21] The near universality of this opinion among the American and British political elite in the late-nineteenth century has meant that it has suffused much of the ensuing analysis. Historical judgement has tended to assume that economic radicalism was a peculiarly Protestant temperament to which most Catholics were immune. 'Catholics', explained Lawrence McCaffrey, 'never have accepted the natural goodness of man, the perfectibility of human nature, or the Enlightenment sources of Anglo-Saxon liberalism'.[22] For Eric Foner, the Land League's republican radicalism was not Catholic in origin, but marked the gradual adoption of a 'Protestant reform tradition'.[23]

This tends to overstate the importance of confessional difference, replicating a Weberian division between an enlightened Protestantism and an insular and regressive 'Romanism'. Not all resistance to ecclesiastical authority implied a decline rather than simply a modification of Catholic belief.[24] The blunt sectarian demarcation does recognise an important feature of Catholic naturalism; namely an acceptance of the frailty of human understanding, which often rejected the implication of progressive liberal and state socialistic thought that humans could safely and benevolently exercise ultimate control over the world. But such an impulse was also a feature of much Protestant thought too, and, significantly, it supported rather than contradicted the metaphysics of natural harmony assumed by republican radicals. So while it is important to identify the intellectual resources and theological paraphernalia that Catholicism offered to

19 Philip H. Bagenal, *The American Irish and Their Influence on Irish Politics* (Boston: Roberts Bros, 1882), 66.

20 Robert T. Rea to Archbishop Michael A. Corrigan, 26 April 1886 (Archbishop Corrigan Papers, C-11, Archives of the Archdiocese of New York); Bishop Francis Silas Chatard to Archbishop Michael A. Corrigan, 30 September 1890 (ACP, C-15, AANY).

21 Horace L. Trauble, 'Freedom and Half-Freedom: The McGlynn Incident', *The Unitarian Review* 29, no. 6 (June 1888): 540.

22 Lawrence J. McCaffrey, 'A Profile of Irish America', in David N. Doyle, and Owen Dudley Edwards (eds.), *America and Ireland, 1776–1976: The American Identity and the Irish Connection* (Westport, CT: Greenwood Press, 1976), 83; David M. Emmons, *Beyond the Pale: The Irish in the West, 1845–1910* (Norman, OK: University of Oklahoma Press, 2010), 10.

23 Foner, 'Class, Ethnicity and Radicalism', 151, 179.

24 David N. Doyle, 'The Irish in Chicago', *Irish Historical Studies* 26, no. 103 (1989): 299–300.

republican radicals just as it did their conservative critics, equally, denominational distinctiveness can obscure the fact that class, social hierarchy, and geopolitical position were also significant drivers of theological interpretation.

Conservative elements in the Catholic hierarchy, whether in Ireland or in the United States, drew heavily on the idea of inherent human weakness from the Fall of man, which, for James O'Connor, the Bishop of Omaha, justified the suffering of poverty.[25] Conservative Catholics followed this lead in laying the evils of poverty at the feet of an ineradicable sin. James A. MacMaster, editor of the *New York Freeman's Journal*, identified the fatal flaw in republican radicals as such, writing: 'Mr. George, with Mr. Powderly's help, strives in vain to lay other foundations for human society than those laid by Christ and his Church. Before they "abolish property", they must abolish original sin, as the root of so many pains besides those of being poor!'.[26] This was by no means a narrowly Catholic perspective of course. A hostility to natural human goodness and the possibility of a naturally just and harmonious social order marked Protestant critiques of radicalism just as strongly. Malthusianism informed the view, as expressed by the Duke of Argyll, that in his natural state, man is 'bowed and bent under the yoke of [...] perverted instincts'.[27] For Protestants as much as Catholics, those who wished to destroy private property in land 'forget that man is depraved and desperately wicked'.[28]

In this way, poverty was both inescapably prescribed and a function of a weakness of character. Not only will 'the great bulk of mankind [...] always be compelled to gain their living, in a close struggle, as it were, with nature', but at the same time, 'so many are poor from their own fault'.[29] Conservative Catholics merged the notion of 'Holy Poverty' – the belief that economic destitution was accompanied by spiritual glories – with a meritocratic or Darwinian inflection in order to blunt its radical edge.[30] Otherwise, through its consequential refusal to deign wealth with virtue and meritocratic righteousness, such ideas offered an implicit and unreconciled challenge to a competitive market society. As one Catholic writer explained, 'the confession of the dignity of poverty [suggests] the unmerited good fortune of wealth'.[31]

The efforts of politically conservative Catholics to position their Church as a bulwark against radicalism or reform of any kind were broadly successful.

[25] Bishop James O'Connor, 'Socialism', *American Catholic Quarterly Review* 8 (1883): 233.

[26] *New York Freeman's Journal*, 13 November 1886.

[27] George Campbell, *The Unity of Nature* (New York: Putnam, 1884), 367.

[28] Alexander W. Terrell, *Land: Its Individuals Ownership and Culture, the Surest Safeguard of Free Government: University of Texas Commencement Address* (Austin: University of Texas, 1898), 21.

[29] Cathrein, *The Champions of Agrarian Socialism*, 122; Rev Henry A. Brann, *Henry George and His Land Theories* (New York: Catholic Publication Society, 1887), 4.

[30] Miller, *Ireland and Irish America*, 265.

[31] Arthur F. Marshall, 'English Manners', *American Catholic Quarterly Review* 5 (1880): 108.

But in Ireland and in Irish-America (and elsewhere in a global context), they were severely hampered by the fact that it remained the spiritual home of a politically and economically subaltern population.[32] So while James Redpath, the crusading Scottish-American journalist who reported sympathetically on the Land War, could observe that the Catholic Church remained, in broad terms, 'the most potent conservative force in our modern society', he found Irish priests to be unremittingly radical when it came to identifying landlords as the cause of Irish suffering.[33] Irish Catholicism, in this way, bore some similarity to dissenting Protestantism due to their shared structural position in opposition to state authority.[34] In Britain, the Anglican Church had long served as the religious arm of the state, offering theological gloss to the secular demands of utilitarian economism.[35] In the United States, the absence of a politically established church did not stymie a religion of the propertied, where much American Protestantism was directed towards a defence of wealth in the same way. The Irish Catholic Church, however, had a more awkward balancing act to perform when a focus on comfortable respectability proved irreconcilable with the social anger incubated by poverty.

Irish priests, like their nonconformist Protestant counterparts, frequently made their theological observations relevant to their economically disenfranchised congregations. Rather than any unique Enlightenment inheritance in Protestant thought unavailable to Catholic thinkers, it was the structural position of these ministries that encouraged scriptural interpretation to regularly veer towards socially radical conclusions. It was this fact that generated W. E. H. Lecky's comparison of Catholic and Nonconformist political tendencies, and his frustration that the radicals in the Land League 'received the support of the great body of the Catholic priests in Ireland, and of the great body of Nonconformist ministers in England'.[36] As with the Free Church in the Scottish Highlands, or Welsh Methodism, a proximity to poverty spurred opposition to evangelical economic utilitarianism.[37] In this context, the Irish Catholic Church had to speak in part as the national church of a state-less and, broadly, powerless people.

Unlike its European counterparts, who knew 'full well how terrible are the passions aroused by political and national aspirations', the Irish Church had

[32] David N. Doyle, 'Irish Elites in North America and Liberal Democracy, 1820–1920', *Radharc* 3 (2002): 32.

[33] James Redpath, *Talks about Ireland* (New York: P. J. Kenedy, 1881), 9.

[34] Biagini, *British Democracy*, 114, 119.

[35] D. M. Thompson, 'The Enlightenment, the Late Eighteenth-Century Revolutions and Their Aftermath: The "Secularising" Implications of Protestantism?' in Ira Katznelson, and Gareth Stedman Jones (eds.), *Religion and the Political Imagination* (Cambridge: Cambridge University Press, 2010), 81.

[36] Lecky, *Democracy and Liberty*, vol. I, 236.

[37] MacColl, *Land, Faith and the Crofting Community*, 213; Matthew Cragoe, 'Conscience or Coercion? Clerical Influence at the General Election of 1868 in Wales', *Past & Present* 149 (1995): 140–169.

also benefited from a cautious acceptance of popular national sentiment.[38] This was perhaps especially true in the United States, where immigrant attachment to Catholicism became intertwined with national aspirations as a singular story of oppression.[39] Priests and, to a lesser but still notable degree, prelates on both sides of the Atlantic were much more responsive to material immiseration than their co-religionists from other countries, seeing that alignment with the political status quo offered fewer advantages than elsewhere. Because of this, neither nationalism nor social radicalism, in Ireland or in Irish-America, embraced a decidedly anticlerical position, unlike in France or Italy.[40] Indeed compared to the Church on the continent, the Irish and Irish-American priesthood were remarkably radical. Of one Irish Jesuit, himself a devoted critic of socialism, it was noted that 'Catholic schools of social ethics on the Continent were startled by his articles [...] on the rights of property. His views seemed to them to savour of socialism'.[41] For Irish labour radicals, priests could sometimes be a hindrance to their more assertive tactics and campaigns, and yet, as one member of the Knights of Labor wrote appreciatively, 'they don't pander to the wealthy and influential, like ministers of other denominations'.[42]

Catholic Republicanism

The distinctive social position of Catholicism in Ireland and Irish-America helped to foster what was, by broader European and American standards, an unusual political alignment. The rough correspondence of Irish Catholicism with republican, home-rule, and nationalist politics over the nineteenth and twentieth centuries stood at odds with the more familiar orientation of liberal-democratic Protestantism juxtaposed against the anti-democratic and imperial tendencies of Catholicism. This was, as has been argued, in part a political necessity. In addition to the structural causes of this specific religio-political alignment, however, there were also important intellectual resources that Catholic teaching offered to republican radicals; genealogies of Catholic thought that supported their

[38] Cardinal Simioni, quoted in Greene, 'The Impact of Henry George's Theories', 117.

[39] Matthew Frye Jacobson, *Special Sorrows: The Diasporic Imagination of Irish, Polish, and Jewish Immigrants in the United States* (Berkeley: University of California Press, 2002), 64; Larkin, *The Roman Catholic Church*, 394.

[40] Robert Stuart, '"Jesus the *Sans-Culotte*": Marxism and Religion during the French *Fin de Siecle*', *The Historical Journal* 42, no. 3 (1999): 705–727; Enrico Dal Lago, 'Lincoln, Cavour, and National Unification: American Republicanism and Italian Liberal Nationalism in Comparative Perspective', *The Journal of the Civil War Era* 3, no. 1 (2013): 85–113; Eric J. Hobsbawm, 'Religion and the Rise of Socialism', in *Worlds of Labour: Further Studies in the History of Labour* (London: Weidenfeld and Nicolson, 1984), 47; Kelley, *The Transatlantic Persuasion*, 48.

[41] M. F. Egan, 'Father Peter Finlay, S.J.', *Studies: An Irish Quarterly Review* 18, no. 72 (1929): 574.

[42] John Hirsch to Terence V. Powderly, 12 May 1880 (Powderly Papers, Series 1: Box 2, Catholic University of America).

approaches to questions of political freedom, property rights, and economic justice. Through Aristotle and Aquinas, Catholic natural law teaching emphasised the underlying harmoniousness of a Divine nature, offering a similar metaphysic of natural purposiveness which was used to press forward claims for a universal right to land.[43] In this respect, both Catholic and republican social critiques shared similar roots for their conviction that the vices of commercial society were due to the atomising and disaggregating tendencies of liberal capitalism, and the (de)construction of a pre-social unencumbered self, dislocated from its basis in a natural harmony, either of law, justice, or community.

Drawing on Aristotle, the Aquinian reservations about the production of wealth for its own sake tied its moral purposiveness to human life and its source to human labour, ensuring that private wealth remained a matter of public consideration.[44] On this point, nineteenth-century Catholics and republicans could both generally (or at least superficially) agree about the corrupting influences of luxury as both a personal and a public vice; as simultaneously and interdependently a politically and morally destabilising force. The problem of how to legitimise luxury, and counter the moral absolutism of Catholic and republican theorists, had animated proponents of liberal commercialism during the previous century, but their victories were uneven.[45] In Ireland, assumptions about the politically insidious consequences of wealth and luxury bubbled under the land question, evident in effusions against landed affluence and urban iniquity. Irish rents were not only taken unjustly from the farmers, but to compound matters, they went 'abroad for expensive luxuries to England or the continent; they meet the demands of fashion and aristocratic dissipation in London; they enrich racecourses, gambling dens, and other haunts of gilded vice'.[46] The framing of the small farmer as the 'soul of the nation', the dominant note of the Land League's vision, suited both Catholic and republican distrust of urbanity and luxury.[47]

43 Fred D. Miller, Jr., *Nature, Justice, and Rights in Aristotle's* Politics (Oxford: Clarendon Press, 1995), 91, 138, 330; George H. Sabine, in Thomas L. Thorson (ed.), *A History of Political Theory*, 4th ed. (London: Harcourt Brace, 1973), 5; William Mathie, 'Property in the Political Science of Aristotle', in Anthony Parel, and Thomas Flanagan (eds.), *Theories of Property: Aristotle to the Present* (Waterloo: Wilfred Laurier Press, 1979), 13; see Tobias Hoffman, Jörn Müller, and Matthias Perkams (eds.), *Aquinas and the Nicomachean Ethics* (Cambridge: Cambridge University Press, 2013).

44 Parel, 'Aquinas' Theory of Property', 88–111.

45 Istvan Hont, 'The Early Enlightenment Debate on Commerce and Luxury', in Mark Goldie, and Robert Wolker (eds.), *The Cambridge History of Eighteenth-Century Political Thought* (Cambridge: Cambridge University Press, 2006), 380.

46 Clancy, *Ireland: As She Is*, 44.

47 Bew, 'The Land League Ideal', 77–92. For a good example of this tendency, see Conyngham, *Ireland Past and Present*. American radicals similarly denounced luxury and conspicuous consumption, although urban life inevitably avoided similar condemnation. Henry George, *Irish World*, 20 December 1879; John L. Thomas, *Alternative America: Henry George, Edward Bellamy, Henry Demarest Lloyd, and the Adversary Tradition* (Cambridge, MA: Harvard University Press, 1983), 2.

Both Catholic and radical republican moralism about wealth tended to meet with accusations of hypocrisy from liberal thinkers, who considered such austere and restrictive attitudes either naïve or disingenuous. The charge that Catholicism itself necessitated hypocrisy was familiar to the work of liberal thinkers from Thomas Hobbes to Henry Sidgwick, who saw 'play-acting' as central to Catholicism.[48] But since both traditions considered individuals as inseparable from their social or natural contexts, Catholic and republican thought viewed the self-seeking desire for wealth, and the personal pride and power that accompanied it, as a socially destabilising force. Pride, the original source of sin in Christian belief, created social disharmony and economic advancement as two sides of the same coin.[49] In an attack on the prevailing scientism of the age, Pope Pius IX identified the sin of pride in particular for 'degrad[ing] man himself to the level of the unreasoning brutes'.[50] For George, it was pride and greed together, driving the unjustified accumulation of land, that had collapsed the Roman Empire.[51] As Irish Catholic thinkers bemoaned the erosion of earlier social and moral restraints on wealth accumulation, they saw the 'pride of superiority' evident in Anglo-American society as the cause of its moral vacuity.[52] Impositions on pride through social shame were a notable feature of life in rural communities, too, because of its disruptive tendencies. Both in Ireland and in the cultural enclaves of the Irish diaspora, hostility towards 'upstarts' and those 'aspiring so blatantly to elite status' was widespread, and such attitudes were drivers of social cohesion.[53]

This was most clearly observable in the practice of boycotting, to which social shaming was foundationally important. Shame was a powerful tool to enforce communal norms, a valuable emotional commodity for social groups seeking to restrain economic exploitation, despite liberal complaints of its repressive toxicity. Parnell's famous declaration on social ostracism was clear that such tactics were only viable where no one was 'so lost to shame' that they would disregard others' disesteem. Shame, and its internalised twin guilt, constituted the emotional apparatus of social responsibility; the psychic mechanisms of civic duty. To Protestant eyes especially, there was no greater purveyor of shame and

[48] David Runciman, *Political Hypocrisy: The Mask of Power, from Hobbes to Orwell and Beyond* (Princeton: Princeton University Press, 2008), 159; Michael P. Zuckert, *Natural Rights and the New Republicanism* (Princeton: Princeton University Press, 1994), 271; Charles H. George, 'English Calvinist Opinion on Usury, 1600–1640', *Journal of the History of Ideas* 18, no. 4 (1957): 457, 474.

[49] Martin Hollis, 'Economic Man and Original Sin', *Political Studies* 29, no. 2 (1981): 179.

[50] Pope Pius IX, quoted in Andrew Dickson White, *A History of the Warfare of Science with Theology in Christendom*, vol. I (New York: Appleton, 1897), 75.

[51] George, *Progress and Poverty*, 336. [52] Marshall, 'English Manners', 109.

[53] Jones, 'The Cleavage between Graziers and Peasants in the Land Struggle', 413; John Belchem, 'Priests, Publicans and the Irish Poor: Ethnic Enterprise and Migrant Networks in Mid-Nineteenth-Century Liverpool', *Immigrants & Minorities* 23, nos. 2–3 (2005): 207–231; John Belchem, *Irish, Catholic and Scouse: The History of the Liverpool-Irish, 1800–1939* (Liverpool: Liverpool University Press, 2007).

guilt than the Catholic Church. Indeed the boycott's conspicuous reliance on moral force led many to assume that the practice had emanated from the teachings of the Church itself. In January 1881, the *Manchester Times* argued that 'the principle acted upon on the shores of Lough Mask are as old as the middle ages; they are a bequest from the Church. The great Boycotters of history are the Popes Gregory VIII and Innocent III'.[54] Later that month, the *Fortnightly Review* carried an article on this new menace of boycotting that suggested it was simply Catholic excommunication in a new guise. Other analyses argued similarly that there was a 'kindred theological hue' to popular disapprobation as a result of a prejudicial Catholicism, which had made 'the bulk of the Irish population [...] instinctively prone to a certain intolerance in their social relations'.[55] Priests came in for particular opprobrium, especially after Pope Leo XIII's encyclical *Saepe Nos* condemning boycotting, for remaining the 'warmest supporters and most industrious instigators' of the practice.[56]

If boycotting represented the pious tyranny of a morally self-righteous and hypocritical Catholicism to many of its critics, it also stood for the despotism of the democratic mob in a way that tied these themes of mental subjugation and mindless democracy together in the imaginations of the Land League's fiercest detractors. To Lecky, for instance, it was not a coincidence that the Catholic Church, what he described as the most democratic institution of Medieval Europe, should use 'the essential spiritual equality of mankind' as 'the most tremendous instrument of spiritual tyranny the world has ever seen'.[57] The Land League's boycotting was an example of such democratic majoritarianism, a 'new Jesuitism' which had 'much real affinity with the old one'.[58] The heavy involvement of local priests in the Land League was not incidental, and a sign, deeply worrying to Lecky, that 'Catholicism will in the future tend more and more to an alliance with democracy'.[59] This was partly a practical matter, a commitment to the social question in order to retain legitimacy and secure 'new elements of power in connection with the questions that most interest the working class'.[60] However, Lecky was also cognisant of the ideological linkages that made it possible; the socialistic language of the early Churchmen, the 'democratic character' of communal worship, the 'communistic life' of the monasteries, 'the long war waged by the Church against slavery', and, in particular, the role of Thomism and the later scholastic thinkers in pressing natural law arguments against political absolutism.[61]

[54] *Manchester Times*, 15 January 1881.
[55] 'Home and Foreign Affairs', *Fortnightly Review* 29, no. 169 (January 1881): 120; William A Hammond, 'The Evolution of the Boycott' *The Forum* (June 1886): 369.
[56] Lecky, *Democracy and Liberty*, vol. II, 11–12.
[57] Lecky, *Democracy and Liberty*, vol. I, 257.
[58] Lecky, *Democracy and Liberty*, vol. I, 224.
[59] Lecky, *Democracy and Liberty*, vol. II, 92.
[60] Lecky, *Democracy and Liberty*, vol. II, 94.
[61] Lecky, *Democracy and Liberty*, vol. II, 92, 233.

Irish Catholicism seemed then, both in practice and in theory, to represent a dangerously democratic, perhaps even proto-socialist force. In this, Lecky was reiterating the view of many Catholic radicals who were similarly keen to view Protestantism as a stepping-stone towards atheism, liberal individualism, and capitalist exploitation.[62] In the face of the dramatic social upheaval of the 1880s, wrought by the land question and George's campaigns, this bore a striking resemblance to the line taken by Rome itself as it sought to carefully balance labour's demands with the Church's own moral authority and a desire to maintain social order. Seeking a way out of the contemporary rhetorical confrontation between 'individualism' and 'collectivism', the Papacy relied heavily on Thomistic expressions of the 'common good' and natural harmony to argue for a limited notion of individual rights that rejected both economic libertarianism and the overarching moral authority of the state.

The most significant of a number of papal interventions on the social question was 1891's *Rerum Novarum*. It was ostensibly a denunciation of the excesses of socialism and a defence of private property inspired in part by the prominent role of Catholics in the land and labour movements in Ireland and the United States.[63] Nevertheless, in seeking to discredit socialist and social liberal thinking, the encyclical developed a number of strongly republican propositions.[64] Pope Leo XIII affirmed that 'the blessings of nature and the gifts of grace belong to the whole human race in common' and restated the Thomist position that labour was the only source of economic value.[65] While well beyond the mainstream of contemporary economic thought, these claims fitted comfortably with radical exegesis on the origins of economic value.[66] Drawing on the Thomistic concept of permissive Natural Law, in which possessive rights, either to property or to the self, were curtailed by the duties and obligations of social existence and subsumed within a broader system of ends, this Catholic critique of socialism had much to offer, albeit inadvertently, to republican radicals trying to draw out the egalitarian and liberationist possibilities of limited property ownership defined and delineated by a theory of natural rights rooted in the needs of the human body.[67]

[62] J. A. MacMahon, 'The Catholic Clergy and the Social Question in Ireland, 1891–1916', *Studies: An Irish Quarterly Review* 70, no. 280 (1981): 266; 'The Reformation was the capitalist idea appearing in the religious field', explained James Connolly, *Labour, Nationality and Religion* [1910] (Dublin: New Books, 1983), 60.

[63] P. Finlay, 'Socialism and Catholic Teaching', *Studies: An Irish Quarterly Review* 8, no. 31 (1919): 353; C. Joseph Nuesse, 'Henry George and "Rerum Novarum"', *The American Journal of Economics and Sociology* 44, no. 2 (1985): 241–254.

[64] Patrick Doyle, 'The Clergy, Economic Democracy, and the Co-operative Movement in Ireland, 1880–1932', *History of European Ideas* 46, no. 7 (2020): 985.

[65] Pope Leo XIII, '*De Rerum Novarum*: On Capital and Labour', 15 May 1891, pt. 8; see also Robert Curran, 'Confronting "The Social Question:" American Catholic Thought and the Socio-Economic Order in the Nineteenth Century', *U.S. Catholic Historian* 5, no. 2 (1986): 191.

[66] Sklansky, *The Soul's Economy*, 106.

[67] Tierney, 'Natural Law and Natural Rights', 401, 404; Tuck, *Natural Rights Theories*, 48–49, 149.

Just as Henry Maine had declared that an excessive focus on natural rights had historically animated the most dangerously radical democratic compulsions, the Church's focus on the very same prompted similar worries.[68] While Thomist thought had occupied a central place within the Church since the sixteenth century, the 'Catholic revival' of natural law thinking in the late-nineteenth century opened the door to the new 'social gospel' as a crusading mission against suffering and deprivation.[69] Although Rome's conception of the 'common good' included deference to ultramontane authority, Thomism also provided significant latitude for resistance to this demand.[70] Pope Leo XIII's declaration, articulated in *Rerum Novarum*, that 'man precedes the State, and possesses, prior to the formation of any State, the right of providing for the substance of his body' was a direct rebuke to the organicist idealism of social liberals that the state was itself the only moral arbiter.[71] As an argument against the natural divinity of the social order, it echoed the attacks of later scholastic Thomists against the divine authority of monarchical absolutists.[72] Apparent parallels between the ultimate authority claimed for the state by Stuart monarchs and that claimed by progressive liberal statesmen two centuries later were seized upon and developed by neo-Thomist thinkers at the turn of the twentieth century, who saw it as evidence of the Catholic origins of popular sovereignty and as a model for contemporary Catholic democracy.[73]

Catholic interpreters of natural rights sough to reconstruct an alternative genealogy to the familiar Protestant lineages, which had been developed by men such as Hugo Grotius and Samuel Pufendorf to fashion a defence of political authority secure from the incursions of Papal influence, and which had increasingly elevated rights over natural law.[74] In this line of thinking, Catholic theologians identified a creeping positivism that would eventually render the recourse to 'nature' as unnecessary as the recourse to the divine. In their alternative account, Catholic intellectuals like the American priest John A. Ryan later sketched a history of Catholic political thought in which, for instance, Thomas Jefferson's ideas on popular sovereignty were taken 'more or less directly' from the Thomistic tradition.[75] Ryan, along with figures such as Jacques Maritain in France, attempted to

68 Maine, *Popular Government*, vii.

69 McGreevy, *Catholicism and American Freedom*, 127–165; Sigmund, *Natural Law in Political Thought*, 180–194.

70 Rose Luminiello, '"Ireland Is Not Going to Take Her Orders from Rome": Leo XIII, Thomism, and the Irish Political Imagination', *History of European Ideas* 46, no. 7 (2020): 964–981.

71 Pope Leo XIII, '*De Rerum Novarum*: On Capital and Labour', 15 May 1891, pt. 7.

72 Skinner, *The Foundations*, 164; Paul E. Sigmund, 'The Catholic Tradition and Modern Democracy', *The Review of Politics* 49, no. 4 (1987): 534.

73 John A. Ryan, *Catholic Doctrine on the Right of Self-Government* (New York: Paulist Press, 1919), 5; O'Rahilly, 'The Catholic Origin of Democracy', 1–18; John Rager, 'The Blessed Cardinal Bellarmine's Defense of Popular Government', *Catholic Historical Review* 10 (1924): 504–515.

74 Haakonssen, and Seidler, 'Natural Law', 447.

75 Ryan, *Catholic Doctrine*, 5.

draw out the radical and communitarian implications of this Aquinian discourse, using the language of natural rights to conceptualise property ownership as limited to need, while also retaining the notion that each person was due a sustaining share in the collective wealth by *right*, since human needs were not an 'impulse towards acquisition', but themselves constituted 'a moral title'.[76]

This was part of a conscious opposition to the more paternalist forms of social liberalism that rejected rights discourses entirely. Merwin-Marie Snell, for instance, a professor at the newly established Catholic University of America in Washington, DC, attacked the Hobbesian core of liberal thought – 'an extreme individualism, limited only by the principle of the absolute unlimited authority of the state' – as being forever drawn to the poles of libertarianism and 'state despotism'.[77] While he characterised liberalism as either 'caesaristic' or 'bureaucratic', it was the term 'democracy' that he identified as a Catholic inheritance.[78] In Ireland, in the early years of the twentieth century, similar ideas were taken up and developed by the Jesuit academic, labour activist, and Sinn Feiner Alfred O'Rahilly, later the president of University College Cork, who observed in the Irish past the origins of a republican-democratic ethos, and an alternative fiction to the Anglo-Saxon 'seed of liberty'.[79] O'Rahilly's rejection of the social liberal claim that collective and individual rights existed only because of the state itself resonated not only with Leo XIII's similar assertions in *Rerum Novarum* but also republican nationalist critiques against the British state. In what could have been a defence of the political philosophy of the boycott, O'Rahilly argued that 'every community which, as a fact of social psychology, acts as a moral whole is a complete society'.[80] O'Rahilly also attacked economic marginalism, rejecting the idea that a science of exchanges could be removed from 'an ethical judgement based on the communal good', since the property being exchanged was itself secondary to the natural right of the individual to the necessities of life – something that could only be secured collectively.[81] For O'Rahilly, as for Ryan, the problem was not natural rights, but rather 'the absolute irresponsible character many have given it in recent times'.[82]

[76] John A. Ryan, *Alleged Socialism of the Church Fathers* (London: Herder, 1913), 18, 48; John A. Ryan, *Distributive Justice: The Right and Wrong of Our Present Distribution of Wealth* (New York: MacMillan, 1916), 316, 332; on this broader Catholic tradition, see Leonard Francis Taylor, *Catholic Cosmopolitanism and Human Rights* (Cambridge: Cambridge University Press, 2020).

[77] Snell, 'The Catholic Social-Reform Movement', 28.

[78] Snell, 'The Catholic Social-Reform Movement', 29.

[79] J. A. Murphy, 'Alfred O'Rahilly', in *Dictionary of Irish Biography* (Cambridge University Press); Alfred O'Rahilly, 'The Sovereignty of the People', *Studies: An Irish Quarterly Review* 10, no. 37 (1921): 39.

[80] Alfred O'Rahilly, 'The Democracy of St. Thomas', *Studies: An Irish Quarterly Review* 9, no. 33 (1920): 5.

[81] Alfred O'Rahilly, 'Aquinas versus Marx, Part II: The So-Called Labour Theory of Value', *Studies: An Irish Quarterly Review* 31, no. 124 (1942): 499; Alfred O'Rahilly, 'St Thomas's Theory of Property', *Studies: An Irish Quarterly Review* 9, no. 35 (1920): 341.

[82] Ryan, *Alleged Socialism of the Church Fathers*, 48.

Priests, Prelates, and the Land League in Ireland

The prominent role played by priests in the Land War only reinforced this connection between Thomist thinking and republican politics. The expanded fifty-three-person executive proposed at the founding of the League included thirteen priests, but their influence at a local level far exceeded this proportion, where they exercised both moral authority and administrative leadership. Using the republican terms of slavery and freedom, of possession rooted in bodily labour, priests sanctified resistance to landlordism as just and righteous and backed by Catholic natural law. The 'sublime morality of St. Paul's teaching' was commonly invoked as 'the main principle of the Land League's teaching', referring especially to St. Paul's Second Epistle which confirmed, Rev Timothy Shanahan explained, 'that the husbandman that laboureth must first partake of the fruits'.[83] This Pauline extract was well worn in the service of the League by Irish ecclesiastics, such as by Archbishop Croke of Cashel, in castigating English misgovernment for rejecting its moral truth.[84] In the history of Irish resistance, there had been, according to Fr Eugene Sheehy at Ballingarry, 'no high, no more sacred principle' than the Land League's call to root out the landlords and fix 'the Irish tenants in their steads'.[85] It was the landlords who were the thieves explained another parish priest at a meeting in Ballymeehan, Co. Leitrim: 'Was there anything more unjust than that one man should appropriate the toil of another'.[86]

In the west of Ireland, as the Land movement began to grow, priests took a lead in local efforts against landlords, even to the frustration of their superiors. James Magee of Castlebar, John O'Malley of The Neale (who, as Chair of the Ballinrobe Land League branch, helped to organise Captain Boycott's boycott), and Eugene Sheehy of Kilmallock were only a handful of the most prominent clergy who led the agitation. There was clerical representation at the vast majority of the League's public meetings, since it was in many cases the presence of supportive priests that determined the location of mass gatherings.[87] As respected local figures, parish priests had much experience interceding on behalf of their parishioners, collecting and petitioning for financial support, and administering the distribution of aid. With the onset of the land crisis, the charitable and clerical functions undertaken by many priests became more difficult to distinguish from directly political activity. Operating as trusted

[83] Timothy Shanahan, P.P. Ballingarry, at Ballingarry, 14 November 1880; M. W. Kirwan, Thurles, 14 November 1880 (MS 11,289, NLI).

[84] Handbill: public letter from the T. W. Croke, the Archbishop of Cashel to Father Ryan, Thurles, 10 August 1880 (Heffernan Papers, MS 21,910, NLI).

[85] Rev Sheehy, Ballingarry, 14 November 1880 (MS 11,289, NLI).

[86] Rev John McManus, Ballymeehan, Leitrim, 22 November 1880, *Freeman's Journal*, 23 November 1880.

[87] See, for instance, D. Ryan, C.C. in Cashel, to Thomas Brennan, 11 April 1881 (LLP, MS 17,693, NLI); Jordan, *Land and Popular Politics*, 243.

intermediaries, the Land League relied on local clergy to distribute relief funds where there was no nearby branch, in some cases simply sending small sums of money directly to priests to dispense as necessary.[88] Local relief committees, many headed by priests, soon morphed into Land League branches, and the humanitarian role of the priest often followed a similar trajectory into a more pointed critique of the causes of such systemic economic deprivation.[89] In their role as community advocates and messengers of popular discontent, George was personally 'very much impressed by the clergy of Ireland as a class'.[90]

Many priests came from farming backgrounds themselves and had little difficulty empathising with the League's grievances, even if some were resistant to its more assertive demands. The clergy also recognised that their significant social and political influence stemmed from their commitment to their community, and so walked a fine line between leading and being led.[91] Priests who adopted a hostile stance to the League could see their influence on their congregations waning.[92] Others, conversely, took pains to vocally proclaim that 'the Irish priest is with the Irish people (cheers). We love the cheer of the multitude'.[93] 'If we were not with the people', one priest proclaimed, 'we would not be Irish priests at all. (cheers)'.[94] Local clergy also had to delicately balance their own political inclinations and loyalties with the authority of their diocesan hierarchy, who were much less likely to be supportive of any radical proclivities. It was George's impression that 'the majority of the clergy are [...] with the people and the no rent fight, but they are for the most part "bulldozed"' by their superiors. He often received supportive and encouraging communications from priests who refused 'to allow their names to be used' publicly for fear of censure.[95] One curate, irate at the lack of support from 'unpatriotic PP's' [parish priests] who 'shamelessly stand with folded arms looking on', believed it was their cowardly concern about institutional reprimand that induced inaction.[96]

88 'Irish National Land League Relief Fund: Sums received for Relief of Distress by Irish National Land League, from 22 December 1879, to 30 April 1880 also Particulars of Grants made by Land League to Local Relief Committees, &c., from 22 December 1879 to 30 April 1880', 4 (Heffernan Papers, MS 21,910, NLI).

89 Moran, 'Near Famine', 164–166.

90 Henry George to Richard George, 10 February 1882 (HGP, Series I: A, Box 3, NYPL).

91 Biagini, *British Democracy*, 119; Jordan, *Land and Popular Politics*, 241.

92 Lucey, *Land, Popular Politics*, 23–24.

93 Rev Boylan, P.P. Crosserlough, at Bailiborough, 21 October 1880 (MS 11,289, NLI); see also 'The Bishops of Ireland', in Aurelius MacSwynie (ed.), *America's Sympathies with Ireland: A Summary of the Indignation Meetings, Speeches, Resolutions of Sympathy, and Letters in Favour of Ireland, Delivered, and Written by Archbishops, Bishops, Priests, Ministers, Governors of States, Senators, Congressmen, Lawyers, and Citizens in General of the United States* (Philadelphia: C. Dorwin Freeman, 1881), 6 (PAHRC, P.001.1830).

94 Rev Timothy Shanahan, Ballingarry, 14 November 1880 (MS 11,289, NLI).

95 Henry George to Patrick Ford, 10 November 1881 (HGP, Series I: B, NYPL); Annie George to Fr Thomas Dawson, 5 June 1887 (HGP, Series I: D, Box 11, NYPL).

96 P. A. MacDonnell, Ballycastle, to Mr. Rourke, 21 September 1880 (LLP, MS 17,693, NLI).

These tensions and difficulties did not hinder the widespread impression that priests were leading actors in the Land War, expressing a loyalty to the cause that was largely returned. While other denominations supported the wealthy, 'we in Ireland', declared Timothy Harrington, 'can boast a ministry, who throw their hat in with the people and against the people's oppressors'.[97] As well as shoring up an often fragile clerical–nationalist alliance, such utterances reinforced the emotive centrality of the priesthood to the mythology of Catholic Irish life. It was a sentiment captured effectively in James Redpath's effusive description of the Irish priest as 'the tongue of the blind Sampson of Ireland [who] toils for them from dawn until midnight'.[98] On the other side of the political divide, conservative critics of the League and government supporters railed against this coalition as evidence of the League's sectarian character, even as its leaders vocally denied any form of religious exclusion.[99] Clerical involvement 'with the forces of anarchy and disorder' of the land agitation elicited accusations of 'a priestly despotism' in which Thomist political language and ecclesiastical supervision combined together as evidence of a radical Catholic conspiracy.[100]

In the face of such condemnations, more senior ecclesiastics were inevitably presented with a daunting equilibrium between the demands of Roman authority, social stability, and lay support. The Irish hierarchy was firmly divided on the appropriate response to the Land League, and indeed the land question itself.[101] Just as with parish priests, the personal experience of particular bishops fashioned their attitudes towards the League's activities. Bishop Duggan of Clonfert, for example, one of the most confidently outspoken supporters of the League among the Catholic hierarchy, had remained closely involved with parish work since his ordination. With first-hand experience of the Famine, a horror that continued to haunt him, Duggan had been involved in the Tenant Right Movements of the late 1840s and 1850s, when his father had suffered eviction.[102] Duggan's political language, excoriating landlords' contractual

97 Quoted in Campbell and Kerr, 'Davitt in Carrickmore', 392.

98 *Connaught Telegraph*, 19 June 1880.

99 W. H. O'Sullivan, Ballingarry, 14 November 1880; David MacAteer, Dungannon, 1 November 1880 (MS 11,289, NLI); Terrence O'Neill to Thomas Brennan [n.d] (LLP, MS 17,693, NLI).

100 Lord Selborne, *Liberal Unionist*, 6 April 1887, repr. in *Claim of the Irish Priesthood to stand above the law* Irish Loyal and Patriotic Union, *Publications issued during the year 1887* (Dublin: Irish Loyal and Patriotic Union, 1887), 38; Lecky, *Democracy and Liberty*, vol. II, 11.

101 The most supportive prelates were Archbishop Croke of Cashel, and Bishops Dorrian, Nulty, MacCormack, and Duggan. Arrayed in opposition were Cardinal McCabe, Archbishop McHale, and Bishop MacEvilly, as well as several others, Larkin, *The Roman Catholic Church*, 24.

102 Thomas Brett, *Life of the Most Reverend Patrick Duggan, Bishop of Clonfert* (Dublin: W. Leckie, 1921), 70; 123; John Bradley, 'Archbishop McGettigan, the Catholic Bishops of Ireland and the Irish Land Bill 1881', *Seanchas Ardmhacha: Journal of the Armagh Diocesan Historical Society* 17, no. 2 (1998): 132.

rights for their 'infringement on the just rights of man', was typical of the Catholic republican response to the land question.[103] While Ireland's problems were the consequence of English blindness and misgovernment Duggan explained, it was only by focussing on universal moral truths grounded in 'principles in conformity with the eternal laws of Equity and Justice' that the land question could be solved.[104]

While only a comparatively small number of prelates evinced such strong and unqualified support for the League, many were keenly aware of the danger posed to their own authority by abstention from political engagement or passive opposition, an approach that Patrick Dorrian, Bishop of Down and Connor, identified as supremely 'short-sighted'.[105] Clerical influence would be severely damaged, argued Duggan, if the Catholic Church in Ireland did not find a way to play a part in the new political scene, and he feared that the intransigent hostility of some of the hierarchy, particularly that of Cardinal McCabe in Dublin, would 'do what persecution could not do – divorce the people from their Church'.[106] Even those critical of the League, such as Archbishop John MacEvilly of Galway, were conscious of popular sympathies and injustices, and alive to the risks of taking too firm a stance against them. MacEvilly wrote to Tobias Kirby of the Irish College in December 1879 to counsel Rome against issuing a denunciation of the League. Despite his opposition, he was forthright about the social and economic suffering in the country and shared his concerns in language similar to the republican tone of the League itself, complaining that the 'poor tenant [is] robbed of the fruit of the sweat of his brow, obliged to pay double rent for the land his own labor reclaimed from utter barren worthlessness'.[107]

A small number of prominent Church figures were outspoken supporters of the League, and the political ambitions of the land struggle as a whole, although such a position naturally invited hostility and condemnation from Church authorities. This was the experience of Thomas Croke, Archbishop of Cashel, who was faced with Roman resistance to his championing of the League. Hailing from a family of prominent religious men, Croke was an academically gifted theologian. He received a doctorate from the Jesuit College in Rome before teaching classics and divinity in Carlow and at the Irish College in Paris.[108] This scholarly stature, as well as his personal popularity, elevated his vocal backing of the Land League and made 'the illustrious Archbishop of

[103] Shields, '"Serving the Farmer"', 59.
[104] Bishop Duggan, quoted in 'The Bishops of Ireland', 7; Brett, *Life of the Most Reverend Patrick Duggan*, 142–143.
[105] Larkin, *The Roman Catholic Church*, 38.
[106] Henry George to Patrick Ford, 8 December 1881 (HGP, Series I: B, NYPL).
[107] 'The Bishops of Ireland', 10; Larkin, *The Roman Catholic Church*, 29.
[108] 'The Bishops of Ireland', 3–4.

Cashel' a major boon to the movement.[109] In the face of Ultramontane criticism, Croke portrayed Irish Catholicism as a distinctly national and demotic religion, acknowledging both the importance of national sentiment to the Church and the necessary accommodation of the League as an alternate centre of moral and political power. After Parnell's imprisonment, Croke was even asked to step in as the nominal head of the League, although he refused this implausible appointment, much to the disappointment of the conservative elements of the league who had hoped his influence would have been a check on its more radical tendencies.[110] This may have been a forlorn hope in any case, as Croke's private expressions reveal an even stronger and more single-minded support for the Land League and opposition to British rule; a 'mean and merciless' power to which the Irish should pledge themselves 'never to make peace with'.[111]

Resisting rather than incorporating the League's social influence was the favoured strategy of Dublin's Cardinal Edward McCabe. Following the death of his predecessor, Cardinal Cullen, the *Irish World* had cautioned that 'it will not do to place in Ireland, under pretence of religion, a Cardinal whose proclivities are against Irish aspirations'.[112] These warnings went unheeded, and, despite his sympathies with the plight of the farmers, the new Archbishop of Dublin expressed his belief that the actions of Parnell had 'brought the country face to face with revolutionary and communistic doctrines'.[113] In response to McCabe's firm grip on the political activities of his priests, he earned the ire of the nationalist movement and was even subjected to threats. His pastoral denouncing the 'No-Rent Manifesto' for destabilising the fundamental rights of property was met with anger among many and served only to highlight how McCabe's intransigent hostility to the implicit radicalism of the land movement endangered the Church's authority in Irish society. This was certainly Croke's opinion as he bemoaned McCabe's distance from popular sentiment.[114]

While McCabe's efforts at suppression were by no means uniformly successful – he admitted himself their unpopularity and his difficulty in keeping 'some of the young priests in this Diocese quiet' – the wider authority of the Church hierarchy did inhibit clerical support for the League.[115] Even tentative endorsements were consequently very significant. The League made the most

[109] Fr McKeogh, P. P. Ballinahinch, Tipperary, 31 October 1880 (MS 11,289, NLI).
[110] Fanny Parnell to Patrick A. Collins, 10 November 1881 (Patrick A. Collins Papers, Series 1, Box 2, Boston College).
[111] T. W. Croke to John Dillon, Thurles, 23 November 1881 (Harrington Papers, MS 8577, NLI).
[112] *Irish World*, 30 November 1878.
[113] C. J. Woods, 'The Politics of Cardinal McCabe, Archbishop of Dublin, 1879–85', *Dublin Historical Record* 26, no. 3 (1973): 103.
[114] Woods, 'The Politics of Cardinal McCabe', 103.
[115] Larkin, *The Roman Catholic Church*, 48.

of favourable pronouncements, publishing and distributing them widely.[116] The more radical prelates, such as Bishop Thomas Nulty of Meath, were under significant pressure from Rome, although there was a tacit understanding in the country at large that their 'free, full opinions' were under ecclesiastical constraint.[117] In long conservations with both Duggan and Nulty, George became clear 'that absolute orders from Rome are holding back such men as [Duggan] and Nulty', and he lamented the fact that they refused to make public their most forthright opinions.[118] Pope Leo XIII's 1883 circular *De Parnellio* was the culmination of this pressure for Roman intervention, but its limited impact demonstrated the inadequacy of such top-down interference in the face of popular support and gave credence to George's opinion that open clerical advocacy would fully ignite the land movement.[119]

Undoubtedly the most significant and far-reaching ecclesiastic intervention was Bishop Nulty's *The Land Question: Letter of the Most Rev Dr Nulty to the Clergy and Laity of the Diocese of Meath*. Written in April 1881, it was in part an anticipation of Gladstone's land act, which the Bishop was 'not very sanguine' about.[120] Nulty's essay began by comparing landlordism to human slavery, 'the most odious and cruel injustice that ever afflicted humanity'.[121] While both moral wrongs had been accepted as economic necessities, the Bishop observed that 'the practical approval [...] which the world has bestowed on a social institution that had lasted for centuries is no proof that is ought to be allowed to live on longer, [if] it be found to be intrinsically unjust and cruel'.[122] Chattel slavery was an analogue to landlordism for the Bishop in a deeper sense, too. Drifting seamlessly into a familiarly republican register, Nulty explained that 'abject, absolute and degrading dependence' of the kind inescapably induced by having to rely 'on the arbitrary and irresponsible will of [a] landlord' was 'the very essence, and is, in fact, the definition of slavery'.[123] Irish peasants were 'dependent for their peace of mind, for their material comforts, [...] and for the right of earning their bread', on the whims and commercial inclinations of the vested land owners, in what he declared to be 'the twin sister of slavery'.[124] Their economic condition was inexcusable, and their need and suffering unconscionable,

[116] Handbill: Public letter from the T. W. Croke, the Archbishop of Cashel to Father Ryan, Thurles, 10 August 1880 (Heffernan Papers, MS 21,910, NLI).

[117] Henry George to Patrick Ford, 22 November 1881 (HGP, Series I: B, NYPL).

[118] Henry George to Patrick Ford, 8 December 1881 (HGP, Series I: B, NYPL).

[119] Vincent Comerford, 'The Parnell Era, 1883–91', in W. E. Vaughan (ed.), *A New History of Ireland, vol VI: Ireland under the Union, 1870–1921* (Oxford: Oxford University Press, 1989), 54; Larkin, *The Roman Catholic Church*, 162–194; Henry George to Patrick Ford, Dublin, 28 December 1881 (HGP, Series I: B, NYPL).

[120] Thomas Nulty, *The Land Question: Letter of the Most Rev. Dr. Nulty to the Clergy and Laity of the Diocese of Meath* (Dublin: Joseph Dollard, 1881), 4.

[121] Nulty, *The Land Question*, 8.

[122] Nulty, *The Land Question*, 9.

[123] Nulty, *The Land Question*, 9.

[124] Nulty, *The Land Question*, 9.

but the Bishop was clear that these ruinous consequences stood downstream from their dependence and effective enslavement.

Nulty's palpable seething anger at the injustice of private monopolisation of the land, as well as the publicity and promotion provided by the *Irish World*, gained the piece widespread notoriety.[125] George described to Patrick Ford how it was 'growing up all over the country [because] the priests are distributing it', and that 'the tory papers and all the English papers are reprinting it as an outrageous official declaration of communism from a Catholic Bishop'.[126] Karl Marx, struck by the remarkable 'declaration against landownership (private) by an Irish bishop', instructed 'the ever faithful Engels' to send a copy of the *Irish World* in which it was reprinted to his daughter Jenny in order that she might 'frighten the French clericals'.[127] After meeting in person, George and Nulty were full of mutual admiration in recognition of their shared principles and purposes. George reported that his 'visit to Bishop Nulty was most delightful', declaring: 'I never met a man that seemed to me to more fill the idea of a Rev Father in God. How I wish he were Pope.'[128] For his part, the Bishop later wrote to George that '*Progress and Poverty* appeared to me to be the best work ever written on the science of Political Economy since the publication of "The Wealth of Nations"'.[129]

Bishop Nulty's pastoral letter was also as clear a statement as could be found connecting the distinctively Thomist and republican strands of thinking that converged on the Irish land question. To George, the Bishop's published opinions on the land question were practically indistinguishable, and 'quite as "Communistic" as my own', and he reused Nulty's turns of phrase in his own subsequent writing.[130] While Nulty saw the 'Three F's' as perhaps the best that could be hoped for in the present circumstances, he demanded that any final settlement of the land question be based on 'the eternal and immutable principles of justice which determine the character of property in land'.[131] From the assumption of a natural right to life and to the use of ownership of that which one has made, the Bishop argued that the singular purpose of land was collective subsistence, a right to which could not be alienated, either individually

125 Henry George, *Irish World*, 28 January 1882.

126 Henry George to Patrick Ford, Dublin, 28 December 1881 (HGP, Series I: B, NYPL).

127 Karl Marx to Jenny Longuet, 7 December 1881, in *Karl Marx and Frederick Engels: Ireland and the Irish Question* (Moscow: Progress Publishers, 1971), 331.

128 Henry George to Patrick Ford, 10 November 1881 (HGP, Series I: B, NYPL); Henry George, 'Visit to Bishop Nulty', 1881 (HGP, Series II, Box 12, NYPL).

129 Thomas Nulty to Henry George, 27 February 1882 (HGP, Series I: A, Box 3, NYPL).

130 Henry George, *Irish World*, 25 March 1882; Henry George, *Irish World*, 2 September 1882; George was convinced, through private conversations, that Bishop Nulty opposed compensation for landlords and supported Davitt's nationalisation scheme, although he refused to publicly endorse these positions. Henry George to Patrick Ford, 6 June 1882 (HGP, Series I: B, NYPL).

131 Nulty, *The Land Question*, 10.

or collectively, since 'that would be tantamount to a nation committing suicide'.[132] In terms redolent of the corporeal republican focus on the body, the Bishop argued that 'no one can have an exceptional right to claim more than a fair share of what was intended equally for all; and what is, indeed, directly or indirectly, a necessary of life for each of them'.[133] Only human labour could create a right of property. The conclusion of this, for Bishop Nulty, was that land could only ever be held privately in usufruct and that 'the people of that country, in their public corporate capacity *are*, and always *must* be, the real owners of the land of their country'.[134]

The prelate added, however, that the right of a farmer to remain undisturbed as long as he was utilising the land productively and 'for the advancement of the general interests of the community' (as well as his absolute right to the 'fruits of his labour') was 'founded on the strictest principles of justice' and stood beyond the reach of the state, whose role was simply 'recognition and protection' of these natural rights.[135] This final recoil from advocating the absolute authority of a (democratic) state over the land was instructive of the wider tensions that land radicals had to confront. Like other republican thinkers, Nulty refused to allow the collective ownership of land, which he believed was implicit in the Aquinian right to life, to dissolve its own ideological foundations. Like the Pope's subsequent declaration in *Rerum Novarum*, Nulty maintained that ultimately, 'man precedes the state'. Much of Nulty's letter was concerned with establishing incontrovertibly that the natural fertility of the soil could and ought to be distinguished from man-made improvements to productivity and that land was not 'an ordinary article of private property'.[136] Such an approach was necessary to the retention of a natural right to land that outweighed both the vested proprietary rights of a landlord and the ultimate authority of a governmental authority, even that acting on behalf of the 'community'.

To support his position, the Bishop drew on familiar passages on land from Mill's *Principles*, as well as other prominent titles such as Arthur Arnold's *Free Land*.[137] It was from this second book in particular that Nulty extracted a number of his key references, such as to Joshua Williams' *Principles of the Law of Real Property*, and it is evident that he relied heavily on the piece for his argument.[138] The author of this work, the radical liberal M.P. for Salford, saw a collective interest in land ownership emerging from an acknowledgement of the individual's right to sustenance. Yet, unlike the Bishop, Arnold insisted

[132] Nulty, *The Land Question*, 14, 18. [133] Nulty, *The Land Question*, 19.
[134] Nulty, *The Land Question*, 19. [135] Nulty, *The Land Question*, 20.
[136] Nulty, *The Land Question*, 24.
[137] Arthur Arnold, *Free Land* (London: Kegan Paul & Co., 1880).
[138] Joshua Williams, *Principles of the Law of Real Property, Intended as a First Book for the Use of Students in Conveyancing* [1845], 9th ed. (London: H. Sweet, 1871).

that any rights to the land were secondary to that of the state, which should facilitate free competition in land for the wider benefit of the community, only suggesting compulsory purchase 'whenever the inalienable joint interest of the public' demanded it.[139] Arnold's analysis was much more in tune with that of progressive liberals like Henry Fawcett, where initial insistence about the uniqueness of property in land tended to become quickly overshadowed by matters of expediency and productivity, thereby deflating that very same claim of distinctiveness. Arnold's work, which was typical of the liberal transition from the land question toward social welfare, was an influential text, but had no place for 'natural rights', and was largely unconcerned with matters of political or social dependence. For the Bishop, however, mirroring George's analysis, the political dimension remained central to the distribution of land. Not only his religious framework, but the Irish context itself, demanded as much.

George and the American Catholic Church

The spiritual tone of *Progress and Poverty* was inescapable. That an economic treatise was 'so percolated with religious phraseology and so profusely adorned with Scriptural quotations' struck many as unusual and provided a convenient explanation for the book's popular success that sidestepped its actual arguments.[140] But the intense religiosity of the work was not, as some critics implied, a pretence or façade designed to lure the gullible. Like many other radicals of the period, George's political arguments were developed through his intellectual engagement with a non-denominational corpus of Christian thought and remained coherently founded within this tradition.[141] It was accessible to both Catholic and Protestant alike; George's recourse to a powerfully egalitarian Christ as familiar and resonant to Catholics such as Terence V. Powderly or Fr Edward McGlynn as much as any Protestant social reformer.[142]

George's early life prepared him well for such cross-confessional religiosity. In the Quaker state of Pennsylvania, his upbringing had been characterised by a firm religious devotion, the family being prominent and active members of St. Paul's Episcopal Church during the height of the second 'great awakening'. While imbibing a heavy diet of biblical study, however, George 'bucked the current of piety at home'.[143] He was intellectually rebellious and found the religious intensity stifling. Instead, George would later find his own personal route to religion, rejecting Episcopalianism for the plain and simplified rituals

[139] Arnold, *Free Land*, 191. [140] Lecky, *Democracy and Liberty*, vol. II, 357.
[141] Claeys, 'Non-Marxian Socialism', 545; Jones, *The Christian Socialist Revival*, 99.
[142] Terence V. Powderly, *The Path I Trod: The Autobiography of Terence V. Powderly* (New York: Columbia University Press, 1940), 39.
[143] Barker, *Henry George*, 10, 12.

of Methodism. His marriage to Annie Corsina Fox, an Australian Catholic of Irish descent, in 1861 only widened his ecumenical outlook. In his own mind, George's political aspirations had deep roots in theology, in the radical implications of scripture, and the example of Christ, that grounded his visceral hatred of economic injustices, and were not confined to any denominational affiliation.[144] His pointed critiques of the 'House of Have' dwelt on religious hypocrisy and spared no institution, observing with frustration that 'many of those who call themselves Christians do not begin to appreciate the deep philosophy of Christ'.[145]

As would be expected for such a prolific orator, George circulated regularly through an extended repertoire of speeches. Among his most trusted and well-received talks – particularly popular in the Scottish Highlands – was his extended reflection on 'Moses'.[146] First presented to the Young Mens' Jewish Society of California, George's appreciation for his subject rested partly on Moses' appeal as a universal authority; as George reminded his audience, 'three great religions place the leader of the Exodus upon the highest plane they allot to man. [...] Moses is the mouthpiece and law-giver of the Most High'.[147] It was through Moses that George attempted to trace the roots of the 'recognition of the common right to land' beyond Aquinas to the very fabric of Abrahamic religion. As he explained, 'it is not the protection of property, but the protection of humanity, that is the aim of the Mosaic code. [...] At every point it interposes its barriers to the selfish greed that if left unchecked will surely differentiate men into landlord and serf, capitalist and workman, millionaire and tramp, ruler and ruled'.[148] The appeal of this talk, for George and his rapt audiences, was in its expansive and inclusive social theology – a biblical endorsement of what George believed were timeless truths.

Despite this ecumenical approach, George continued to endure an uneasy relationship with the Catholic Church in the United States. Seeing a radical theology encased within a reactionary institution, his appeals to American Catholics showed little reverence for ecclesiastical authority, and he sought instead to highlight 'the distinction Catholic theology makes between the Church and Church officialism'.[149] Unsurprisingly, this was not an approach well calculated to win him many supporters among the hierarchy. In 1891, writing after over a decade of both cooperation and conflict with many Catholic clergy, George forlornly hoped 'that the spirituality of the Church could in

[144] Hilton, *The Age of Atonement*, 299.
[145] Henry George to Patrick Ford, 17 May 1882 (HGP, Series I: A, Box 3, NYPL).
[146] Barker, *Henry George*, 248–250.
[147] Henry George, 'Moses' (HGP, Series II, Box 13, NYPL).
[148] Henry George, 'Moses' (HGP, Series II, Box 13, NYPL); George, *Progress and Poverty*, 333.
[149] Henry George to Fr Thomas Dawson, 9 December 1888; Henry George to Fr Thomas Dawson, 22 December 1891 (HGP, Series I: D, Box 11, NYPL).

some way be separated from its political and corrupt machines'.[150] At the same time, however, George's own skirmishes with the Church only accelerated and exacerbated existing tensions within the institution itself over what its role in American public life should be. George's popularity, along with the power and influence of the Land League and organisations like the Knights of Labor, forced the American Catholic Church to become more involved in what was delicately termed the 'social question'.[151] Conservative and progressive wings of the hierarchy were already at loggerheads over the level of acculturation and accommodation the Church should afford to American civic institutions.[152] As the 1880s dawned, the most pressing issue became the Church's response to simmering economic and political unrest; unrest in which Irish Catholics, both at home and abroad, were prominent players.

At first, things were relatively simple. The American hierarchy was broadly positive towards the general aims of the Land League. During Parnell's tour of the United States in the early months of 1880, John Ireland, the Bishop of St. Paul, was of the opinion that 'no fault can be found with the agitation [...] the means are legal, the demands reasonable'.[153] Cardinal McCloskey of New York offered a much more reserved endorsement, but affirmed the value of charitable support for the suffering Irish poor, a theme which Parnell emphasised in his speeches. Yet, cautioned the Cardinal, the money should only be used to 'keep bodily distress from the homes of the Irish peasant', and not for 'any political projects for the attempted bettering of his holding in the land'.[154] As Parnellism gave way to Georgism, and relief to 'no rent', the attitude of the conservative Catholic hierarchy towards the agitation in Ireland hardened considerably.

In McCloskey's opinion, the social radicalism of the Land League, just as with the vocal nationalism of the Fenian movement, drew undue attention to Irish Catholics in America. His long-standing worry, shared by many others even within broadly nationalist circles, was that supporting radicalism and potentially violent agitation might 'incite perhaps the anger and disgust of the American people against us'.[155] Fomenting revolution in Ireland served no

150 Henry George to Fr Thomas Dawson, 22 December 1891 (HGP, Series I: D, Box 11, NYPL).
151 Robert E. Curran, 'Confronting "The Social Question:" American Catholic Thought and the Socio-Economic Order in the Nineteenth Century', *U.S. Catholic Historian* 5, no. 2 (1986): 165–193; Foner, 'Class, Ethnicity, and Radicalism', 170; Brown, *Irish American Nationalism*, 148.
152 John T. McGreevy, Catholicism and American Freedom: A History (New York: Norton, 2003), 112–122.
153 *The Pilot*, 13 March 1880; on Parnell's Tour: F. S. L. Lyons, *Charles Stuart Parnell* (Dublin: Gill and Macmillan, 1977), 100–105.
154 'Interview with Cardinal McCloskey on the Irish Relief Fund', *New York Herald*, 3 January 1880 (Cardinal McCloskey Papers, A-32, Archives of the Archdiocese of New York).
155 Cardinal McCloskey and the Fenian Movement, *New York Herald*, 3 March 1866 (CMP, A-31, AANY).

valuable purpose, as he saw it, to improve the lives of American Catholics. It 'seems unwise', he reflected, to press Irish politics into American public life, since 'the political interests of our people are here'.[156] Yet McCloskey knew, not least from his own experiences of trying to supress Fenianism in the 1860s, that the hierarchy's control over their priests and their congregations was never rigid, and that, to a greater or lesser degree, the Church must yield to some social demands.[157] Very quickly after Parnell's American tour and the establishment of the American wing of the Land League, the organisation became closely associated with and supported by local priests, much like it was in Ireland.[158]

McCloskey and his successor as Archbishop and then Cardinal of New York Michael A. Corrigan were keenly aware of the appeal of the Land League, labour radicalism, and George's social philosophy among their extensive working-class flock. Indeed, some Irish-American Catholics, confronted by the ostensible conflict between their political ideals and religious loyalties, wrote directly to their Archbishop for clarification on these matters. It was clear that for some of these correspondents, their deep religious faith and personal understanding of Catholic theology was the primary impetus for their interest in labour politics. Was it not true that the 'Church forbids the taking of Usury', queried one parishioner.[159] Another asked straightforwardly: 'Can I remain in communion with the Catholic Church, while accepting the land theories of Henry George?', explaining that his support for these ideas derived from the hope that 'there would be a more equal division of the land which God undoubtedly made for all'.[160] Similar enquires were made on behalf of labour organisations, which many Catholics perceived to offer a meaningful realisation of the principles of natural justice.[161] The deeply Christian worldview that informed George's ideas, and the perception, resulting from this, that 'Mr. George is not a socialist in the sense condemned by right reason and the Church' was of particular concern to the American hierarchy.[162] Grounding his proposals for the emancipation of land in a religious discourse not only made George more appealing to many Irish Catholics, but far more threatening to the Church itself.

156 'Interview with Cardinal McCloskey on the Irish Relief Fund', *New York Herald*, 3 January 1880 (CMP, A-32, AANY).

157 Oliver Rafferty, 'Fenianism in North America in the 1860s: The Problems for Church and State', *History* 84, no. 274 (1999): 276; Cardinal McCloskey and the Fenian Movement, *New York Herald*, 3 March 1866 (McCloskey CMP, A-31, AANY).

158 John Talbot Smith, *The Catholic Church in New York: A History of the New York Diocese from Its Establishment in 1808 to the Present Time*, vol. II (New York: Hall & Locke, 1905), 387.

159 James Vincent to Cardinal McCloskey [n.d.] (CMP, A-30, AANY).

160 Richard M. Carney to Michael A. Corrigan, 14 December 1884 (Archbishop Corrigan Papers, C-7, Archives of the Archdiocese of New York).

161 Thomas J. Doyle to Michael A. Corrigan, 15 April 1886 (ACP, C-7, AANY).

162 *Catholic Herald*, 4 December 1886, quoted in Green, 'The Impact of Henry George's Theories', 152.

No other episode demonstrated this more forcefully, and stirred conservative prelates to defensive action, than the 'McGlynn Affair'. The ideological alliance between Henry George and the immensely popular New York priest Rev Dr Edward McGlynn drove home the potential synchronicity between Georgite ideas and Catholic social thought, and the danger that George's association with the radical wing of the Land League and similarly adjacent labour organisations could pose to the intellectual authority of the Catholic Church. Edward McGlynn was the parish priest of St. Stephen's Church on East 29th Street, a heavily Irish area of Manhattan. Born on the Lower East Side of New York in 1837, McGlynn's early life had been financially comfortable. His parents, Peter and Sarah, had left Donegal thirteen years earlier and made their money in construction. Earmarked early for the priesthood on account of his intellect, the young Edward was sent for study to the Urban College of the Propaganda in Rome before his ordination in 1860.[163] He was only twenty-nine years old when he became the pastor of St. Stephen's, where he set about developing local welfare institutions, such as the establishment of an orphan asylum, that would support the growing tide of new Catholic immigrants into his parish. McGlynn's fame, and his notoriety among his superiors, grew as a result of his involvement in questions of public welfare and social justice. His resistance to Catholic parochial education in favour of public schools and his progressive racial politics (one parishioner complained to the Archbishop that McGlynn had told his congregation 'that the Blessed Virgin was a color'd women') were but some of the political episodes that brought him to public prominence.[164] Indeed, McGlynn's reputation as 'the best known priest of the time' and his widespread popularity reaching far beyond New York meant that Cardinal McCloskey, who remained in post until his death in the autumn of 1885, recognised the propriety of handling his most rebellious priest delicately.[165]

McGlynn was not an anomaly, however. By the 1870s, he was a leading member of New York's *Academia*, an informal collective of well-educated, impassioned, and socially radical priests. His friends and confidants in this circle, many of whom had known him since his days in Rome, included the popular Fr Sylvester Malone of the Church of SS. Peter and Paul in Williamsburgh, Brooklyn, as well as Frs Crimmins, Ducey, Farrell, and McGlynn's clerical lawyer and adviser Rev Dr Richard Lalor Burtsell.[166] This radical nucleus became, in the 1880s, active and vigorous supporters of both George and the

[163] Stephen Bell, *Rebel, Priest and Prophet: A Biography of Dr. Edward McGlynn* (New York: Devin-Adair, 1937), 1–6.
[164] Anon to Cardinal McCloskey, 21 January 1871 (CMP, A-28, AANY).
[165] Talbot Smith, *The Catholic Church in New York*, 305–306; Bell, *Rebel, Priest and Prophet*, 21; Brown, *Irish-American Nationalism*, 122.
[166] Robert E. Curran, 'Prelude to "Americanism": The New York *Academia* and Clerical Radicalism in the Late Nineteenth Century', *Church History* 47, no. 1 (1978): 48–65.

Land League. Malone, for instance, used his pulpit to campaign for the League and explained, in terms that laid bare the worrisome nature of George's theories for the Catholic hierarchy, that Henry George had 'translated into political economy and civil government the doctrines always inculcated by my Church'.[167] This coterie, just like the priests on Land League platforms in Ireland, moved seamlessly between a Thomistic language of natural law and the republican claims for all to possess the 'fruits of their labors' by right.[168] McGlynn introduced his most careful statement of political principles, which he was required to present to the Papal envoy Msgr Francis Satolli as a condition of his readmittance to the Church in 1892, with the affirmation of this natural right to life which brought with it, inescapably, a common right to land. He began: 'All men are endowed by the law of nature with the right to life and to the pursuit of happiness, and therefore with the right to exert their energies upon those natural bounties without which labor or life is impossible.'[169]

As this would suggest, McGlynn's ideological alignment with George was almost absolute. His work was a thunderous echo of George's, replete with references to 'industrial slavery', the 'rights of men for universal justice', and the 'monopoly of natural bounties'.[170] Like Bishop Nulty, too, McGlynn emphasised the parallels between slavery and land monopoly. The divine source of each person's right to the land 'requires no parchment to prove', explained McGlynn, but was inalienably rooted in the innate needs of the human body. 'The mere fact that he is here, a human being endowed with this nature is the one indispensable title to this joint, equal usufruct of all the bounties of nature.'[171] Like George, McGlynn's radical politics was deeply invested in a republican construction of liberty, viewing 'absolute dependence of one person upon another' as 'against the law of nature', and drew consciously on the history of American radical republicanism.[172] Land's 'unearned increment' produced the only ethical tax, which would grow 'by a natural law proportionately with the growth of civilization' and allow all other taxes to be abolished.[173]

[167] Fr Sylvester Malone, *The Standard*, 9 April 1887, cited in Greene, 'The Impact of Henry George's Theories', 203.

[168] Fr John Crimmins, *New York Tablet*, 18 February 1882; Fr Sylvester Malone, *New York Tablet*, 2 April 1881.

[169] 'Doctrinal Statement of Revered Doctor Edward McGlynn, Presented by him to the Papal Ablegate Monsignor Francis Satolli, by whose direction it was examined by four Professors of the Catholic University, Washington, DC, December 1892. Declared to contain nothing contrary to Catholic Teaching', in Fr Sylvester Malone, *Dr. Edward McGlynn* (New York: Dr. McGlynn Monument Association, 1918), 47.

[170] 'Thoughts of Dr. McGlynn', in Sylvester L. Malone, *Dr. Edward McGlynn*, 106, 105, 57.

[171] 'Thoughts of Dr. McGlynn', in Sylvester L. Malone, *Dr. Edward McGlynn*, 56.

[172] 'Thoughts of Dr. McGlynn', in Sylvester L. Malone, *Dr. Edward McGlynn*, 90.

[173] 'Doctrinal Statement of Revered Doctor Edward McGlynn', in Fr Sylvester Malone, *Dr. Edward McGlynn*, 49.

McGlynn's famous address 'The Cross of a New Crusade' inaugurated his Anti-Poverty Society in the spring of 1887 and was accompanied by commemorative souvenirs depicting 'The People's Priest' on a stars-and-stripes shield, swathed in oak laurels reminiscent of the Roman *Corona Civica* ('Civic Crown'). On the soil below lay not only a spade and pickaxe, but a copy of *Progress and Poverty* and two Mosaic tablets bearing the inscription: 'The earth belongs in usufruct to the living – Tom Jefferson.'

The experience of ministering to the grinding poverty around him had left McGlynn searching for solutions, and in George's book, he had found 'so clear an exposition of the cause of the trouble, involuntary poverty, and its remedy' that he 'became all aglow with a new and clearer light'.[174] As he would explain at George's funeral in 1897, McGlynn viewed the social philosopher as 'a seer, a forerunner, a prophet; a teacher sent from God'.[175] McGlynn had been involved in the American Land League right from its inception and was a member of the Provisional Central Council of the organisation established during Parnell's American tour.[176] Yet his direct involvement with George's campaign came, as with so many other relationships in the Irish-American labour world, through the connections made by Patrick Ford, editor of the *Irish World*. At Ford's invitation, McGlynn spoke at New York's Cooper Union in the summer of 1882 alongside Michael Davitt after the latter's arrival from Ireland. It was here where McGlynn encouraged the Irish leader to abandon his cautious approach and publically embrace George's ideas, which were, he noted, simply the 'same platform' as 'Bishop Nulty of Meath'.[177]

Georgists and labour radicals alike hoped that McGlynn would quickly become an active agitator, dedicated to spreading the light across industrial America, but the intervention of Cardinal McCloskey put paid to such prospects.[178] Fearful of losing all he had built at St. Stephen's, and under pressure from Rome, McGlynn agreed to refrain from public political interventions. This détente largely held until 1886, when George's campaign for the mayoralty of New York under the banner of a united labour front drew McGlynn back out into political advocacy. Ignoring several warnings from the new Archbishop of New York, Michael A. Corrigan, to desist, McGlynn continued to attack the allure of wealth and power within the Church and, even more dangerously, insist

174 Edward McGlynn, quoted in Bell, *Rebel, Priest and Prophet*, 23.

175 'Address of the Rev. Edward McGlynn, D.D.' in Edmund Yardley (ed.), *Addresses at the Funeral of Henry George, Sunday, October 31, 1897, At the Grand Central Palace, New York City* (Chicago: The Public Publishing Company, 1905), 35.

176 Printed letter dated 30 March 1880 (Devoy Papers, MS 18,048(3), National Library of Ireland).

177 *Irish World*, 15 July 1882.

178 'I have been advocating the idea among the K. of L. [Knights of Labor] that they try to hire you and Father McGlynn for the campaign and keep you in the field all the time', G. Y. Malcolm to Henry George, Flint, Michigan, 8 December 1882 (HGP, Series I: A, Box 3, NYPL); Henry George to Fr Thomas Dawson, 1 February 1883 (HGP, Series I: A, Box 4, NYPL).

that land was common property.[179] After being invited to Rome by Cardinal Simeoni, the Prefect of the Propaganda, to explain himself, the radical priest declined. He replied to Simeoni: 'I have taught, and I shall continue to teach, in speeches and writings, as long as I live, that land is rightfully the property of the people in common, and that private ownership of land is against natural justice, no matter by what civil or ecclesiastical laws it may be sanctioned.'[180]

Further summons and snubs followed, before McGlynn was officially excommunicated in July 1887.[181] This lengthy episode pitted the radical social thought and popularity of the 'the people's priest', as McGlynn came to be known, against the authority of Archbishop Corrigan and the Church's ultramontane establishment. It was a dangerous tactic for the conservative hierarchy and risked deepening extant fissures in the Church. When McGlynn was removed from his post at St. Stephen's, accounts suggest that tens of thousands gathered to protest this clerical authoritarianism.[182] Annie George, Henry's Catholic wife, observed with some dismay the popular hostility that the Archbishop's punishments had elicited. 'It is sad to hear', she wrote, 'as I did last night the name of the highest dignitary, hissed loudly and strongly by Irish Catholics men and women'.[183]

Corrigan insisted that it was McGlynn's insubordination that led to his censure, that it was a matter of his 'rebellion'.[184] It is true that the prelate, as the youngest ever American bishop, had a strict and domineering attitude, and adopted an uncompromising, authoritarian approach.[185] McGlynn's involvement in George's campaigns was particularly problematic since it provided the imprint of clerical consent. His intellectual charisma was also deeply worrying, and he 'was leading many young priests astray by his ability to fascinate them', as well as coordinating the visits of radical priests from Ireland.[186] But the attack on McGlynn for disobedience had the significant advantage of circumventing more thorny theological questions. George, certainly, was in

179 Edward McGlynn, 'The Pope in Politics' (ACP, G-67, AANY).

180 Edward McGlynn to Cardinal Simeoni, 20 December 1886 (Public record of McGlynn Case, MSS: L.3, AANY).

181 Talbot Smith, *The Catholic Church in New York*, vol. II, 544–545.

182 Edward T. O'Donnell, '*Soggarth Aroon*, The Rise and Fall of Rev. Edward McGlynn', in Terry Golway (ed.), *Catholics in New York: Society, Culture, and Politics, 1808–1946* (New York: Fordham University Press, 2008), 158; Robert E. Curran, 'The McGlynn Affair and the Shaping of the New Conservatism in American Catholicism, 1886–1894', *The Catholic Historical Review* 66, no. 2 (1980), 184.

183 Annie George to Fr Thomas Dawson, 5 June 1887 (HGP, Series I: D, Box 11, NYPL).

184 Archbishop Corrigan to Anon., 24 December 1889 (Public record of McGlynn Case, MSS:L.3, AANY).

185 Greene, 'The Impact of Henry George's Theories', 146.

186 Bernard McQuaid to Michael A. Corrigan, 27 December 1886 (ACP, C-16, AANY); Frances Silas Chatard to Michael A. Corrigan, 10 August 1882 (ACP, C-2, AANY); James A. Healy to Michael A. Corrigan, 15 November 1881 (ACP, C-2, AANY).

little doubt that the attacks on McGlynn were driven primarily by a desire to sever Catholic support for his ideas without the unenviable challenge of having to explicitly condemn them as morally unsound. In the wake of McGlynn's excommunication, Archbishop Corrigan disingenuously proclaimed that the Church now 'has no quarrel with the George land doctrine except that it considers it poor political economy'.[187] James Healy, Bishop of Portland, Maine, subsequently wrote with incredulity to Corrigan, rightly unable to believe that this was his position, but Corrigan's need to distance George's land theories from theological consideration was itself revealing.[188]

Archbishop Corrigan, alongside his close ally Bishop Bernard McQuaid of Rochester, made concerted efforts to undermine and discredit McGlynn. McQuaid shrewdly advised Corrigan not to fight McGlynn on theological grounds, but to attack his character. He suggested dwelling instead on the difficulties 'he has brought on the cause of Catholic education by neglecting to provide schools for his children, [...] and be careful to make known how easy it would have been for him, with his large and able congregation, to pay off the heavy debt that still weighs down the parish'. McQuaid went on to suggest accusing McGlynn of embezzlement.[189] Animosity towards McGlynn seems to have been an invigorating experience for McQuaid in particular, who warned Corrigan after the removal of McGlynn that 'the next one you will have to gag or squelch will be [Fr.] Ducey', adding on another occasion that at least the episode had brought 'to the surface much scum that it is good to get rid of'.[190] Vindictiveness was evident in the firing of Ellen Garvin, a maid in the rectory at St. Stephen's, who had been reported by a member of the congregation for expressing her continued support for the exiled McGlynn.[191] The Archbishop even sought out theological opinion in Rome on the possibility of excommunication for those who attended a McGlynn meeting.[192]

Such intrigue only appeared necessary to Archbishop Corrigan because of the challenges involved in refuting McGlynn's public statements on their own terms. In Rome, Corrigan and his allies worked hard to get George's book condemned by the Holy See, but were resisted by those, such as Cardinal Gibbons of Baltimore and Cardinal Manning of Westminster who were concerned

[187] 'The Catholic Church's Position Toward McGlynn, Henry George and Powderly', newspaper clipping (ACP, C-15, AANY).

[188] James A. Healy to Michael A. Corrigan, 27 March 1888 (ACP, C-15, AANY).

[189] Bernard McQuaid to Michael A. Corrigan, 11 December 1886 (ACP, C-16, AANY).

[190] Bernard McQuaid to Michael A. Corrigan, 17 January 1887 (ACP, C-16, AANY); Bernard McQuaid to Michael A. Corrigan, 13 January 1887 (ACP, C-16, AANY).

[191] Thomas F. Lynch to Michael A. Corrigan, 20 January 1888 (ACP, C-19, AANY).

[192] Rev Elias F. Schauer, C.SS.R to Archbishop Corrigan, 20 May 1888 (ACP, C-20, AANY). The archives also show the existence of a poorly forged confession from McGlynn supposedly showing that he had been married to a women named Anna Salomon in 1886, 'Enclosed purportedly written by Edward McGlynn' (G.67, folder 2, AANY).

about the damaging effects of an open Catholic censure of George (as well as being more sympathetic towards the general thrust of his ideas).[193] Writing to Corrigan personally, George warned that an outright condemnation of McGlynn and himself 'would but give point to the assertions of those who are striving to alienate workingmen from the Church'.[194] One priest counselled similarly that hostility to labour activism would make it seem as though 'the Church takes sides with the rich and powerful against them, and imprudent action would be [likely] to alienate many of them'.[195]

To the more conservative members of the American hierarchy, the sympathetic tone taken by many prelates towards Georgism, and the labour movement more broadly, was shocking. Explicit radicalism of the type espoused by Bishop Nulty caused one Corrigan ally to exclaim: 'They have all gone crazy!'[196] But as the liberal modernisers in the American Church recognised, not only did active opposition to George and McGlynn run the risk of 'array[ing] the labor party and the Irish national party against the Church', but in fact their ideas merited no such Catholic condemnation, and indeed exhibited a striking intellectual reciprocity with developing Catholic social teaching.[197] Cardinal Gibbons felt compelled to remind Rome that 'the theories of Henry George differ from those ordinarily called socialism or communism' and held out no grounds for condemnation.[198] The ever-enervated McQuaid fumed at such distinctions, and was appalled by the sympathetic approach towards the radical Irish nexus taken by Cardinal Gibbons and others.[199] He went as far as to claim, with an element of justification, that 'Cardinal Manning and Bp. Nulty [are] responsible for much of George's influence'.[200]

Nevertheless, and despite the challenges it presented, Corrigan and his allies in the American Church were at the forefront of constructing a Catholic refutation of George's ideas. The social philosopher's popularity, particularly during

193 Charles E. McDonnell to Michael A. Corrigan, 9 February 1888 (ACP, C-19, AANY). Denis O'Connell, the Cork born rector of the North American College in Rome, and former secretary of Cardinal Gibbons in Baltimore, worked to ensure that the sympathetic interpretations of Cardinals Gibbons and Manning were received by the Pope prior to any decision.

194 Henry George to Michael A. Corrigan, 30 September 1886 (ACP, C-8, AANY).

195 Rev Msgr George A. Doane, to Michael A. Corrigan, 3 June 1886 (ACP, C-7, AANY).

196 'I cannot believe that he means all that his words [imply]', Henry A. Brann to Michael A. Corrigan, 19 January 1887 (ACP, C-6, AANY); James A. Healy to Michael A. Corrigan, 18 March 1891 (ACP, C-15, AANY).

197 Patrick W. Riordan, Bishop of San Francisco to John J. Keane, 24 January 1887, cited in Greene, 'The Impact of Henry George's Theories', 159.

198 Cardinal Gibbons to Cardinal Simeoni, 26 February 1887, quoted in the *Standard*, 9 April 1887.

199 Bernard McQuaid to Michael A. Corrigan, 28 December 1887 (ACP, C-16, AANY); Bernard McQuaid to Michael A. Corrigan, 1 February 1887 (ACP, C-16, AANY). For his part, Gibbons rejected claims that he was an active supporter of McGlynn in his battle with Corrigan, but the impression was certainly present. Cardinal Gibbons to Michael A. Corrigan, 30 April 1887 (ACP, C-15, AANY).

200 Bernard McQuaid to Michael A. Corrigan, 22 January 1887 (ACP, C-16, AANY).

1886, provoked a flurry of articles and pamphlets which attempted to repudiate his views on property in distinctly Catholic terms. The threat of the 1886 mayoral election had prompted Archbishop Corrigan to issue a pastoral letter denouncing the labour campaign and correcting those lost, disenchanted souls 'led astray by Mr. George', although he largely left the theological detail to other clerics.[201] The Archbishop's interest in formulating logically coherent critiques of George's political economy was not merely theoretical, of course, given the wealth that the Church extracted from rent. While hoping for 'Divine Providence to thwart the machinations of evil minds' like McGlynn and George, Archbishop Corrigan added a positive conclusion to one missive; he had heard from the Bahamas that 'they have discovered a gold mine there in the shape of fibre manufacture which yield a large profit', to which he had 'secured 1,000 acres at $1.20 per acre'.[202]

Many Catholic critiques were scattergun in their approach, simply condemning socialism generally, or demonstrating their unfamiliarity with George's work by attacking his atheism and scientism, or his centralising unpatriotic politics, despite all evidence to the contrary.[203] If misrepresentation was unerringly common, so was a failure to grapple with the critical distinction George made between land and other forms of property, or between land values and human labour. Bishop James O'Connor of Omaha, for instance, accepted that the right to land rested upon the 'right to live, and, therefore a right to the means of living', but took this as a simple defence of all forms of property.[204] Like the theologian Victor Cathrein, O'Connor defended private individuation of land on the basis of a morally justifiable first occupancy ('a thing without an owner becomes the property of the first occupant'), and in this way the private possession of land need not be distinguished from the right to its fruits.[205] Cathrein, a notable Swiss-German Jesuit whose refutations of socialism and social-democracy were translated into at least eight languages, accepted the Thomistic principle that 'all men indeed have the same right to exist', but denied that this had anything to do with possession of the land, reverting to a narrower liberal argument that 'this right implies nothing more than that every one's life is sacred and inviolable against every unjust attack'.[206]

Some condemnations exhibited a pervasive sense of complacent authority in their glib and imprecise criticisms, while others gave the impression of a harried

[201] E. Ellery Anderson, to Michael A. Corrigan, 23 November 1886 (ACP, C-6, AANY).
[202] Michael A. Corrigan to Bernard McQuaid, 12 March 1889 (ACP, C-18, AANY).
[203] O'Connor, 'Socialism', 224; Greene, 'The Impact of Henry George's Theories', 161; Cathrein, *The Champions of Agrarian Socialism*, 10, 15, 14; Brann, *Henry George and his Land Theories*, 3, 4.
[204] O'Connor, 'Socialism', 225.
[205] Cathrein, *The Champions of Agrarian Socialism*, 44, 104; O'Connor, 'Socialism', 225.
[206] Cathrein, *The Champions of Agrarian Socialism*, 108; see also Victor Cathrein, *Socialism: Exposed and Refuted* (New York: Benziger Brother, 1982); Victor Cathrein, *Socialism: Its Theoretical Basis and Practical Application*, 8th ed. (New York: Benziger Brothers, 1904).

rummage through a clutch of intellectual snares, which were presented to the reader and then quickly discarded before their inconsistencies became too evident. While Cathrein accepted that 'every man has a natural right to appropriate for his use as much as is strictly necessary for the immediate preservation of his life', for obvious reasons, he demurred from developing this point further.[207] Dr Henry A. Brann, contra Cathrein, accepted that 'the authority of the state is from God, and that the state has the right of eminent domain [...] to curtail private ownership for the benefit of the whole community', before adding, 'how far this right of eminent domain may extend we are not going to discuss'.[208] This was clearly a surprising admission in a work purporting to deal precisely with that question. It spoke to a familiar circularity, common to many hostile evaluations, in which George's claims were attacked on moral grounds, but private property only defended on the basis of its greater productive utility.[209]

The most frequent point of contention, just as in non-Catholic critiques, was the idea that land could be considered separately from other forms of property. Rev Edward Higgins, president of St. Xavier College in Cincinnati, rejected this possibility since all objects were, directly or indirectly, products of the soil.[210] Brann similarly denied that land could ever be considered separately from either its products or its social values. 'Must we for the future build our houses on stilts, to keep the improvement separate from the thing improved', he inquired facetiously.[211] Increasing values were only 'accidentally' caused by the community, according to Brann, and therefore incurred no commensurate social repayment. He privately confided to Archbishop Corrigan what was clearly evident from his work, that he had 'read a good deal' to fully understand what he was critiquing, 'except on the "unearned increment", on that I could find nothing'.[212] The same obstacle had confronted Higgins, who, evidently not a reader of Mill, dismissed the issue as nonsense: 'nor can we stop to analyze that ingenious but visionary speculation which Mr. George styles the "unearned increment"'.[213] This refusal to countenance the distinction between land and moveable property, and between the use and exchange value of land, was pervasive. As one presumptuous correspondent explained to Archbishop Corrigan, there was a difference between 'the products of labor on one hand', and 'land' on the other, but 'in your case they are very often confused, [...] and confounded'.[214]

207 Cathrein, *The Champions of Agrarian Socialism*, 46.

208 Brann, *Henry George and His Land Theories*, 6.

209 Brann, *Henry George and His Land Theories*, 5–8; Rev Edward A. Higgins, *Fallacies of Henry George, Exposed and Refuted: The True Philosophy of the Land Question* (Cincinnati: Keating & Co., 1887), 16.

210 Higgins, *Fallacies of Henry George*, 11–12.

211 Brann, *Henry George and His Land Theories*, 15.

212 Henry A. Brann to Michael A. Corrigan, 19 January 1887 (ACP, C-6, AANY).

213 Higgins, *Fallacies of Henry George*, 8.

214 George E. Swani to Michael A. Corrigan, 22 November 1885 (ACP, C-12, AANY).

Constructing a solid theological refutation of George's claims on their own terms proved to be an insurmountable challenge for Corrigan and his allies, a fact that accounts for the Archbishop's subsequent restraint on George's social philosophy, as well as his allies' chaotic condemnations. George's personal popularity among Irish-American Catholics, together with his coherent radical theology, was wildly disorientating for the conservative hierarchy in America.[215] In the light of such rhetorical flailing, the acceptance of McGlynn's political declaration by Rome in 1892 and his return to the Church was something of a vindication both for the *Soggarth Aroon* ('the dear priest') himself and for the Catholicity of his (and George's) ideas on land. The encyclical *Rerum Novarum* the previous year, in acknowledging that land was divinely given 'to minister to the needs of all', had given enough latitude to enable McGlynn to accommodate his political principles, and to which he gave his 'full adhesion'.[216] Although not solely a direct response to George, *Rerum Novarum* was prompted by the theological uncertainty that George provoked. The question of denouncing George's work was consciously diverted by the Papacy into the development of a broader encyclical on labour and capital, and both Corrigan and George himself believed that it was a reaction to his ideas.[217] The grounding of a common ownership of land in a natural right to life, which drew on both Thomist and republican ideas, appeared far more threatening to the Catholic Church, at least in the United States and Ireland, than the atheistic claims of Marxism.

[215] Brann, *Henry George and His Land Theories*, 17; Henry A. Brann to Michael A. Corrigan, 8 December 1886 (ACP, C-6, AANY).

[216] Pope Leo XIII, '*De Rerum Novarum*: On Capital and Labour', 15 May 1891, pt. 8; Edward McGlynn to Msgr Francis Satolli, 23 December 1892, in Malone, *Dr. Edward McGlynn*, 52.

[217] Rev Charles E. McDonnell to Michael A. Corrigan, 25 January 1888 (ACP, C-19, AANY); Michael A. Corrigan to Thomas S. Preston, 22 December 1891 (ACP, C-18, AANY).

5 Transatlantic Radicalism and the Land Question

'For English readers', explained Eleanor Marx and Edward Aveling, detailing the contours of American socialism in 1891, 'it is not necessary to give any description of George or his views'.[1] Such was the towering reputation of the man within radical circles by the end of the 1880s. But his focus on 'land alone' had been, in the assessment of these socialist luminaries, entirely 'played out' – a dead end: 'As far as a real working class movement is concerned, he is a ruined man.'[2] George's familiar radical reasoning, in which a right to life, through the necessities of the human body, justified a universal right to natural resources – his corporeal republicanism – had achieved remarkable success, replicated in the work of Bishop Nulty and Edward McGlynn. For socialists like the Marx-Avelings, Fabians like the Webbs, as well as new liberals like J. A. Hobson, George's importance, however, like that of the land question more broadly, remained limited to that of an accidental instigator of both working-class mobilisation and greater state intervention in social questions.

This narrative reaffirmed George's obsolescence while subsuming the land question into a politics of class or social welfare, allowing both socialists and new liberals to regard Georgism and the Irish land agitation as the inchoate stirrings of their own new, transformative politics. Largely discarded in both interpretations were the decentralist, participatory, naturalised rights claims that underwrote George's radical politics. As it has been shown, since property in land was both rooted in the rights of the individual and universal to all, democratic political participation was a necessary feature of this political economy, theoretically immune from the intercession of either a specific class of proprietors or the state as representing the community as a whole. George's moralist crusade refused property in land on 'the very principle of the right to property', and it paradoxically demanded in response a rejection of such rights in order to protect property from its own dangerously destabilising logic.[3] This

[1] Edward Aveling, and Eleanor Marx, in Paul LeBlanc (ed.), *The Working Class Movement in America* [1891] (Amherst: Humanity Books, 2000), 171.

[2] Aveling, and Marx, *The Working Class Movement in America*, 175, 204.

[3] Eugenio Biagini, *Liberty, Retrenchment and Reform: Popular Liberalism in the Age of Gladstone*, 1860–1880 (Cambridge: Cambridge University Press, 1992), 10.

severed the radical agrarian thread by which land connected all humans to political power

The meanings of 'socialism' and 'liberalism' were also subject to fierce contestation during the 1880s: George had begun the decade aligned with socialists and was marked as an aberrant and obsolete individualist at its end. This was less a matter of any personal adjustment (his obdurate focus on the land question was a firm restraint in this respect), than what was effectively an ideological revolution. George's republicanism, one that carried with it echoes of its hopeful eighteenth-century revolutions, was discarded as naïve and laughably insufficient to meet the problems of the time. Moreover, the agrarian radicalism typified by George and the Irish Land League, albeit in different ways, came to be seen as a retrogressive force by both socialists and social liberals alike, who were soon distrustful of its intransigent individualism and archaic natural rights arguments. This chapter looks to trace the significance of the Irish Land War and George in the defeat of this lost liberalism.

Radicalisms

The idea that land was distinct from other forms of property was a defining feature of the Paineite democratic radicalism that dominated transatlantic working-class resistance for most of the nineteenth century.[4] Landlords and financiers, those who neither toiled nor spun, remained the most familiar foes, condemned for their appropriation of the earth and unnatural profiteering.[5] British, Irish, and American radicals grounded their ideas of political and economic justice on what they saw as the unimpeachable natural right to labour on the land for sustenance and security. This underwrote their distinction of the productive as opposed to unproductive classes of society, and the appropriation not only of wealth but of rightful political power from the former by the latter.

In Britain, these ideas drove the Chartist campaigns of the 1830s and 1840s. Ending the monopoly of land would not only secure to the workers the fruits of their labour, but break their political oppression by ensuring their independence. 'We consider that the monopoly of land is the source of every social and political evil', explained the Chartist newspaper *The Poor Man's Guardian* in April 1834.[6] Hostile to Malthusian analyses just like their transatlantic cousins, the Chartists, and particularly Irish leader Fergus O'Connor, assumed a corrupted but recoverable natural harmony existed and that simply the removal of impediments to justice would be sufficient to enable economic and political

[4] Thompson, *The Making of the English Working Class*, 105. On Thompson's own relationship to this intellectual lineage, see Tim Rogan, *The Moral Economists: R. H. Tawney, Karl Polanyi, E. P. Thompson, and the Critique of Capitalism* (Princeton: Princeton University Press, 2017).

[5] Jones, *Languages of Class*, 134, 157.

[6] *Poor Man's Guardian*, 148 (4 April 1834), quoted in Chase, *The People's Farm*, 8.

emancipation.[7] While the Chartist 'Land Plan', which drew heavily on Irish experiences and traditions, was largely unsuccessful, limited in scale and ambition in contrast to similar American projects, the legacies of Chartism moulded the late-nineteenth-century radical imagination.[8] Michael Davitt's formative years growing up in the Lancashire mill town of Haslingden, and his education at the Mechanics Institute there, were steeped in this radical tradition.[9] Even into the 1870s and the mobilisation of English agricultural labourers known as the 'Revolt of the Field', did Chartist agrarian ideas remain prominent points of reference and the matter of land nationalisation central to socialist organising.[10] In Scotland in particular, owing to the acuity of Highland struggles, land retained its totemic significance well into the early twentieth century.[11]

A similar philosophy of agrarian producerism was if anything more dominant in the United States. Antebellum America boasted an array of labour radicals who explained, in a language of nonconformist Protestantism and Jeffersonian republicanism, that all social and economic oppression stemmed from the iniquitous distribution of land.[12] For these radicals, men such as Thomas Skidmore and Cornelius Blatchley, the idea that land should not be a commodity that facilitated acquisitive individualism, and that workers should own the full product of their labours themselves, were two sides of the same coin.[13] Fearing both political and moral dissolution, these Georgist predecessors reshaped republican concerns into an explicitly labour-orientated programme – Skidmore led, in the form of the New York Workingmen's Party of 1829, what Marx believed to be the world's first labour party – and focussed their ire on the soul crushing effects of a relentless competition for survival.[14] Land offered an escape and a way to reclaim a natural harmony in society.

[7] Malcolm Chase, '"Wholesome Object Lessons": The Chartist Land Plan in Retrospect', *The English Historical Review* 118, no. 475 (2003): 59–85.

[8] Bronstein, 'Land Reform and Political Traditions', 35; David Lloyd, 'The Clachan and the Chartists: Irish Models for Fergus O'Connor's Land Plan', *Irish Review* 47 (2013): 34.

[9] King, *Michael Davitt*, 5; John Dunleavy, 'Michael Davitt's Lancashire Apprenticeship', *Journal of the Galway Archaeological and Historical Society* 59 (2007): 109–121.

[10] J. P. D. Dunbabin, 'The "Revolt of the Field": The Agricultural Labourers' Movement in the 1870s', *Past & Present* 26 (1963): 68–97; H. J. Perkin, 'Land Reform and Class Conflict in Victorian Britain', in J. Butt, and I. F. Clarke (eds.), *The Victorians and Social Protest: A Symposium* (Newton Abbot: David & Charles Archon, 1973), 177–212; R. Harrison, 'The Land and Labour League', *Bulletin of the International Institute of Social History* 8, no. 3 (1953): 169–195.

[11] The Scottish section of the SDF was called the Scottish Land and Labour League. See also James Hunter, 'The Politics of Highland Land Reform, 1873–1895', *The Scottish Historical Review* 53, no. 155 (1974): 45–68.

[12] Sean Wilentz, *Chants Democratic: New York City & the Rise of the American Working Class, 1788–1850* (New York: Oxford University Press, 1984), 184–185; Pessen, *Most Uncommon Jacksonians*, 108.

[13] Wilentz, *Chants Democratic*, 159; Sklansky, *The Soul's Economy*, 114.

[14] Lewis S. Feuer, 'The North American Origin of Marx's Socialism', *The Western Political Quarterly* 16, no. 1 (1963): 61, 65; Wilentz, *Chants Democratic*, 183, 160–161; Edward Pessen, 'Thomas Skidmore, Agrarian Reformer in the Early American Labor Movement', *New York History* 35, no. 3 (1954): 280–296.

Although Skidmore's ideas lay at the extremities of popular opinion, similar political claims and republican language, denouncing middlemen, bankers, financiers, and various incarnations of speculators, found a home nearer the mainstream in the 'Locofoco' wing of the Jacksonian Democrats.[15] During the middle of the century, a multiplicity of artisan and farmers organisations could claim the mantle of this democratic republican radicalism. George Henry Evans, who, alongside Thomas Skidmore had been instrumental in the Workingmen's Party, later founded the National Reform Association with the Irish Chartist Thomas Ainge Devyr. Aiming to resettle urban workers on western lands, the dream was to create a patchwork of small townships with landholding restrictions; communities of self-sufficient farmers and craftsmen that would develop model participatory democracies and escape 'the cringing, the fawning and the lying' endemic to urban wage labour.[16] They were, according to one newspaper, 'neither more nor less than English Chartists transported to this country'.[17] In the 1870s, this agrarian impulse found an outlet in farmers' movements such as The Grange, which sought railroad and financial regulation and the establishment of cooperative enterprises, and propelled future Populist leader Ignatius Donnelly to prominence, and the Greenback-Labor Party.[18] Donnelly, author of the Populists' 'Omaha Platform', which demanded a return of the 'fruits of the toil' to the labourer, shared George Henry Evans' belief that land ownership should be limited.[19] He expressed the immutable connection between land, productive fertility, and human need, when he explained that it was 'right and wise and proper for men to accumulate sufficient wealth to maintain their age in peace, dignity and plenty', but that there should be 'a maximum beyond which no man could own property'.[20]

Many of the same radicals populated these movements and organisations, and a shared political language mirrored this shared recruitment. Front and centre, supporting the analysis of exploitation by land monopoly, was a discourse of natural rights. Thomas Ainge Devyr, after his active involvement in Chartism and the National Reform Association, would later write polemics

15 Alexander Saxton, *The Rise and Fall of the White Republic: Class Politics and Mass Culture in Nineteenth-Century America* (London: Verso, 1990), 206.

16 *The Landmark*, quoted in Bronstein, 'Land Reform and Political Traditions', 32; Feuer, 'The North American Origin', 53; Ellis, 'Radical Lockeanism', 831.

17 *The Sun* (New York), quoted in Devyr, *The Odd Book*, pt. II., 139.

18 Paul Crawford, 'The Farmer Assesses His Role in Society' in Paul H. Boase (ed.), *The Rhetoric of Protest and Reform, 1878–1898* (Athens, OH: Ohio University Press, 1980), 101–131.

19 The Omaha Platform of the People's Party of America (4 July 1892), in Howard Zinn, and Anthony Arnove (eds.), *Voices of a People's History*, 229–230.

20 Ignatius Donnelly, *Caesar's Column: A Story of the Twentieth Century* [1890], Walter B. Rideout (ed.), (Cambridge, MA: Harvard University Press, 1960), 104.

on the land question for the New York *Irish World* and become a cautious supporter of George.[21] Devyr's first political tract, self-published in Belfast in 1835 when he was still largely unknown, was entitled simply *Our Natural Rights*. It was intent on demonstrating to the 'famished tillers of the soil' 'and my brothers of industry and toil' that the roots of their oppression lay not in sectarian dominance, but in the 'absolute ownership of land', which gave to the landlord an exacting and demeaning political power.[22] 'The land was indisputable [sic] given to supply the natural wants of man', and, inquired Devyr, could there by anyone 'so stultified as to deny the self-evident truth of this position?'[23] Inevitably, Devyr devoted considerable attention to delineating the differences between land and moveables, arguing that, evident from the law of Moses, there was a 'complete line of demarcation' between the two, as well as an obvious distinction between 'the land itself' and the 'productions' on it.[24] Accordingly, it was both the needs and the correspondent productive capabilities of the body, Devyr explained, that justified access but not ownership of the land. To the landlord he declaimed: 'NOTHING *but your wants and nakedness appealing to its Creator* could give you a claim on it [land] – those wants supplied, the claim is discharged'.[25] Even Devyr's solution was a prototype of George's: 'An inconsiderable levy off the land which GOD has bestowed on us, would support a vigilant and efficient Government.'[26]

Constructing a popular republican government funded by the communal right to labour on the land appeared to Devyr, as it later would to McGlynn, a system of such perfect, beautiful simplicity and harmony that it must have been divinely ordained. Like the needs and abilities of the human body, the intent discernable in the natural world provided a model for society that was both commonly perceptible and secure from sophistries and twisted justifications. The 'natural state of things', free from landlord exploitation and enjoying 'the providence of Nature', would be, according to Devyr, a bucolic vista of happy and productive small farms, each interdependent on each other, so that if one sought advantage over another, 'the indignant reply of the clan' would be exile and alienation (or, to commit a small anachronism, boycotting).[27] Tying the

[21] Michael A. Gordon, 'Studies in Irish and Irish American Thought and Behaviour in Gilded Age New York City' (PhD dissertation, University of Rochester, 1977), 480; Wilentz, *Chants Democratic*, 373; *Irish World*, 23 November 1878; Devyr formed the opinion that George was a centraliser, seeking to vest all rents in a powerful machinery of the state, and decried this tendency, although obviously so did George himself. On Devyr, see Whelehan, *Changing Land*, 121–145.

[22] Thomas Ainge Devyr, *Our Natural Rights: A Pamphlet for the People* [1835] (Williamsburg, NY: T. A. Devyr, 1842), 3, 5, 6.

[23] Devyr, *Our Natural Rights*, 24–25. [24] Devyr, *Our Natural Rights*, 25–26.

[25] Devyr, *Our Natural Rights*, 25. [26] Devyr, *Our Natural Rights*, 9.

[27] Devyr, *Our Natural Rights*, 23–24, 35.

culturally specific to the universal by means of their material connection to the natural world, Devyr explained that it was 'the nature-taught peasant of Ireland and the North of Scotland' that had secured republican freedom during the American Revolution.[28] In the battle to reclaim humanity's rightful natural inheritance, Ireland (and to a lesser extent Scotland) had again been in the vanguard for this same reason, fighting against 'those who impiously counteract the beneficent designs of God and Nature'.[29]

In 1840, five years after he had arrived from Ireland, Devyr left England for America. In his new homeland, he encountered a 'great *popular* error', which, owing to the vast expanses of potential land, assumed that 'every individual must be free to accumulate as much as he pleases'.[30] Devyr rejected such 'speciousness', explaining that those who advocated for unlimited acquisition were actually 'the violators of, and tramplers on, the rights of property', and immediately set to work correcting this misconception.[31] He began writing for Brooklyn's *Democratic Review*, producing articles attacking public debts, land monopoly, private railroad ownership, and the 'distressing [...] crush and struggle of life'.[32] Finding conflict with his fellow countrymen over the role of religion in politics, he became involved in the New York anti-rent agitation, made contact with former Chartist colleagues in America, such as a County Durham schoolmaster named Edward Lawson, and started the National Reform Association with Evans. Drawn back to Irish matters by the Famine, Devyr remained congenitally irate at Irish nationalists who failed to exhibit sufficient radical purpose, castigating Thomas Francis Meagher for failing to acknowledge that every citizen has 'the right to dig bread out of that Republican soil', and reminding William Smith O'Brien that 'Ireland for the Irish' should mean nothing less than collective ownership of the land.[33] He later wrote articles on the land question for the Fenian paper *The Irish People*, although his caustic personality tended to make him more enemies than friends in the movement for Irish self-government.

In the late 1850s, Devyr founded the Tax-Payers Association, seeking to secure a Constitutional limit to taxation, before sailing for Ireland and England in 1860 to reconnect with former Chartist and radical friends such as Bronterre O'Brien and George Jacob Holyoake. The outbreak of the American Civil War was conflicting for Devyr, for although he despised the 'horde of anti-Christian inhuman planters' and 'insolent, inflated aristocrats' of the South, he recoiled at the idea of preventing succession by force of federal government, and was deflated by the subsequent relegation of the land question.[34] To Devyr, unchained labour

[28] Devyr, *Our Natural Rights,* 11. [29] Devyr, *Our Natural Rights,* 36.
[30] Devyr, *Our Natural Rights,* 43. [31] Devyr, *Our Natural Rights,* 44.
[32] Devyr, *The Odd Book*, pt. I., 156; pt. II., 33. [33] Devyr, *The Odd Book*, pt. II. 62, 64.
[34] Devyr, *The Odd Book*, pt. II, 111–112.

without land remained an insidious slavery itself, and he castigated the failure to follow emancipation with the natural inheritance of land for all.[35] The Land War, however, provided Devyr with the opportunity to reconnect the Irish republican cause with his passion to reclaim the universal and natural right to land, and on discovering that the *Irish World* was also a firm advocate of paper money and land reform, he joined the staff of the paper in 1877. From this perch, Devyr continued to inveigh against landlordism as the inversion of nature.[36]

All through his long, polemical career, which involved friendships and fights with radicals and reformers from Gerrit Smith to Orestes Brownson, Devyr remain fixed upon the ownership of land as the key to reclaiming natural rights and a natural harmony. 'Social, as well as political salvation', he explained, 'depends upon finding out what Natural Right is, and bravely adopting it'.[37] Devyr was by no means the only radical to embody the ideological triumvirate of land reform, natural rights, and the cause of Ireland, a country where, as many argued, the worst of legalised feudalism still reigned supreme. John Francis Bray, author of the influential 1839 book *Labour's Wrongs and Labour's Remedy*, traversed the Atlantic too, becoming involved in Chartism, and latterly, the Knights of Labor and the Populists – Bray was archetypical in his attacks on national debt, centralised state power, and the private ownership of natural resources which ensured that property in land is always followed by '*property in man*'.[38] In Britain, George had encountered his work, scribbling a revealing quote in his notes to be used in subsequent speeches: 'As nature and wants of all men are alike, the rights of all must be equal.'[39] A corporeal republicanism again providing the outline for an egalitarian politics.

By the late nineteenth century, these ideological commitments remained central to radical politics in the United States. They inspired Hendrick B. Wright, a Pennsylvanian lawyer and Democratic (and latterly Greenback) congressman, who had become well known for his attempts to modify the 1862 Homestead Act with the provision of government loans to enable workers to take advantage of western resettlement.[40] As Wright explained, the Irish fight for land and independence had, throughout the century, been a mirror to his own republican convictions. It was Wright's view that any person 'living under a republican government' who did not support the Land League lacked 'exalted manhood',

35 Devyr, *The Odd Book*, pt. II, 116. 36 Devyr, *The Odd Book*, pt. II, 181.
37 Devyr, *The Odd Book*, pt. II, 140.
38 Jamie Bronstein, *John Francis Bray: Transatlantic Radical* (Pontypool: Merlin Press, 2009), 32, 35, 51; John Francis Bray, *Labour's Wrongs and Labour's Remedy*, 33–34.
39 A handwritten transcript by Henry George from *Labor's Wrongs and Labor's Remedy*, 'Notes and Extracts Re: Britain' (HGP, Series II, Box 12, NYPL).
40 William F. Deverell, 'To Loosen the Safety Value: Eastern Workers and Western Lands', *Western Historical Quarterly* 19, no. 3 (1988): 273; see also, Hendrick B. Wright, *A Practical Treatise on Labor* (New York: G. W. Carlton, 1871).

since land was a 'common inheritance', and its monopolisation was 'subverting the cherished theories of our fathers'.[41] Wright viewed his own involvement in the Land League, right at the end of his life, as a culmination of his political commitments. Not only did he link the Irish land struggle with earlier radicalism, but he saw it as part of a more universal emancipation in which 'there is quite as much necessity for an American, as an Irish Land League'.[42] Irish land had played a significant and continuing role in transatlantic republicanism for several generations of radicals, but it is clear that the 'residual but ineradicable individualist presuppositions' of the demand for 'natural rights' remained far closer to the surface of political discussion in Ireland and the United States than they did in Britain.[43]

Other impulses tended to dominate the question of land reform in Britain, often expressing more spiritual, paternalist, or nationalist dimensions that would soften its radical democratic edges. While drawing on hostility towards technology, economic centralisation, and the deskilling of artisans, the notion of a particular rural spirituality, of communing with nature, often governed urban and suburban calls to go 'back to the land' in Britain. John Ruskin's vision of a 'quasi-feudal agrarian society', for instance, highlighted that rural idealism need not be connected to a political democratic-agrarianism.[44] Access to land was also framed as a palliative solution, which would improve health and well-being without necessarily drawing localised democracy in its wake, or as a matter of economic nationalism.[45] The Commons Preservation Society, which later developed into the National Trust, viewed land as a unique inheritance, working to ensure access to public spaces and rights of way on the grounds of national interest and, like the development of Garden Cities, improvements in public health and well-being.[46] Important though these impulses were, they carried no democratic implications. Echoes of the older vision of the solidaristic but independent smallholder could still be found, plans which hoped to revive 'the old-fashioned English family life, each family established in its own cottage [with] just so much ground as is necessary for that

[41] Hendrick B. Wright to Terence V. Powderly, 11 March 1881 (PP, Series I, Box 2, CUA).

[42] Hendrick B. Wright to Terence V. Powderly, 11 March 1881 (PP, Series I, Box 2, CUA).

[43] Tuck, *Natural Rights Theories*, 3; Rodgers, *Contested Truths*, 72; James L. Huston, 'The American Revolutionaries, the Political Economy of Aristocracy, and the American Concept of the Distribution of Wealth, 1765–1900', *The American Historical Review* 98, no. 4 (1993): 1088; Furner, 'The Republican Tradition and the New Liberalism', 172.

[44] Jan Marsh, *Back to the Land: The Pastoral Impulse in Victorian England from 1880–1914* (London: Quarter Books, 1982), 9.

[45] Leslie Stephen, 'Commons Preservation', in *The Life of Henry Fawcett* (London: Smith, Elder & Co., 1885), 293–340; George Shaw-Lefevre, *English and Irish Land Questions: Collected Essays* (London: Cassell, Petter, Galpin & Co., 1881).

[46] Paul Readman, *Land and Nation in England: Patriotism, National Identity, and the Politics of Land, 1880–1914* (Woodbridge: The Boydell Press, 2008), 114–116; Marsh, *Back to the Land*, 39–35; Jo Guldi, 'Global Questions about Rent and the Longue Durée of Urban Power, 1848 to the Present', *Southern Methodist University History Faculty Publications* 13 (2018): 8–9.

livelihood, and no more', but their impact was limited.[47] Interest in the land question by all political tendencies was determined more by its 'patriotic resonance', as appeal was made to an English 'birthright' and preserving 'racial' health rather than any universalistic rights.[48] As a prominent atheist, Charles Bradlaugh could hardly be expected to champion 'natural rights', but his scheme of land reclamation was more focussed on the efficient utilisation of uncultivated land to alleviate poverty than any political restitution.[49] Bradlaugh's Malthusianism, what Devyr referred to with characteristic acidity as his 'war against the *uncreated*', was an uneasy fit with republican radicalism too.[50]

This is not to say that spiritual communitarian tendencies could not elicit radical democratic or socialist responses. Indeed, George himself was deeply imbued with the tradition of American romanticism, represented by Emerson, Thoreau, and Whitman, which was suffused with a nebulous yearning for rural and communitarian lifestyles and, blending the individual and the collective, often emphasised a unity of man and nature.[51] Indulging his own Thoreau-esque inclinations, George once wrote to his sister of his dream 'to get away from cities and businesses, with their jostlings and strainings and causes, altogether, and find some place on one of the hill sides, [...] where I could gather those I love and live content with what nature and our own resources would furnish'.[52] Although there was little talk of 'natural rights' in these longings, nature itself occupied a prominent position in the work of romantic English socialists like William Morris and Edward Carpenter, and helped to legitimise suspicion towards the capacity and demand of modern science to categorise, organise, dominate, and control, inevitably eliciting a decentralist and anarchic political philosophy.[53] 'The attempt to explain Man by Mechanics',

47 Rev John Burrows, 'Settlements of Six Acre Farms', in John Allet Hobson (ed.), *Co-operative Labour upon the Land, and Other Papers; The Report of a Conference upon 'Land, Co-operation and the Unemployed', Held at Holborn Town Hall in October, 1894* (London: Swan Sonnenshein & Co., 1895), 13–14.

48 Readman, *Land and Nation*, 206–207.

49 For Bradlaugh, all rights to the land were subject to the authority of the State as the final authority. Charles Bradlaugh, *Compulsory Cultivation of Land: What It Means, and Why It Ought to Be Enforced* (London: Freethought Publishing, 1887), 21; Charles Bradlaugh, *The Land, the People, and the Coming Struggle* [1871] (London: Freethought Publishing, 1880), 12; see also, Wolfe, *From Radicalism*, 80–81; Gareth Stedman Jones, *An End to Poverty? A Historical Debate* (London: Profile Books, 2004), 210–211.

50 Devyr, *The Odd Book*, pt. II, 87–88.

51 Bevir, 'British Socialism and American Romanticism'; On Unitarian theology and republican politics in the US, see Eric Foner, *Free Soil, Free Labor, Free Men: The Ideology of the Republican Party before the Civil War* (New York: Oxford University Press, 1970), 106.

52 Henry George to his sister, San Francisco, 15 September 1861 (HGP, Series I: A, Box 1, NYPL); see also George's work 'The Poetry of Life', which exalted 'the beautiful and ennobling in nature'. Henry George, 'The Poetry of Life' (1857) (HGP, Series II, Box 12, NYPL).

53 Morris had 'some misgiving' about George's tours of Britain and Ireland because he believed that 'the capitalists of this country [...] would make common cause with Mr. George'. William

complained Edward Carpenter, was 'a huge vicious circle' in which 'ethics has been made a question of utility and inherited experience'.[54] Carpenter was, alongside George Bernard Shaw and Ramsay Macdonald, a member of Thomas Davidson's *Fellowship of the New Life*, a group which saw socialism as the outgrowth of a more esoteric immanentism – the 'spiritual recognition that we are all one'.[55]

This idyllic naturalism, a romantic reaction against industrial production and endless consumerism, found a common cause with Christian socialists in their shared recognition of universal brotherhood and distrust of claims of scientific authority in politics. George's support was drawn heavily from this milieu. Rev Stuart Headlam, perhaps best described as an Anglican McGlynn, Rev John Elliotson Symes, Professor of English at the newly established University College Nottingham, and the economist and Unitarian minister Philip Wicksteed all became close to George, facilitating his tours of Britain and Ireland, and forming the nucleus of the Georgist English Land Restoration League.[56] Traversing Scotland George met with Unitarian minister E. L. Macdonald in Aberdeen, and Rev Malcolm MacCallum, author of *Religion as Social Justice*, and his brother Donald, a Church of Scotland minister and Land Leaguer at his parish in Waternish, Skye.[57] These networks were built upon the intellectual affinity between George's ideas and the moral critique of acquisitive land ownership that flowed from these religious sources.

In Ireland, Land League speakers were not averse to using romantic pastoral imagery in concert with demands for the restoration of their natural rights. The peasant proprietors of northern France, Switzerland, and the Low countries, 'these men as happy as princes, resting under the shade of their own vine, independent of everything about them', were often called upon to invoke the agrarian ideal.[58] There was a confluence of these tendencies in Irish-America too, inflamed by a sense of longing and loss, where native Irish spirituality and the beauty of the land came to stand in opposition to a soulless Anglo-American materialism. Ralph Waldo Emerson took this as his topic when writing in the

Morris, 'Useful Work versus Useless Toil' [1884], in A. L. Morton (ed.), *Political Writings of William Morris* (New York: International Publishers, 1973), 91, 99.

54 Edward Carpenter, 'Modern Science: A Criticism' [1885] in *Civilisation, Its Cause and Cure, and Other Essays* (London: G. Allen & Unwin, 1921), 79.

55 Bevir, 'British Socialism and American Romanticism', 83.

56 Henry George to Patrick Ford, 28 December 1881 (HGP, Series I: A, Box 3, NYPL); Jones, *The Christian Socialist Revival*; A. W. Coats, 'John Elliotson Symes, Henry George and Academic Freedom in Nottingham during the 1880s', in A. W. Coats (ed.), *The Sociology and Professionalization of Economics*, vol. II, *British & American Essays* (London: Routledge, 2003), 157–168.

57 Henry George, Diary, 1884 (HGP, Series III, NYPL); MacColl, *Land, Faith and the Crofting Community*, 73–74; On the MacCallum brothers, see D. E. Meek, 'The Prophet of Waternish', *West Highland Free Press*, 8 July 1977.

58 Dean Quirke, P.P. of Cashel at Tipperary, 31 October 1880 (MS 11,289, NLI).

Irish World, issuing a condemnation of the present state of American society as being simultaneously 'favourable to Progress and antique inequalities'.[59] In Britain, both the producerist radical republicanism of the type expressed by Devyr and Bray, and the religious and spiritual critiques of social conditions articulated by Headlam and Symes alighted upon the land question as their political cause. Perhaps the most illuminating description of these radicals was an observation offered by Hobson:

> The spirit of humanitarian and religious appeal which suffuses Progress and Poverty wrought powerfully upon a large section of what I may call typical English moralists. In my lectures upon Political Economy about the country, I have found in almost every centre a certain little knot of men of the lower-middle or upper-working class, men of grit and character, largely self-educated, keen citizens, mostly nonconformists in religion, to whom Land Nationalisation, taxation of unearned increment, or other radical reforms of land tenure are doctrines resting upon a plain moral sanction. These free-trading Radical dissenters regard common ownership of land and equal access to the land as a 'natural right', essential to individual freedom. It is this attitude of mind which serves to explain why, when both theoretic students of society and the man in the street regard Land Nationalisation as a first large step in the direction of Socialism, organized Socialists regard the followers of Henry George with undisguised hostility and contempt.[60]

A natural right of access to land based on the needs of the human body was the keystone for these 'English moralists', but, as Hobson intimated, it was precisely this vision that was under severe pressure from conservative, progressive liberal, and socialist analysis that would soon cause it to collapse.

In the United States, it was the Knights of Labor who held the mantle of this tradition during the early 1880s. Founded in 1869 in George's home city of Philadelphia, from 1879, the Knights were headed by Terence V. Powderly, a second-generation Irish-American machinist, and, from a base of around 10,000 in 1878 developed, by the middle of the 1880s, a membership of around 750,000.[61] Beginning in the 1880s, concurrent with the rise of Land League activity in America, the Knights experienced a surge. Proportionally their primary support came from smaller industrial cities rather than the major metropolises, with their heartland the anthracite mining regions of Pennsylvania, where Irish-Americans dominated the membership. Assembly 426 of Luzerne County, Pennsylvania, for instance, boasted a membership of 122, comprising 89 miners, 2 carpenters, 20 labourers, and 1 engineer. The officers of this

[59] Ralph Waldo Emerson, *Irish World*, 4 January 1879.

[60] J. A. Hobson, 'The Influence of Henry George in England', *The Fortnightly Review* 62, no. 372 (1897): 841–842.

[61] Eric Arnesen, 'American Workers and the Labor Movement', in C. W. Calhoun (ed.), *The Gilded Age: Essays on the Origins of Modern America* (Wilmington, DE: Scholarly Resources, 1996), 47; O'Donnell, 'Henry George and the "New Political Forces"', 189.

particular branch consisted of a McDonnell, Callaghan, McOwen, Logan, Kelly, and McMullen.[62] Similarly, in Massachusetts, the leadership was drawn primarily from the industrial towns of Lynn, Worcester, and Cambridge rather than Boston itself.[63]

In their forms of protest (the Knights were enthusiastic adopters of boycotting), their medieval ritualism, their diffuse and semi-autonomous structure of local assemblies, and their universalist rather than class-based membership, the Knights of Labor offered a 'distinctly pre-Marxist critique' of capitalism.[64] As one member explained, the Knights were there to defend 'the liberty that was bequeathed to us by Jeferson [sic] and the fathers of the republic'.[65] The organisation's constitution attested to 'an inevitable and irresistible conflict between the wage-system of labor and republican system of government'.[66] Correspondingly, the ideal of self-improvement and auto-didacticism suffused the Knights just as it did the Irish Land League.[67] The Knights committed its members to defending 'the nobility of all who earn their bread by the sweat of their brow' and denied any inevitable conflict between 'the interests of labor and capital', attacking only those who 'violate the rights' of others.[68] In taking members from skilled and unskilled labourers, rural and urban, engineers and craftsmen, excluding only publicans, land speculators, lawyers, and financiers, the Knights were not only a movement of the dispossessed but offered instead a hopeful vision of a harmonious republic of producers.[69]

Key to the Knights' political vision was a limitation on wealth accumulation. The organisation's Declaration of Principles began by laying out the 'imperative' of restricting 'unjust accumulation' by obeying 'the divine injunction, "In the sweat of thy face shalt thou eat bread"'.[70] Although the Knights were ideologically diffuse owing to the emphasis on self-education within partially independent local assemblies and sought some ameliorative legislation over working conditions and income tax, their central principles remained clearly indebted to the politics of land: the republican harmony of

[62] The monthly report of Assembly 426 of Luzerne County, Pennsylvania, D.A. 16 for the month ending 28 February 1878 (PP, Series 1: Box 2, CUA).

[63] *Irish World*, 8 February 1879; Frank K. Foster to Henry George, 27 April 1884 (HGP, Series I: C, Box 11, NYPL).

[64] Gordon, 'Studies in Irish and Irish American Thought', 505, 512–513; Fink, *Workingmen's Democracy*, 6.

[65] J. P. Conway to Terence V. Powderly, 7 April 1880 (PP, Series 1: Box 2, CUA).

[66] Fink, *Workingmen's Democracy*, 4.

[67] Terence Powderly to John M. Davis, 28 November 1879; Fink, *Workingmen's Democracy*, 11; The Constitution of the Irish National League (Heffernan Papers, MS 21,910, NLI).

[68] Carroll D. Wright, 'An Historical Sketch of the Knights of Labor', *The Quarterly Journal of Economics* 1, no. 2 (1887): 143.

[69] Henry Pelling, 'The Knights of Labor in Britain, 1880–1901', *The Economic History Review* 9, no. 2 (1956): 313–331.

[70] 'Declaration of Principles', reproduced in Wright, 'An Historical Sketch', 157.

the human body in nature which underwrote all associated claims of value, right, possession, and flourishing. The insistence that public land, 'the heritage of the people', be possessed by producers rather than speculators was only one of many demands made by the Knights, yet it grounded their political vision: first among the 'higher duties that should be taught', according to their constitutional regulations for local assemblies, was 'man's inalienable inheritance and right to a share, for use, of the soil; and that the right to life carries with it the right to the *means* of living'.[71] Even while focussed on industrial rather than agrarian emancipation, the Knights' participatory, localised politics, in which every member 'is a part of the government in the country', and their commitment to moral and intellectual flourishing were rooted ultimately in the land.

The Knights were a formidable force by the 1880s, in size and influence.[72] Tentative alliances with both George and the Irish Land League of America strengthened their reach, but also brought to the fore splits and divisions within the organisation that would eventually, by the end of the decade, wither its power. From 1882 until George's campaign for mayor of New York, which was directly supported by the Knights under the United Labor banner, George enjoyed a great deal of support from the organisation. Despite some disagreements, Powderly was personally keen on George's ideas, and *Progress and Poverty* quickly became a key text in Knights' reading rooms. George, for his part, advocated consistently for the Knights, speaking under their imprimatur on occasion.[73] He enjoyed a good relationship with Powderly in the main, their association fostered by mutual friendships with Patrick Ford and Michael Davitt.

Yet even from the beginning, signs of division were evident. George's individualism and his fixation on land as a distinct form of property prompted caution from avowed socialists in the organisation. On 12 December 1880, George was invited to deliver the inaugural address at the Brooklyn 'Spread the Light Club'.[74] Adopting its name from one of the *Irish World*'s favourite slogans, the club was an outgrowth of the Knights' Local Assembly 1562, a politically advanced and socialistically minded group led by Theodore Cuno, William Horan, and Matthew Maguire.[75] With publicity and support from the *Irish World* and the local *Brooklyn Eagle*, the club ran public lectures in order to educate the population and 'enable them to assert their rights against

[71] 'Constitutional Regulations for Local Assemblies', reproduced in Wright, 'An Historical Sketch', 160.

[72] Kirkup, *An Inquiry into Socialism*, 10–11.

[73] Robert E. Weir, 'A Fragile Alliance: Henry George and the Knights of Labor', *The American Journal of Economics and Sociology* 56, no. 4 (1997): 423.

[74] Handbill advertising George's inaugural talk at the Brooklyn Spread the Light Club, 12 December 1880 (PP, Series I: Box 2, CUA).

[75] Theodore F. Cuno to Terence V. Powderly, 25 February 1881 (PP, Series I: Box 2, CUA).

the universally felt influence of domineering corporations and monopolies'.[76] George's talk, naturally on the ownership of land, was well received by his 'humble friends' in the group. But early in 1881, Cuno, Maguire, and Horan wrote to George to express their disagreement with his ideas. While they were pleased that George's increasing popularity was opening 'the eyes of the intelligent men who edit the better class of American newspapers', they felt compelled to explain that 'Ricardo's theory has long been exploded by Karl Marx long before Progress and Poverty was written, and consequently, your method to conclude from Ricardo's sophistry that "interest" for the use of tools (capital) should be paid, cannot hold water'.[77]

The 'Spread the Light Club' acknowledged that George 'mean[t] well enough', but argued that any defence of interest risked enshrining idle wealth: it is 'this misconception we desire to dispel'.[78] For George, returns to capital were simply returns to stored labour, and he would not budge from the contention that 'Nature gives nothing to man without labour, and he can transfer that right to whoever he pleases', remaining 'convinced that the sins that are attributed to capital are simply the results of monopoly'.[79] At this early point in the decade, the 'Spread the Light Club' was sure that radicals such as George were at an infant stage of their ideological development. 'We know very well that you are an individualist' they wrote to George, 'while we have placed ourselves upon the side of collectivism'. Yet they were confident that, since 'no one is infallible', 'you will some day or other advance with Patrick Ford, Michael Davitt, and other humanitarian philosophers and liberty lovers "toward higher ground"'.[80]

Subsequent events would only draw them further apart. By the end of the decade, the equivalence of socialism with statism was harder to escape, and questions about centralisation became issues of contention. The Knights of Labor disintegrated over disagreements about tactics and objectives as the republican principles that had bound them together appeared insufficient and pallid to many.[81] George's failed mayoral candidacy and the collapse

[76] Handbill advertising George's inaugural talk at the Brooklyn Spread the Light Club, 12 December 1880 (PP, Series I: Box 2, CUA).

[77] 'Spread the Light Club', Matthew Maguire, William Horan, and Theodore F. Cuno, to Henry George, 17 April 1881 (HGP, Series I: A, Box 3, NYPL).

[78] 'Spread the Light Club', Matthew Maguire, William Horan, and Theodore F. Cuno, to Henry George, 17 April 1881 (HGP, Series I: A, Box 3, NYPL).

[79] Henry George, 'Lecture at Midland Institute', Birmingham, 23 January 1884 (HGP, Series II, Box 13, NYPL).

[80] 'Spread the Light Club', Matthew Maguire, William Horan, and Theodore F. Cuno, to Henry George, 17 April 1881 (HGP, Series I: A, Box 3, NYPL).

[81] Kim Voss, *The Making of American Exceptionalism: The Knights of Labor and Class Formation in the Nineteenth Century* (Ithaca, NY: Cornell University Press, 1993), 79; Fink, *Workingmen's Democracy*, 228–289.

of New York's Central Labor Union, alongside the Haymarket affair in 1886, accelerated this process with the concurrent growth of the American Federation of Labor and, into the 1890s, Daniel de Leon's Socialist Labor Party. Powderly's Knights were left as a 'conservative, reactionary' rump, according to Eleanor Marx, while the 'best elements' of the organisation, former Knights P. J. Maguire and Samuel Gompers, helped lead the American Federation of Labor.[82] Socialism appeared to have left George, the Knights, and the radical vision behind. For some, there was a sense of inevitability about such a trajectory; the tendency of the age being towards more effective, efficient, and centralised administration. As early as 1879, the eclectic and influential labour radical Joseph Labadie, a Knight and a supporter of George, observed that 'the true labor men [...] have left the party and joined the Socialists. [...] I have no hesitancy in saying that that is the future party'. Labadie's republican principles meant that he did 'not concur in some of their idealistic theories', but in the battle between individualism and collectivism, he thought it was a matter of certainty that 'their fundamental principles will eventually prevail'.[83]

Socialisms

By the end of the decade, then, George was not a socialist; his republicanism and the radical politics of land could no longer be easily accommodated by the term. On his first tour of Britain and Ireland, George had made no attempt to downplay the socialistic implications of his ideas. Speaking on platforms with land nationalisers, he often discussed 'true socialism' as the goal of his crusade and barely mentioned the concept of the 'single-tax'.[84] In 1883, a branch of the American Socialist Labor Party even purchased a bulk order of *Progress and* Poverty for distribution.[85] His use of the terms 'cooperative' and 'socialist' as almost interchangeable echoed Mill's, and his language, as we have seen, was that of a Christian socialist.[86] By 1889, in a debate with SDF leader Henry Hyndman, George was adamant that socialism and statism were equivalent and that it repudiated the virtue forming necessity of self-directed activity,

82 Aveling, and Marx, *The Working Class Movement in America*, 203–204.
83 Joseph Labadie to Terence V. Powderly, 7 December 1879 (PP, Series 1: Box 2, CUA).
84 Wolfe, *From Radicalism*, 85.
85 Charles Thompson to Henry George, 9 April 1879 (HGP, Series I: A, Box 2, NYPL); Socialist Labor Party of New Haven, CT, 30 January 1883 (HGP, Series I: A, Box 4, NYPL).
86 Mill, 'Chapters on Socialism' [1869], 375–376; John Plowright, 'Political Economy and Christian Polity: The Influence of Henry George in England Reassessed', *Victorian Studies* 30, no. 2 (1987): 235–252; Claeys, *Money, Machinery and the Millennium*, 131; Stedman Jones, 'Religion and the Origins of Socialism', 171–189; Henry George, 'Lecture on the New Constitution' [1877] (HGP, Series II: Box 12, NYPL).

complaining that 'socialism begins at the wrong end; it pre-supposes pure government; its dream is simply of a benevolent tyranny'.[87]

George's definitional certainties were misplaced, covering over the nuances that still proliferated, and owed much to his own personal disappointments. Socialism remained, in the mid-1880s, 'to a very large degree unfixed'.[88] Many, like Kirkup or John Swinton, the Scottish-American radical journalist, for instance, remained wedded to more moralistic assumptions and rejected Marxist orthodoxy.[89] Among the ideologically varied list of British socialist leaders compiled in 1894 by Robert Flint, Professor of Divinity at the University of Edinburgh, George shared an affinity with many.[90] Yet George was correct to observe, as others did similarly, the shift towards greater emphasis on state administration rather than personal independence that went hand in hand with the declining focus on the land question. Socialism was simply 'the extension of the protection of the State' to men as well as women and children, according to Arnold Toynbee.[91] This idea that state administration was the defining feature of socialism was shared by Henry Fawcett, Émile de Laveleye, John Elliot Cairnes, and Richard T. Ely among many others.[92] The entrancing optimism of frictionless state administration had persuaded 'both Conservative and Radical [...] to raise the banner of socialism'.[93] Given its apparent ubiquity, many observers simply portrayed this as the inescapable tendency of the age, appealing across the political spectrum. 'Society is reforming itself on Collectivist, not on individualist principles', explained Sidney Webb, producing 'an increasing social momentum in the same general direction'.[94]

The cause of this 'momentum' appeared too deeply rooted in all facets of social organisation and intellectual life to be questioned. 'It is scarcely necessary to attempt to prove that there has been an almost uninterrupted increase in the functions of the modern State ever since its existence began', asserted

[87] Henry George, in Henry George, and Henry M. Hyndman, *The Single-Tax versus Social Democracy: Which Will Most Benefit the People, Verbatim Report of the Debate in St. James's Hall, July 2, 1889* (London: The Twentieth Century Press, 1906), 30. George Bernard Shaw's acerbic and excoriating review of the debate declared George's ideas 'a mere academic fossil dug up from the Quesnay-Mirabeau stratum'. George Bernard Shaw, 'The Hyndman-George Debate', *International Review* (August 1889): 33–44.

[88] Kirkup, *An Inquiry into Socialism*, 1.

[89] G. A. Cohen, *Karl Marx's Theory of History: A Defence* (Princeton: Princeton University Press, 2000), 146.

[90] 'Hyndman, Champion, Joynes, John Burns, Miss Helen Taylor, Morris, Bax, Dr. and Mrs. Aveling, Mrs. Besant, Bernard Shaw, and Rev. Stewart Headlam', Flint, *Socialism*, 43.

[91] Toynbee, *'Progress and Poverty'*, 24.

[92] Fawcett, *State Socialism*, 3; Émile de Laveleye, *The Socialism of To-Day* (London: The Leadenhall Press, 1886), xv; Cairnes, *Some Leading Principles*, 265; Rev Aug. J. Thebaud, S. J., 'Socialism at the Present Day', *American Catholic Quarterly Review* 5 (1880): 48–49; Ely, *Recent American Socialism*, 48.

[93] Kirkup, *An Inquiry into Socialism*, 177.

[94] Webb, *Socialism in England*, 16.

Ely in 1886.[95] It was a product of 'contemporary industrial evolution', which had replaced 'the Individual by the Community as the starting point of social investigation'.[96] It attained this 'irresistible momentum' from the increasing 'centralisation of industrial processes' which caused 'the prevailing system of individualism' to break down.[97] The construction of socialism as a 'scientific' proposition, a matter of careful, informed administration for social amelioration not only provided an aura of inevitability but also narrowed the distance between avowed socialists and progressive liberalism.[98] Arnold Toynbee would have been in positive agreement, at least in rhetorical terms, with August Bebel's definition of socialism as simply 'science applied with full understanding to all the fields of human activity'.[99]

So although George was accorded a prominent position in the early and prototypical histories of British and American socialism – his *Progress and Poverty* alongside the Irish Land War had 'completely revolutionised' socialist thought and organisation – these interlinked movements had simply served, in the minds of both socialists and progressive liberals, to finally deflate radicalism.[100] 'Mr. George was, almost in his own despite', explained the Webbs, 'driving Peasant Proprietorship [...] out of the political field'.[101] Figures like Henry Hyndman, the former Tory turned socialist and leader of the SDF who had been strongly influenced by George and by agrarian principles, moved inexorably away from the land question. Despite George's best efforts to resist this process, a focus on the potentialities of state administration was too great a pull. The firm localism and hostility to centralisation that had characterised radicalism – J. Morrison Davidson of the Georgist English Land Restoration League saw their goal as moving society 'from feudalism to municipalisation' – could not be easily reconciled to this.[102] As some of his more perceptive critics observed, a sole focus on the land question served only to 'denationalis[e] a country', devolving political power away from those institutions most capable

95 Richard T. Ely, 'Administration', *Christian Union*, 16 December 1886.

96 Webb, *Socialism in England*, 9–10. 97 Kirkup, *An Inquiry into Socialism*, 184, 13.

98 Adcock, *Liberalism and the Emergence of American Political Science*, 152.

99 August Bebel, *Women under Socialism* [1879], trans. Daniel de Leon (New York: Labor News Company, 1904), 371.

100 Webb, *Socialism in England*, 21–22; Webb and Webb, *The History of Trade Unionism*, 362; Kirkup, *A History of Socialism*, 328.

101 Webb and Webb, *The History of Trade Unionism*, 362.

102 J. Morrison Davidson was the brother of Thomas Davidson, founder of *The Fellowship of the New Life*. Son of Aberdeenshire farm labourers, Morrison became a lawyer, radical journalist, and land nationaliser. *The Times*, 20 December 1916; see J. Morrison Davidson, *Concerning Four Precursors of Henry George and the Single Tax, as also the Land Gospel according to Winstanley 'The Digger'* (London: Labour Leader Publishing, 1899); Flint, *Socialism*, 158. George had long been at pains to explain that no 'new machinery' of state administration was required, and instead that 'all we have to do is simplify and reduce it', George, *Progress and Poverty*, 364.

of legislating for better social conditions.[103] Georgists, meanwhile, continued to decry what Sidney Webb described as the 'subordination of individual ends to the common good', seeing an unnecessary demarcation between individualism and socialism that was really just 'a phantom of language'.[104]

Also set firmly against such divisions was the radical wing of the Land League, best represented by Patrick Ford's *Irish World*, a paper practically unrivalled in its influence and reach in both Ireland and Irish-America. Ford, who grew up in Boston having emigrated there from Galway as a child, deeply impressed George with his strength of character, and the two men would share an enormously fruitful working relationship.[105] He was, in George's mind, 'a single hearted devotee to principle', or, in William O'Brien's more colourful description, a 'solemn, self-immolating, remorseless, yet intensely religious' figure, 'whom you might expect to see either recommended for beatification as a saint or blown up by an infernal machine [...] fired by his own hand'.[106] Ford had enjoyed a long career in radical journalism before the *Irish World*. His ideas as well as his forthright editorial style were forged in the crucible of abolitionist politics, during his time working for William Lloyd Garrison's *Liberator*, a title he would meaningfully appropriate for his own paper's masthead.[107]

Ford came to occupy a pivotal place in the intersection of Irish nationalism and social radicalism. Through the *Irish World*, his influence was extensive; in one assessment 'the only man, who ever exercised any considerable influence over the Irish race, who has never made a public speech' in the country.[108] While Ford's paper rapidly accelerated George's influence and acclaim, its own radical credentials were already firm, having previously declared in favour of land nationalisation in some form.[109] The imprint of agrarian republicanism was clear in the *Irish World*'s political demands, which, even into the 1880s, continued to argue for the dissolution of the standing army, abolition of senate and presidential veto, and refusal to contract a national debt, echoing the anti-federalists of the early American republic.[110] The spectral presence of Thomas Jefferson haunted radicals' political dreams. Many saw themselves reliving the ideological battle between Alexander Hamilton and Jefferson; a continuous

[103] Flint, *Socialism*, 158; Lecky, *Democracy and Liberty*, vol. II, 356; Biagini, *Liberty, Retrenchment and Reform*, 64.
[104] Webb, *Socialism in England*, 10; Grant Allen, *Individualism and Socialism* (Glasgow: Land Values Publication Department, 1889), 3.
[105] Henry George to McClatchy, 27 January 1881 (HGP, Series I: A, Box 3, NYPL); Rev John Talbot Smith, *Patrick Ford of the Irish World* (AIA.047, NYU).
[106] O'Brien, *Recollections*, 274.
[107] Greene, 'The Impact of Henry George's Theories', 80; Rodechko, *Patrick Ford and His Search for America*, 30.
[108] O'Brien, *Recollections*, 274. [109] *Irish World*, 16 November 1878.
[110] *Irish World*, 16 November 1878; *Pilot*, 17 January 1880; *Irish World*, 25 March 1882.

struggle between 'the money power' – aristocratic, centralised, revelling in bureaucracy and authority – and popular republican sovereignty.[111] For Patrick Ford, Hamilton's 'English Party' were the ideological kin of contemporary enemies of republicanism.[112]

This republican nostalgia was a meaningful indication of a deeper political divergence.[113] The *Irish World*, of course, framed its politics in the republican language of natural rights; arguing that equal entitlement to 'the opportunities of Nature' was a 'self evident' and 'inalienable right'.[114] In point of fact, Ford's newspaper helped to construct this conceptual universe and was key in reinforcing the idea that the Land War was not just about rents and debts, but about natural rights, popular democracy, and the creeping authoritarianism of elite, technocratic rule. While open to a variety of socialist opinions on the role of the state, giving column inches to Philip Van Patten of the Socialist Labor Party for instance, the paper cautioned that 'there are some things [the state] can never do. Things that the individual himself can do if he is only given what belongs to him'.[115] 'German socialism', what one Catholic journal described as a materialist and evolutionary theory that deified the state 'to the total exclusion of free will and moral accountability' was viewed suspiciously.[116] Just as public Land League meetings in Ireland sought to characterise their own demands as not only distinct from, but in direct opposition to, the 'sophistry' and utopianism of 'the vicious vocabulary of the continent', the *Irish World* argued that, outside of Germany, 'the Individualists, or, as they style themselves, the anarchical collectivists, are not only in the right, but in the majority'.[117]

As some contemporaries noted, Ireland had found 'the means of its agitation' in an anarchistic form of socialism which 'holds to individual sovereignty

[111] Henry George, 'Speech made during Presidential campaign, 1876' (HGP, Series II, Box 12, NYPL); Henry George, 'To the voters of San Francisco', newspaper clipping, 3 May 1878 (HGP, Series I: A, Box 2, NYPL); Henry George, 'Wanted: A Democratic Party', 12 March 1883 (HGP, Series II, Box 13, NYPL); Dunne, *Ireland: Rights, Wrongs and Remedies*, 29 (103, Box 34, P.001.1804, PAHRC).

[112] *Irish World*, 12 October 1872; see also Gordon, 'Studies in Irish and Irish American Thought', 425.

[113] Rodgers, *Contested Truths*, 39, 72.

[114] *Irish World*, 16 November 1878; 27 December 1879; 23 April 1881; 19 August 1882; 9 September 1882.

[115] *Irish World*, 14 December 1878.

[116] Rev Aug. J. Thebaud, S. J., 'Socialism at the Present Day', 47; Henry George to John Swinton, San Francisco, 6 May 1879 (HGP, Series I: A, Box 2, NYPL); Marxists were, for their part, equally suspicious of what they saw as the plebeian moralism and bourgeois ambitions of organisations like the Knights and the Greenbackers: Philip Van Patten to Terence V. Powderly, 20 May 1880 (PP, Series 1: Box 2, CUA); Philip Van Patten to Terence V. Powderly, 15 July 1880 (PP, Series 1: Box 2, CUA).

[117] Patrick Meehan, Cloneen, 13 June 1880, and John Walsh, Straide, 1 February 1880, in Timothy Daniel Sullivan (ed.), *Condemnations of Crime: Compiled from Speeches Delivered at Meetings of the Land League and National League in Ireland, 1879–1887* (London: The Irish Press Agency,

as its watchword'.[118] The *Irish World* was itself home to a number of anarchist writers such as Henry Appleton, Joshua King Ingalls, Sidney H. Morse, and Dyer Lum, who were also associated with Benjamin Tucker and his anarchist paper *Liberty*.[119] Ingalls, for instance, was another veteran land reformer who had been active with George Henry Evans' NRA and was sympathetic to George (even if, like Devyr, he was critical of what he considered to be his excessive reliance on the state).[120] Emphasising the centrality of land to his anarchist politics, Ingalls explained 'that laws conferring upon wealth unlimited power to monopolize the soil are in violation of clearly-defined relations existing in nature, [and] are incompatible with civil rights and the social and moral instincts of mankind'.[121] The cross-pollination between Georgist, Irish radical, and anarchist networks rested upon a close ideological affinity; a shared focus on individual sovereignty, an optimistic view of human sociability, and the communality of natural resources.[122] It is no surprise that the practice of boycotting appeared to anarchists as a perfect example of precisely this unstructured harmonisation of human interaction against economic centralisation.[123] For anarchists, the land and 'free intercourse with nature' offered resistance against 'the body-and-soul destroying factories of England and America' that left behind them a trail of 'demoralized people'.[124]

At the core of the anarchist political claim was the same faith in the ultimate natural harmony of the individual and society that drove radical republican, and even Catholic social teaching, to reject liberal managerial and technocratic solutions to the problems of social deprivation in favour of a simple reclamation of lost freedoms. The dichotomy between individualism and collectivism was therefore a false choice.[125] As one writer in the *Irish World* explained, 'I am a socialist and an individualist – I do not believe in the old dogma of surrendering

1888), 46, 48; Similar statements proliferate, see 'we don't want anything Communistic', only 'justice for the tenants, to root them in the soil which God created for their benefit', Rev Joyce, Westport, 9 June 1879, in Sullivan (ed.), *Condemnations of Crime*, 52; *Irish World*, 2 October 1880.

118 'Anarchic Socialism', *New Englander* 7, no. 178 (January 1884): 113, 116.

119 Whelehan, *The Dynamiters*, 286–288; David DeLeon, *The American as Anarchist: Reflections on Indigenous Radicalism* (Baltimore, MD: Johns Hopkins University Press, 1978).

120 J. K. Ingalls, 'Land Reform in 1848 and 1888', in Frank H. Brooks (ed.), *The Individualist Anarchists: An Anthology of Liberty (1881–1908)* (New Brunswick, NJ: Transaction, 1994), 151–152; J. K. Ingalls, *Reminiscences of an Octogenarian in the Field of Industrial and Social Reform* (New York: Holbrook, 1897).

121 Ingalls, *Land and Labor*, 11. George, too, sometimes noted the parallels between his ideas and that of anarchic socialists. Henry George, 'Lecture notes for Cambridge', 10 March 1884 (HGP, Series II, Box 12, NYPL); Henry George to John Swinton, 29 April 1880 (HGP, Series I: A, Box 2, NYPL).

122 Hodgskin, *The Natural and Artificial Right*, 36; Vincent, 'Visions of a Stateless Society', 433–476.

123 *Liberty*, 31 October 1891.

124 Peter Kropotkin, *Fields, Factories and Workshops* [1899] (New York: G P Putnam's Sons, 1913), 19; TRANSATLANTIC, *Irish World*, 14 December 1878; *Irish World* 20 December 1879.

125 *Liberty*, 17 July 1886.

individual rights or liberty on which to establish a society or general government', but, at the same time, 'no true individualism [...] can ever exist in the world without socialism'.[126] The same can be said of George's political vision, in which communality was inseparable from individual liberty, and did not involve a rejection of social duties, norms, and even restrictions. He spoke of 'the truth that each individual must act upon and be acted upon by the society of which he is a part [...] and the life of each be dominated by the conditions imposed by all'.[127] His articulation of liberalism did not reject the communality imposed by social ties, but resisted any devaluation of the individual caused by hierarchies. This was its own form of anarchic socialism, 'a commonwealth in which the family affections might knit their tendrils around each member, binding with links stronger than steel the various parts into the living whole'.[128]

Liberalisms

On the evening of 8 March 1884, as part of his second transatlantic tour, George dined in the Great Hall of Trinity College, Cambridge. He had been invited to talk at the university by a group of undergraduates, including a young Frederick Scott Oliver, the future advocate of imperial federalism.[129] After a rambunctious and exhausting encounter at the Oxford Union the day before, George found a more sympathetic audience here, including the prime minister's daughter, Mary Gladstone, who had been deeply impressed by *Progress and Poverty* after reading it the previous summer.[130] Among his dinner companions were the progressive liberal M.P. Professor James Stuart, and Sedley Taylor, the academic polymath who had recently completed a treatise on cooperative enterprise.[131] Unsurprisingly, the conversation turned to the work of Taylor's friend Henry Fawcett. The renowned liberal politician had been Professor of Political Economy at nearby Trinity Hall and an active advocate of common access to land and industrial cooperation. George was particularly taken by Fawcett's illustrative observation in his book on *Pauperism*, which mirrored the American's own complaint, about 'the direst poverty always accompanying the greatest wealth'.[132]

126 *Irish World*, 2 October 1880; Kate Gannett Wells, 'The Pathos of Socialism', *The Unitarian Review and Religious Magazine* 25, no. 4 (1886): 347.
127 Henry George, 'Moses' (HGP, Series II: Box 13, NYPL).
128 George, 'Moses' (HGP, Series II: Box 13, NYPL).
129 Henry George, 'Diary Entry: 8 March 1884' (HGP, Series III, NYPL); Henry George, lecture notes for Cambridge, 10 March 1884 (HGP, Series II, Box 12, NYPL). Frederick Scott Oliver, *The Irish Question: Federation or Secession* (New York: Press of the Civil Service Print Co., 1918).
130 Barker, *Henry George*, 404.
131 Sedley Taylor, *Proft-Sharing between Capital and Labour* (London: Kegan Paul, Trench and Co., 1884).
132 Henry Fawcett, *Pauperism: Its Causes and Remedies* (London: Macmillan, 1871), 2. George had written this quote in his diary after the Cambridge meeting.

His friendly interlocutors at Cambridge shared George's moral disgust with human deprivation and purposelessness, his frustration that 'men everywhere [are] being changed into machines', but demurred from his analysis and his conclusions.[133] Their differences were well encapsulated by Fawcett, who was to a large degree representative of the direction of British liberalism at the time.[134] A political economist indebted to Mill, Fawcett had moulded his older, individualist assumptions to fit a politics of utility in line with a cautious, gradualist reformism. These intellectual predilections tracked Fawcett's opinions on the land question. Writing in 1871, Fawcett exhibited many of the same concerns as George as to the tendency of land to become monopolised into sites for speculation.[135] But while he bemoaned seventeenth- and eighteenth-century enclosures for curtailing the 'rude abundance' of the English peasantry, Fawcett's solution was not a direct reclamation of these lost rights.[136] Sympathetic to the logic of peasant proprietorship, and keen to ensure occupiers of land possessed 'some proprietary rights', he nevertheless rejected Mill's idea of the 'unearned increment' as detrimental to the necessary capitalisation of agriculture, preferring instead simply the removal of impediments to the sale of land.[137] Opposing the extent of enclosures of common land had to be based on 'a principle of economic science', rather than any claim to natural right.[138] By 1883, his response to George and the Irish crisis was to firmly disavow any scheme of land nationalisation on the basis of its financial impropriety.[139] Critically, he believed that 'the ownership of land was in this respect in precisely the same position as other kinds of property, and that it was therefore grossly unjust to subject it to special burdens'.[140]

This refusal to view land as a distinct form of property freed it from claims of natural right. Its political valence dimmed; the question of its possession was simply one feature of the broader, judicious management of the social problem. Leslie Stephen, Fawcett's close friend and biographer, noted appositely in 1885 that Fawcett and George were distinguished by the latter's narrowness and naivety. 'Mr. George has recently excited the public mind by asking' the same question that had vexed Fawcett, explained Stephen, but Fawcett's solutions relied upon 'the method of a man of science, not that of an inspired reformer'.[141] A keen Malthusian, Fawcett, like many of his contemporary

[133] Henry George, lecture notes for Cambridge, 10 March 1884 (HGP, Series II, Box 12, NYPL); Barker, *Henry George*, 405.

[134] See Lawrence Goldman (ed.), *The Blind Victorian: Henry Fawcett and British Liberalism* (Cambridge: Cambridge University Press, 1989).

[135] Fawcett, *Pauperism*, 213. [136] Fawcett, *Pauperism*, 234.

[137] Fawcett, *Pauperism*, 208. [138] Fawcett, *Pauperism*, 247.

[139] Fawcett, *State Socialism*.

[140] Leslie Stephen, *The Life of Henry Fawcett* (London: Smith, Elder & Co., 1885), 166.

[141] Stephen, *The Life of Henry Fawcett*, 141.

progressive liberals, believed that radical dreams of natural equality, of 'a vast population governed only by pure laws of reason', were tragically and dangerously naïve for not accounting for 'adequate checks upon population'.[142] For Fawcett, 'poverty and its attendant evils may be diminished, but diminished only by judicious measures'.[143] He was not a slave to principle, but was rather 'a consistent empiricist' – for him, 'the one general principle is that Government should do what experience proves it can do efficiently'.[144]

Fawcett's ability to reorient the presumptions of liberal individualism through a lens of practical state management, as a matter of efficient political science, was mirrored by the wider shifts in Anglo-American liberalism, which still contained significant, but increasingly awkward, traces of its radical and Chartist legacies.[145] In Britain, many of these competing forces were held together by the popular appeal of Gladstonian liberalism, but the issue of land forced a significant disjuncture.[146] Although the conservative leader Lord Salisbury complained that the Liberal Party was 'on an inclined plane leading from the position of Lord Hartington to that of Mr. Chamberlain and so on the depths over which Mr. Henry George rules supreme', there was still important ideological divergence here.[147] On the invitation of another progressive liberal, Walter Wren, George had dined at the Reform Club with John Bright and Joseph Chamberlain. And while he was personally well disposed to the liberal politicians, and noted that 'Chamberlain is an extremely bright man' who has 'evidently been reading the *Irish World*', George was disappointed with what he perceived as their restraint on the land issue.[148]

The solution for many progressive liberals when it came to the land question was greater democracy and freedom of trade in land.[149] This was certainly Fawcett's solution in 1883, when he argued that 'the chief end to be sought in the reform of land tenure is to free the land from all restrictions which limit the amount of land which is brought into the market'.[150] The Land Tenure Reform Association, of which Fawcett had been a founding member, took as its guiding principle Richard Cobden's well-worn quip that a League for free trade in land had, by the early 1860s, become more necessary than the one for free trade

142 Fawcett, *Pauperism*, 205; Stephen, *The Life of Henry Fawcett*, 152.
143 Stephen, *The Life of Henry Fawcett*, 152. 144 Stephen, *The Life of Henry Fawcett*, 150.
145 Antony Taylor, '"The Old Chartist": Radical Veterans on the Late Nineteenth- and Early Twentieth-Century Political Platform', *History* 95, no. 4 (2010): 462; Jon Lawrence, 'Popular Radicalism and the Socialist Revival in Britain', *Journal of British Studies* 31, no. 2 (1992): 169.
146 Biagini, *Liberty, Retrenchment and Reform*, 425.
147 Lord Salisbury at Dorchester, 16 January 1884, quoted in J. L. Garvin, *The Life of Joseph Chamberlain*, vol. I, *Chamberlain and Democracy* (London: Macmillan, 1932), 462.
148 Henry George to Patrick Ford, 22 April 1882 (HGP, Series I: B, NYPL); Henry George, 'Lecture Notes: Britain', reply to John Bright (HGP, Series II, Box 12, NYPL); Chamberlain opposed George's remedies, even as he agreed with his analysis of the symptoms. Garvin, *Chamberlain*, 385.
149 See Arnold, *Free Land*. 150 Fawcett, *State Socialism*, 11.

in corn over which he had presided. Yet this was not a doctrine of *laissez-faire* and individual rights. Fawcett's arguments for free trade in land rested on the ground of expediency rather than rights or a moral or naturalistic claim for harmony in trade.[151] Insofar as 'free trade' was a positive, it was not synonymous with *laissez-faire* and did not demand the exclusion of the state from the economic sphere. It was simply a matter of careful balance and deliberation. The 'rash reformers' who eschewed 'a careful examination' of necessary institutional equilibrium, observed Leslie Stephen, were ignorant of the fact that 'society is not a mere aggregate of independent atoms, but a complex living organism'.[152]

In this respect, the free trade in land arguments were able to integrate an older radical rhetoric into progressive liberal perspectives, which provided an alternative to 'the growing influence of Henry George within Radical circles'.[153] Disavowing individual rights while maintaining a commitment to free trade in land on the basis of utility and efficiency opened the door to ameliorative counterbalancing economic interventions from a liberal state where necessary, while closing it on a reclamation of inalienable rights to natural resources based on the radical argument of a 'right to life'.[154] While this perspective preceded George, it took on a much greater prominence as a result of its effectiveness in countering and diluting his arguments. On the other side of the political divide, and operating in parallel, individualist claims became increasingly hollowed defences of property in land against all social restrictions. Fractured by the problem of the private possession of land, the individualist, classical liberalism of the mid-Victorian era, with its focus on the 'rights' of property, largely became the preserve of libertarian conservatives such as inhabited the Liberty and Property Defence League, for whom Gladstonian interventionism in Ireland represented 'the germ of socialism in the way of dealing with property'.[155]

Another member of the Land Tenure Reform Association who disagreed sharply with George's analysis was the economist J. E. Thorold Rogers, most notable for his ground-breaking work, *Six Centuries of Work and Wages*.[156] For Rogers, assertive and absolutist landlords like those in the Liberty and Property Defence League were, unfortunately, sowing the seeds of their own downfall in their recalcitrant individualism. If George and other land nationalisers were

[151] Stephen, *The Life of Henry Fawcett*, 148. [152] Stephen, *The Life of Henry Fawcett*, 150.

[153] Howe, *Free Trade and Liberal England*, 139; Frank Trentmann, 'Wealth versus Welfare: The British Left between Free Trade and National Political Economy before the First World War', *Historical Research* 70, no. 171 (1997): 71.

[154] Howe, *Free Trade*, 138.

[155] Francis Richard Charteris (The Earl of Wemyss), HC Deb, 31 July 1885, vol. 300, c. 637; Edward Bristow, 'The Liberty and Property Defence League and Individualism', *The Historical Journal* 18, no. 4 (1975): 761; Michael Taylor, *Herbert Spencer and the Limits of the State: The Late Nineteenth Century Debate between Individualism and Collectivism* (Bristol: Thoemmes Press, 1996), xiv.

[156] Taylor, 'Richard Cobden', 146–166.

successful, warned Rogers, landlords would only have themselves to blame for not limiting themselves to only 'their defensible rights'.[157] There was, he cautioned, 'an increasing number' of dangerous radicals 'who credit the private ownership of land with being the source of all [...] the social mischiefs of modern civilisation', and, 'as long as landowners cling to anti-social expedients', calmer advocates of judicious reform like Rogers himself would be overwhelmed by those who 'assail the institution' of private property in land itself, leaving the landlords' rent-rolls entirely unprotected.[158]

Like Fawcett and many other liberal critics of George, Rogers refused a solid distinction between land and other forms of property. He did so on the basis that, since land had been purchased as property, attempts to appropriate rent would be both unfair and inexpedient to further investment and enterprise, and as such it was 'impossible to distinguish between the sanctity of different kinds of property'.[159] Writing in 1873, Rogers had already laid out his opposition to schemes of land nationalisation and had explained that protecting private property from the 'projects of those who desire to make the State the owner of the whole soil', meant, paradoxically, abandoning absolute notions of individual ownership.[160] In a mirror image of the radical position, Rogers extrapolated an individualist politics from a collectivist metaphysics, explaining that 'there is no economical problem in which abstract reasoning and practical wisdom are so completely at variance' as the ownership of land.[161]

Anticipating subsequent new liberal arguments, Rogers had explained that it would be unnecessary and counterproductive to nationalise the land precisely because the state was already its ultimate and final owner. Like all forms of property, the possession of land was dependent on the 'discretion' of 'public opinion' – and the idea of 'an inalienable right to the possession' of land a dangerous and misleading sophistry.[162] All questions of ownership, in land or otherwise, were equal insofar as they always 'must yield to considerations of public defence, and even public utility'.[163] Like the issue of free trade, the ownership of land was a matter of broadly viewed 'national interest', embracing matters of economic efficiency and public welfare, and not reducible to a simplistic demand

[157] J. E. Thorold Rogers, 'Contemporary Socialism', *The Contemporary Review* 47 (1885): 58; This, he had explained, was simply a 'purchased [...] right to received interest on the money which his land cost him'. James E. Thorold Rogers, *The Irish Land Question: A Letter Written in Sept., 1869, to the Late Sir John Gray, M. P.* (Oxford: E. C. Alden, 1881), 13.

[158] Thorold Rogers, 'Contemporary Socialism', 59.

[159] Thorold Rogers, 'Contemporary Socialism', 57–58.

[160] J. E. Thorold Rogers, *Cobden and Modern Political Opinion: Essays on Certain Political Topics* (London: Macmillan, 1873), 107.

[161] Thorold Rogers, *Cobden and Modern Political Opinion*, 107.

[162] Thorold Rogers, *Cobden and Modern Political Opinion*, 107.

[163] Thorold Rogers, *Cobden and Modern Political Opinion*, 107–108.

for rights. In this way, the nominal assumption of collective authority over all private property in land became the most effective means by which the radical 'right to life' argument could be bypassed in favour of an appeal to utility, an intellectual manoeuvre which had the added advantage of obscuring the claims for localised participatory democracy that the radical argument contained.

Rogers was by no means alone here. Versions of this argument were put forward by Catholic, conservative, and progressive liberal critics alike.[164] Robert Flint, a liberal, professorial critic of socialism, who had taken it upon himself to present a series of lectures on the seductive dangers of socialism to Edinburgh's workingmen and women, explained the peculiar appeal of land nationalisation by way of biographical experience. 'In early youth', Flint recalled, 'I myself held the views which they maintain', having been acquainted with and influenced by Patrick Edward Dove, 'a man of talent, almost of genius'.[165] Dove's arguments that 'the rent value of the soil is not the creation of the cultivator, nor of the landlord [... and] should be allocated to the nation' had thoroughly persuaded Flint until he realised that all rights and values were social arrangements that 'cannot possibly be absolute and unlimited as against society'.[166] Any right to land therefore stood exposed to questions of public utility, and, since it was no longer a moral question, any attempt to remove landlordism was also subject to the issue of compensation, rendering it economically imprudent.[167]

If the land question, and in particular George and the Irish Land War, helped to push liberals like Flint away from naturalistic claims to harmony and individual rights, and indeed towards a more traditionally conservative position, it rejuvenated and energised radicals precisely because of these foundational metaphysical claims. As has been argued, to a large degree, the Land War took place in the rhetorical universe of late-eighteenth-century liberalism. George's own views on free trade, for instance, which were frequently a matter of contention with his Irish and Irish-American support, owed much to the Paineite idealism of natural harmony and economic emancipation.[168] George was opposed to protectionism simply because 'it is wasteful; it is demoralizing; it is opposed to liberty'.[169] Michael Davitt, similarly, although more open to practical possibilities of a protective tariff, shared this radical inclination.

[164] See, for example, Brann, *Henry George and His Land Theories*; Mallock, *Property and Progress*; Lecky, *Democracy and Liberty*; Fawcett, *State Socialism*.

[165] Flint, *Socialism*, 204. [166] Flint, *Socialism*, 204, 206.

[167] Flint, *Socialism*, 221.

[168] Frank Trentmann, 'National Identity and Consumer Politics: Free Trade and Tariff Reform', in D. Winch, and P. K. O'Brien (eds.), *The Political Economy of British Historical Experience*, 1688–1914 (Oxford: Oxford University Press, 2002), 217.

[169] Henry George, 'Lecture Notes: Brooklyn Revenue Reform Club', 14 February 1883 (HGP, Series II, Box 13, NYPL).

'I am a free trader', he wrote, 'because I believe in freedom – freedom political, racial, and economic for all'.[170]

Irish communities who had been exposed to the jagged consequences of 'free trade' often met this particular radical nostrum with short shrift, however. Richard Burke, originally of Roscommon but now of West Virginia, wrote to George that while he 'heartily' endorsed his 'idea of land tenure', 'I am unable to concur with the free trade theory'. Burke had left Ireland and the Catholic ministry there for the United States, 'rather than abide the miseries of Ireland under the land system'.[171] The painful economic suffering exacted under the guise of the freedom of the market coloured powerful and lasting perceptions of this particular doctrine as an Anglo-American ideology that sought to undermine 'national husbandry' and therefore the security and sustenance of local communities.[172] A similar answer came from Charles O'Brien, editor of *The American Celt*. It was O'Brien's view that above all else, George's commitment to free trade would impair his Irish support. There were some staff at his paper, he conceded, who were favourable to the policy, 'but the great majority of Irishmen who are acquainted with the issue are tariff men, chiefly because, as you say, it is against English interests'.[173] The issue represented one of the few areas of disagreement between George and the *Irish World*, which supported protection as a means to achieve 'independence and self-reliance', and eliminate the speculators who thrived on the 'Free Trade sophistries'.[174]

The effect of George and the Land League can be detected in the increasing focus, during the 1880s, on the interlocking triumvirate of land, natural rights, and participatory democracy as a particularly potent, mutually reinforcing threat to the stability and order of the state and the security of property. In his polemic against the dangers of democracy, the noted jurist and historical anthropologist Henry Sumner Maine observed that, as 'popular government has steadily extended itself in the Western world', 'no form of property [had become] so much menaced in such societies as property in land'.[175] Malthusianism, 'the central truth of all biological science', was 'evidently disliked by the multitude', who were reasoning with false 'deductions from the assumption of a State of Nature' in which all possessed a priori rights.[176] This not only led them to anti-scientific conclusions about the natural rectitude

[170] Michael Davitt to John D. Fitzgerald, quoted in Marley, *Michael Davitt*, 152.

[171] Richard Burke to Henry George, 2 February 1883 (HGP, Series I: A, Box 4, NYPL).

[172] Trentmann, 'National Identity and Consumer Politics', 223; Marc-William Palen, *The 'Conspiracy' of Free Trade: The Anglo-American Struggle over Empire and Economic Globalisation, 1846–1896* (Cambridge: Cambridge University Press, 2016), 267. Parnell favoured protectionism, and Davitt recognised its occasional necessity too: Bew, *Enigma*, 122; Marley, *Michael Davitt*, 147, 153.

[173] Charles O'Brien to Henry George, 16 February 1883 (HGP, Series I: A, Box 4, NYPL).

[174] *Irish World*, 16 November 1878; *Irish World*, 6 April 1889, clipping in (DP, MS 9368, TCD).

[175] Maine, *Popular Government*, 228. [176] Maine, *Popular Government*, 37, vii.

of participatory democracy – making 'every form of government, except Democracy, illegitimate' – but also, explained Maine, the misguided assumption that land presupposed a natural right to life. Maine's critique was directly shaped by both George and the Land League; the central argument in *Popular Government* was developed from a series of anonymous articles on the land question and boycotting he had authored for the *St. James Gazette* in 1880 and 1881.[177] These influences were evident in his dismissal of 'schemes founded on the assumption that, through legislative experiments on society, a given space of land may always be made to support in comfort the population which from historical causes has come to be settled on it'.[178]

What would become a familiar progressive liberal concern with the political instability threatened by natural rights approaches to the land had earlier been a mainstay of paternalistic mid-century Whig liberalism. Maine's close friend James Fitzjames Stephen, brother of Leslie Stephen, demonstrated this progression. A university friend of William Harcourt, later Home Secretary during the Land War, Stephen was associated with the *Pall Mall Gazette*, a paper defined by its hostility to the liberalism of Mill and Gladstone.[179] Stephen's intellectual fame, such as it was, stemmed from a critical examination of the work of John Stuart Mill, published in 1873, the year of the philosopher's death. In *Liberty, Equality, Fraternity*, Stephen attacked Mill's socialistic tendencies as stemming from his individualistic preoccupation with an innate and antecedent theory of the 'rights of man'.[180] To Stephen, just as with the new liberals who would subsequently echo his arguments both on the question of property and the interrelated issue of boycotting, the state derived its authority to determine both individual liberties and property rights from the fact that all social collectives exerted control (through various mechanisms) over their members.[181] The schemers 'of abstract and so-called natural rights', warned Stephen, made a meaningless distinction between state authority and collective social action, leading to an unnecessary firm 'line between social and legal penalties' and imbuing dangerously anarchic participatory politics with far too much power.[182]

In 1886, Stephen would use these arguments against Irish boycotting, the conservatively minded jurist articulating the social liberal position that the practice was an offence, not against individual liberty (for such a thing could

177 Séamas Ó Síocháin, 'Henry Maine and the Survival of the Fittest', in Séamas Ó Síocháin (ed.), *Social Thought on Ireland in the Nineteenth Century* (Dublin: University College Dublin Press, 2009), 68, 73.

178 Maine, *Popular Government*, 37.

179 John Morley, *Recollections*, vol I (London: Macmillan, 1918), 168.

180 James Fitzjames Stephen, *Liberty, Equality, Fraternity* [1873] (New York: Henry Holt, 1882), 196.

181 Stephen, *Liberty*, 10; see also James A. Colaiaco, *James Fitzjames Stephen and the Crisis of Victorian Thought* (Basingstoke: Palgrave, 1983).

182 James Fitzjames Stephen, 'On the Suppression of Boycotting', *Nineteenth Century* 20, no. 118 (1886): 766; Stephen, *Liberty*, 15.

not exist outside of society), but against the order and stability of the state.[183] As an expression of democratic action, boycotting, just like the demand for land, relied in principle on an *a priori* natural right, normatively distinguishable from legal or governmental authority. But, as Stephen explained, the 'distinction between an unjust and an inexpedient law' relied on nothing firmer than a meaningless moralism, they were 'simply two names for one and the same thing'.[184] This would become a key feature of social liberal thought, used to resist both boycotting and the agrarian radicals' arguments for the land. As the positivist Frederic Harrison wrote to the liberal statesman John Morley, 'what [Stephen] says of Liberty is right. Mill has talked about abstract and absolute right, and has idealized the individual in a way that is metaphysical nonsense and also extremely anarchical [...] Mill's plea for the sacredness of individual liberty is a dangerous sophism'.[185]

George and the agrarian crisis in Ireland made such opposition to 'natural rights' more necessary and more pronounced. On both sides of the Atlantic, progressive liberals were not only concerned with how to justify ameliorative interventions in social and economic life but also how to quell anarchic political and industrial action like boycotting. In the United States, the progressive economist Richard T. Ely, whom Eleanor Marx had described as 'most favourably disposed to the labourers as a class', explained that claims for natural rights were futile, instead 'there are three chief agencies through which we must work for the amelioration of the labouring class, [...] these are Science, the State and the Church'.[186] Natural rights, Woodrow Wilson warned his students at Princeton similarly, were 'false and artificial [and] un-American'.[187] The 'common will' had been the prime governing force of both ancient and modern societies, acting in dialectic fashion with the demands of its leaders.[188] At root, government 'rests upon authority and force', but force mediated through 'the acquiescence of the general will', Wilson explained. As such, government was 'merely the executive organ of society', forming 'a compact, living whole.[189] It followed, therefore, that the damaging effects of industrial capitalism were to be mitigated through rigorous scientific analysis and state management – they were, as Arnold Toynbee told an audience of workingmen, 'problems of administration [that] can be solved if men will

183 Stephen, 'On the Suppression of Boycotting', 765–784.
184 Stephen *Liberty*, 196, 197.
185 Frederic Harrison to John Morley, 8 April 1873, quoted in Colaiaco, *James Fitzjames Stephen*, 163.
186 Aveling, and Marx, *The Working Class Movement in America*, 135; Ely, *Recent American Socialism*, 72.
187 Quoted in Rodgers, *Contested Truths*, 159. See also Saxton, *The Rise and Fall*, 206; Ross, 'Socialism and American Liberalism', 27, 42, 74; Rodgers, *Atlantic Crossings*, 98, 101.
188 Woodrow Wilson, *The State: Elements of Historical and Practical Politics* [1898], rev. ed. (London: D. C. Heath, 1919), 28.
189 Wilson, *The State*, 30.

only have patience' – rather than the chimerical focus on stolen land and lost rights.[190] The language of personal independence often remained, a nod to the older individualist liberalism many wished to protect, but it was now a narrower version, shorn of any claim to direct political power.

In Britain, the work of Thomas Hill Green pressed on with James Fitzjames Stephen's call to dissolve the hazardous distinction between justice and expediency. Although his short academic career was abruptly ended by illness and an untimely death in 1882, Green's ideas proved remarkably influential. His *Principles of Political Obligation* became a key textbook for students of political theory, and his profound impact on liberal politicians extended widely.[191] For Green, natural rights claims were inextricably bound up with possessive acquisitiveness and resistance to social development. By eliding the distinction between socially dependent freedoms and state institutions, that is, making the state itself the extrapolated pinnacle of all anterior forms of social organisation, Green's central achievement was to transpose popular republican notions of social existence and public virtue onto the state, whereby its authority became a distilled and sanitised expression of collective instinct. The social practices of interdependence which constituted individuals' claims on each other – what the radical vision saw as a messy, anarchic, and reflexive process involving shame, duty, affection, and empathy – Green reconstituted as institutional legitimacy; such 'forms of community [...] do not continue to exist outside [the state], nor yet are they superseded by it. They are carried on into it'.[192]

Green's work crystallised and cohered the social liberal response to the radical argument put forward by George and the Land League, articulated in their natural rights demands for land and exemplified in their practices of boycotting. Like Rogers and Fawcett before him, Green explained that any right to land or property of any kind was a social institution, granted for 'good reasons of social expediency' by the state as the guarantor of the common good.[193] In this view, assumptions of a 'law of nature, prescribing the freedom of equality of all', positioned social consciousness as distinct from political authority, 'revers[ing] the true process' and delegitimising the state.[194] Moreover, since Green equated governmental authority with all forms of community, there could be no room for alternative, popular conceptions of land rights – 'the institutions by which

190 Toynbee, *'Progress and Poverty'*, 24.

191 Bernard Bosanquet, 'Preface' in Thomas Hill Green, *Lectures on the Principles of Political Obligation* (London: Longmans, Green, and Co., 1895), v; James Bryce, 'Professor T. H. Green: In Memoriam' *Contemporary Review* 41 (1882): 861.

192 Thomas Hill Green, *Lectures on the Principles of Political Obligation* (London: Longmans, Green, and Co., 1895), 146.

193 Green, *Lectures on the Principles*, 127; Thomas Hill Green, *Liberal Legislation and Freedom of Contract* (Oxford: Slatter and Rose, 1881), 11.

194 Green, *Principles of Political Obligation*, 72.

man is moralised' were embodied within the state, not by some independent social life.[195] Indeed, this meant that resistance, such as represented by the boycott and other radical practices, was fundamentally illegitimate and antisocial. Although the state might not always live up to its role as 'the sustainer and harmoniser of social relations', there could be no natural harmony beyond it.[196] As such, the priority should always rest with the maintenance of order rather than the demand for rights, 'because public interest, on which all rights are founded, is more concerned in the general obedience to law'.[197]

Green's ideas reframed freedom as submission to the general will rather than participation in it.[198] By excising the radical right to life on the land, and subsuming social cooperation into an argument for governmental legitimacy, the question of popular power was superseded by that of public welfare. While he recognised that land 'had its characteristics' which distinguished it from 'ordinary commodities', this was relevant only insofar as it necessitated a greater degree of supervision from legislators.[199] Naturally, Green was pleased with Gladstone's Land Act of 1881, an intervention which offered compromise and conciliation, embedding property rights within an apparatus of technocratic management rather than endangering them. For him, it was an epoch defining measure, a sign that 'the era of administration has come'.[200] His students and disciples agreed that social progress was surely now dependent on careful, scientific management, led by a thoughtful and humane intellectual class.[201] Men such as the Fabian David George Ritchie, a philosopher at St. Andrews who had studied under Green at Oxford, embraced this positivist logic, completely recasting older radical evils such as Malthusianism and utilitarianism as the key to the resolution of social ills.[202] As Hobson later explained, reflecting back on the period: all the 'ruling principles' of the old liberal politics, 'absolute individualism, complete equalitarianism, mechanical rationality', and natural harmonies had been 'justly discredited', leading to 'a complete recasting of the theory and art of government' and the rejection of 'the older democratic doctrines' in order to achieve 'a clearer conception of human welfare'.[203]

Natural rights had long provided a firm grounding for moral demands that was hard to shake off, however. T. H. Green's theory of politics left so little

195 Green, *Principles of Political Obligation*, 122.
196 Green, *Principles of Political Obligation*, 48.
197 Green, *Principles of Political Obligation*, 150. 198 Green, *Liberal Legislation*, 10.
199 Green, *Liberal Legislation*, 15, 11; Green, *Principles of Political Obligation*, 229.
200 Green, *Liberal Legislation*, 23. 201 Claeys, 'Non-Marxian Socialism', 551.
202 Sandra den Otter, *British Idealism and Social Explanation: A Study in late Victorian Thought* (Oxford: Oxford University Press, 1996), 108; see also Stefan Collini, *Liberalism and Sociology: L. T. Hobhouse and Political Argument in England, 1880–1914* (Cambridge: Cambridge University Press, 1979).
203 J. A. Hobson, *Free-Thought in the Social Sciences* (London: George Allen & Unwin, 1926), 268–269. On Hobson, see Michael Freeden (ed.), *Reappraising J. A. Hobson: Humanism and*

room for collective action against governmental authority that he struggled to justify resistance to slavery without almost inadvertently naturalising a right to personal liberty.[204] Progressive liberals sometimes lapsed, by necessity, into the older radical register of justice, harmony, and rights. Carl C. Plehn, Professor of Political Economy at Berkeley, referring to the heavy burden of property tax on Californian farmers, called it an 'injustice, or, better, [an] inexpedient method of taxation'.[205] Plehn, who rejected any reliance on natural rights to confer ownership when he insisted that 'private property in land, as in any other form of wealth, rests on the same basis of expediency', still tripped into this language, before correcting himself.[206] As his Georgist interlocutor correctly observed, in 'denying Natural Rights, although using the words "just" and "unjust," you [can only] rest your arguments on expediency'.[207] Similarly, Arnold Toynbee, cautioning an audience of workingmen and women about the dangers of Georgism, declared 'you have no right – well, it is superfluous to talk about right – I say that it is highly inexpedient in the interests of this community' to take someone's property.[208] Such missteps reflected the difficulty of fully discarding a powerful moral vision.

Pressed by the agrarian crises of the 1880s, this shift also necessitated a reframing of the idea of democracy. Where the land question had, in radical hands, served to legitimate popular political participation, its abandonment by liberals facilitated a theory of public welfare that embraced mass politics only as a passive expression of collective will, to be moulded and directed as required, and had very little to say about the connection between economic and political power. Threats to property were therefore threats to the social order upon which all rights rested and without which 'I literally should not have a life to call my own'.[209] Protecting property, 'the first and most valuable' aspect of 'the progress of civilization', should therefore always take precedence over popular participation.[210] The 'fierce anarchy' of the Land League was in this way reframed as a danger to popular rights. For William Gladstone, it was the 'confiscation', 'spoliation', and 'sheer rapine' of the League that made the Land War 'a conflict for the very first and elementary principles upon which

Welfare (London: Unwin Hyman, 1990); Michael Freeden, 'J. A. Hobson as a New Liberal Theorist: Some Aspects of his Social Thought until 1914', *Journal of the History of Ideas* 34, no. 3 (1973): 421–433.

204 Green, *Principles of Political Obligation*, 137–138, 145, 149, 153.

205 Professor Carl Plehn, in T. H. Benton De Witt (ed.), *A Correspondence between an Amateur and a Professor of Political Economy* (Philadelphia: J. B. Lippincott, 1898), 10.

206 Professor Carl Plehn, in Benton De Witt (ed.), *A Correspondence*, 9.

207 James Love, in T. H. Benton De Witt (ed.), *A Correspondence between an Amateur and a Professor of Political Economy* (Philadelphia: J. B. Lippincott, 1898), 11.

208 Toynbee, *'Progress and Poverty'*, 40.

209 Green, *Principles of Political Obligation*, 122.

210 Lecky, *Democracy and Liberty*, vol. I, li, 212; J. R. Seeley, *The Expansion of England: Two Courses of Lectures* [1883] (Boston: Little, Brown, and Company, 1905), 67.

civil society is constituted'.[211] In justifying coercive policies against popular action, liberal politicians relied heavily on the same logic that T. H. Green utilised. Although there were no natural rights to land, property must be protected in order to secure the principle of 'civilization'. This meant that sometimes, for 'a civilised government to be really advantageous to the people, [it] must be in a considerable degree despotic', explained the radical liberal M.P. Thomas Burt.[212] Exposing these contradictions between liberty and property – between natural freedoms and private accumulation – the Land War forced liberalism to finally and more fully dispose of its older individualistic assumptions in order to protect social order, property, 'progress', and 'civilization'.[213] The consequence of this, as Hobson would explain in the early twentieth century, was an entire revision of 'the doctrine of Democracy'.[214]

In the economic sphere, the marginal revolution echoed this process, edging out normative and moral concerns from economic analysis. The distinction between land, in the form of rent, and other property, in the form of profit, was erased in neoclassical marginalism, as use and exchange value collapsed into each other under the banner of marginal utility.[215] Here, too, George had a role to play. As Edwin Cannan intimated, George's use of Ricardian economics, directing it towards the politics of 'confiscation', had helped to discredit classical economic theory.[216] From the progressive liberal perspective, the law of rent had been, at best, 'a very naïve piece of improvisation' intended to serve 'some useful purpose as a lightning conductor' for the protection of capitalists, which Mill, and later George, had inadvertently turned against its creators.[217] But neoclassical theory could circumvent this: Alfred Marshall, the leading English marginalist, was keen to show, in his dismissal of George, that land should not be considered distinct from moveable property.[218] In drawing out the somewhat latent socialistic tendencies that classical economic theory contained with regard to land, hereditary traits from its republican ancestry, many

211 *Freeman's Journal*, 28 October 1881.

212 Thomas Burt, *The Government and the Land League* (Birmingham: National Liberal Foundation, 1881), 9, 15.

213 Woodrow Wilson, 'What Is Progress?' [1912], in *The New Freedom: A Call for the Emancipation of the Generous Energies of a People* (New York: Doubleday, Page and Co., 1918), 42, 45–46.

214 John Allet Hobson, *The Crisis of Liberalism: New Issues of Democracy* (London: P.S. King & Son, 1909), 77–78.

215 Sklansky, *The Soul's Economy*, 106.

216 Cannan, *A History of the Theories of Production*, 393.

217 Hobson, *Free-Thought*, 87–90.

218 Marshall, 'Three Lectures on *Progress and Poverty*', 224; James J. Shaw, 'The Nationalization of the Land', *Journal of the Social and Statistical Inquiry Society of Ireland* 8, no. 62 (1884): 492–508; Elwood P. Lawrence, 'Henry George's Oxford Speech', *California Historical Society Quarterly* 30, no. 2 (1951): 117–123.

marginalists later identified George, and so indirectly the Irish Land War as well, as the key factors in its destruction.[219]

Like the politics of social liberalism, neoclassical economics benefitted from its claims to professional and scientific authority, mathematical precision, and moral neutrality.[220] Professionalisation and the cover of scientific objectivity helped to insulate economists from the moral critique of 'powerful amateurs' like George.[221] In both spheres, the political and the economic, the concept of utility came to evince a certain circularity, representing not only a central organising principle, but an intellectual horizon under which all competing measurements of value were collapsed. Peering beyond this meant discovering that 'ethical science' could unearth nothing more solid than selfishness as the only scientifically proven moral maxim.[222] It was through the corporeal politics of land that radicals resisted these moral foundations of the scientific management of the social order. Such selfishness still remained, in the moralistic view of the *Irish World*, 'the essence of all evil in the world'.[223] The practical application of mechanistic and hedonistic reasoning was turning man 'into an exquisite automaton', offering nothing but 'the science of second causes' and leaving 'nothing but unconscious force' in its wake.[224] This was the essence of George's fundamental disagreement with Herbert Spencer and the other 'high priests of positivism'.[225] Spencer's disavowal of land nationalisation in favour of social Darwinian individualism was an unconscionable intellectual treachery to George.[226] Considering the English philosopher to have been cowed by economic interests, George attacked his evolutionary ethics as hollow and meaningless, lacking any 'basis for moral ideas': 'All his efforts to obtain something like a moral sanction reach no further than expediency', he complained.[227] An important conclusion that George drew from Spencer's

219 John Maloney, *Marshall, Orthodoxy and the Professionalisation of Economics* (Cambridge: Cambridge University Press, 1985), 207.

220 Furner, 'The Republican Tradition and the New Liberalism', 185; Rothschild, 'Political Economy', 767; Philip Mirowski, 'Physics and the "Marginalist Revolution"', *Cambridge Journal of Economics* 8 (1984): 361–379.

221 Church, 'Economists as Experts', 573, 592.

222 Henry Sidgwick, *The Methods of Ethics* [1874], 7th ed. (London: Macmillan, 1907), vi, xv; Francis Y. Edgeworth, *Mathematical Psychics: An Essay on the Application of Mathematics to the Moral Sciences* (London: Kegan Paul, 1881), 16.

223 *Irish World*, 23 November 1878.

224 Edward Carpenter, 'Modern Science: A Criticism' [1885] in *Civilisation, Its Cause and Cure, and Other Essays* (London: G. Allen & Unwin, 1921), 79; A. de. G., 'Position of the Intellectual World as Regards Religion', *American Catholic Quarterly Review* 5 (1880): 442; *Irish World*, 23 November 1878.

225 Ransom B. Welch, *Faith and Modern Thought* (New York: G. P. Putnam's Sons, 1876), 271.

226 George, *A Perplexed Philosopher,* 167; Alfred Russel Wallace, 'Herbert Spencer on the Land Question: A Criticism' [1892], in *Studies: Scientific and Social,* vol I (London: Macmillan, 1900), 333.

227 George, *A Perplexed Philosopher,* 116–117.

duplicitous intellectual manoeuvres was that no individual should accept the conclusions of academics without personal investigation, for 'while we may not be scientists or philosophers we too are men'.[228] 'On such subjects' as politics and economics, George warned, 'the masses of men cannot safely trust authority', as it rested on 'the views and wishes of those who profit or imagine they profit from the wrong'.[229]

Land provided a site of resistance against these attempts to 'smother natural rights with conventional technicalities' and exclude public participation.[230] It could be a secure ground against the danger that, without access to natural resources by right, 'every extension and application of systematized knowledge to the arts seems to tend to the concentration of power and wealth'.[231] The agrarian movement that encompassed George and the League resisted these processes, but also inadvertently propelled them. It was a perverse but remarkable achievement that such campaigns managed to unite opponents from across the political spectrum in agreement that land was not a unique form of property; that actually all forms of property were social creations. Albeit with wildly differing conclusions, socialists, liberals, and conservatives could agree on that. This confluence provided valuable cover and protection for property in land on the slippery and elusive basis of utility. In an unending circularity, the right to land was *already* held on the final authority of the state; therefore, there was no need to indulge schemes of nationalisation. It would be economically counterproductive to expropriate or to recompensate landlords. Even Lecky, defending civilisation from George's proposed upheavals, paused to add that he had 'no wish to put forward any extreme or exaggerated view of the sanctity of landed property. In my own opinion, the Legislature has a perfect right, if the public welfare requires it, to take possession of all such property'.[232] The Liberty and Property Defence League agreed: all property, including land, was 'held subject [to] public interest' and could be taken by the state.[233] It was simply that, just as Robert Flint, Henry Fawcett, J. E. Thorold Rogers, and many others noted similarly, it was inexpedient to do so.

[228] George, *A Perplexed Philosopher*, 238. [229] George, *A Perplexed Philosopher*, 235.
[230] Ingalls, *Land and Labor*, 3; *Irish World*, 12 July 1879.
[231] Henry George, 'Garfield or Hancock', 1880 (HGP, Series II, Box 12, NYPL).
[232] Lecky, *Democracy and Liberty*, vol I, 191.
[233] Liberty and Property Defence League, *Land*, 20.

6 Class, Culture, and Place

Writing in 1887, the prominent American jurist A. Lawrence Lowell, a well-heeled scion of New England's Brahmin elite and latterly president of Harvard University, expressed his unease with the growing numbers of Irish immigrants in US cities. Keen for new arrivals to 'merge indistinguishably in the body of the people', Lowell's particular concern was the intractability of Irish identity. 'Among the various European races whose members have become citizens of the United States in large numbers', he complained, 'there is, perhaps, none from which it has been more difficult to erase the foreign sentiments and qualities [...] than the Irish'.[1] From Lowell's vantage, three interlinked tendencies among the Irish had combined to make them peculiarly aggravating to Anglo-American cultural sensibilities and dangerous to the stability of its political institutions. First, there was their 'clannish nature' which caused them to congregate in cities and allowed them exert undue political influence; second, their Catholicism, an ostensibly superstitious and intolerant creed; and finally, and perhaps most importantly, their political subalternism. For not only were the majority of Irish immigrants desperately poor, they also lacked 'the views and sentiments of the capitalist'.[2]

Lowell's observations, despite their hostility, recognised something meaningful. The ideological baggage of Irish culture, even in its variation, carried within it a means of resistance to the imposing structures of capitalist life.[3] For Irish immigrants in industrial America, just as for those in northwest England or the west of Scotland, the experiences of their transplanted communal life, inscribed upon and reinforced by expressions of Irish national identity, offered a means to refuse the instrumentality of their new urban and capitalist environments. While the discourses of agrarian radicalism emanated from the practices and experiences of life on the land, and were supported by features of Catholic and republican thought, they were also tethered quite effectively to Irish identity and figured prominently in the languages of Irish nationalism. The physical displacement of emigration laid bare a corresponding emotional

[1] A. Lawrence Lowell, 'Irish Agitation in America', *Forum* 4, no. 4 (December 1887): 401.
[2] Lowell, 'Irish Agitation in America', 401. [3] Lloyd, 'The Clachan and the Chartists', 33.

and ideological dislocation. Not only for recent arrivals but for second- and third-generation Irish-Americans, the romantic appeal of a spiritual home free from the corrupting struggles of life in America held out a strong attraction. It was in this way that Irishness could easily become, as Lowell realised, the vehicle for political radicalism. As Ireland itself came to be viewed by British and American elites as a dangerous place apart, a malignant sore disfiguring the harmony of the Anglo-American North Atlantic, so too did Irish identity become a 'creative irritant', and a conduit for radical ideas.[4]

The Politics of Place

Each year the invitations to the annual ball held by Boston's Fenian Brotherhood grew more and more ornate and ostentatious, developing gilded edges and elaborate designs.[5] These cards were material indications of the increasing wealth and power among an Irish-American middle class who, despite success in their business and professional lives, were still often deeply and personally invested in the cause of Irish nationalism. How was it that this nationalism still paid emotive deference to the superior spirituality of the oppressed Irishman and woman and still framed Irish identity as a form of resistance to the debasing materialism of Anglo-American culture? In this regard, the reflexive identification of Irishness with political and economic subjugation and an unshakable anti-materialism appeared to sit uneasily alongside the commercial preoccupations of prosperous and respectable Irish-Americans. At the very least, there was a degree of tension between the 'fanatic heart' of the Irish nationalist and the demands of bourgeois gentility. Some have interpreted this as hypocrisy, or at least a collective self-deception, in which 'radical rhetoric' disguised the 'fundamentally conservative demands' of inclusion and elevation within the status hierarchy of American social and commercial life.[6]

Certainly the successful career trajectories of Boston Fenians like George D. Cahill or Patrick A. Collins, who would later serve in the US Congress, would support this hypothesis. There is no doubt that ethnic and nationalist associationalism of this type was in part motivated by a desire for assimilation into the host culture; to secure Irish independence as a means to secure American acceptance.[7] It is also true that nationalist organisations offered the opportunity for intra-group leadership, where middle-class Irish-Americans could exert social control and influence that might hold back the more radical

[4] Doyle, 'Irish Elites in North America', 31.

[5] Invitations to Annual Ball of the Fenian Brotherhood (GDCP, Series II, Box 5, BC).

[6] Miller, *Ireland and Irish-America*, 267; Brown, *Irish-American Nationalism*, 46, 153–154.

[7] Enda Delaney and Donald MacRaild, 'Irish Migration, Networks and Ethnic Identities since 1750: An Introduction', *Immigrants & Minorities* 23, nos. 2–3 (2005): 130.

elements among their compatriots.[8] Nevertheless, just as in Ireland where the acquisitive ambitions of large graziers remained constrained by the egalitarian rhetoric of the smaller farmers and labourers, middle-class Irish-Americans were also beholden to the political radicalism of a large and influential section of the Irish working class.[9]

What the language of Irish nationalism showed was not an inauthentic radical veneer disguising hypocrisy and power lust, but that Irish identity remained transfixed by and unable to escape from the moralistic, romantic, and egalitarian tones of agrarian republicanism.[10] This intersection of national and radical premises meant that even cultural activities which aimed at the 'de-Anglicization of the Irish people' were by necessity premised on the existence of dramatic differences between Anglo-American and Irish cultural mores, and so ended up repudiating liberal-capitalist modes of rationality as irredeemably 'Anglo-Saxon'.[11] Reinforcing and reifying 'Irishness' also meant rejecting as cold and inhuman the perceived individualism of Anglo-American political culture. Such were the tendencies that caused Michael Davitt to worry about the 'demoralising influences' of English 'civilization' as it 'infuse[d] its views into those [cultures] with which it is brought into contact';[12] or Matthew Harris' observation that wealthier Irish people abandoned their national identification as incompatible with their social status.[13] Irish identity became inescapably subaltern.

This conflagration of national identity and radical politics mapped on to the peculiarities of place in uneven ways. Depending on the features of the host community and the levels of Irish immigration, such political identities could be subsumed, synthesised, come to coexist with or even dominate local political cultures.[14] In some places across the North Atlantic, such as Liverpool, or Butte, Montana, where the Irish community reached a critical mass, such Irish cultural forms took hold and persisted, shaping politics and dominating wider social life.[15] Within culturally contained areas of larger cities, this process was

[8] John Belchem, 'Ethnicity and Labour History: With Special Reference to Irish Migration', in van Voss, and van der Linden (eds.), *Class and Other Identities: Gender, Religion and Ethnicity in the Writing of European Labour History* (New York: Berghahn Books, 2002), 92–93.

[9] Miller, *Ireland and Irish America*, 251.

[10] Gordon, 'Studies in Irish and Irish American Thought', 385.

[11] Jacobson, *Special Sorrows*, 31.

[12] Michael Davitt, 'English Civilisation', in Carla King (ed.), *Jottings in Solitary* (Dublin: University College Dublin Press, 2003), 19.

[13] Matthew Harris, letter to the *Irishman*, Ballinasloe, 19 June 1880, Pamphlet (HP, MS 21,910, NLI); Frederick Engels complained similarly that 'the worst [thing] about the Irish is that they become corruptible as soon as they stop being peasants and turn bourgeois', Engels to Marx, 27 September 1869, in Karl Marx, and Frederick Engels, *Ireland and the Irish Question*, 274.

[14] Meagher, 'From the World to the Village', 132; Belchem, 'Ethnicity and Labour History', 88–100.

[15] David M. Emmons, 'Exiles, "Evangelizers", and Anti-imperialists: Ireland's Disputed American "Empire"', *American Journal of Irish Studies* 9 (2012): 65; David Emmons, *The Butte Irish: Class and Ethnicity in an American Mining Town, 1875–1925* (Urbana: University of Illinois Press, 1990).

also visible. The survival and development of boycotting, which was only possible where shared moral norms persisted, demonstrated that places such as Wilkes-Barre in the Pennsylvanian coalfields, or lower Manhattan, were incubators of Irish cultural politics.[16] To the more hostile elements in the contemporary American press, places like Boston and New York even appeared to be 'virtually Irish cities'.[17]

Yet such a significant number of Irish immigrants did not easily translate into political unity. As Patrick Ford complained to Michael Davitt at the end of the 1890s, 'there are fully 25,000,000 of Irish blood in the United States, [if only they] understood themselves and would come together, things would be as we could wish them to be'.[18] There was wide variation across the country. In New England, as a bastion of establishment Anglo-America, the Irish community found fewer avenues for municipal political influence than in the metropolis of New York.[19] The mining towns of Pennsylvania's anthracite region fostered an industrial solidarity that was hugely different to Irish-American culture in California, where Chinese immigration and the absence of a long established community were formative influences. In the American South, intra-Irish competition and religious distinction became less important in the face of a unifying Confederate and 'Southern' identity.[20] Across the west in general, where the image of the rugged frontiersman was preferred to strictures of eastern gentility, more socially radical ambitions for Irish national and agrarian liberation tended to be embraced.[21]

In smaller towns, such as Worcester, Massachusetts, the Irish-American community often sought incremental integration, adopting American cultural forms while maintaining a distinct but sanitised Irish identity. A community not large or concentrated enough to secure direct political representation itself, the Irish in Worcester required interaction and affiliation with pre-existing institutions in contrast to larger industrial centres such as nearby Fall River, where the political hue of Irish politics was often more radical, and interest in local integration less pronounced.[22] The iron and steel mills of Pittsburgh, as Victor Walsh argued,

16 *New York Times*, 27 July 1902.

17 E. E. Hale, 'Social Forces in the United States', *North American Review* 137, no. 323 (1883): 406.

18 Patrick Ford to Michael Davitt, 19 January 1899 (DP, MS 9483/6742, TCD).

19 Thomas H. O'Connor, *The Boston Irish: A Political History* (Boston: Back Bay Books, 1995); Ronald H. Bayor, and Timothy J. Meagher (eds.), *The New York Irish* (Baltimore, MD: Johns Hopkins University Press, 1997).

20 David T. Gleeson, 'Smaller Differences: "Scotch Irish" and "Real Irish" in the Nineteenth-Century American South', *New Hibernia Review* 10, no. 2 (2006): 68–91; Kevin Kenny, 'Twenty Years of Irish American Historiography', *Journal of American Ethnic History*, 28, no. 4 (2009): 67–75; Malcolm Campbell, 'Ireland's Furthest Shores: Irish Immigrant Settlement in Nineteenth-Century California and Eastern Australia', *Pacific Historical Review* 71, no. 1 (2002): 59–90

21 Emmons, *The Butte Irish*, 293–295.

22 Timothy J. Meagher, *Inventing Irish America: Generation, Class, and Ethnic Identity in a New England City, 1880–1928* (Notre Dame, IN: University of Notre Dame Press, 2001), 135–154.

acted as 'cultural crucibles', drawing together Irish immigrants under a nationalist and radical political identity.[23] In centres such as this, the various ethnic, nationalist, and labour associations often blended together quite closely, sharing overlapping membership and interests.[24] Naturally, Land League branches drew their members from existing labour and nationalist groups, particularly the Knight of Labor. As Terence Powderly recalled, 'a secret meeting of the Knights of Labor would follow' on from Land League meetings on occasion, such was the symbiotic relationship between Irish nationalist and radical labour movements.[25] In Ireland and in the United States, senior leadership and regular members often belonged to both the League and the Knights. In places, such as Randolph, Massachusetts, where the subsequent National League was unable to sustain itself, the existence of thriving local assemblies of Knights served to explain the diversion of radical energies.[26]

Such associationalism, what Lowell derided as 'clannish' behaviour, was taken as evidence that 'the Irish are much addicted to politics'.[27] Nowhere was this assumption more clearly manifest than in the local democratic politics of New York and Philadelphia, which Irish-Americans dominated during the second half of the nineteenth century. New York's famous Tammany Hall, the local 'Democratic-Republican' political machine founded in 1789, came to function as a 'miniature, private welfare state', concerned with practical gains for the ethnic community.[28] Operating on the basis of reciprocal loyalties, Irish dominance of urban machine politics represented less a desire for power and influence than an attempt to firm up social cohesion through mutualism and protection.[29] Local politics provided an opportunity to institutionalise support for otherwise precarious Irish workers, in what was later described as 'the social system of an Irish village writ large'.[30] It was not simply a means for individual self-aggrandizement, but bore similarities to the proliferate web of mutual aid,

[23] Victor A. Walsh, 'A Fanatic Heart: The Cause of Irish American Nationalism in Pittsburgh during the Gilded Age', *Journal of Social History* 15 (1981): 195.

[24] Walsh, 'A Fanatic Heart', 192–193.

[25] Powderly, *The Path I Trod*, 179; Foner, 'Class, Ethnicity, and Radicalism', 169–170.

[26] Thomas Dolan to George D. Cahill, 22 June 1887 (George D. Cahill Papers, Box 4, Boston College).

[27] Lowell, 'Irish Agitation in America', 402.

[28] Melvyn Dubofsky, *When Workers Organize: New York City in the Progressive Era* (Amherst: University of Massachusetts Press, 1968), 21; see also, Peter McCaffery, *When Bosses Ruled Philadelphia: The Emergence of the Republican Machine, 1867–1933* (University Park: Pennsylvania State University Press, 1993).

[29] Steven P. Erie, 'Politics, the Public Sector and Irish Social Mobility: San Francisco, 1870–1900', *The Western Political Quarterly* 31, no. 2 (1978): 275–276; Steven P. Erie, *Rainbow's End: Irish-Americans and the Dilemmas of Urban Machine Politics, 1840–1985* (Berkeley: University of California Press, 1988), 25; Lawrence McCaffrey, 'Ireland and Irish-America: Connections and Disconnections', *U.S. Catholic Historian* 22, no. 3 (2004): 10.

[30] Nathan Glazer and Daniel Patrick Moynihan, *Beyond the Melting Pot: The Negroes, Puerto Ricans, Jews, Italians, and Irish of New York City* (Cambridge, MA: MIT and Harvard University Press, 1963), 226.

charitable, and benefit societies that flourished in Irish immigrant communities across the diaspora.[31] Community support could provide resistance to the dislocation caused by the 'peripatetic quest' for individual success.[32]

Shifting with the tides of Irish-American opinion, Tammany's opportunistic support for the Land League from 1881 onwards was a sign of the agrarian movement's power and reach among New York's working-class Irish.[33] But it was not such explicit radicalism that first drew the chagrin of wealthy and powerful Anglo-American elites like Lowell towards Irish political power in urban America. The expansion of the industrial and financial sectors had, Lowell noted, demanded greater administrative organisation, requiring legislators to discard 'the exploded doctrine of the natural rights of man' and enact 'the complete reform of the civil service'.[34] As such, a more systematic and professionalised approach to local governance was required, adopting the informed and expedient managerial techniques of commercial life to rationalise the messiness of local democracy. This meant that the chaotic and informal structures of urban Irish politics, often grounded in local and interpersonal loyalties, needed to be swept away and replaced with a more logical system of local authority.

In New York, the city's wealthy social elite enthusiastically led the charge for civil service reform.[35] Attacking demagoguery and despotism, and the slavish tendencies of an imported Catholicism, the civil service reformers were not only overwhelmingly Protestant and Anglo-American, but their professional networks, in which philanthropy and civil reform appeared as merely an adjunct of finance and industry, gave this group the appearance of a pseudo-aristocratic establishment; the great and good devoted to patrician principles of improvement. Emerging from the city's exclusive Union League Club, an organisation devoted to the idea that 'eminent men with ancestors in Colonial stock had too long retreated from public life', the New York Committee of

[31] Deborah S. Skok, 'Organized Almsgiving: Scientific Charity and the Society of St. Vincent de Paul in Chicago, 1871–1918', *U.S. Catholic Historian* 16 (1998): 19–35; Belchem, *Irish, Catholic and Scouse*, 70–94.

[32] John Belchem, 'The Immigrant Alternative: Ethnic and Sectarian Mutuality among the Liverpool Irish during the Nineteenth Century', in Owen Ashton, Robert Fyson, and Stephen Roberts (eds.), *The Duty of Discontent: Essays for Dorothy Thompson* (London: Mansell Publishing, 1995), 232.

[33] Foner, 'Class, Ethnicity, and Radicalism', 166, 177.

[34] A. Lawrence Lowell, *Essays on Government* (Boston: Houghton, Mifflin and Company, 1890), 48, 9, 50.

[35] Brown, *Irish-American Nationalism*, 140; see also, Leslie Butler, *Critical Americans: Victorian Intellectuals and Transatlantic Liberal Reform* (Chapel Hill: UNC Press, 2007), 191–200; Robert H. Wiebe, *The Search for Order, 1877–1920* (New York: Hill and Wang, 1967); John G. Sproat, *"The Best Men": Liberal Reformers in the Gilded Age* (New York: Oxford University Press, 1968); Edward H. Miller, 'They Vote Only for the Spoils: Massachusetts Reformers, Suffrage Restriction, and the 1884 Civil Service Law', *The Journal of the Gilded Age and Progressive Era* 8, no. 3 (2009): 341–363.

Seventy declared, in 1871, its intention to purge the 'official corruption which has made such cheering progress in this city' and 'bribed the toiling masses' into acquiescence.[36] Regardless of the embezzlement by 'Boss' Tweed and his ring, to Irish-Americans in New York, this appeared to be an attempt to exclude them from political office by pretentious, Anglicised, aristocratic elites.[37] It was the intention of such reformers, Patrick Ford warned his readers, 'to import and slavishly imitate the manners of the English aristocracy, deride republican simplicity, [and] bring into contempt democratic institutions'.[38]

What was, from one side, an attempt to rationalise and de-personalise political life, to expunge sentiment in public affairs in favour of an ordered administration, appeared on the other as centralisation and bureaucratic control. These characteristics were comfortably mapped on to cultural stereotypes. The Irish dealt 'too much in sentiment and too little in cold facts' and were 'guided almost exclusively by sentiment and passion', complained Anglo-American liberals who had isolated the problem of sentimentality as a primary affliction of the country's democracy.[39] If sentiment should remain only in 'the sphere of private and personal relations' rather than political life, then it was axiomatic that the Irish, 'a people renowned for careless generosity regardless of [the] consequences', should not possess undue political power.[40] Not least since this 'unfortunate emotional bias' was the primary cause of erroneous views on the uniqueness of property in land.[41] In the realm of philanthropy and charity, too, Irish cultural mores chaffed against the developing propensity for more ordered, systematised, and efficient relief, seeing it as a distasteful and hollow replacement for social obligation and human feeling; what John Boyle O'Reilly, former Fenian and editor of the Boston *Pilot*, mocked as 'That Organised Charity, scrimped and iced, in the name of a cautious, statistical Christ'.[42]

Conversely, an obsession with centralisation and bureaucracy, what John Mitchel had described as the 'British System', featured prominently in Irish analyses of English political thought.[43] Drawing heavily on republican and

[36] *Appeal to the People of the State of New York, Adopted by the Executive Committee of Citizens and Taxpayers for the Financial Reform of the City and County of New York* (New York: The "Free Press" Association, 1871), 11; Gordon, 'Studies in Irish and Irish American Thought', 405; O'Donnell, 'Henry George and the "New Political Forces"', 198.

[37] Brown, *Irish-American Nationalism*, 140.

[38] *Irish World*, 1 January 1877.

[39] *Boston Daily Advertiser*, quoted in *Boston Pilot*, 17 January 1880; Stephen, 'On the Suppression of Boycotting', 775.

[40] Sumner, *What Social Classes Owe*, 25. 'Ireland Under Ordinary Law', 271; Goldwin Smith, 'Great Britain, America, and Ireland', *Princeton Review* (July–December 1882): 283.

[41] Molesworth, *Land as Property*, 2.

[42] John Boyle O'Reilly, *In Bohemia* (Boston: Cashman, Keating & Co., 1886), 15;. Skok, 'Organized Almsgiving', 19–20; Belchem, *Irish, Catholic and Scouse*, 91.

[43] John Mitchel to Fr Kenyon, in Dillon, *Life of John Mitchel*, 106.

anti-imperial arguments, political centralisation was considered an English tendency. Grounded, explained Henry George, in 'aristocratic and monarchical ideals', it sought to disempower local communities while obfuscating economic exploitation.[44] Arguing through their experiences of British rule, Irish nationalists often denounced unitary and centralised power as being '*of necessity* a failure', and made local self-government a primary goal.[45] The administrative structure of the British Empire was seen to have created a tyrannical but invisible economic machine, detaching duty and responsibility from the exercise of power, making it less visible and resistible. Causing political and civic life to wilt, centralised bureaucracy served only financial power through what Davitt described as 'the mercenary class of officials who are seldom heard of by the public'.[46] It was the Famine, perhaps above all, which had provided the most painful manifestation of this type of deaf power in the Irish imagination. 'The poor man on whom the coroner holds an inquest has been murdered, but no one killed him', Archbishop John Hughes famously said during the Famine, 'Who did it? No one did it. Yet it was done'.[47]

These two cultural and ideological tendencies also clashed firmly over the meaning of America itself. In line with a broader shift in the Anglophone world towards an emphasis on the commonalities and unity of the 'white' settler empire, many Anglo-Americans sought to stress the cultural significance of the British connection to the United States.[48] For some, this involved accentuating the 'Teutonic' influences on American liberty, rather than according too much prominence to an awkward, anti-British revolution.[49] The final decades of the nineteenth century even saw tentative suggestions for some form of confederation between the United States and its former imperial ruler, provoking fears among Irish-Americans that 'the actual physical reunion of Britain and America may be consummated'.[50] The British historian Goldwin Smith, who had held a Professorship at Cornell during the previous decade, lamented in 1882 that 'the anti-British feeling

44 Henry George, *Irish World*, 1 April 1882; E. E. Hale, 'Social Forces in the United States', 405.

45 Justin McCarthy, M.P., quoted in Conyngham, *Ireland Past and Present*, 241; 'Constitution of the Irish National League' (Heffernan Papers, MS 21,910, NLI); Biagini, *British Democracy*, 108; *Irish World*, 13 September 1879; 2 September 1882.

46 Michael Davitt, 'Ireland's Share of the British Constitution', in Carla King (ed.), *Jottings in Solitary* (Dublin: University College Dublin Press, 2003), 60–61.

47 This version of the Archbishop's speech, delivered in New York, 20 March 1847, is recounted in Michael Davitt, *The Fall of Feudalism in Ireland or the Story of the Land League Revolution* (New York: Harper and Brothers, 1904), 51–52.

48 Duncan Bell, 'Empire and International Relations in Victorian Political Thought', *The Historical Journal* 49, no. 1 (2006): 297.

49 Craig Bruce Smith, 'Claiming the Centennial: The American Revolution's Blood and Spirit in Boston, 1870–1876', *Massachusetts Historical Review* 15 (2013): 7–53.

50 *New York Times*, 9 April 1902; Edward F. McSweeney, 'De-Americanizing Young America: Poisoning the Source of our National History and Traditions', 1920 (AIA.047, NYU).

of the Irish in the United States' was the 'sole impediment' to 'the existence of perfect amity, and a union as entire as the severing Atlantic will permit' between Britain and America.[51]

Responding to these tendencies, the *Irish World* fumed that 'the Republic bequeathed to us by the Revolutionary War and republican statesmen is not to the liking of our snobs'.[52] For Irish-Americans, the American War of Independence provided a potent historical memory upon which to fix their claims to American identity, as well as their struggle for Irish self-government. The imagery of the American Revolution was tossed back and forth across the Atlantic; used in Ireland to justify resistance, in the United States to demand acceptance, and called upon to secure the support of non-Irish-Americans in the cause.[53] Jefferson's old warning that 'in spite of treaties, England is still our enemy' was given a fresh new lease of life in Irish-American pamphlets, where the diaspora and those back home in Ireland were enjoined to follow 'Washington's example [against] England's consistent perversity'.[54] Speaking at a National League reception in Chicago, the Irish nationalist leader Alexander Sullivan called upon Americans not to forget that 'in this struggle the people of Ireland were but following the example of those here, who enjoyed no liberty, no prosperity, until they drove English authority from their shores'.[55] In Ireland, too, the image of America performed a critical role as a political archetype and a counterweight to British imperial influence. The 'Great Western Republic', or the 'great Republic beyond the Atlantic', not only set a political example, however, but offered promise of protection as 'the moral avenger of Ireland'.[56] The 'rent tax' would, like the 'tea tax', lead similarly to 'national independence'.[57] Some nationalists even entertained the idea of federation with the United States in lieu of independence, causing the *Irish*

[51] Smith, 'Great Britain, America, and Ireland', 283. [52] *Irish World*, 7 December 1878.

[53] David Sim, *A Union Forever: The Irish Question and U.S. Foreign Relations in the Victorian Age* (Ithaca, NY: Cornell University Press, 2013).

[54] Clancy, *Ireland: As She Is*, 27.

[55] Alexander Sullivan, speech reprinted in *Irish World*, 16 February 1883 (Davitt Papers, TCD, MS 9368); T. L. McCarthy, *Irish World*, 8 February 1879; Thomas Sexton, 'Proceedings of the Second Annual Convention of the Irish National league of America, held at Boston, Mass., 13 and 14 August 1884', 14 (PAHRC, 103, Box 40, AC0129). See also Dr. William B. Wallace, 'Address to the Representatives of the Irish Societies of the Empire State' (Devoy Papers, NLI, MS 18,048); United States Senator Jones of Florida, in 'Report of the Second Annual Convention of the Irish National League of America', Boston 13–14 August 1884 (Devoy Papers, MS 18,048, NLI).

[56] Clancy, *Ireland: As She Is*, 304; quote from 'Irish National Land League Relief Fund: Sums received for Relief of Distress by Irish National Land League, from 22 December 1879 to 30 April 1880 also Particulars of Grants made by Land League to Local Relief Committees, &c., from 22 December 1879 to 30 April 1880' (Heffernan papers, MS 21,910, NLI); Rev James Cantwell at INLL meeting at Thurles Co. Tipperary, 14 November 1880 (MS 11,289, NLI); Father O'Boyle, speaking in Belfast, *Ulster Examiner*, 4 February 1882.

[57] Matthew Harris, letter to the *Irishman*, Ballinasloe, 19 June 1880, Pamphlet (MS 21,910, NLI); see also comments by J. B. McHugh, Bailieborough, 21 October 1880 (MS 11,289, NLI).

World to fantasise that such a 'consummation would render Ireland immediately free, happy, and prosperous'.[58]

The Revolution was not the only formative American historical parallel conscripted into service for the Irish cause. With comparisons between landlordism and slavery commonplace, favoured by George, Nulty, Davitt, and a host of Land League orators and writers, it is not surprising that the US Civil War also became a key point of reference.[59] Not only did the Land War rely on a rhetoric of enslavement, as when T. P. O'Connor later described the conflict as heralding 'the last day of slavery and the dawn of emancipation', but in making the explicit comparison with chattel slavery, agrarian radicals expressed their distinctly republican conceptions of freedom as a matter of political and economic independence.[60] 'Away, then, with the name of freedom!' Devyr had declared, 'we are *slaves*, and let us not, by assuming the name of freemen, stamp ourselves idiots, too'.[61] It was the 'yoke of slavery' that landlordism had weighed on Ireland, since 'without land, slavery is inevitable and will be as enduring as the land itself'.[62] In the United States, despite the best efforts of radical republicans like Thaddeus Stevens, post–Civil War Reconstruction had not included the redistribution of former plantation land to freedmen and women.[63] This catastrophic failure to restructure the political economy of the American South had laid bare the necessity of land reform to many radicals, as the experiences of former slaves turned sharecroppers served to capture the painfully pyrrhic freedom of economic subjugation, and they frequently returned to the plight of freedmen and the deep failure of Reconstruction to drive home their arguments.[64]

It was these intellectual echoes that drew so many prominent former abolitionists and grandees of the anti-slavery movement, particularly Radical Republicans, into support for the Irish agrarian agitation. James Redpath, Wendell Phillips, Henry Ward Beecher, William Lloyd Garrison Jr., and Francis G. Shaw were just some of the more prominent supporters of the Land League. Redpath, of Scottish Presbyterian heritage, campaigned enthusiastically for the League and played an important role in popularising the boycott

58 *Irish World*, 30 November 1878; Matthew Kelly, *The Fenian Ideal and Irish Nationalism, 1882–1916* (Woodbridge: Boydell and Brewer, 2006), 25.

59 James Walker, *The National Inheritance* (London: F. Farrah, 1873), 16; *Irish World*, 9 July 1881; Henry George, 'Lecture Notes and Text: "Malthusian Theory"' (HGP, Series II, Box 12, NYPL); Nulty, *The Land Question*, 9; Account of Land League meeting at Thurles, Co. Tipperary, 14 November 1880 (MS 11,289, NLI).

60 T. P. O'Connor, *Memoirs of an Old Parliamentarian* (London: Ernest Benn, 1929), 114.

61 Devyr, *Our Natural Rights*, 9.

62 Fr Mulcahy, Ballingarry, 14 November 1880 (MS 11,289, NLI); Thomas Ainge Devyr, *John Swinton's Paper*, 23 March 1884.

63 Foner, *Reconstruction*, 235–236.

64 George, *Progress and Poverty*, 319; Henry Ward Beecher, *The Pilot*, 17 January 1880.

in the America, earning the honour of several branches adopting his name.[65] For Shaw, a wealthy New England abolitionist in the twilight of his life, the question of land reform inspired by the Irish agitation 'gripped [him] as nothing had since the last days of the Civil War'.[66] The old abolitionists and antislavery republicans approached the Irish cause as they had the question of slavery; as a moral crusade, 'in which compromise with sin was itself a sin'.[67] Palpable echoes of the radicals' argument that 'in principle the two systems of appropriating the labor of other men are essentially the same' could be found in Henry Ward Beecher's observation, at a reception for Parnell in Brooklyn, that 'he that possesses the land possesses the people'.[68] In Boston, the eminent abolitionist Wendell Phillips, who had in 1879 bemoaned the failure to expropriate and redistribute the lands of former slaveholders, became a firm ally and advocate for the Irish Land League.[69] It was a distinguished endorsement, and proudly publicised, but what Phillips saw in the Irish agrarian movement was something more profound, radical, and universal: 'one of the last battles between democracy and aristocracy'.[70] The same fight for freedom that had animated abolitionists, one grounded firmly in a demand for natural rights, found a new field of action, albeit briefly, in the Irish Land War.

Together, the revolutionary republicanism of 1776 and the US Civil War not only allowed Irish-Americans access to foundational elements of American national identity, combining loyalty to their adoptive homeland with the fight for Irish independence and carving out a place for themselves separate from an Anglo-American establishment, but it yoked the politics of democratic republicanism, with its division between an elitist, centralised, and bureaucratic English liberalism and a demotic, localised, and public-spirited American one, firmly on to Irish-American identity. As useful as these confluences were for George, they were also something of a double-edged sword. While Irish identity politics had been fused with the agrarian radicalism that informed his own plan, it also trafficked in a form of particularism that ran counter to George's universal vision. And while Irish republicans often skilfully traversed the

65 Greene, 'The Impact of Henry George's Theories', 69; Redpath, *Talks about Ireland*; *New York Tribune* 11 January 1881; *Washington Post,* 29 January 1881; There were Redpath branches in Arctic, Rhode Island; Lawlor, Iowa; Ithaca, New York; and Carmelton, Pennsylvania. Wendell Phillips also had one in his native Boston.

66 Lorien Foote, *Seeking the One Great Remedy: Francis George Shaw and Nineteenth Century Reform* (Athens, OH: University of Ohio Press, 2003), 173.

67 Foner, *Free Soil*, 109.

68 George, 'The "Reduction to Iniquity"', 70; Henry Ward Beecher, *The Pilot,* 17 January 1880.

69 Wendell Phillips, 'Ought the Negro to Be Disenfranchised? Ought He to Have Been Enfranchised', *North American Review* 128, no. 268 (1879): 160; Wendell Phillips to P. J. Flatley, 9 May 1882 (PACP, Box 4, BC).

70 Wendell Phillips, *Irish World*, 9 November 1878; Wendell Phillips, *Daniel O'Connell: The Irish Patriot*, 5–6 (AIA.047, NYU).

chasm between the particular and the universal, the issue still raised its head occasionally. George was critical of nationalism's 'little hatreds', and his refusal to make sufficient allowances for national sentiment certainly harmed his cause in Ireland.[71] Naturally, he supported Irish independence, denouncing in unequivocal terms the horrors and injustices of British misrule, and he was of course politically inclined towards devolving power in any case.[72] He was happy to praise Ireland, its past, and the 'greatness of the Irish nation abroad' for their 'strength of family and patriotic attachments'.[73] So strong was his fear, however, that legislative independence would obscure and undermine the land question, he was often at pains to deny the distinctiveness of Irish malaise. While nationalists claimed that English rule had been particularly injurious to Ireland, maintaining the opposite was central to George's thesis, in which Ireland was his exemplar. George's opinion was that, 'such little differences, if they exist do not affect the general fact'.[74] For his confidante Fr Thomas Dawson, it was clear that this had 'prejudiced your Irish readers against you'. He gently encouraged George to 'make more allowances for "mere Irish Nationalists", as you playfully called them in conversation'.[75]

The Politics of Class

Although the animating ideals of the American Revolution provided a cultural focal point around which the various and competing class identities in Irish-America could orientate themselves, the prospect of unity that it held up was ultimately difficult to achieve. Nationalist politics offered the possibility of bourgeois assimilation for an upwardly mobile middle-class, as well as shelter and support for political radicalism.[76] And, just as in Ireland, the Land League in America was able to hold together these elements for a time under one, sometimes tense, umbrella.[77] On the invitation of Charles Stuart Parnell, during his tour of the United States in early 1880, the disparate political factions and semi-autonomous groups of agrarian radicals that were already supporting the agitation were drawn together with the creation of a centralised executive committee and administration of the Irish National Land League of America,

71 Henry George to Thomas Briggs, 29 October 1881 (HGP, Series I: A, Box 3, NYPL).

72 Henry George, 'Lecture Notes, Britain' (HGP, Series II, Box 12, NYPL).

73 Henry George, 'Lecture Notes, 1882', Glasgow, 17 March 1882 (HGP, Series II, Box 13, NYPL).

74 Fr Thomas Dawson to Henry George, 21 September 1882 (HGP, Series I: A, Box 3, NYPL), annotation.

75 Fr Thomas Dawson to Henry George, 21 September 1882 (HGP, Series I: A, Box 3, NYPL).

76 Miller, *Ireland and Irish-America*, 270.

77 Victor A. Walsh, 'Irish Nationalism and Land Reform: The Role of the Irish in America', in P. J. Drudy (ed.), *The Irish in America: Emigration, Assimilation and Impact* (Cambridge: Cambridge University Press, 1985), 256.

'for the purpose of rendering moral and financial aid' to its Irish counterpart.[78] At the first conference, a provisional Central Council was selected, which included three Manhattan priests: one of whom was Rev Dr Edward McGlynn. Also selected were John Devoy; the Fenian poet and journalist John Boyle O'Reilly; Fr Lawrence Walsh, who would act as treasurer; Alexander Sullivan; and Terence Powderly, Grand Master Workman of the Knights of Labor.

The involvement of men such as McGlynn and Powderly portended a politically radical agenda, and to head off such an eventuality, the constitution for the new organisation explicitly disavowed any desire to dictate Irish strategy or to encourage the transmission of agrarian agitation into the United States.[79] This enforced neutrality never held strongly, but it reflected the concerns of more conservative members that the organisation should be mindful of retaining an aura of respectability in the United States.[80] Some found that a homeland in political turmoil, and where radical attacks on the institution of property were becoming normalised, was not serving their purposes of assimilation in America very well, drawing the ire of many non-Irish-Americans.[81] Even the behaviour of the Irish clergy was too much for some. One New York Leaguer wrote to the official President Patrick A. Collins complaining that 'the priests of Ireland are permitted to take too much upon themselves' and that 'it is over to you as President of the Land League in this country to take immediate action about the unwise and unpatriotic letter of Archbishop Croke'.[82]

The figurehead of the radical wing of the League was Patrick Ford, who through his influential newspaper had, many feared, assumed *de facto* ideological control over the direction of the American organisation. As the League in Ireland appeared to take a more radical turn in the autumn of 1881 with the expansion of boycotting and the No Rent Manifesto (something that the *Irish World* had previously called for), these divisions would intensify and indeed persist through the lifetime of the Land League and into the subsequent National League, where the agrarian aspect was explicitly demoted in importance. John Byrne, serving as vice-President of the National League, later publicly attacked Ford and his politics, announcing that the 'commercial and professional' Irish 'cannot believe in wild theories and schemes which business training teaches us are usually actuated by selfish, and oftimes dishonest motives'.[83] These class divisions had geographical manifestations

[78] Printed untitled handbill, New York, 30 March 1880 (Devoy Papers, MS 18,048, NLI).
[79] *Constitution of the Land League Adopted at Buffalo*, New York, 12 and 13 January 1881 (Richmond, VA: P. Keenan, 1881), 6 (George D. Cahill Papers, Series III, Box 5, Boston College).
[80] 'Proceedings of the First Annual Convention of the Irish National Land League, held at Buffalo, New York, 12 and 13 January 1881', 23 (GDCP, Series III, Box 5, BC).
[81] Anon to Patrick A. Collins, 20 October 1881 (PACP, Series I, Box 1, BC).
[82] C. F. Moonan to Patrick A. Collins, 22 October 1881 (PACP, Series I, Box 1, BC).
[83] John Byrne, 'A Manly Protest', newspaper clipping (Devoy Papers, MS 18,049(5), NLI).

too, exacerbating the discord that plagued the American Land League. One Massachusetts Land Leaguer ascribed the difference to the more genteel temperament possessed by the Boston Irish; living 'among the Yankees' he said, 'one of the things we have learned from them is steadiness of purpose'.[84] Such attitudes were, to the agrarian radicals, simply examples of cowardly, duplicitous, and snobbish 'whiggery'. Denoting an elitist, un-principled, and economically self-interested liberalism, the epithet of Whig was one commonly aimed at Gladstone's administration, but there was as well, complained George, 'a great deal of "whiggery" in this Land League'.[85] The influence of Ford's paper, however, gave the radical wing unrivalled clout both in America and back in Ireland. As one supporter stressed: 'Patrick Ford is the man and to his noble paper and not to Boston whiggery is due the success of the Land League in America.'[86]

Ford's newspaper was a remarkable success, joining a long tradition of Irish influence in American journalism stretching back to the eighteenth century. Journalistic and literary precociousness had long been a familiar Irish conceit, and Ford, along with the Boston *Pilot*'s editor John Boyle O'Reilly, prided himself on the high moral and political value of the press, choosing to develop a distinctive tone of principled campaigning in his paper.[87] Contrasting itself with the American press, Ford's *Irish World* proclaimed its purpose to 'take a new departure from expediency, which gives to the world only shams, and build upon Principle, which upholds reality. We must go to work prepared to recognize and to act up to *all* the demands of justice'.[88] Ford regularly published serious and complex articles on moral, philosophical, and economic topics, offering 'a weekly education in the trans-Atlantic radical tradition', that the *Tipperary Advocate* welcomed as 'advanced philosophy in the most interesting guise'.[89] A trenchant critical voice directed against both major political parties, supporting the Greenback-Labor movement over the 'Wall Street Democrats'

[84] George D. Cahill to Alexander Sullivan, 18 May 1883 (GDCP, Series I, Box 4, BC).

[85] Henry George to Patrick Ford, 28 December 1881 (HGP, Series I: B, NYPL); Michael Davitt to John Devoy, 16 December 1880, in William O'Brien, and Desmond Ryan (eds.), *Devoy's Post Bag, 1871–1928*, vol. II (Dublin: Fallon, 1948), 23; Patrick Egan to John Devoy, 17 February 1881, in William O'Brien, and Desmond Ryan (eds.), *Devoy's Post Bag*, 108; Patrick Egan to INLL Dublin office, 31 July 1881 (Harrington Papers, MS 8583, NLI); on political connotations of 'Whig' in the United States, Paul K. Conkin, *Prophets of Prosperity: America's First Political Economists* (Bloomington: Indiana University Press, 1980), 202.

[86] Quoted in Meagher, *Inventing Irish America*, 191.

[87] John Talbot Smith, *Patrick Ford of the Irish World* (AIA.047, NYU); John Boyle O'Reilly, Inaugural address as President of the Boston Press Club, 8 November 1879, in James Jeffrey Roche (ed.), *Life of John Boyle O'Reilly; Together with His Complete Poems and Speeches* (New York: Cassell Publishing Co., 1891), 195; Doyle, 'Irish Elites in North America', 42.

[88] *Irish World*, 16 November 1878.

[89] Foner, 'Class, Ethnicity, and Radicalism', 158; *Tipperary Advocate*, quoted in *Irish World*, 5 April 1879.

and a 'republican party [that had] outlived its usefulness', the *Irish World* was explicitly both an ethnic and a labour paper.[90]

In this way, the paper combined a tone of ethnic self-reliance with the language of republican individualism. It vigorously opposed anti-Catholicism in American public life, defending the Church from nativist attacks, all while pressing the hierarchy to give more latitude to labour radicals.[91] Ford was keen to maintain cordial links with the New York Archdiocese even as he condemned its narrow view of the labour question. In 1881, he wrote to Cardinal McCloskey to apologise for an article which had attacked 'practices which seemed to be a deviation from the spirit of the simplicity of the Church'.[92] In the years that followed, Ford cultivated a more sympathetic attitude to the Church, even swapping New Year's cards with McCloskey's successor, Archbishop Corrigan.[93] Like the Knights of Labor, the *Irish World* also supported the temperance movement, advocating for abstinence over prohibitive legislation, since the former would cultivate 'moral courage' and the latter 'take from man the power to do either good or evil'.[94] Like the Boston *Pilot*, Ford's paper encouraged western resettlement and the Catholic Colonisation movement as part of its mission to improve the employment opportunities and moral and intellectual habits of the Irish working class. The 'yearning to "occupy and possess the land"' was to be cultivated, since it would free 'Irish immigrants who would otherwise be compelled to toil without hope of competence in the larger cities'.[95]

These interests and tendencies coalesced to produce a paper of remarkable popularity. With a weekly circulation of between 60,000 and 125,000 during the 1880s, it dwarfed other Irish Catholic papers and indeed most labour papers too.[96] Ford paid high wages to his staff and struggled to secure sustainable advertising revenue, making the solvency of his newspaper entirely dependent on a large and expanding readership.[97] During the late 1870s, he dramatically developed his printing and distribution operation, making the paper available

[90] *Irish World*, 16 November 1878.

[91] Rodechko, 'An Irish-American Journalist and Catholicism', 527.

[92] Patrick Ford to Cardinal McCloskey, 31 March 1881 (CMP, A-27, AANY).

[93] Patrick Ford to Michael A. Corrigan, 5 January 1885 (ACP, C-8, AANY).

[94] *Irish World*, 23 November 1878; Meagher, *Inventing Irish America*, 165–166.

[95] 'The Catholic Movement in Western Colonization – Colonization in Nebraska', *American Catholic Quarterly Review* 6 (1881), 434; 'Catholic colony, Greeley County, Nebraska' (103, Box 34, P008.880, PAHRC); 'Resolutions adopted at the Boston Convention of the Irish National League of America, August 1884' (103, Box 40, AC0129, PAHRC); Egbert Hazard to Terence V. Powderly, 21 August 1880 (PP, Series 1: Box 2, CUA).

[96] Jacobson, *Special Sorrows*, 57; Rodechko, *Patrick Ford and His Search for America*, 48; John M. Davis, editor of the Philadelphia Labour Paper, *The Trades*, spoke of his ambition 'to make a second *Irish World*'. John M. Davis to Terence V. Powderly, 19 December 1879 (PP, Series I: Box 2, CUA).

[97] Rodechko, *Patrick Ford and His Search for America*, 40–46.

on the day of its publication in all major American east coast cities.[98] Rather than relying solely on press association dispatches from Ireland, with their pro-British bent, Ford also maintained an impressive journalistic network and had 'original cables', giving his paper a significant advantage.[99] While its influence in the United States unnerved the official leadership of the American Land League, it was its transatlantic reach that was truly profound. In Ireland, it was 'some vast Irish-American invasion', declared William O'Brien, 'sweeping the country with new and irresistible principles of Liberty and Democracy'; Ford's 'Spread the Light' fund, an initiative to finance the distribution of free copies of the paper in Ireland, and which could be directed at specific locations, meant that 'there was scarcely a cabin the West to which some relative in America did not despatch a weekly copy of the Irish World'.[100] Devyr, a regular contributor, thought it the 'only publication' that the British government saw as 'a terror to them'.[101] It was an opinion endorsed by George Trevelyan, Chief Secretary for Ireland, who was quoted as declaring Ford 'not only the most powerful newspaper editor in America, but of all time'.[102]

The paper's reputation, combined with its intellectual sophistication, gestured towards the remarkable appeal of radical ideas. George's own popularity in Ireland was inseparable from that of the paper itself. At St Mary's Hall in Belfast, George was introduced on to the stage by a local priest, who remarked that the American was 'even more welcome to us in that he is closely connected with a paper that has championed our cause with sincerity and power'.[103] In Liverpool, George reported back to Ford with delight that 'nothing could exceed the enthusiasm with which they received your name'. It was a situation replicated 'wherever the *Irish World* has reached'.[104] And it had reached very far, even despite attempts by the government to stem the flood of copies into Britain and Ireland (George warned Ford that the Post Office, under Postmaster General Henry Fawcett, had 'no scruple about opening anything', advising him to 'change the style of wrapping' of the paper).[105] Undeterred, the paper continued to spread 'its peculiar light in every nook and corner of the land', according to the Anglo-Irish writer Standish O'Grady, who noted that

98 *Irish World*, 8 February 1879.

99 T. M. Healy to Patrick A. Collins, 1 January 1882 (PACP, Series I, Box 2, BC).

100 O'Brien, *Recollections*, 273. 101 Devyr, *The Odd Book*, pt. II, 176.

102 George O. Trevelyan, quoted in Smith, *Patrick Ford of the Irish World* (AIA.047, NYU).

103 Fr O'Boyle at St. Mary's Hall, Belfast, *Irish World*, 25 March 1882.

104 Henry George to Patrick Ford, 9 March 1882 (HGP, Series I: B, NYPL); Foner, 'Class, Ethnicity, and Radicalism', 161.

105 Henry George to Patrick Ford, 7 January 1882; 4 February 1882; 18 February 1882; Henry George to John Denvir, 14 February 188 (HGP, Series I: B, NYPL); Devyr, *The Odd Book*, 186; Henry Labouchere and Henry Fawcett, HC Deb 17 February 1881, vol. 258, cc.1080–1; Alexander Sullivan and Henry Fawcett, HC Deb 31 March 1881, vol. 260, cc. 343–4; T. M. Healy and Henry Fawcett, HC Deb 4 April 1881, vol. 260, cc. 564–5.

it was 'through the agency of the *Irish World*' that the idea of 'the land for the people' had 'seized the democratic imagination'.[106] There was no doubt that its political heft was in part a consequence of its strident moral tone and its appeal to the central tenets of republican radicalism. Fanny Parnell, Charles' sister and a key figure among the moderates in the American Land League, worried that 'while the paper is safe enough for educated people and contains some excellent ideas, it is a paper calculated to do much mischief in the hands of an only partially educated and simple-minded peasantry'.[107]

Such powerful and subversive political influence was deeply concerning to those Irish nationalists not enamoured with the radical vision. As George sensed in Ireland, the Parnellite wing of the Land League was 'afraid of the radical element in the U.S. dictating and radicalizing the movement here'.[108] Yet they were also beholden to it, recognising the significant financial influence wielded by the *Irish World*, as well as its popular appeal.[109] This meant that there could not be any open hostility towards 'our friends at the Irish World of New York', for fear of jeopardising an essential revenue stream.[110] Consequently, the Irish leadership, for whom the class tensions bedevilling the American movement were not as transparent, frequently aggravated the status sensitivities of the American executive. As President, Patrick A. Collins was alive to any perceived slight in favour of Patrick Ford, such as resolutions of thanks from Ireland being sent only to the *Irish World* by those who believed the paper to be 'representative' of the movement in America.[111]

The Irish leadership soon became aware of the need to spread their affections more cautiously. Land League treasurer Patrick Egan found himself apologising to Collins for sending Ford 'a more lengthy telegram than I forwarded to you', and had to reassure the president of the League that there was not 'the slightest intention of in any way passing over your organization or giving any special recognition to the Irish World'.[112] He reassured Collins that they would send future official communications though his organisation, but reminded him that 'the Irish World has been an exceedingly powerful ally and a very good friend of our movement from the very beginning and we could not nor would not do anything like throwing them over'.[113] Egan also defended Thomas Brennan's right to contact Ford directly as a private arrangement, 'not to be taken in any sense as official'.[114]

106 O'Grady, *The Crisis in Ireland*, 25.
107 Ely M. Janis, 'Petticoat Revolutionaries: Gender, Ethnic Nationalism, and the Irish Ladies' Land League in the United States', *Journal of American Ethnic History* 27, no. 2 (2008): 21.
108 Henry George to Patrick Ford, 28 February 1882 (HGP, Series I: B, NYPL).
109 Foner, 'Class, Ethnicity, and Radicalism', 168.
110 Patrick Egan to Thomas Brennan, 22 May 1881 (Harrington Papers, MS 8577(1), NLI).
111 Thomas Walsh to Patrick A. Collins, 27 April 1881 (PACP, Box 1, BC).
112 Patrick Egan to Patrick A. Collins, 7 March 1881 (PACP, Box 1, BC).
113 Patrick Egan to Patrick A. Collins, 7 March 1881 (PACP, Box 1, BC).
114 Patrick Egan to Patrick A. Collins, 7 March 1881 (PACP, Box 1, BC).

The Irish leadership had clumsily stumbled into a vicious internecine conflict and was able to do little to resolve matters. Attempts at neutrality simply gave the impression of acknowledging Ford's *de facto* authority. Ford, having the upper hand in popular support and visibility, was able to take the moral high ground and force the official leadership to precipitate the open division, while maintaining an apparently conciliatory tone. He even offered Collins a perceptibly demeaning hand of friendship to create 'a union of the two sections of the land league' at the Chicago convention in 1882; Collins did not reply.[115] Collins, on the other hand, seeming at the end of his tether with fighting to assert his 'official' dominance of the American Land League, refused calls from the leadership in Ireland to stand on a national platform with Ford. T. P. O'Connor wrote that Ford would put his name to it without mentioning the *Irish World* and that Collins should sign 'without any title appended', adding that he thought 'Mr Ford's request reasonable under the circumstances'.[116] Such a deprivation of Collins' official status was a clear insult; not to mention that Ford had insisted on extending the resolution beyond a vague reference to the 'Irish question' to the inclusion of the plank 'That the land in Ireland belongs of right to the people of Ireland'.[117] The political power Ford possessed was plain, and O'Connor was left to plead that Collins 'for the sake of unity accept conditions'.[118]

This political battle between the radical agrarian vision and the political authority of the conservative leadership was also played out at branch level. Writing to congratulate Collins on his successful deposition of 'the "claimant" Patrick Ford' and victory over the 'enemy within' (specifically regarding, more prosaically, Collins' reassurances from Patrick Egan), the secretary of the Manchester, New Hampshire branch also lamented that 'we have been pestered with a few men from the Celtic Debating Club – a Fenian organisation who seem to have come into our league with the purpose of preventing it from getting the free support of our Irish citizens'. As a result of this entryism, 'we have scarcely had a meeting lately in which they have not dragged in the name of the Irish World'.[119] By September, the struggle for the soul of the League in America had permeated the Ladies Land League too, where after an open conflict with Anna Ford, Patrick's sister, Fanny Parnell confessed that 'it will require my utmost efforts to keep it [the Ladies League] from falling under the control of the Irish World, and I may fail'. 'I think that an open rupture with the

[115] Patrick Ford to Patrick A. Collins [two cables], 7 January 1882; James Mooney to Patrick A. Collins, 17 April 1882 (PACP, Box 2, BC).
[116] T. P. O'Connor to Patrick A. Collins [cable no.2], 8 November 1881 (PACP, Box 2, BC).
[117] T. M. Healy and Eugene Sheehy to Patrick A. Collins [cable], 9 November 1881; Patrick A. Collins to T. P. O'Connor, 16 November 1881 (PACP, Box 2, BC).
[118] T. P. O'Connor to Patrick A. Collins [cable no.2], 8 November 1881 (PACP, Box 2, BC).
[119] Christopher A. Gallagher to Patrick A. Collins, 17 March 1881 (PACP, Box 1, BC).

I. W. is now not only inevitable, but a duty, and not only a duty, but a measure of good policy.'[120]

By early November 1881, Parnell had emerged victorious. She had succeeded in removing Anna Ford and other supporters of the *Irish World* from the books of her local branch. 'It was only a local victory over the I.W. but still I feel proud of it.'[121] The vituperative campaign against the *Irish World* demonstrated the depth of feeling and sense of marginalisation among the conservative wing. But while Collins remained frustrated at the lack of support, the leadership in Ireland was quickly becoming bored of the squabbles. They were more concerned about not alienating *Irish World* money and support and, perhaps significantly, remained oblivious to the degree to which the middle-class Irish-American imperative of respectability was important.[122] It was evident when Egan wrote to Collins in March 1882, appealing to him to 'avoid quarrel with [the] Irish World [as] any public scandal [in] America would simply ruin [the] cause at home can you not meet them half way'.[123]

'The home people', commiserated James Redpath with Patrick Collins, 'are tied like a tin-kettle to Ford's coat tails'.[124] But it could not be otherwise, since it was only the radical faction, with its mass working-class support, that was willing and able to finance the League in Ireland. Amid the sneers and insults aimed at Ford and his support, the conservative leadership was keenly aware that they were involved in a financial competition, and this involved making sure that no money they raised went near the *Irish World* funds.[125] But it was a financial competition that they could not win. The largest contributing areas in the United States matched the concentrations of working-class Irish communities, particularly San Francisco and Oakland in the West, Chicago in the mid-West, and the industrial cities of Philadelphia, Brooklyn, Jersey City, Lowell, and Fall River. These regions provided tremendous financial aid. Between December 1879 and April 1880, Pittston, Pennsylvania, alone contributed more than treble the amount that the British cities of Manchester or Glasgow could offer.[126]

The financial geographies of the Land League in America were predominantly shaped by the class compositions of particular communities, as well as

120 Fanny Parnell to Patrick A. Collins, 25 September 1881 (PACP, Box 1, BC).
121 Fanny Parnell to Patrick A. Collins, 10 November 1881 (PACP, Box 2, BC).
122 Patrick Egan to Patrick A. Collins, 28 November 1881 (PACP, Box 2, BC); Quincy Branch (Boston), INLL to its President John Cavanagh [n.d.] (GDCP, Series I, Box 4, BC).
123 Patrick Egan to Patrick A. Collins [cable], 13 March 1882 (PACP, Box 2, BC).
124 James Redpath to Patrick A. Collins, 8 May 1881 (PACP, Box 1, BC).
125 George D. Cahill to Rev Laurence Walsh, 14 March 1883 (GDCP, Series I, Box 4, BC); Patrick Egan to Land League executive, 19 June 1881; 3 July 1881 (Harrington Papers, MS 8583, NLI).
126 'Irish National Land League Relief Fund: Sums received for Relief of Distress by Irish National Land League, from 22 December 1879 to 30 April 1880 also Particulars of Grants made by Land League to Local Relief Committees, &c., from 22 December 1879 to 30 April 1880', 4 (Heffernan Papers, MS 21,910, NLI).

the opportunities for middle-class leadership. So, for instance, while contributions from Boston to the Land League in Ireland tended to come in fewer but larger and rounded sums of as much as £1,000 or £2,000 through John Boyle O'Reilly, New York's Irish communities sent money through a multiplicity of channels, frequently the *Irish World* or the New York Irish Relief Fund, as well as many other individual donations varying wildly in size.[127] In 1881, New York as a whole contributed $23,472 to the League's treasurer Rev Laurence Walsh, but sent $36,524 directly to Ireland, bypassing official channels.[128] The *Irish World* claimed a significant amount of the money raised for Land League causes and was itself a powerful funding machine. By 1884, according to the paper's own estimates, it had received and distributed over half a million dollars for 'patriotic objects' over the preceding eight years. Of this total, an impressive $343,072.92 was accounted for by the Land League fund alone.[129]

Other significant variations are evident from the financial reports of the Land League in America. For the thirteen months between January 1881 and February 1882, a total of $200,000 was sent back to Ireland through official channels.[130] After this point, however, there was a significant collapse in donations made through the League's executive. Massachusetts had raised $81,000 in 1881, a figure which fell to under $16,000 in 1882. In fact as early as July, Thomas Flatley was forced to deny the 'alleged falling off of the Land League in this country'.[131] The quarterly reports reveal the sums raised in 1882 to be around a third of those achieved in 1881. Individual branches demonstrate this collapse well. The South Boston branch managed to extract $1,400 dollars from its 308 members in 1881, but a meagre $55 was collected the following year; so too in Connecticut where the Ansonia branch proffered only $100 dollars to the national treasurer, despite amassing an impressive total of $2,635 the previous year. In Bridgeport, Connecticut, the Parnell branch's respectable total of $376, one of the highest for that state in 1882, paled into comparison with its previous effort of over $1,000. Working-class Irish communities, particularly in downtown Manhattan, across the Pennsylvanian coalfields and industrial towns, and far out west in California were far less likely to send their money through the League's official channels than those in Massachusetts and Connecticut, the home state of official treasurer Laurence Walsh. No branches

[127] 'Irish National Land League Relief Fund: Sums received for Relief of Distress by Irish National Land League, from 22 December 1879, to 30 April 1880 also Particulars of Grants made by Land League to Local Relief Committees, &c., from 22 December 1879 to 30 April 1880', 4 (Heffernan Papers, MS 21,910, NLI).

[128] 'Annual Report of Thomas Flatley' (1882) (P.001.1876, PAHRC).

[129] *Irish World*, 16 February 1884.

[130] Circular from Thomas Flatley, Boston, 24 February 1882 (GDCP, Series III, Box 5, BC).

[131] Thomas Flatley, 'Second Quarterly Report of the Irish National Land League of the United States for quarter ending July 10, 1881' (GDCP, Series III, Box 5, BC); 'Annual Report of Thomas Flatley' (1882) (P.001.1876, PAHRC).

from California even appeared in the League's reports from the first quarter of 1881, and the fifty that appeared in the next quarterly report sent their money direct to the League's treasurer Patrick Egan in Paris.[132] Pennsylvania sent only $12,516 to Rev Walsh in 1881, significantly below Connecticut and Massachusetts even on a per branch basis.

Perhaps the starkest demonstration of the numerical and financial power of working-class Irish-America, harnessed and channelled through the *Irish World*, was in New York. Here, the size and number of the city's branches gave them considerable independence from the national leadership. The vast numbers of Irish-Americans in the city, and in nearby Brooklyn, meant that most branches were affiliated under a municipal executive. In Brooklyn, the city's twenty-eight centralised branches together sent $6,200 directly to Patrick Egan in 1881. New York City was divided into the Parnell Land League council, with thirty-eight numbered subsidiary branches, and the INLL Executive council with around thirty branches. The Parnell council had more branches located on the outskirts of the city compared with its INLL counterpart, which was focussed primarily on lower Manhattan. The Parnell council mostly, although not exclusively, remitted its monies to Rev Walsh in modest sums recorded quarterly. Membership of its branches ranged from high double to low treble figures, much like most other branches across the rest of the eastern coastal states. In stark contrast, the INLL cohort boasted extraordinary membership numbers, with individual branches containing many hundreds of members. For example, Ward 23 on West 45th Street claimed 1,383 members, while a mere 10 blocks south on West 35th Street a 'Michael Davitt' branch recorded 1,460 members. The INLL council of New York City sent its money in two large sums, totalling nearly $21,000 for 1881, straight to Egan in Paris, bypassing the official American leadership. Unsurprisingly, this was much more than the Parnell council could muster. Even for the subsequent lean year, the INLL cohort raised $4,932.50 set against the Parnell council's $3,549.46.[133]

The politics of place and the politics of class were clearly evident in the undulating financial power of the American Land League. The influence of the radical wing on the economic and ideological direction of the League, most directly and visibly through the *Irish World*, gave credence to concerns about Ford's remarkable (and to his critics dangerous and demagogic) influence. At no time was this more evident than at the end of 1881 when, after his arrest, Parnell acquiesced to the No Rent Manifesto, a radical tactic of rent refusal that the *Irish World* had long advocated. For the radical faction, it was better late than never, and under the leadership of Anna Parnell, the Ladies' Land

[132] 'Third Quarterly report of the Irish National Land League of the United States, Boston, Mass., 8 November 1881' (GDCP, Series III, Box 5, BC).

[133] 'Annual Report of Thomas Flatley' (1882) (P.001.1876, PAHRC).

League in Ireland took the battle in a more determined direction.[134] In the United States, the American radicals who had huddled round the Irish cause as the vanguard of a new political future were also enthused. Louis F. Post, Georgist and editor of the labour paper *Truth*, compared the Manifesto to the Declaration of Independence and the Emancipation Proclamation and as 'the beginning of a contest between defrauded industry and luxurious idleness which will soon overleap all political boundaries'.[135] At a No Rent Rally in New York, attended by over forty-one different trades unions, the Manifesto was described as 'the death knell of thralldom sounding from the little Isle of Erin' as the gathering resolved to advocate for its universal extension.[136] Again, the conservative wing found itself on the back foot. Patrick Egan was forced to assure Collins that, although Ford had telegrammed to suggest a rent strike, 'the "No Rent" Manifesto was deliberately decided upon and actually written before Mr. Ford's telegram reached me'.[137] Under the headline, 'The Real Aim for Ireland', the Boston *Pilot* editorialised that it was 'time for Irishmen to take their attention off the Land Act and the "No Rent" policy', for the 'outside world', presumably Anglo-America in particular, 'will sympathize far more with an open demand for Home Rule than with an organized war on landlords'.[138] The paper even insinuated that Patrick Egan was a 'paid servant' of Patrick Ford.[139]

But much as they resisted, radicalism was baked into the Land War. Inevitably and inescapably the Land League of America made valuable use of the subtle cultural inflections built into the intertwined histories of American and Irish republicanism, and underneath which lay the latent logics of agrarian radicalism. Branch names demonstrated the seamless coalescence, the overlapping affinities and parallels, of transatlantic republicanism. Thomas Davis, Emmet, Mitchel, Tone, Davitt, Andrew Jackson, Sarsfield, Sexton, Liberty, Ironsides, and Free Soil were all commemorated as branch names.[140] Davitt's was the most popular name for a branch by a considerable distance, followed by Parnell and Emmet. Working-class Pittsburgh boasted one named for the *Irish World*. And it was in Philadelphia where invocations of the American revolutionary generation were most common. The city had branches named

[134] Henry George to Patrick Ford, 22 November 1881 (HGP, Series I: B, NYPL); Fanny Parnell to Patrick A. Collins, 10 November 1881 (PACP, Series I, Box 2, BC); Henry George to Annie George, 3 May 1882 (HGP, Series I: A, Box 3, NYPL).

[135] *Truth*, 30 January 1882.

[136] Matthew Maguire, *Irish Nation*, 2 February 1882.

[137] *Irish World*, 29 October 1881; Patrick Egan to Patrick A. Collins, 6 December 1881 (PACP, Series I, Box 2, BC).

[138] *The Pilot*, 5 November 1881.

[139] Patrick Egan to Patrick A. Collins [cable], 21 November 1881 (PACP, Series I, Box 2, BC).

[140] Irish National League, Philadelphia, 'Financial Report of the Treasurer of Municipal Council I.N.L of Phila., for fiscal year ending May 31, 1886' (103, Box 40, AC0130a, PAHRC).

for Commodore Barry and Commodore Stewart, both naval commanders who fought Britain in the American Revolutionary War and the War of 1812, respectively, with the latter having the added advantage of being an ancestor of Parnell.[141] It was clear: as well as being able to wield huge financial power, the agrarian radicals of the Irish Land League also controlled the cultural and emotional terrain.

Romanticism and Resistance

The political sediments of agrarian republicanism infused the cultures of Irish nationalist thought so pervasively that even Fenianism, largely an urban phenomenon, wrapped itself in the small farmer ideal.[142] Sustained, during the course of the nineteenth century, in the political thought of the Young Irelanders, the connection between imperialism, commercialism, and British cultural hegemony fertilised a rich imaginative landscape in which rural Ireland embodied its inversion; a romantic, spiritual, and poetic place, a land of saints, scholars, and heroic soldiers doggedly resisting the encroachments of British 'civilization'.[143] The Waterford-born Fenian James J. Clancy, a participant in the rising of 1867 before becoming, like many others, a journalist in the United States, explained that this antithetical stance 'placed her [England] and Ireland at opposite ends of the balance. As either rises, so the other sinks'.[144]

Land stood at the very epicentre of this contrast, not just politically and economically, but also woven into the emotional texture of the romantic vision. The uncorrupted beauty and harmonious naturalism of the Irish countryside gave an aesthetic expression to resistance against British liberal modernity. The strains of urban industrial life, the moral compromises of commerce, were escaped in an idealised rural Ireland in which the human and the natural ran seamlessly into one another – a land where 'the verdant hedge, the smooth, white roads, the bubbling spring, the running brooks, and the larger streams where the trout and salmon play; the magic lakes, the mossy ruins, the forts and raths, the holy wells and ancient towers' evinced together 'an

[141] 'Annual Report of Thomas Flatley, Secretary of the Irish National Land League of the United States, submitted at the Second Annual Convention held in the City of Washington, D.C., 12 and 13 April 1882' (Buffalo: Union and Times Print, 1882) (P.001.1876, PAHRC).

[142] Bew, 'The Land League Ideal'; Kelly, *The Fenian Ideal*, 239; Whelehan, *The Dynamiters*, 249.

[143] Dwan, *The Great Community*, 23–50; on long tradition of Irishness and British commercial imperialism: David A. Wilson, *United Irishmen, United States: Immigrant Radicals in the Early American Republic* (Ithaca, NY: Cornell University Press, 1998); Kevin Whelan, *The Tree of Liberty: Radicalism, Catholicism and the Construction of Irish Identity, 1760–1830* (Cork: Cork University Press, 1996); Michael Drury, 'Thomas Paine's Apostles: Radical Emigres and the Triumph of Jeffersonian Republicanism', *William and Mary Quarterly* 4 (1987): 661–688.

[144] Clancy, *Ireland: As She Is*, 27, 62; on Clancy: Sean McConville, *Irish Political Prisoners, 1848–1922: Theatres of War* (London: Routledge, 2003), 166.

ever living halo of beauty'.[145] It was not uncommon for political polemics to describe Ireland's 'green and fertile fields, her grassy slopes, her flowing rivers and luxuriant plains', framing such natural splendour as a moral rebuke to British misrule, as 'the glittering robe that hides the wounds and sores of an afflicted nation'.[146] Natural harmony suggested moral harmony and, potentially, a political harmony; both reflecting and generating 'a more elevated system of morality' than now existed anywhere else and creating 'the land of scholars and the nurse of arms'.[147] This romantic naturalism, with its focus on a pre-existing harmonious order, translated into the political sphere. Ireland's 'air of romance and chivalry' had invested 'her with an unconquerable resolve never to give up the struggle until they place the diadem of liberty upon her brow'.[148] It meant that Ireland's fight against English rule represented, as James Clancy explained, 'a rude, unorganized Democracy resisting an aggressive, piratical Feudalism'.[149]

This anarchic 'unorganized Democracy' was a political reflection of the harmony evident in the natural world. The roots of this moral presumption of harmony spread widely, binding together agrarian radical and romantic nationalist tropes. Traditional conceptions of masculinity and femininity were nurtured by it, and themselves fed into a vision of a rugged and honest demotic sensibility, which could be effectively contrasted against an unnaturally effete and aristocratic affect. Ireland's moral superiority was understood through the gendered division of the 'genius of Irishmen' and the 'virtue' of its daughters, which had 'for ages been the theme of universal admiration'.[150] As Davitt explained, established social roles were part of 'the moral instincts of our people', a commonly intelligible morality, 'in obedience to the law of Nature'.[151] It was as essential to republican society that men would develop the 'qualities that are essential to the part which he has to perform in the duties of life', as it was that women transmitted such values to the next generation.[152]

[145] Dunne, *Ireland: Rights, Wrongs and Remedies*, 3 (PAHRC, 103, Box 34, P.001.1804).
[146] Conyngham, *Ireland Past and Present*, 202.
[147] Rev James Joseph Moriarty, *The Mystic Key to Ireland's History: A Lecture Delivered on St. Patrick's Day, 1881* (Chatham, NY: The Courier Printing House, 1881), 5, 14; M. W. Kirwan, *Lecture by M. W. Kirwan, Editor of the True Witness, in reply to Reverend Mr. Bray, on the "Romish" Church, Delivered in the Mechanics' Hall, March 13, 1877* (Montreal: True Witness Office, 1877), 2; Conyngham, *Ireland Past and Present*, 18.
[148] Conyngham, *Ireland Past and Present*, 18. [149] Clancy, *The Land League Manual*, 30.
[150] Kirwan, *Lecture*, 2.
[151] Davitt, *The Fall of Feudalism*, 155; Davitt, 'Random Thoughts on the Irish Land War', 187.
[152] Davitt, 'Random Thoughts on the Irish Land War', 187; Eileen J. Yeo, 'Gender and Homeland in the Irish and Jewish Diasporas, 1850–1930', in Marlou Schrover, and Eileen Yeo (eds.), *Gender, Migration and the Public Sphere, 1850–2005* (New York: Taylor & Francis, 2010), 23; Alison Kibler, 'The Stage Irishwoman', *Journal of American Ethnic History* 24, no. 3 (2005): 5–30.

Irish masculinity in particular was conceptually utilised to resist standards of Anglo-American gentility.[153] It was called upon to foster solidarity, as when boycotting was described as standing 'together like men', rather than 'bowing and scraping before every little shoneen in the country'.[154] The Land League had helped, explained George, re-energise a 'new manhood [...] into the down trodden people'.[155] But evocations of Irish masculinity also possessed a sharper, more critical character in the inverse condemnation of the 'withering' manhood of those 'too cowardly and mean to stand up boldly in assertion of their country's liberties'.[156] These strictures came together in attacks on the 'manners and customs of aristocracies', through which English power 'has returned upon us in spirit'.[157] Not only did this construction of Irish republican masculinity enable Irish-American men to call claim to a familiar image in the United States – the hardy and practical man of demotic and unaffected manners, the American *par excellence* – but this construct also emphasised maxims of patriotism and honesty over material wealth. While poverty meant struggle, which fostered masculinity and other virtues, wealth and luxury always threatened to breed effeminacy and vice.[158] The American Revolution had been, therefore, a struggle between 'manhood and monarchy', and of course Ireland's landlords were, *sui generis*, 'a small class of effeminate aristocrats'.[159]

The confluence of these cultural streams was a central site of resistance to liberal capitalism. Confronting Anglo-American cultural mores formed part of the battle against English imperial and commercial power. In 1883, in an address to the Irish societies of New York State, one speaker observed how wealthy Americans had tried to 'impress us at this side of the ocean with the greatness of the debt we owe Old England; how generously her capitalists treat us! – how affectionately her aristocracy marries us! But Irishmen, all this will

[153] Patricia Kelleher, 'Class and Catholic Irish Masculinity in Antebellum America: Young Men on the Make in Chicago', *Journal of American Ethnic History* 28, no. 4 (2009): 11; William Jenkins, 'Remapping: "Irish America": Circuits, Places, Performances', *Journal of American Ethnic History* 28, no. 4 (2009): 92.

[154] Richard Lalor at Maryborough [Port Laoise], 5 October 1879, in T. D. Sullivan (ed.), *Condemnations of Crime*, 46.

[155] Henry George, 'Visit to Bishop Nulty', 1881 (HGP, Series II, Box 12, NYPL).

[156] Fintan Lalor, Tenants' Right and Landlord's Law' [1847], 143; Conyngham, *Ireland Past and Present*, 229; John O'Connor Power at Ballinasloe, *Freeman's Journal*, 4 November 1878; Bill Poster: 'Scandalous Flunkeyism and Gross Misrepresentation' (HP, MS 21,910, NLI); Paul Bew, and Patrick Maume, 'Michael Davitt and the Personality of the Irish Agrarian Revolution', in Lane Fintan, and Andrew G. Newby (eds.), *Michael Davitt: New Perspectives* (Dublin: Irish Academic Press, 2009), 65.

[157] *Irish World*, 7 December 1878; 22 May 1880; T. P. O'Connor, 'The Irish Situation', *American Catholic Quarterly Review* 8 (1883): 76; Jacobson, *Special Sorrows*, 25.

[158] *Irish World*, 23 November 1878.

[159] Irish World, 20 December 1879; Bell, *Peasant Proprietary for Ireland*, 24.

not do. The brawn of America is yet manly'.[160] Ford's *Irish World*, too, brashly rejected the 'knickerbocker respectability' of genteel Anglo-America, with its aristocratic pretentions, taking deliberate aim at the 'superficial pharisaism of the British snobs on either side of the Atlantic'.[161] Indeed, the paper even gleefully cheered on the Sino-phobic, anti-Semitic Californian rabble-rouser Denis Kearney, who both Henry George and Terence Powderly considered a demagogue with 'no principle whatever', primarily because 'when Denis Kearney was East, New England culture was shocked at his awful adjectives'.[162] The appeal of this cathartic rejection of the respectable 'civilised' social order, one that seemed to conceal economic dominance through displays of refinement and educated sophistication, was well expressed by Rev John Talbot Smith, who recalled that the *Irish World* was 'the first really vivid expression of my own feelings, the first proper expression of my natural rage against the horde of elegant Oxford and Cambridge and Harvard and Yale liars'.[163]

In this way, the cultures of Irish nationalism at home and across the diaspora – romantic, poetic, sentimental, particularist, demotic, and hardy – were not simply aligned with agrarian republican politics, but sprang from the same sources. They were mutually dependent aspects of the same opposition and signalled a rejection of what was perceived as a peculiarly English (or more precisely Anglo-American) liberal commercialism and imperialism. Britain's place in the vanguard of economic and imperial power suffused economic opposition with cultural antagonism, and vice versa, as 'Englishness' came to operate as an ideological category to be confronted.[164] Irish nationalists, often unwittingly, adopted Marx's demand that 'England cannot be treated simply as a country along with other countries. She must be treated as the *metropolis of capital*'.[165] The Fenian writer Patrick J. Flatley exhibited this tendency when he suggested that 'English' national identity was devoid of moral, emotional, or spiritual depth, the English, he opined, 'do not appear to have been mastered by any deepened conviction other than the conviction of self-interest'.[166]

160 Dr. William B. Wallace, 'Address to the Representatives of the Irish Societies of the Empire State' (Devoy Papers, MS 18,048, NLI).

161 *Irish World*, 31 October 1874; *Irish World*, 12 April 1879.

162 Denis Kearney [unsigned] to Terence V. Powderly, 29 March 1878 (PP, Series 1: Box 2, CUA); Charles H. Litchman to Terence V. Powderly, 26 June, and 29 August 1878 (PP, Series 1: Box 2, CUA); Henry George to John Swinton [n.d.], 1880 (HGP, Series I: A, Box 2, NYPL); Henry George, *Irish World*, 9 July 1882; *Irish World*, 24 May 1879.

163 Smith, *Patrick Ford of the Irish World* (AIA.047, NYU).

164 Bevir, and Trentmann, 'Critique within Capitalism'; Rothschild, 'Political Economy', 266; Similarities in Indian context developed in Kaushal Kishore Mishra, 'Problem of Sovereignty in Gandhian Thought', *The Indian Journal of Political Science* 66, no. 3 (2005): 515–530.

165 Karl Marx, 'Confidential Communication', in Karl Marx and Frederick Engels, *Ireland and the Irish Question* (Moscow: Progress Publishers, 1971),161.

166 Patrick J. Flatley, *Ireland and the Land League: Key to the Irish Question* (Boston: D. O'Loughlin and Co., 1881), 24–25.

This critical, anti-capitalist interpretation of 'Englishness' provided fertile ground for transnational co-operation and the development of an idiom of pan-Celtic solidarity. It was, as James Hunter has described, 'a belief that Ireland and Scotland stood in similar relation to England's imperial power'.[167] Fighting against both economic globalisation and cultural imperialism, this radical pan-Celticism tied the imperial to the commercial in similar ways that Mitchel and Davis had earlier done, viewing the centralisation of both culture and political control as an impulse intimately connected with liberal British and Anglo-American political discourse. Here again, land took centre stage as the legacies of Highland clearances drew striking parallels with Ireland. A shared radical theology seamlessly knit together Irish and Scottish views of land ownership regardless of confessional distinction, something also evident in Welsh Methodism at the same time.[168] Davitt, in particular, led the way, emphasising the shared struggles of the Irish tenant and Scottish crofter in his speeches at Scottish Land League meetings, but he was joined by many more among the radical wing of the Land League.[169] In the west of Scotland, Irish radicals such as John Ferguson, Edward McHugh, and Richard McGee were vocal proponents of the Land League's necessity in Scotland and soon became, like Davitt, ardent admirers of Henry George.[170] For George himself, Scotland would later become almost as important as Ireland to his political activism.[171] In Wales, although land agitation did not achieve the same proportions as in Ireland or Scotland, the terms of critique were identical.[172]

167 James Hunter, 'The Gaelic Connection: The Highlands, Ireland and Nationalism, 1873–1922', *The Scottish Historical Review* 54, no. 158 (1975): 181.

168 Ewen A. Cameron, 'Communication or Separation? Reactions to Irish Land Agitation and Legislation in the Highlands of Scotland c.1870–1910', *The English Historical Review* 120, no. 487 (2005): 633–666; Andrew G. Newby, *Ireland, Radicalism and the Scottish Highlands, c. 1870–1912* (Edinburgh: Edinburgh University Press, 2007); Andy Wightman, *The Poor Had No Lawyers: Who Owns Scotland (And How They Got It)* (Edinburgh: Birlinn, 2010); David Howell, 'The Land Question in Nineteenth-Century Wales, Ireland and Scotland: A Comparative Perspective', *Agricultural History Review* 61, no. 1 (2013): 83–110.

169 Máirtín Ó Catháin, 'Michael Davitt in Scotland', *Saothar: Journal of Irish Labour History* 25 (2000): 19–26.

170 Andrew G. Newby, 'Edward McHugh, the National Land League of Great Britain and the "Crofters' War", 1879–1882', *Scottish Historical Review* 82 (2003): 74–91; on Ferguson see, McFarland, *John Ferguson.*

171 *Glasgow Herald*, 18 March 1882; Henry George to Edward Robeson Taylor, 30 May 1882 (HGP, Series I: A, Box 3, NYPL); Terence McBride, 'John Ferguson, Michael Davitt and Henry George – Land for the People', *Irish Studies Review* 14, no. 4 (2006): 421–430.

172 Landlords were 'devourers of the marrow' according to the Denbigh *Baner*, 24 November 1886, reprod. in J. E. Vincent, *The Land Question in North Wales, Being a Brief Survey of the History, Origin, and Character of the Agrarian Agitation, and of the Nature and Effect of the Proceedings of the Welsh Land Commission* (London: Longmans, Green and Co., 1896), 15. See also David Howell, *Land and People in Nineteenth Century Wales* (London: Routledge and Kegan Paul, 1977); Matthew Cragoe, '"A Contemptible Mimic of the Irish": The Land Question in Victorian Wales', in Matthew Cragoe, and Paul Readman (eds.), *The Land Question in Britain*, 1750–1950 (Basingstoke: Palgrave Macmillan, 2010), 92–108.

Scotland, like Wales, occupied a more complex position than Ireland, however. On the one hand, the country had been more comprehensively overrun by British state power, but it was also much more fully incorporated into the machinery of government, leaving less residual cultural resistance or interest in nationalism. Scotland was considered to have compromised its nationhood for 'comparative prosperity', while Ireland had 'preferred rags and an unconquered spirit of liberty to favors won by national dishonor'.[173] Yet even in this analysis, Scotland's relationship with England and the British Empire was still somewhat analogous with Ireland's. The Scottish nationalist and land radical John Murdoch found great support from the coterie of social radicals that adjoined the broader Land League movement, despite the comparative unpopularity of his cause at home.[174] Parnell, the Philadelphia Fenian William Carroll, and Terence V. Powderly all helped to facilitate a speaking tour in the United States for Murdoch, allowing him to access a well-established network of Irish nationalist and American labour audiences. The place occupied by Scotland and Wales in the radical analysis was well summed up by an *Irish World* cartoon, in which the British Empire was represented as a crumbing classical Greek temple. While the column labelled India, Ireland, and Afghanistan was breaking apart, Scotland and Wales, along with Canada and Australia, formed parts of the weakened but structurally intact columns.[175] England had no column of its own, while Scotland and Wales took their places alongside Ireland with other members of the Empire.

Pan-Celtic sympathies relied upon a belief in the importance of cultural particularity, often residing in a spiritual or emotive-aesthetic connection to place and land, in forming a barrier against the unanchored and demoralised freedoms of a market-based or paternalist liberalism. Professor John Stuart Blackie of the University of Edinburgh, an active supporter of the Scottish land agitation, and a respected figure quoted liberally by Irish Land Leaguers, including Parnell in front of the US House of Representatives, put it in this way: 'In all countries the land was the quarry out of which the possibility of existence was evolved. [...] The land was the scene on which the great drama of social life was enacted; the root out of which the most necessary element of popular well-being firmly grew.' It was the sense of belonging 'to a definite spot' that could produce the manifested loyalties needed to resist the economic exploitations of 'the man with gold in his pocket [who] may prosper anywhere' and the 'sagacious capitalist'.[176]

173 'Proceedings of the Third General Convention of the Irish National League of America, held at, Chicago, Illinois, August, 18 and 19, 1886', 28 (103, Box 40, AC0129, PAHRC).

174 John D. Wood, 'Transatlantic Land Reform: America and the Crofters' Revolt, 1878–1888', *The Scottish Historical Review* 63, no. 175 (1984): 92; Hunter, 'The Gaelic Connection', 180.

175 *Irish World*, 15 November 1879.

176 John Stuart Blackie, 'Land Laws and Landlords', *Contemporary Review* 37 (1880): 31; Parnell's references to Blackie, in Healy, *Why There Is an Irish Land Question*, 58; Davitt discussed Blackie in Aberdeen, Aberdeen *Daily Free Press*, 30 October 1882 (DP, MS 9351.679, TCD).

In this way, land again provided that universal element upon which to construct alternative economic visions to a deracinating and demoralising 'Englishness'; a localism that evinced a universalism. It helped Irish nationalism look outwards, taking tentative and uneven steps towards developing an internationalist and even anti-colonial character. Indeed, the wider imperial context was never too far away from the radical analysis of Ireland's condition and could be viewed in expressions of sympathy for African and Asian peoples suffering under British rule, the 'millions crushed' under the 'juggernaut car' of imperialism.[177] On Land League platforms, it was possible to learn that Ireland's cause was held in common with 'the world and of all countries now and forever' and be reminded that 'there is a greater Ireland wherever the curse of England's civilisation exists'.[178]

Inseparable from 'England's civilisation', indeed practically synonymous with it, was the institution of legal contract, and its political equivalent, constitutionalism. In Britain and the United States, the second half of the nineteenth century saw the continued formalisation of the idea of 'free labour' as equivalent with security of contract.[179] For both supporters and opponents, the sanctity of contract was frequently held up as the apotheosis of Anglo-American political economy.[180] It was 'that which the whole world recognized as essential Anglo-Saxonism; not the Anglo-Saxonism of mere brute force, but ideal Anglo-Saxonism, legal and constitutional Anglo-Saxonism', explained Alexander Sullivan.[181] The cold legalistic malevolence that Sullivan saw as construing 'legal and constitutional Anglo-Saxonism' gave Irish discussions of 'constitutionalism' a decidedly schizophrenic character, oscillating between condemnations of this legalistic formalism, and a demand to improve upon and perfect constitutional guarantees. As one small American pamphlet on Irish politics conceded, 'It seems curious that it should be necessary to define here the term "constitutionalism" or "constitutional freedom". But in dealing with the Irish question it is necessary to have an absolutely clear understanding on this point, for the term has been used in Ireland in very strange connections'. In Ireland, the author continued, since the authority of Dublin Castle rested on its claim to constitutionality, the word itself had 'come to have in Ireland, not only a different meaning from what it has in the dictionary, but the exactly opposition meaning. It means what in America

[177] Clancy, *Ireland: As She Is*, 63; *Irish World* 12 April 1879; M. W. Kirwan speaking at INLL meeting, Thurles, Co. Tipperary, 14 November 1880 (MS 11,289, NLI).

[178] *Irish World*, 20 December 1879; Rev Sheehy, Ballingarry, 14 November 1880 (MS 11,289, NLI).

[179] Lowell, *Essays*, 14; Leon Fink, *The Long Gilded Age: American Capitalism and the Lessons of a New World Order* (Philadelphia: University of Pennsylvania Press, 2015), 16.

[180] William Graham Sumner, 'Do We Want Industrial Peace' [1889], in *War and Other Essays*, Albert Galloway Keller (ed.), (New Haven: Yale University Press, 1911), 233–234; Offer, *Property and Politics*, 189.

[181] Alexander Sullivan, 'The American Republic and the Irish National League of America', *American Catholic Quarterly Review* 9 (1884), 4–5.

would be called despotic. The more constitutional a man's views are held to be, the more despotic they are'.[182] But while English constitutionalism was a 'monstrous mockery', which had 'triumphed over every moral law', the constitutional idiom retained a point of appeal for Davitt, Parnell, and many other Land Leaguers, who demanded 'English constitutional freedom of speech' live up to its expressed principles.[183]

The romantic invocations of subaltern suffering, the elevation of the spiritual over the materialistic, and the hostility to bureaucratic or legalistic formalism which characterised the Pan-Celtic agrarian imaginary were manifest most clearly in a proclivity for poetics. Verse and song offered the creative freedom to reconstruct political life beyond the bounds of technical language, and without the constraints of an imposed economic rationality.[184] The connection between the moral and emotional affect of national identity and the egalitarianism of radical politics could be constructed and affirmed here, without the awkward compromises of more detailed and prosaic explanations, and in a medium in which meaning was tied to the 'somatic aspects of language'.[185] Poetry was recited at public Land League meetings, with speakers sometimes quoting short verses from the platform.[186] Songs, too, played a similarly important role in transmitting ideals and sustaining shared commitments, passed on orally or through published work like Richard K. Fox's *Land League Songster*.[187] The work of Boston *Pilot* editor and former Fenian prisoner John Boyle O'Reilly, who published three volumes of verse later in life, was a stark example of this relationship between poetry and political imagination. His poems, characterised by an emotionally effusive idolisation of the subaltern and a mournful longing for a more emotionally stable and just community, were later claimed as 'socialistic' in one sympathetic appraisal, and evidence that Fenian political culture 'clearly saw that [revolution] was through the proletariat alone'.[188]

182 'Irish National League of America', *What Is "Castle Government?" A Question Answered, for Americans Interested in the Irish Question* (Chicago: Irish National League of America, 1884), 4–5 (103, Box 40, AC0129, PAHRC).

183 Clancy, *Ireland: As She Is*, 7; *Irish World*, 20 December 1879; Michael Davitt and Charles Stewart Parnell, quoted in Aurelius MacSwynie (ed.), *America's Sympathies with Ireland*, 27–28; Father McKeogh, P.P. of Ballinahinch, at Tipperary, 31 October 1880 (MS 11,289, NLI); Rev Sheehy, Ballingarry, 14 November 1880 (MS 11,289, NLI).

184 Richard Parfitt, *Musical Culture and the Spirit of Irish Nationalism, 1848–1972* (London: Routledge, 2020).

185 Terry Eagleton, *Materialism* (New Haven: Yale University Press, 2016), 132.

186 Patrick Brady at Ballinagleragh, 5 September 1880 (MS 11,289, NLI).

187 'Song Composed at the Time of the Boycott by the Late William Murray' (Irish Folklore Collection, 0741/3/60, University College Dublin); Richard K. Fox, *Land League Songster: A Collection of Patriotic Irish Ballads Celebrating Deeds of Valor Performed by Erin's Sons in the Past, and Suited to The Present Land Agitation, Wit, Sentiment and Patriotism* (New York: Richard K. Fox, 1880).

188 Thomas Brady, *Historical Basis of Socialism in Ireland* (New York: Socialist Labor Party, 1921) (AIA.047, NYU).

O'Reilly's hostility towards liberal capitalism, despite his own social and economic success, shows just how integral these ideas remained to Irish-American identity. His poetry is an example of the variety of mediums through which these ideas and political markers were sustained and collectively internalised as a central element of cultural identity. The title poem of the collection *In Bohemia*, published in 1886, radiated a deep antipathy towards the hubris of Gilded Age conspicuous consumption, criticising:

The moistureless froth of the social show;
The vulgar sham of the pompous feast
Where the heaviest purse is the highest priest[189]

Social and spiritual ambitions were lauded over more worldly and economic concerns in the verse of 'The Priceless Things' and 'The Old Vagabond'. In the later, O'Reilly offered the comforting utopianism of self-imposed poverty as the eponymous speaker informed his audience:

And a man to be free must a poor man be, for unhappy is he who thrives:
[...]
A man's higher being is knowing and seeing, not having and toiling for more;
In the senses and soul is the joy of control, not in pride or luxurious store.[190]

O'Reilly's poetic energies were not rationed to an anti-materialist spirituality, but also attacked structural economic issues as well. His poem 'The City Streets' was a Gilded Age lament over the rampant inequality of the era that, were it not for the rhyming meter, could have been taken directly from George's own work. In it, O'Reilly described 'palaces built for trade [...] where fabulous gains are made', with 'miles of glass [...and] polished brass'. He wrote of the social dislocation that such wealth inequalities generated; that there was 'No need to speak of what's out of sight: let us take what is pleasant, and leave the rest'. After a vivid and angry description of the personal horror of poverty and the apathy it induced, O'Reilly confronted 'progress':

The strong and the selfish are sure to rise, while the simple and generous die obscure.
And these are the virtues and social gifts by which Progress and Property rank over Man!
Look there, O woe! where a lost soul drifts on the stream where such virtues overran[191]

189 O'Reilly, 'In Bohemia', *In Bohemia* (Boston: Cashman, Keating & Co., 1886), 15.
190 O'Reilly, 'An Old Vagabond', *In Bohemia* (Boston: Cashman, Keating & Co., 1886), 61–63.
191 O'Reilly, 'The City Streets', *In Bohemia* (Boston: Cashman, Keating & Co., 1886), 70–76.

Not only 'progress', but 'civilization' too (inextricably bound to the contractualism of '*statutes*'), found itself in the dock, condemned as a deficient yardstick for measuring social or moral value, as opposed to matters of Natural Right:

'Tis Civilization, so they say, and it cannot be changed for the
weakness of men.
Take care! take care! 'tis a desperate way to goad the wolf to the end
of his den.
Take heed of your Civilization, ye, on your pyramids built of
quivering hearts;
There are stages, like Paris in '93, where the commonest men play
most terrible parts.
Your statutes may crush but they cannot kill the patient sense of a
natural right;
It may slowly move, but the People's will, like the ocean o'er
Holland, is always in sight.[192]

Running in parallel was a perception of the loss of moral certainty in an economistic and utilitarian view of value. Thomas J. Mooney had written scathingly in the *Irish World* of the pretention of attempts 'to measure production and its value, life and its duties, society and its laws, God and His love, man and his soul'.[193] Similarly, O'Reilly opined:

Common debts are scored and cancelled, weighed
and measured out for gold;
But the debts from men to ages, their account is
never told.[194]

Ireland naturally provided another central theme of O'Reilly's poetry. He emphasised the diaspora as a central aspect of Irish nationality, a collective identity that involved those who left as much as those who stayed, describing Ireland as the: 'Mustard seed of the nations! they scattered thy leaves to the air'.[195] This took an anti-imperialist form, which sought to bind Ireland to the United States and situated Irishness in direct contrast to English values:

And wherever the flag of the pirate flew, the Eng-
lish slur was heard,
[...]
That strangles the rights of others, and only itself
endures.[196]
[...]
Till the world comes to know that the test of a cause
Is the hatred of tyrants, and Erin's applause![197]

[192] O'Reilly, 'The City Streets', 70–76. [193] *Irish World*, 30 November 1878.
[194] O'Reilly, 'The Priceless Things', *In Bohemia* (Boston: Cashman, Keating & Co., 1886), 29–32.
[195] O'Reilly, 'Ireland – 1882', *In Bohemia* (Boston: Cashman, Keating & Co., 1886), 47–51.
[196] O'Reilly, 'Ireland – 1882', 47–51.
[197] O'Reilly, 'Erin', *In Bohemia* (Boston: Cashman, Keating & Co., 1886), 55–58.

Drawing most heavily on the republican themes of natural harmony and justice was O'Reilly's poem *The Three Queens*. In it, he reconstructed a prelapsarian golden age, a 'time traditioned!', when 'Men owned the world, and every man was free; The lowest life was noble; all were equal', under the stewardship of Queen Liberty.[198] She was followed by Queen Law:

> *Her new code read: "The earth is for the able"*
> *(And able meant the selfish, strong, and shrewd);*
> *"Equality and freedom are a fable;*
> *To take and keep the largest share is good."*
> *Her teachers taught the justice of oppression,*
> *That taxed the poor on all but air and sun;*
> *Her preachers preached the gospel of possession,*
> *That hoards had rights while human souls had none.*

The context of land coursed through the verse. From 'earth' in the first line, to being taxed 'on all but air and sun' and 'the gospel of possession', land rent was a central thread. Queen Law also inveighed against normative naturalism. Under her reign:

> *Then all things changed their object and relation;*
> *Commerce instead of Nature—Progress instead of Men;*

The reordering of values away from 'Nature' signified an inversion of the divinely ordained order. However, the third Queen was Learning, soon to offer emancipation from the restrictions imposed by Queen Law. As the poem reached its conclusion, the centrality of the United States became clear:

> *And men are learning, grain by grain, the knowledge*
> *That worlds exist for higher ends than trade.*
> *[...]*
> *To guard the deep republican foundations*
> *Of our majestic freedom of the West!*[199]

O'Reilly's work tied together the various themes examined in this chapter. It dwelt confidently on a number of established Irish republican tropes: masculinity, romanticism, public virtue, the oppositional nature and Englishness and Irishness, an ambivalence with commerce and materialism, a spiritual elevation of poverty, a faith in learning, and a suspicion of centralisation, bureaucracy, and utility, among others. As well as this, his poetry signified the importance of cultural and literary forms in sustaining these values, even in the face of compromise with contemporary society. Land underpinned all

198 O'Reilly, 'The Three Queens', *In Bohemia* (Boston: Cashman, Keating & Co., 1886), 77–83.
199 O'Reilly, 'The Three Queens', 77–83.

of this. In some ways, even his most strident and hopeful poems were laments for an agrarian ideal, for it was in the context of a great social upheaval that they were written.

'He was Irish and American; intensely both, but more than both. The world was his country and mankind was his kin.'[200] Patrick A. Collins' eulogy at the funeral of John Boyle O'Reilly was a fitting epitaph for the man, but it might also serve as an accurate illustration of the transatlantic life of this republican tradition. The relationship between the cultures of Irish republican nationalism and radical agrarianism was deep rooted and interdependent, rather than contingent or opportunistic. They too were Irish and American, 'intensely both, but more than both'.

[200] Patrick A. Collins, eulogy at the funeral of John Boyle O'Reilly (PACP, Series II: Box 4, BC).

Conclusion

> Now, observe, the doctrine of Mr. George, that the land of a people belongs to the whole people, has been and still is, the watch-word of the Irish Land League agitation, and observe also, that not the farmers only, but the whole mass of the population have projected themselves into this movement.[1]

In his capacity as a foreign correspondent for the *Irish World*, George's reportage from Ireland during the Land War drove home the idea that this conflict was a battle for the meaning of 'liberalism'. Horrified by the widespread poverty, and surprised by the comfortable wealth that sat alongside it, he was indignant and dismayed at the 'reign of terror I found here', where 'the first principles of human belief are being trodden under foot by an irresponsible dictatorship'.[2] He reported to his commissioning newspaper that 'there were two great Englishmen whom I wished could have been alive' to see the state of Ireland's misgovernance, Charles Dickens and John Stuart Mill, for 'it would require the author of "On Liberty" to fitly warn his countrymen' of the disastrous and illiberal policies being pursued.[3] George would experience this first hand, twice being arrested on his tours around Ireland. Although he was warned on arrival to use a pseudonym in order to avoid arrest, George enjoyed his encounters with the police as providing useful evidence of British despotism and an opportunity for self-promotion (the American handed out copies of his book to the local magistrate and 'one each to the sub-inspector and the constables who had personally been very polite to me').[4]

[1] O'Grady, *The Crisis in Ireland*, 23–24.

[2] Henry George to Thomas Briggs, 29 October 1881 (HGP, Series I: A, Box 3, NYPL); Henry George, 'Jailed in Ireland', draft copy for *Irish World* (HGP, Series II, Box 13, NYPL); *The Nation*, 16 September 1882.

[3] Henry George, *Irish World*, 10 December 1881.

[4] Henry George to Patrick Ford, 10 November 1881 (HGP, Series I: B, NYPL); Anna George de Mille, 'Henry George: The Fight for Irish Freedom', *The American Journal of Economics and Sociology* 3, no. 2 (1944): 270; Henry George to Annie George, August 1882 (HGP, Series I: A, Box 3, NYPL); *Irish World*, 22 August 1882.

George's second arrest provoked a minor political affair, with demands for public apologies and questions in parliament.[5] But it was simply fuel for both George and the Land League to their complaint that British liberalism had abandoned its own principles.[6] 'A great many of your so-called Liberals are, in my opinion, a very conservative sort [...] and are rather Tories in disguise', remarked George at a lecture in Birmingham, a view of the remarkable resemblance between 'English Liberals and English Tories' that was repeatedly echoed by the Land League.[7] It was a signal tragedy that coercion in Ireland had been enacted by 'those who have the cant of liberalism on their lips', he complained.[8] In George's opinion, British liberalism was 'paternal rather than democratic or even constitutional', and although there existed liberal tendencies, he deemed them to be 'anything but democratic'.[9] That the Irish Land War elicited this 'paternal and patronising' liberalism was inescapable given the central contradictions it evinced between liberalism and the land.[10]

Ireland was soon to disappoint George. After working hard during the spring and summer of 1882 to ensure that 'money contributed by radical men for radical purposes' achieved radical aims, events soon overtook George's ambitions.[11] Charles Stuart Parnell's agreement with Gladstone to end rural violence and rent strikes in return for his release from prison and the 1882 Arrears of Rent Act coincided with the Phoenix Park murders of the newly appointed Chief Secretary and Undersecretary for Ireland. Faced with the dual blow of the Kilmainham Treaty, as it became known, and the political assassinations, the Land League was buried under a new coercion act. Davitt may have complained that the Arrears Act simply replicated the errors of the 1881 Act – 'another experimental measure by which landlord and tenant, instead of being legally divorced, are both turned over into the hands of the lawyers' – and mocked the idea that 'the Land League movement is about to efface itself all the world over because he [Gladstone] has been converted to Mr. Parnell's views upon the Arrears question', but it was Parnell's release and his reasserted authority that side-lined the radical energy of the League, which had, until that point, been driven forward primarily by the Ladies' Land League.[12]

5 Congressman C. C. Mason (Indiana) to Patrick Ford, 28 August 1882, *Irish World*, 9 September 1882; Frank O'Donnell, M.P., HC Deb. 10 August 1882, vol. 273, col. 1383.

6 Biagini, *British Democracy*, 138.

7 Henry George, 'Lecture at Midland Institute, Birmingham', 23 January 1884 (HGP, Series II, Box 13, NYPL); Col. John W. Forney, quoted in MacSwynie (ed.), *America's Sympathies with Ireland*, 24; Clancy, *Ireland: As She Is*, 29.

8 Henry George, *Irish World*, 14 January 1882; 28 January 1882; 25 March 1882.

9 Henry George, *Irish World*, 1 April 1882.

10 Henry George, *Irish World*, 21 January 1882.

11 Henry George to Patrick Ford, 20 April 1882; Henry George to Patrick Ford, 24 May 1882 (HGP, Series I: B, NYPL).

12 Michael Davitt, *The Land League Proposal: A Statement for Honest and Thoughtful Men* (Glasgow: Cameron and Ferguson, 1882), 10–11.

According to George, who was in Dublin at the time, news of Parnell's release turned the offices of the Ladies' Land League into something resembling a wake.[13] As Parnell shifted focus from agrarian to constitutional matters in order to 'prevent the spread of radical ideas and to bring the people into lines of thought and of action which agreed with the notions of the English liberals', the radical leadership was marginalised, with Dillon, Egan, and, later, Thomas Brennan leaving for the more hospitable climate of the United States.[14] In George's opinion, the move away from the land represented 'the surrendering of a great principle [...] and the giving up of vantage which had been won by much effort and sacrifice'.[15]

Corresponding changes occurred in the United States, where the conservative leadership of the League happily took advantage of the move away from agrarian radicalism, portraying the land question as narrow, class based, and complete: 'As the Land League accomplished the relief of a class, the National league represents the aspirations and the resolve of an entire people.'[16] Over the course of the decade, internecine rivalry and interstate conflict became its primary business.[17] For George, however, although he was hugely disappointed 'with the Irish business' after the summer of 1882, harbouring only a hope that 'our ideas are steadily [...] spreading', his own political fortunes elsewhere were improving.[18] He returned to New York to find Edward McGlynn in full voice and a radical movement pinning their hopes to his fame.[19] The formation of the Central Labor Union (CLU) provided the organisational hub of this broad labour church in the city, and its growth owed much to the concomitant withering of American Land League, as Irish radicals transferred their allegiances.[20] The centrality of the land question carried over too, at least initially. Bishop Nulty's influential pastoral letter, quoted liberally by agrarian radicals, including by Davitt during his final speeches before travelling to the United States in the summer of 1882, saw its most powerful phrase become the first resolution on the CLU's platform. With a couple of minor grammatical changes, the Declaration of the Principles of the Central Labor Union of New York followed the Irish Bishop in declaring that:

[13] Henry George, 'Interview on Irish Nationalist Politics', 1882 (HGP, Series II, Box 13, NYPL); Henry George to Patrick Ford, 6 June 1882 (HGP, Series I: B, NYPL).
[14] Henry George, 'Interview on Irish Nationalist Politics', 1882 (HGP, Series II, Box 13, NYPL).
[15] Henry George to Terence V. Powderly, 25 July 1883 (PP, Series I, Box 8, CUA).
[16] Alexander Sullivan, 'Second Annual Convention of the Irish National League of America; Boston 13–14 August 1884' (Devoy Papers, MS 18,048, NLI).
[17] 'An Exposure of the Reprehensible Means employed by John Fitzgerald, of Lincoln, Neb. and Alexander Sullivan, of Chicago, Ills. to prevent Mr William O'Brien, from lecturing for the Irish National League of Philadelphia' (1887) (103, Box 40, AC0130a, PAHRC).
[18] Henry George to Annie George, 22 May 1882 (HGP, Series I: A, Box 3, NYPL).
[19] Henry George to Fr Thomas Dawson, October 1882, NYPL, HGP (HGP, Series I: A, Box 3, NYPL).
[20] Jeremiah Murphy, *Irish World*, 28 October 1882; see too O'Donnell, 'Henry George and the "New Political Forces"', 276.

as every individual in every country is a creature and a child of God, and as all his creatures are equal in his sight, any settlement of the land of this or any other country that would exclude the humblest man in that country from his share in the common inheritance would not only be an injustice and a wrong to that man, but would, moreover, be an impious resistance to the benevolent intentions of the Creator.[21]

George's campaign to become Mayor of New York in 1886 for the United Labor Party was, according to David Montgomery, the 'high-water mark of that decade's labor struggles'.[22] Drawing together various labour factions, and supported by Samuel Gompers, Terence Powderly, and Daniel de Leon, George came a close second to local industrialist, congressman, and civil service reformer Abram Hewitt.[23] Hewitt's nomination on an explicitly anti-labour platform was the result of an awkward and temporary alliance between the Tammany Democratic machine and its Anglo-American enemies to stop the radicals gaining power, but it was clear even to his opponents that George's popular support represented 'in many ways a revolt against present political methods'.[24]

It was also to be a high point of George's own political career. With the labour movement on both sides of the Atlantic largely moving away from radicalism, George's influence waned. Increasing conflict with socialists who no longer considered his ideas a help but a hindrance to their cause also contributed.[25] The question of land reform most certainly did not disappear, but it was no longer entirely in his shadow. While agrarian agitation in Ireland and Scotland during the later part of the decade continued in the grooves made by events in the early 1880s, Fabian socialist and progressive liberal collaboration in urban Britain over increased taxation of ground rents was marked by a conscious distancing from Georgism.[26] The problem remained George's moralistic natural rights arguments, and as the Liberal Party gradually adopted more 'equitable taxation of land values', it did so on the basis that urban landlords needed to contribute their 'fair share'.[27] Even then, however, George remained a haunting spectre during debates over the 'unearned increment' and the rights of ownership of land. 'There was, a few years ago, great agitation

21 Declaration of Principles of the Central Labor Union of New York [and platform of the United Labor Party of New York City, 1882 and 1883], *Truth*, 17 April 1882; Nulty, *The Land Question*, 14.

22 Montgomery, *Citizen Worker*, 112.

23 Louis F. Post, and Fred C. Leubuscher, *Henry George's 1886 Campaign: An Account of the George-Hewitt Campaign in the New York Municipal Election of 1886* (New York: John W. Lovell, 1887).

24 Bleecker Miller, *Trade Organization in Politics*, 154.

25 Sidney Webb to Henry George, 8 March 1889, in *The Letters of Sidney and Beatrice Webb*, vol. I, Norman Mackenzie (ed.) (Cambridge: Cambridge University Press, 1978), 125–126.

26 George Bernard Shaw, 'The Economic Basis of Socialism', in George Bernard Shaw (ed.), *Fabian Essays in Socialism* (London: Fabian Society, 1889), 26.

27 *The Times* 2 October 1891; Thorold Rogers, HC Deb. 23 March 1886, vol. 303, c. 1643; Sidney Webb, *A Plea for the Taxation of Ground Rents* (London: The 'United Committee' for the Taxation of Ground Rents and Values, 1887). See also Barker, *Henry George*, 402; Offer, *Property and Politics*, 190–195. Readman, *Land and Nation*, 130–131.

on the subject of the land', recalled progressive liberal M.P. Richard Haldane, bringing forward a bill to increase local authority powers of land purchase in 1892. 'There came to this country a gentleman of great oratorical ability, who went through the land rather in the character of a preacher than in any other guise, and he preached the doctrine of the iniquity of private ownership of land, and the doctrine of expropriation without compensation. I bring forward this bill', continued Haldane, 'not because I agree with Mr. Henry George, but because I disagree with him'.[28] Georgist ideas about land monopoly, at least in specific urban settings, filtered heavily into Liberal analysis, but proposals for change bore only a homeopathic resemblance to his plans as the moral foundation of his vision had been excised entirely.[29]

In Ireland, the question of land ownership remained critical to the political upheavals of the Irish revolutionary years, but the terms of any settlement had largely been set by the precedent of Gladstone's 1881 Land Act. The United Irish League's attack on grazing during the Ranch War in the early twentieth century and the land redistribution of the Irish Civil War years were driven in part by the same small farmer ideal that had spurred the Land War.[30] At the same time, however, successive state-assisted purchase bills were ultimately of greatest benefit to larger farmers and served to consolidate both land and political power in a Catholic nationalist middle class.[31] The success of this rural class was a reminder of the umbilical connection between land and political power, even if the hopeful and expansively egalitarian rhetoric of the Land League went unfulfilled. Even so, demand for access to land remained a key driver of continued agrarian unrest and violence, as the most unwieldy dynamic of the Land War, the tensions between small farmers and labourers on the one hand, and larger agricultural interests on the other, continued to shape the political and economic life of the country.[32]

[28] Richard Haldane, HC Deb, 4 May 1892, vol. 4, c. 78.

[29] Ian Packer, *Lloyd George, Liberalism and the Land: The Land Issue and Party Politics in England, 1906–1914* (Woodbridge: Boydell and Brewer, 2001), 30; see also James Dundas White, 'The A. B. C of the Land Question: A Handbook for Students and Speakers' (Cincinnati: Joseph Fels Fund of America, 1912).

[30] David Seth Jones, 'Land Reform Legislation and Security of Tenure in Ireland after Independence', *Eire-Ireland* 33, no. 1 (1997): 116–143; David Seth Jones, *Graziers, Land Reform and Political Conflict in Ireland* (Washington, DC: Catholic University of American Press, 1995); Tony Varley, 'A Region of Sturdy Smallholders? Western Nationalists and Agrarian Politics during the First World War', *Journal of the Galway Archaeological and Historical Society* 55 (2003): 127–150; M. A. G. Ó Tuathaigh, 'The Land Question, Politics and Irish Society, 1922–1960', in P. J. Drudy (ed.), *Ireland: Land Politics and People* (Cambridge: Cambridge University Press, 1982).

[31] Terence Dooley, 'Irish Land Questions, 1879–1923', in Thomas Bartlett (ed.), *The Cambridge History of Ireland, vol. IV: 1880 to the Present* (Cambridge: Cambridge University Press, 2018), 126.

[32] Fergus Campbell, 'Irish Popular Politics and the Making of the Wyndham Land Act, 1901–1903', *The Historical Journal* 45, no. 4 (2002): 755–773; Fergus Campbell, *Land and Revolution: Nationalist Politics in the West of Ireland, 1891–1921* (Oxford: Oxford University Press,

It was precisely this apparent continuity that has made it possible to miss the impact of the Land War in its international and intellectual contexts. As the momentum for home rule found a surer footing among the agricultural middle class and became cloaked in a new Gaelic 'Irish-Irelandism', it also foreclosed on the radical republican vision expressed by the Land League. But Ireland's agrarian revolt, allied to George's campaigning, had fundamentally reshaped liberal political thought across the Atlantic in the early part of the 1880s, and the collapse of the radical hopes becomes clearer in this perspective. Some interpretations have suggested that George only 'appeared like a return to the pre-Malthusian perspectives of the late Enlightenment reformers', but for the popular constituency he animated, this appearance was a reality.[33] Together with Ireland's distinctive rural economy and geopolitics, Georgist radicalism and the republican praxis of the Land League conspired to challenge liberal political economy by isolating, and forcing attention towards, the instability of natural rights justifications for the private and acquisitive possession of land. It was this aspect of the conflict that engaged the attention of republican radicals on both sides of the Atlantic and provided intellectual ballast for the developing labour movement. It was not only Irish republican socialist James Connolly who would later explain that the Land League was the 'mental pabulum' on which he was 'nourished', but, as Knights of Labor Grandmaster Workman Terence Powderly argued, the connection between 'the alien land lord who first drives his victims from Irish soil' and the industrial poverty in America for want of the 'land which God made for all honest men instead of for thieves' was 'the key note that will reach the American heart'.[34]

In response to the claims made by George and the League, the languages of natural rights and natural law were firmly excised from political discourse. George Bernard Shaw, stumbling upon a Henry George lecture in Memorial Hall, Farringdon Street, London, later recalled that he knew the orator was an American because 'he spoke of Liberty, Justice, Truth, Natural Law, and other strange eighteenth century superstitions'.[35] Shaw's cultured cynicism appeared to mock these pieties, but it betrayed, at the same time, a sardonic recognition of the challenge involved in escaping this ideological matrix. Largely exiled from liberal politics in favour of an organicist deification of 'progress' (which was, in Woodrow Wilson's terms, 'almost synonymous with life itself'), these ideas, and the linguistic nodes of popular republicanism, found redoubts in the early

2005); Terence Dooley 'Land and Politics in Independent Ireland, 1923–48: The Case for Reappraisal', *Irish Historical Studies* 34, no. 134 (2004): 175–197.

33 Stedman Jones, *An End to Poverty?*, 208.

34 James Connolly in Paul Dillon, 'James Connolly and the Kerry Famine of 1898', *Saothar: Journal of Irish Labour History* 25 (1998): 29; Terence V. Powderly to Hannah Dever, September 22 1883, quoted in Montgomery, *Citizen Worker*, 113.

35 George Bernard Shaw to Hamlin Garland, 29 December 1904, in George Bernard Shaw, *Collected Letters, 1898–1910*, Dan H. Laurence (ed.) (London: Max Reinhardt, 1972), 476.

twentieth century in a variety of political subcultures, such as R. H. Tawney's Christian socialism and in Catholic social teaching.[36] But they were also allied to a new political conservatism, most notably from the 1960s onwards, which pointedly made use of conceptions of 'natural law' and individual rights to yoke a reclamation of the 'fruits of [individual] labor' to a libertarian economic programme that gained a good deal of support from Irish-Americans though its appeals to 'traditional social values'.[37] Subsequently, contemporary analysis of rights discourse has often assumed, with much justification, that it is either too fragile to resist, or even complicit with, modern 'market fundamentalism', and that, as Shaw would have agreed, the histories of natural rights claims remain inexorably bound to bourgeois possessiveness and capitalist accumulation.[38]

Yet the land question, and agrarian agitation, complicates this picture. When applied to land, natural rights claims tended to be limiting, non-acquisitive, and egalitarian. The finiteness of land and its divine purpose for the support of humans made it distinctive as a form of property and opened up the radical argument that self-preservation was the purpose of its possession. Popular forms of protest, such as boycotting, reinforced this in their anarchic rejection of any external, hierarchical political authority. Here again, embodied in practical political action, was an implicit reliance on individual rights rooted in the nature of human beings, constrained only by a counterbalancing harmony of others' identical rights. Faced with this intellectual challenge gaining widespread popular traction during the Land War, defenders of property and accumulation moved rapidly away from claims of natural right. This often led to a striking convergence between conservative and social liberal arguments on land and agrarian resistance. To defend property in land as 'actual capital, just as much as money, coal, iron, cattle, or any other disposable commodity', meant defending it all on the basis of being 'consistent with the general good'.[39] The question of land helped to further drive liberals, conservatives, and socialists towards an organicist utilitarian politics.

Conversely, as the liberal M.P. Robert Wallace noted in 1881, 'the very wildest schemes of land reform are those which, on the face of them, promise to do most for establishing property as an institution'.[40] In his view, such a position was absurd. There was no 'natural right' to property, it was simply 'an arrangement justified by the good of society, and may be infringed when

[36] Wilson, 'What Is Progress?', 42, 48.

[37] Barry Goldwater, *The Conscience of a Conservative* (Shepherdsville, KY: Victor Publishing, 1960), 11, 61; Kim Phillips-Fein, *Invisible Hands: The Making of the Conservative Movement from the New Deal to Reagan* (New York: W. W. Norton, 2009), 215; Michael Kazin, *The Populist Persuasion: An American History* [1995], rev. ed. (Ithaca: Cornell University Press, 2017), 173–178.

[38] Samuel Moyn, *Not Enough – Human Rights in an Unequal World* (Cambridge, MA: Harvard University Press, 2018), 218.

[39] Molesworth, *Land as Property*, 21.

[40] Robert Wallace, 'The Philosophy of Liberalism', *The Nineteenth Century: A Monthly Review* 9, no. 48 (1881): 320.

and as far as the good of society demands'.[41] Yet, as Malcolm Chase once observed, this 'ostensibly Janus-headed stance' of agrarian radicalism, 'at once critical of private property in the soil and yet jealous for rights of property in land', makes sense 'if we view it as a bid not for the ownership of the means of production, but rather for a control of them'.[42] In other words, if it is seen not as a liberal claim but a republican one; not, as James Connolly scoffed, 'rights in the thin and attenuated meaning of the term to which we have been accustomed', but ones connected to political power.[43]

The ideological and metaphysical ruptures of the late-nineteenth-century Atlantic world have long been the source of much historiographical and terminological disagreement, and analysis has usually involved navigating the disputed territory of 'liberalism'.[44] The question of continuity or discontinuity between political languages, of which ideological lineages filtered into what tradition, has been of particular interest because of more contemporary questions over the contested state of liberalism in the second half of the twentieth century and beyond[45] – and not least because the last decades of the nineteenth century have often been seen as the critical boiling point for the internal contradictions of the 'Enlightenment project'.[46] In this, land has played a unique role, underpinning the 'naturalist cosmology' of republican thought which was embedded in agrarian social practices, and so providing a unique lens through which to view the shifts in late-nineteenth-century political thought.[47]

41 Wallace, 'The Philosophy of Liberalism', 318.

42 Chase, *People's Farm*, 183.

43 James Connolly, 'The Re-conquest of Ireland [1915]', in James Connolly, *Labour in Ireland* (Dublin: Maunsel and Roberts, 1922), 293–294.

44 Nancy Cohen, *The Reconstruction of American Liberalism, 1865–1914* (Chapel Hill: University of North Carolina Press, 2002); Polanyi, *The Great Transformation*, 149–153; Ross, 'Socialism and American Liberalism', 7–79; Furner, 'The Republican Tradition and the New Liberalism', 171–241; Daniel T. Rodgers, 'Republicanism: The Career of a Concept', *The Journal of American History* 79, no. 1 (1992): 11–38; Sklansky, *Soul's Economy*, 105–136; Glickman, *A Living Wage*.

45 Shadia Drury, 'Robert Nozick and the Right to Property', in Anthony Parel and Thomas Flanagan (eds.), *Theories of Property: Aristotle to the Present* (Waterloo: Wilfred Laurier Press, 1979), 361; Here the concept of liberal alienation played a key role: Michael Sandel, *Liberalism and the Limits of Justice* [1982], 2nd ed. (Cambridge: Cambridge University Press, 1998), 184–218; Hannah Arendt, *The Human Condition* (Chicago: University of Chicago Press, 1958), 262–266; Habermas, *The Philosophical Discourses*, 83.

46 MacIntyre, *After Virtue*, 62, 113–130; Peter Dews, 'Postmodernism: Pathologies of Modernity from Nietzsche to the Post-structuralists', in Terence Ball and Richard Bellamy (eds.), *The Cambridge History of Twentieth Century Political Thought* (Cambridge: Cambridge University Press, 2003); The 'rediscovery' of the republican thesis naturally owed a great deal to these contemporary concerns. Pocock's work relied on 'terms borrowed from or suggested by the language of Hannah Arendt', J. G. A., Pocock, 'Afterword', in *The Machiavellian Moment: Florentine Political Thought and the Atlantic Republican Tradition* [1975] (Princeton: Princeton University Press, 2003), 566.

47 Chappey and Vincent, 'A Republican Ecology?', 114; 'What we call land is an element of nature inextricably interwoven with man's institutions. To isolate it and form a market out of it was perhaps the weirdest of all undertakings of our ancestors', Polanyi, *The Great Transformation*, 178.

'Until the 1880s', E. P. Thompson observed, 'working-class Radicalism remained transfixed' by the question of land.[48] But that was about to change. Agrarian visions of decentralised democracy, self-sufficient independence, and a levelling egalitarianism had been familiar across Europe and the United States.[49] 'The passion of Irish peasants for the possession of the land', which presented, according to A. V. Dicey, an enduring 'puzzle' for the British, was a sentiment 'familiar' and 'natural' in many other societies, he conceded.[50] Yet it was not a puzzle to many radicals, particularly working-class radicals like Keir Hardie, Edward McHugh, or John Morrison Davidson, for whom the land represented the keystone of a much more comprehensible and morally coherent political economy.[51] Moral and metaphysical issues were at the core of this political divergence as radicalism gave way to socialism – it was not simply, as critical writers claimed, the demotic appeal of Christian moralism that gave George and the Land League their popular force, but a whole cosmology grounded in a belief in harmony, the purposiveness of nature, and the origins of value in labour and fertility alone. It was this that formed the basis of what Hobson complained of as 'the individualist basis of land nationalisation': precariously balanced 'upon the "natural rights" of the individual', and seeing land and labour as 'the only original requisites of wealth-production'.[52] It was through these ideas that the Irish Land War acquired its powerful international resonance. Seen in the broader context inhabited by contemporaries, George and the Land War were inseparable, 'the two were like hand and glove' – 'it was the terrible object lesson of Ireland writhing in the grasp of a relentless landlordism' that gave *Progress and Poverty* 'nine-tenths of its significance'.[53] Together they represented both a theoretical and a practical defence of these propositions, and elicited an equally firm countervailing resistance among liberal thinkers and politicians; a key nexus in a long-standing battle of ideas about rights, centralisation, Malthusianism, utilitarianism, and, underneath it all, land.

Even though the 1880s did not mark the end of the land question, it did see a wilting of its attendant democratic implications. While many liberals in Britain and the United States still perceived the unique spiritual and

48 Thompson, *The Making*, 105.

49 Biagini, *Liberty, Retrenchment and Reform*, 11; Chase, *People's Farm*, 15.

50 A. V. Dicey, *England's Case against Home Rule* (London: John Murray, 1886), 80.

51 The working-class composition of those attracted to Georgism, as against the aristocratic and upper middle-class appeal of Fabianism and progressive liberalism, was striking. See Jones, 'Henry George and British Socialism', 486–487.

52 J. A. Hobson, 'The Influence of Henry George in England', *The Fortnightly Review* 62, no. 372 (1897): 842.

53 J. Morrison Davidson, *Concerning Four Precursors of Henry George and the Single Tax, as also The Land Gospel according to Winstanley 'The Digger'* (London: Labour Leader Publishing, 1899), 2.

emotive importance of access to and preservation of the natural world, as evident in the movements for commons preservation and John Muir's Sierra Club, for instance, these were primarily inspired by romantic or psychosocial imperatives divorced from the exercise of political power.[54] The natural right to life and self-preservation, the normative naturalism of corporeal republicanism, which had underpinned radical belief for the previous century, had carried with it an attendant right to land and therefore also to political participation. In the new understanding, 'a clear grasp of society as an economic organism completely explodes the notion of property as an inherent individual right' and, correspondingly, 'the idea of natural individual rights as the basis of Democracy disappears'.[55] Without such archaic concepts as natural rights, 'the general will and wisdom of the Society, as embodied in the State' would now be the driving force of political life, and 'the perfect and fitting development of each individual' would no longer mean the cultivation of virtue through political participation, but 'the filling, in the best possible way, of his humble function in the great social machine'.[56]

There were other factors that helped to push the older republican radicalism, and its notions of natural right and popular democracy, out of the political sphere and contributed to the disjointed relationship of liberalism with democracy.[57] Urbanisation, enfranchisement and imperialism, and associated languages of 'character' and 'civilization' also helped to recast the meaning of liberalism, although clearly none of these issues were entirely separate from that of land either.[58] It was also true that George and the Land War had carried along their own contradictions with regard to the role of the state. When it came to refuting the core assumptions of this radical republican politics, however, one man loomed as the largest obstacle. 'Mr. Henry George, educated under the American Constitution, may share the familiarity of its framers with the intentions of the Creator and the natural rights of Man', mocked the Fabian writer Sydney Olivier, but such beliefs were dangerously anarchic nonsense. While the Land League, too, unquestionably radical in its assertive

[54] Jedediah Purdy, *After Nature: A Politics for the Anthropocene* (Cambridge, MA: Harvard University Press, 2015), 116–119.

[55] Hobson, *The Crisis of Liberalism*, 77.

[56] Hobson, *The Crisis of Liberalism*, 78; Sidney Webb, 'Historic: The Development of the Democratic Ideal', in Bernard Shaw (ed.), *Fabian Essays in Socialism* (London: Fabian Society, 1889), 58.

[57] Honohan, 'Irish Republicanism in a Wider Context', in Iseult Honohan (ed.), *Republicanism in Ireland*, 6.

[58] See Richard Bellamy, *Liberalism and Modern Society: An Historical Argument* (Oxford: Polity, 1992); Michael Freeden, *The New Liberalism: An Ideology of Social Reform* (Oxford: Oxford University Press, 1978); Uday Singh Mehta, *Liberalism and Empire: A Study in Nineteenth-Century*

agrarianism, avowed that 'The Land for the People' meant that 'the land was made for the people', theorists from across the political spectrum moved to reject these naively outdated a priori convictions.[59] Olivier assured his readers instead that 'positive ethical science knows nothing of natural and fundamental rights: it knows nothing of individual liberty, nothing of equality, nothing of underlying unity'.[60]

British Liberal Thought (Chicago: University of Chicago Press, 1999); Duncan Bell, *Reordering the World: Essays on Liberalism and Empire* (Princeton: Princeton University Press, 2016); Peter Cain, 'Empire and the Languages of Character and Virtue in Later Victorian and Edwardian Britain', *Modern Intellectual History* 4, no. 2 (2007): 1–25; Sankar Muthu (ed.), *Empire and Modern Political Thought* (Cambridge: Cambridge University Press, 2012); Jennifer Pitts, *A Turn to Empire: The Rise of Imperial Liberalism in Britain and France* (Princeton: Princeton University Press, 2005).

59 *Connaught Telegraph*, 12 May 1877.

60 Sydney Olivier, 'The Moral Basis of Socialism', in Bernard Shaw (ed.), *Fabian Essays in Socialism* (London: Fabian Society, 1889), 104.

Bibliography

Manuscript Sources

Boston

John J. Burns Library, Boston College
  George D. Cahill Papers
  Patrick A. Collins Papers
  John Boyle O'Reilly Papers
  James Jeffrey Roche Papers

Dublin

National Library of Ireland
  John Devoy Papers
  Timothy M. Harrington Papers
  John T. Heffernan Papers
  Irish National Land League Papers
  S. L. Anderson Papers
Trinity College Dublin
  Michael Davitt Papers

Philadelphia

Philadelphia Archdiocesan Historical Research Center, St. Charles Borromeo Seminary
  Pamphlet Collection
  Newspaper Collection

London

British Library
  Balfour Papers
National Archives
  Irish Office Papers
  Records of the Chief Secretary of Ireland

New York

Archives of the Archdiocese of New York, St. Joseph's Seminary, Dunwoodie
Richard Burtsell Papers
Archbishop Michael A. Corrigan Papers
Cardinal John McCloskey Papers
Manuscripts and Archives Division, New York Public Library
Henry George Papers
Tamiment Library and Robert F. Wagner Labor Archives, New York University
Archives of Irish America Pamphlet Collection

Washington, DC

American Catholic History Research Center and University Archives, Catholic University of America
Terence Powderly Papers

Newspapers

Belfast News-Letter
Brooklyn Examiner
Catholic Herald
Catholic Universe
Connaught Telegraph
Freeman's Journal and Daily Commercial Advertiser
Glasgow Herald
Irish Nation
Irish World
Irish World and Industrial Liberator
John Swinton's Paper
Kerry Sentinel
Liberty (Not the Daughter but the Mother of Order)
Liverpool Mercury
Manchester Guardian
Massachusetts Ploughman and New England Journal of Agriculture
The Nation
New York Freeman's Journal
New York Herald
New York Tablet
New York Times
New York Tribune
Newcastle Courant
The Pilot
The Times
Truth
Washington Post

Periodicals

The Albany Law Journal
American Catholic Quarterly Review
American Journal of Sociology
The American Law Review
The Arena
Blackwood's Edinburgh Magazine
Catholic Historical Review
Catholic World: A Monthly Magazine of General Literature and Science
Century Illustrated Magazine
Contemporary Review
Christian Advocate
Christian Union
Donahoe's Magazine
The Dublin Review
The Eclectic Magazine of Foreign Literature
Edinburgh Review
The Examiner
The Fortnightly Review
The Forum
Harper's Magazine
The Independent
International Journal of Ethics
The International Review
Journal of the Social and Statistical Inquiry Society of Ireland
The Literary World: A Monthly Review of Current Literature
The Methodist Review
New England and Yale Review
New Englander
The Nineteenth Century: A Monthly Review
The North American Review
Political Science Quarterly
Princeton Review
The Quarterly Journal of Economics
The Review of Reviews
The Saturday Review of Politics, Literature, Science, and Art
Scribner's Monthly
Studies: An Irish Quarterly Review
The Unitarian Review and Religious Magazine

Contemporary Works

'A Capitalist' [Alonzo Van Deusen], *Rational Communism: The Present and Future Republic of North America* (New York: The Social Science Publishing Co., 1885).
'A Guardian of the Poor', *The Irish Peasant: A Sociological Study* (London: Swan Sonnenschein and Co., 1892).

'A Land Valuer' [Murrough O'Brien], *Fixity of Tenure at Fair Rents Impracticable as a Final Settlement of the Irish Land Question* (Dublin: M. H. Gill and Son, 1881).

'Aliquis', *Landlords, Land Laws, and Land Leagues in Scotland; Being a Humble Contribution to Contemporary Politics* (Edinburgh: David Douglas, 1881).

'Cork Defence Union', *Boycotting in the County of Cork* (Cork: Purcell, 1886).

'Editor of the Citizen and Irish Artisan', *An Aspect of the Land Question Forgotten! Will the Land League Solution Wipe Out What Remains of Skilled Industry?* (Dublin: Hastings and Co., 1880).

'Irish Loyal and Patriot Union', *The Other 'Coercion' as Now in Operation* (Dublin: Hodges, Figgis, 1886).

'Irish National League of America', *What Is 'Castle Government?' A Question Answered, for Americans Interested in the Irish Question* (Chicago: Irish National League of America, 1884).

'Liberty and Property Defence League', *Land* (London: Parliamentary Committee of the Liberty and Property Defence League, 1885).

'M. R.', *A Review of Henry George's 'Progress and Poverty'* (London: William Reeves, 1884).

'One Who Knows' [Hugh Oakeley Arnold-Forster], *The Truth about the Land League, Its Leaders, and Its Teaching* (London: National Press Agency, 1882).

Report of the Trial of the Queen, at the Prosecution of the Rt Hon. The Attorney-General, against Charles Stuart Parnell, John Dillon, Joseph Gillis Biggar, Timothy Daniel Sullivan, Thomas Sexton, Patrick Egan, Thomas Brennan, Michael O'Sullivan, Michael P. Boynton, Patrick Joseph Sheridan, Patrick Joseph Gordon, Mathew Harris, John W. Walsh, and John W. Nally, for Conspiracy in Inciting Tenants Not to Pay Rents Contracted for, and Deterring Tenants from Payment of Rent (Dublin: Alex Thom & Co., 1881).

Adams, Rev. Thomas, *The Morality of the Irish Land League to the Patriotic Sons of Ireland* (Brooklyn: Thomas Adams, 1881).

Allen, Grant, *Individualism and Socialism* (Glasgow: Land Values Publication Department, 1889).

Aristotle, *The Politics and the Constitution of Athens,* Stephen Everson (ed.), (Cambridge: Cambridge University Press, 1996).

Aristotle, *Nicomachean Ethics*, Lesley Brown (ed.), (Oxford: Oxford University Press, 2009).

Arnold, Arthur, *Free Land* (London: Kegan Paul & Co., 1880).

Aveling, Edward and Eleanor Marx, *The Working Class Movement in America* [1891] Paul LeBlanc (ed.), (Amherst: Humanity Books, 2000).

Bagenal, Philip H., *The American Irish and Their Influence on Irish Politics* (Boston: Roberts Brothers, 1882).

Begg, James, *Social Reform: How Every Man May Become His Own Landlord; or, A Way by Which to Elevate the Condition of the Masses of Britain, and Develop the Resources of the Country: Being A Lecture, Delivered in Newington Free Church, at the Request of the 'Scottish Social Reform Association,' on the 6th of March 1851* (Edinburgh: Johnstone and Hunter, 1851).

Bell, George W., *Peasant Proprietary for Ireland: A Communication from Captain George W. Bell, Lawyer and Journalist, Ottawa, Illinois, U.S.A., to Thomas Sexton, Esq., M.P.* (Dublin: Irish National Land League, 1881).

Bence Jones, William, *The Life's Work in Ireland of a Landlord Who Tried to Do His Duty* (London: Macmillan, 1880).

Benton De Witt, T. H. (ed.), *A Correspondence between an Amateur and a Professor of Political Economy* (Philadelphia: J. B. Lippincott, 1898).

Bernard, William Leigh, *The Irish Land Question: Suggestions for the Extended Establishment of a Peasant Proprietary in Ireland* (Dublin: Hodges, Foster & Figgis, 1880).

Blacker, Rev. Robert Shapland Carew, *Erin: Her Sisters, Her Nurse, and Her Doctors* (London: William Ridgeway, 1881).

Blackstone, William, *The Commentaries on the Laws of England Vol. II: Of the Rights of Things* [1765] Robert Malcolm Kerr (ed.), (London: John Murray, 1876).

Blatchford, Robert, *Land Nationalisation* (London: Clarion Press, 1906).

Bleecker Miller, John, *Trade Organizations in Politics, Also Progress and Robbery, an Answer to Henry George* (New York: Baker & Taylor Co., 1887).

Bradlaugh, Charles, *The Land, the People, and the Coming Struggle* [1871] (London: Freethought Publishing, 1880).

Bradlaugh, Charles, *Compulsory Cultivation of Land: What It Means, and Why It Ought to Be Enforced* (London: Freethought Publishing, 1887).

Brann, Henry A., *Gladstone and Irish Grievances: An Essay on the Irish Land Laws, Tenures and Grievances; Their Proposed Solution; the Gladstone Coercion Act and Land Bill; and the Land League* (New York: Benjamin H. Tyrrel, 1881).

Brann, Henry A., *Henry George and His Land Theories* (New York: The Catholic Publication Society, 1887).

Bray, John Francis, *Labour's Wrongs and Labour's Remedy; or, the Age of Might and the Age of Right* (Leeds: David Green, 1839).

Briggs, M. C., *Regress and Slavery vs. 'Progress and Poverty': The Single-Tax Theory Shown to Be Unjust, Impracticable, and Absurd* (New York: Hunt and Eaton, 1891).

Brownson, Orestes A., *The Works of Orestes A. Brownson*, vol. XIII, Henry F. Brownson (ed.), (Detroit: Thorndike Nourse, 1884).

Bryant, Elizabeth, *Types of Mankind, as Affecting the Financial History of the World: Delivered before the Greenback Labor Club of the District of Columbia, October 7, 1879* (Washington, DC: Rufus H. Darby, 1879).

Budd, Henry, and Ardemus Stewart (eds.), *American and English Decisions in Equity: Being Select Cases Decided in the Appellate Courts of America and England* vol. II (Philadelphia: M. Murphy, 1896).

Budd, Henry, and Ardemus Stewart (eds.), *American and English Decisions in Equity: Being Select Cases Decided in the Appellate Courts of America and England*, vol. III (Philadelphia: M. Murphy, 1897)

Burgess, Rev. William, *Land, Labor and Liquor: A Chapter in the Political Economy of the Present Day* (Toronto: S. R. Briggs, 1887).

Burt, Thomas, *The Government and the Land League* (Birmingham: National Liberal Foundation, 1881).

Butt, Isaac, *Land Tenure in Ireland: A Plea for the Celtic Race* (Dublin: John Falconer, 1866).

Butt, Isaac, *The Irish People and the Irish land: A Letter to Lord Lifford* (Dublin: John Falconer, 1867).

Cairnes, John Elliot, *Essays in Political Economy: Theoretical and Applied* (London: Macmillan and Co., 1873).

Cairnes, John Elliot, *Some Leading Principles of Political Economy* (New York: Harper and Brothers Co., 1878).

Campbell, George, *The Unity of Nature* (New York: G. P. Putnam's Sons, 1884).

Cannan, Edwin, *A History of the Theories of Production and Distribution in English Political Economy from 1776 to 1848*, 2nd ed. [1893], (London: P. S. King, 1903).

Carpenter, Edward, *Civilisation: Its Cause and Cure, and Other Essays* (London: George Allen and Unwin, 1889).

Cathrein, Rev. Victor, *Socialism: Exposed and Refuted* (New York: Benziger Brother, 1982).
Cathrein, Rev. Victor, *Socialism: Its Theoretical Basis and Practical Application*, 8th ed. (New York: Benziger Brothers, 1904).
Cathrein, Rev. Victor, *The Champions of Agrarian Socialism: A Refutation of Émile de Laveleye and Henry George* (Buffalo: P. Paul and Bro., 1889).
Chatard, Rt. Rev. Francis Silas, *Tenure of Land and Eminent Domain: A Lecture before the Leonine Union, of Indianapolis, October 3. 1887* (Indianapolis, IN: Carlon & Hollenbeck, 1887).
Clancy, James J., *Ireland: As She Is, as She Has Been, and As She Ought to Be* (New York: Thomas Kelly, 1877).
Clancy, James J., *The Land League Manual* (New York: Thomas Kelly, 1881).
Clancy, James J., *Who Are the Conspirators? Or, the True Story of the Boycotting Prosecutions* (London: Irish Press Agency, 1889).
Connolly, James, *Labour in Ireland* (Dublin: Maunsel and Roberts, 1922).
Connolly, James, *Labour, Nationality and Religion* [1910], (Dublin: New Books, 1983).
Conyngham, David Power, *Ireland Past and Present: Embracing a Complete History of the Land Question from the Earliest Period to the Present Time* (New York: James Sheehy, 1884).
Crilly, Daniel, *Irish Evictions* (London: The Irish Press Agency, 1887).
Davidson, John Morrison, *Concerning Four Precursors of Henry George and the Single Tax, as also the Land Gospel according to Winstanley 'The Digger'* (London: Labour Leader Publishing, 1899).
Davidson, John Morrison (ed.), *Land for the Landless: Spence and 'Spence's Plan,' (1775) with Neo-Spencean Appendix (1896)* (London: William Reeves, 1896).
Davitt, Michael, *Jottings in Solitary*, Carla King (ed.), (Dublin: University College Dublin Press, 2003).
Davitt, Michael, *Land Nationalization; or, National Peasant Proprietary. Michael Davitt's Lectures in Scotland* (Glasgow: Cameron & Ferguson, 1884).
Davitt, Michael, *Reasons Why Home Rule Should Be Granted to Ireland: An Appeal to the Commonsense of the British Democracy* (London: The National Press Agency, 1886).
Davitt, Michael, *Speech Delivered by Michael Davitt in Defence of the Land League* (London: Kegan Paul, Trench, Trubner, & Co., 1890).
Davitt, Michael, *Speech of Michael Davitt at the Meeting in Favour of Land Nationalisation, Held at St. James's Hall, October 30th, 1883* (London: W. Reeves, 1883).
Davitt, Michael, *The Castle Government of Ireland: A Lecture by Michael Davitt* (Glasgow: Cameron & Ferguson, 1882).
Davitt, Michael, *The Fall of Feudalism in Ireland or the Story of the Land League Revolution* (New York: Harper and Brothers, 1904).
Davitt, Michael, *The Land League Proposal: A Statement for Honest and Thoughtful Men* (Glasgow: Cameron & Ferguson, 1882).
Devoy, John, *Michael Davitt: From the Gaelic American* [1906], Carla King, and William John McCormack (eds.), (Dublin: University College Dublin Press, 2008).
Devyr, Thomas Ainge, *Our Natural Rights: A Pamphlet for the People* [1835] (Williamsburg, NY: T. A. Devyr, 1842).
Devyr, Thomas Ainge, *The Odd Book of the Nineteenth Century, or, 'Chivalry' in Modern Days, A Personal Record of Reform – Chiefly Land Reform, for the Last Fifty Years* (New York: T. A. Devyr, 1882).

Dewey, John, and James H. Tufts, *Ethics* (New York: Henry Holt and Company, 1908).
Dicey, Arthur Venn., *England's Case against Home Rule* (London: John Murray, 1886).
Dillon, William, *Life of John Mitchel*, vol. II (London: Kegan Paul, Trench and Co., 1888).
Dillon, William, *The Dismal Science: A Criticism on Modern English Political Economy* (Dublin: M. H. Gill & Son, 1882).
Dixwell, George Basil, *'Progress and Poverty'. A Review of the Doctrines of Henry George* (Cambridge: John Wilson and Son, 1882).
Dixwell, George Basil, *The Premises of Free Trade Examined* (Cambridge: John Wilson and Son, 1881).
Donnelly, Ignatius, *Caesar's Column: A Story of the Twentieth Century* [1890], Walter B. Rideout (ed.), (Cambridge, MA: Harvard University Press, 1960).
Dove, Patrick Edward, *The Elements of Political Science*, vol. II (Edinburgh: Johnstone and Hunter, 1854).
Dove, Patrick Edward, *The Theory of Human Progression*, (abr.) Julia A. Kellogg [1850], (New York: Isaac H. Blanchard, 1910).
Dunne, Edmund Francis, *Ireland: Rights, Wrongs and Remedies: An Address delivered before the Fort Wayne, Indiana, U.S.A. Branch of the National Land League of Ireland, on St. Patrick's Day, 1881* (Chicago: S. W. Roth, 1881).
Dunne, Finley Peter, *Mr. Dooley and the Chicago Irish: The Autobiography of a Nineteenth-Century Ethnic Group,* Charles Fanning (ed.), (Washington, DC: Catholic University of America Press, 1976).
Edgeworth, Francis Ysidro, *Mathematical Psychics: An Essay on the Application of Mathematics to the Moral Sciences* (London: Kegan Paul, 1881).
Ely, Richard T., *Recent American Socialism* (Baltimore: N. Murray, Johns Hopkins University Press, 1885).
Ely, Richard T., *The Labor Movement in America* [1886] (New York: Macmillan, 1905).
Fawcett, Henry, *Pauperism: Its Causes and Remedies* (London: Macmillan and Co., 1871).
Fawcett, Henry, *State Socialism and the Nationalisation of the Land* (London: Macmillan, 1883).
Flatley, Patrick J., *Ireland and the Land League: Key to the Irish Question* (Boston: D. O'Loughlin and Co., 1881).
Filmer, Robert, *Patriarcha and Other Political Works of Sir Robert Filmer,* Peter Laslett (ed.), (Oxford: Basil Blackwell, 1949).
Finn, Rev. Thomas, *Notes on the History of Two Irish Estates* (Dublin: Irish National Land League, 1881).
Flint, Robert, *Socialism*, 2nd ed. [1894], (London: Isaac Pitman & Sons, 1908).
Ford, Patrick, *The Criminal History of the British Empire* [1881], (New York: The Irish World, 1915).
Fothingham, Octavius Brooks, *Farewell Sermon of the Rev. O. B. Frothingham, 27th April, 1879* (New York: G. P. Putnam's Sons, 1879).
Fox, Richard K. (ed.), *Parnell's Land League Songster: A Collection of Patriotic Irish Ballads Celebrating Deeds of Valor Performed by Erin's Sons in the Past, and Suited to The Present Land Agitation; Wit, Sentiment and Patriotism* (New York: Richard K. Fox, 1880).

Gast, John, *Calumny Defeated, or a Complete Vindication of the Conduct of the Working Shipwrights, during the Late Disputes with Their Employers* (London: J. Delahoy, 1802).

Geary, Rev. James A., *The Irish Land Question: The Story of a Confiscated Country* (Washington, DC: Friends of Irish Freedom National Bureau of Information, 1920).

George, Henry, *A Perplexed Philosopher* [1892], (London: Vacher and Sons, 1937).

George, Henry, *Land and People* (London: William Reeves, 1888).

George, Henry, *Our Land and Land Policy: Speeches, Lectures and Miscellaneous Writings* (New York: Doubleday and McClure, 1901).

George, Henry, *Protection or Free Trade: An Examination of the Tariff Question, with Especial Regard to the Interests of Labor* [1886], (New York: Doubleday Page & Company, 1904).

George, Henry, *Progress and Poverty: An Inquiry into the Cause of Industrial Depressions, and of Increase of Want with Increase of Wealth. The Remedy,* 10th ed. [1879], (New York: D. Appleton and Co., 1882).

George, Henry, *Social Problems* [1883], (New York: Doubleday and McClure Co., 1898).

George, Henry, *The Irish Land Question: What It Involves, and How Alone It Can Be Settled. An Appeal to the Land Leagues* (London: Cameron & Ferguson, 1881).

George, Henry, and George Campbell, *Property in Land: A Passage-at-Arms between the Duke of Argyll and Henry George* (New York: Funk & Wagnalls, 1884).

George, Henry, and Henry Hyndman, *The Single-Tax versus Social Democracy: Which Will Most Benefit the People, Verbatim Report of the Debate in St. James's Hall, July 2, 1889* (London: The Twentieth Century Press, 1906).

Gilmour, Rt. Rev. Richard, *Lecture on the Land League, Delivered at the Tabernacle, Cleveland, Ohio, February 6th, 1882* (Cleveland: J. B. Savage, 1882).

Ginnell, Laurence, *The Brehon Laws: A Legal Handbook* (London: T. Fisher Unwin, 1894).

Grant, Daniel, *Land Tenure in Ireland* (London: William Ridgeway, 1881).

Green, Thomas Hill, *Lectures on the Principles of Political Obligation* (London: Longmans, Green, and Co., 1895).

Green, Thomas Hill, *Liberal Legislation and Freedom of Contract: A Lecture* (Oxford: Slatter and Rose, 1881).

Gronlund, Laurence, *The Cooperative Commonwealth in Its Outlines: An Exposition of Modern Socialism* (Boston: Lee and Shepard, 1884).

Hackner, Rev. Willibald, *Socialism and the Church; or, Henry George vs. Archbishop Corrigan* (New York: Catholic Publication Society, 1887).

Hancock, William Neilson (ed.), *Ancient Laws of Ireland. Senchus Mor: Introduction to Senchus Mor, and Achgabail; or Law of Distress, as Contained in the Harleian Manuscripts*, vol. I (Dublin: Alexander Thomas, 1865).

Hancock, William Neilson, *The Difference between English and Irish Poor Law as to the Treatment of Women and Unemployed Workmen* (Dublin: R. D. Webb and Son, 1862).

Hancock, William Neilson, *The Journeyman Bakers' Case* (London: Emily Faithful, 1862).

Hazlitt, William, *A Reply to the Essay on Population by the Rev. T. R. Malthus* (London: Longman, Hurst, Rees and Orme, 1807).

Healy, Timothy M., *Why There Is an Irish Land Question and an Irish Land League* (Boston: Kiley, 1881).

Higgins, Rev. Edward A., *Fallacies of Henry George, Exposed and Refuted: The True Philosophy of the Land Question* (Cincinnati: Keating & Co., 1887).

Hobhouse, Leonard T., *Social Evolution and Political Theory* (New York: Columbia University Press, 1911).

Hobson, John Allet (ed.), *Co-operative Labour upon the Land, and Other Papers; The Report of a Conference upon 'Land, Co-operation and the Unemployed,' Held at Holborn Town Hall in October, 1894* (London: Swan Sonnenshein & Co., 1895).

Hobson, John Allet, *Free-Thought in the Social Sciences* (London: George Allen & Unwin, 1926).

Hobson, John Allet, *The Crisis of Liberalism: New Issues of Democracy* (London: P. S. King & Son, 1909).

Hobson, John Allet, *Towards International Government* (London: George Allen and Unwin, 1916).

Hodgskin, Thomas, *The Natural and Artificial Right of Property Contrasted* (London: B. Steil, 1832).

Howard, James, *The Tenant Farmer: Land Laws and Landlords* (London: Macmillan and Co., 1879).

Humphrys, Rev. David, *The Justice of the Land League* (London: Kegan Paul & Co., 1881).

Hutcheson, Francis, *A System of Moral Philosophy*, vol. II (Glasgow: R & A. Foulis, 1755).

Hyndman, Henry M. (ed.), *The Nationalization of the Land in 1775 and 1882* (London: E. W. Allen, 1882).

Hyndman, Henry M., *The Record of an Adventurous Life* (London: Macmillan, 1911).

Ingalls, Joshua K., *Land and Labor; Their Relations in Nature – How Violated by Monopoly* (Princeton, MA: Co-operative Publishing Co., 1877).

Ingalls, Joshua K., *Reminiscences of an Octogenarian in the Field of Industrial and Social Reform* (New York: Holbrook, 1897).

Ingram, John Kells, *A History of Political Economy* (London: A. & C. Black, Ltd., 1888).

Jefferson, Thomas, *Jefferson: Political Writings,* Joyce Appleby and Terence Ball (eds.), (Cambridge: Cambridge University Press, 1999).

Johnson, Thomas L., *Twenty-Eight Years a Slave, or the Story of My Life in Three Continents* (Bournemouth: W. Mate & Sons, 1909).

Kirkup, Thomas, *A History of Socialism*, 4th ed. [1892], (London: Adam and Charles Black, 1909).

Kirkup, Thomas, *An Inquiry into Socialism*, 2nd ed. [1887], (London: Longmans, Green, and Co., 1888).

Kirwan, M. W., *Lecture by M. W. Kirwan, Editor of the True Witness, in Reply to Reverend Mr. Bray, on the 'Romish' Church, Delivered in the Mechanics' Hall, March 13, 1877* (Montreal: True Witness Office, 1877).

Kropotkin, Peter, *Fields, Factories and Workshops* [1899], (New York: G. P. Putnam's Sons, 1913).

Laing, Samuel, *Boycotting* (London: National Press Agency, 1888).

Lalor, James Fintan, *'The Faith of a Felon' and Other Writings*, Marta Ramón (ed.), (Dublin: University College Dublin Press, 2012).

Lalor, James Fintan, *The Rights of Ireland and the Faith of a Felon,* James Connolly (ed.), (Dublin: Socialist Party of Ireland, 1900).

Laveleye, Émile de, *Primitive Property* (London: Macmillan and Co., 1878).

Laveleye, Émile de, *Protestantism and Catholicism in Their Bearing upon the Liberty and Prosperity of Nations: A Study of Social Economy* (Toronto: Belford Brothers, 1876).

Laveleye, Émile de, *The Socialism of To-Day* (London: The Leadenhall Press, 1886).

Lecky, Walter, *Père Monnier's Ward: A Novel* (New York: Benzigner Brothers, 1898).

Lecky, William Edward Hartpole, *Democracy and Liberty*, vol. I [1896], (New York: Longmans, Green, and Co., 1903).

Lecky, William Edward Hartpole, *Democracy and Liberty*, vol. II [1896], (London: Longmans, Green, and Co., 1913).

Lewis, George Cornewall, *On Local Disturbances in Ireland, and on the Irish Church Question* (London: B. Fellowes, 1836).

Ley, Henry W., *Land Nationalisation: Who Shows the Way? Henry George, Thomas Spence, Thomas Paine or Alfred Russel Wallace* (London: W. Reeves, 1888).

Lowell, A. Lawrence, *Essays on Government* (Boston: Houghton, Mifflin and Company, 1890).

Lynch, John, *The Land Laws of Ireland: A Paper Read before the Ballarat Eclectic Association, on 7th August, 1882* (Ballarat: Luplau, Henwood, & Rider, 1882).

MacSwynie, Aurelius (ed.), *America's Sympathies with Ireland: A summary of the Indignation Meetings, Speeches, Resolutions of Sympathy, and Letters in favour of Ireland, delivered, and written by Archbishops, Bishops, Priests, Ministers, Governors of States, Senators, Congressmen, Lawyers, and Citizens in general of the United States* (Philadelphia: C. Dorwin Freeman, 1881).

Maine, Henry Sumner, *Popular Government: Four Essays* (London: John Murray, 1885).

Makgill, George, *Rent No Robbery: An Examination of Some Erroneous Doctrines Regarding Property in Land* (Edinburgh: William Blackwood, 1851).

Mallock, William Hurrell, *Property and Progress, or a Brief Inquiry into Contemporary Social Agitation in England* (New York: G. P. Putnam's Sons, 1884).

Malone, Sylvester L., *Dr. Edward McGlynn* (New York: Dr. McGlynn Monument Association, 1918).

Malthus, Rev. Thomas R., *An Essay on the Principle of Population; or, a View of Its Past and Present Effects on Human Happiness; with an Inquiry into Our Prospects Respecting the Future Removal or Mitigation of the Evils Which It Occasions*, 6th ed. [1798], (London: John Murray, 1826).

Marshall, Alfred, 'Three Lectures on Progress and Poverty' [1883], *The Journal of Law and Economics* 12, no. 1 (1969): 184–226.

Marx, Karl, and Frederick Engels, *Ireland and the Irish Question* (Moscow: Progress Publishers, 1971).

McSweeny, Edward F., *De-Americanizing Young America: Poisoning the Source of Our National History and Traditions* (New York: Friends of Irish Freedom National Bureau of Information, 1920).

McSweeny, Edward F., *Ireland Is an American Question* (New York: Friends of Irish Freedom National Bureau of Information, 1919).

Mill, John Stuart, *Autobiography* [1873], (New York: P. F. Collier and Son, 1919).

Mill, John Stuart, *Chapters and Speeches on the Irish Land Question* (London: Longmans, Green, Reader, and Dyer, 1870).

Mill, John Stuart, *Principles of Political Economy* [1848], Jonathan Riley (ed.), (Oxford: Oxford University Press, 1994).

Mill, John Stuart, *Programme of the Land Tenure Reform Association* (London: Longmans, Green, Reader, and Dyer, 1871).

Mill, John Stuart, *The Letters of John Stuart Mill*, vol. II, Hugh S. R. Elliot (ed.), (London: Longmans, Green, and Co., 1910).

Molesworth, Guilford L., *Land as Property* (London: E. & F. N. Spon, 1885).

Moriarty, Rev. James Joseph, *The Mystic Key to Ireland's History: A Lecture Delivered on St. Patrick's Day, 1881* (Chatham, NY: The Courier Printing House, 1881).

Morley, John, *Recollections*, vol. I. (London: Macmillan, 1918).

Morris, William, *Political Writings of William Morris,* Arthur Leslie Morton (ed.), (New York: International Publishers, 1973).

Nulty, Most Rev. Dr. Thomas, *Letter of Most Rev. Dr. Nulty, Bishop of Meath, to Joseph Cowen, Esq., M.P., Newcastle-on-Tyne, on the State of Public Affairs in Ireland* (Dublin: Joseph Dollard, 1881).

Nulty, Most Rev. Dr. Thomas, *The Land Question: Letter of the Most Rev. Dr. Nulty, to the Clergy and Laity of the Diocese of Meath* (Dublin: Joseph Dollard, 1881).

O'Brien, William, *Recollections* (London: Macmillan and Co., 1905).

O'Connor, Thomas Power, *Memoirs of an Old Parliamentarian* (London: Ernest Benn, 1929).

O'Grady, Standish, *The Crisis in Ireland* (Dublin: E. Ponsonby, 1882).

O'Reilly, John Boyle, *In Bohemia* (Boston: Cashman, Keating and Co., 1886).

Ogilvie, William, 'The Right of Property in Land' [1781], in *The Pioneers of Land Reform, Thomas Spence, William Ogilvie and Thomas Paine,* Max Beer (ed.), (London: G. Bell and Sons, 1920).

Oliver, Frederick Scott, *The Irish Question: Federation or Secession* (New York: Press of the Civil Service Print Co., 1918).

Olivier, Sydney, *Sydney Olivier: Letters and Selected Writings,* Margaret Olivier (ed.), (London: George Allen & Unwin, 1948).

Overton, Richard, 'An Appeal from the Degenerate Representative Body' [1647], in *Leveller Manifestoes of the Puritan Revolution,* Don M. Wolfe (ed.), (New York: Thomas Nelson, 1944).

Paine, Thomas, 'Agrarian Justice' [1796], in *The Pioneers of Land Reform, Thomas Spence, William Ogilvie and Thomas Paine,* Max Beer (ed.), (London: G. Bell and Sons, 1920).

Philip, Kenward, *Boycotting: Or Avenging Ireland's Wrongs* (New York: Richard K. Fox, 1881).

Phillips, Wendell, *Daniel O'Connell: The Irish Patriot* (Boston: Lee and Shepard, 1884).

Phillips, Wendell, *The Scholar in a Republic: Address at the Centennial Anniversary of the Phi Beta Kappa of Harvard College, June 30, 1881* (Boston: Lee and Shepard, 1881).

Post, Louis F. and Fred C. Leubuscher, *Henry George's 1886 Campaign: An Account of the George-Hewitt Campaign in the New York Municipal Election of 1886* (New York: John W. Lovell, 1887).

Powderly, Terence V., *The Path I Trod: The Autobiography of Terence V. Powderly* (New York: Columbia University Press, 1940).

Rae, John, *Contemporary Socialism* (New York: Charles Scribner's Sons, 1884).

Redpath, James, *Talks About Ireland* (New York; P. J. Kenedy, 1881).

Richey, Alexander George (ed.), *Ancient Laws of Ireland: Din Tectugad, and Certain Other Selected Brehon Law Tracts*, vol. IV, (Dublin: Alex Thom & Co., 1879).

Roche, James Jeffrey, *Life of John Boyle O'Reilly; together with his complete poems and speeches* (New York: Cassell Publishing Co., 1891).

Rogers, John Rankin, *The Inalienable Rights of Man* (Olympia, WA: J. R. Rogers, 1900).

Rolleston, T. W., *Boycotting: A Reply to Mr. S. Laing* (Dublin: E. Ponsonby, 1888).

Rose, Henry, *The New Political Economy: The Social Teaching of Thomas Carlyle, John Ruskin, and Henry George; with observation on Joseph Mazzini* (London: James Speirs, 1891).

Rousseau, Jean-Jacques, *The Discourses and Other Early Political Writings,* Victor Gourevitch (ed.), (Cambridge: Cambridge University Press, 1997).

Rousseau, Jean-Jacques, *The Social Contract and Other Later Political Writings,* Victor Gourevitch (ed.), (Cambridge: Cambridge University Press, 1997).

Russell, Thomas, *A Letter to the People of Ireland on the Present Situation of the Country* (Belfast: Northern Star, 1796).

Ryan, John A., *A Living Wage: Its Ethical and Economic Aspects* (New York: MacMillan, 1906).

Ryan, John A., *Alleged Socialism of the Church Fathers* (London: Herder, 1913).

Ryan, John A., *Catholic Doctrine on the Right of Self-Government* (New York: Paulist Press, 1919).

Ryan, John A., *Distributive Justice: The Right and Wrong of Our Present Distribution of Wealth* (New York: MacMillan, 1916).

Ryan, John A., *Henry George and Private Property* (New York: The Columbus Press, 1910).

Seeley, J. R., *The Expansion of England: Two Courses of Lectures* [1883], (Boston: Little, Brown, and Company, 1905).

Sedgwick, Arthur George, *The Democratic Mistake: Godkin Lectures of 1909, Delivered at Harvard University* (New York: Charles Scribner's Sons, 1912).

Shaw, George Bernard, *Collected Letters, 1898–1910,* Dan. H. Laurence (ed.), (London: Max Reinhardt, 1972).

Shaw, George Bernard (ed.), *Fabian Essays in Socialism* (London: Fabian Society, 1889).

Shaw-Lefevre, George, *English and Irish Land Questions: Collected Essays* (London: Cassell, Petter, Galpin & Co., 1881).

Sidgwick, Henry, *Lectures on the Ethics of T. H. Green, Mr. Herbert Spencer, and J. Martineau* (London: Macmillan and Co., 1902).

Sidgwick, Henry, *The Methods of Ethics*, 7th ed. [1874], (London: Macmillan and Co., 1907).

Simon, Richard, *An Examination of Some of Mr. Henry George's Doctrines on Progress and Poverty* (London: Bemrose & Sons, 1880).

Skeat, Walter W., *Principles of English Etymology*, 1st Ser., 2nd ed. (Oxford: Clarendon Press, 1892).

Smith, Samuel, *The Nationalisation of the Land* (London: Kegan Paul, Trench & Co., 1884).

Spence, Thomas, 'The Real Rights of Man' [1793], in *The Pioneers of Land Reform, Thomas Spence, William Ogilvie and Thomas Paine,* Max Beer (ed.), (London: G. Bell and Sons, 1920).

Spencer, Herbert, *Social Statics: Or, the Condition Essential to Human Happiness Specified, and the First of them Developed* [1850], (New York: D. Appleton and Co., 1883).

Spencer, Herbert, *The Man versus The State* [1884], (New York: Mitchell Kennerley, 1916).
Stephen, James Fitzjames, *Liberty, Equality, Fraternity* [1873], (New York: Henry Holt and Company, 1882).
Stephen, Leslie, *The Life of Henry Fawcett* (London: Smith, Elder & Co., 1885).
Sullivan, Alexander Martin, *Ireland at the Bar! The State Trials – 1881. Speech of A. M. Sullivan, Esq., M. P. on Behalf of Mr. Patrick Egan* (Dublin: J. J. Lalor, 1881).
Sullivan, Michael F., *Ireland of To-Day: The Causes and Aims of Irish Agitation* (Philadelphia: J. C. McCurdy & Co., 1881).
Sullivan, Timothy Daniel (ed.), *Condemnations of Crime: Compiled from Speeches delivered at meetings of the Land League and National League in Ireland, 1879–1887* (London: The Irish Press Agency, 1888).
Sumner, William Graham, *Problems in Political Economy* (New York: Henry Holt and Company, 1883).
Sumner, William Graham, *War and Other Essays,* Albert Galloway Keller (ed.), (New Haven: Yale University Press, 1911).
Sumner, William Graham, *What Social Classes Owe to Each Other* (New York: Harper & Brothers, 1883).
Talbot Smith, John, *Patrick Ford of the Irish World* ([n.p.]:[n.d.]).
Talbot Smith, John, *The Catholic Church in New York: A History of the New York Diocese from Its Establishment in 1808 to the Present Time*, vols. I & II (New York: Hall & Locke, 1905).
Taylor, Sedley, *Profit-Sharing between Capital and Labour, Six Essays* (London: Kegan Paul, Trench & Co., 1884).
Terrell, Alexander W., *Land: Its Individuals Ownership and Culture, the Surest Safeguard of Free Government: University of Texas Commencement Address* (Austin: University of Texas Press, 1898).
Thelwall, John, *The Rights of Nature, against the Usurpations of Establishments* (London: H. D. Symonds, 1796).
Thorold Rogers, James Edwin, *Cobden and Modern Political Opinion: Essays on Certain Political Topics* (London: Macmillan, 1873).
Thorold Rogers, James Edwin, *The Irish Land Question: A Letter Written in Sept., 1869, to the Late Sir John Gray, M. P.* (Oxford: E. C. Alden, 1881).
Tobin, Rev. F. L., *Notes on 'Progress and Poverty,' A Reply to Henry George* (Pittsburgh: John M. Welsh, 1887).
Toynbee, Arnold, *'Progress and Poverty,' A Criticism of Mr. Henry George, Being Two Lectures Delivered in St. Andrew's Hall, Newman Street, London* (London: Kegan Paul, Trench and Co., 1883).
Trench, W. Steuart, *Realities of Irish Life* (London: Longmans, Green, and Co., 1869).
Vincent, J. E., *The Land Question in North Wales, Being a Brief Survey of the History, Origin, and Character of the Agrarian Agitation, and of the Nature and Effect of the Proceedings of the Welsh Land Commission* (London: Longmans, Green, and Co., 1896).
Walker, James, *The National Inheritance* (London: F. Farrah, 1873).
Wallace, Alfred Russel, *Studies: Scientific and Social*, vol. I (London: Macmillan and Co., 1900).
Webb, Sidney, *A Plea for the Taxation of Ground Rents* (London: The 'United Committee' for the Taxation of Ground Rents and Values, 1887).
Webb, Sidney, *Socialism in England* (London: Swan Sonnenschein, 1890).

Webb, Sidney, and Beatrice Webb, *The History of Trade Unionism*, 2nd ed. [1894], (London: Longmans, Green, and Co., 1896).

Webb, Sidney, and Beatrice Webb, *The Letters of Sidney and Beatrice Webb*, vol. I, Norman Mackenzie (ed.), (Cambridge: Cambridge University Press, 1978).

Welch, Ransom B., *Faith and Modern Thought* (New York: G. P. Putnam's Sons, 1876).

White, Andrew Dickson, *A History of the Warfare of Science with Theology in Christendom*, vol. I (New York: Appleton, 1897).

White, James Dundas, *The A. B. C. of the Land Question: A Handbook for Students and Speakers* (Cincinnati: Joseph Fels Fund of America, 1912).

Whitman, Walt, *Specimen Days & Collect* (Philadelphia: Rees Welsh, 1882).

Williams, Joshua, *Principles of the Law of Real Property, Intended as a First Book for the Use of Students in Conveyancing*, 9th ed. [1845], (London: H. Sweet, 1871).

Wilson, Woodrow, *The New Freedom: A Call for the Emancipation of the Generous Energies of a People* [1913], (New York: Doubleday, Page & Company, 1918).

Wilson, Woodrow, *The Papers of Woodrow Wilson*, Arthur S. Link (ed.), vol. VII (Princeton: Princeton University Press, 1968).

Wilson, Woodrow, *The State: Elements of Historical and Practical Politics*, rev. ed. [1898], (London: D. C. Heath, 1919).

Wolman, Leo, *The Boycott in American Trade Unions* (Baltimore: Johns Hopkins University Press, 1916).

Wright, Hendrick B., *A Practical Treatise on Labor* (New York: G. W. Carlton, 1871).

Yardley, Edmund (ed.), *Addresses at the Funeral of Henry George* (Chicago: Public Publishing Company, 1905).

Secondary Sources

Adcock, Robert, *Liberalism and the Emergence of American Political Science: A Transatlantic Tale* (Oxford: Oxford University Press, 2014).

Adorno, Theodor W., and Max Horkheimer, *Dialectic of Enlightenment* [1944], (London: Verso, 1997).

Andelson, Robert V., 'Msgr. John A. Ryan's Critique of Henry George', *The American Journal of Economics and Sociology* 33, no. 3 (1974): 273–286.

Andersen, Heine, 'Morality in Three Social Theories: Parsons, Analytical Marxism and Habermas', *Acta Sociologica* 33, no. 4 (1990): 321–339.

Appleby, Joyce, *Liberalism and Republicanism in the Historical Imagination* (Cambridge, MA: Harvard University Press, 1992).

Arendt, Hannah, *The Human Condition* (Chicago: University of Chicago Press, 1958).

Arendt, Hannah, *On Violence* (New York: Harcourt Brace, 1970).

Arnesen, Eric, 'Comparing Urban Crises: Race, Migration and the Transformation of the Modern American City', *Social History* 30, no. 4 (2005): 499–507.

Ashton, Owen, Robert Fyson, and Stephen Roberts (eds.), *The Duty of Discontent: Essays for Dorothy Thompson* (London: Mansell Publishing, 1995).

Ball, Terence, and Richard Bellamy (eds.), *The Cambridge History of Twentieth Century Political Thought* (Cambridge: Cambridge University Press, 2003).

Ball, Terence, James Farr, and Russell L. Hanson (eds.), *Political Innovation and Conceptual Change* (Cambridge: Cambridge University Press, 1989).

Barker, Charles A., *Henry George* (New York: Oxford University Press, 1955).

Barker, Charles A., 'Henry George and the California Background of Progress and Poverty', *California Historical Society Quarterly* 24, no. 2 (1945): 97–115.

Barrera, Albino, 'Exchange-Vale Determinism: Scholastic *Just Price*, Economic Theory, and Modern Catholic Social Thought', *History of Political Economy* 29, no. 1 (1997): 83–116.

Barrett, James R., 'Americanisation from the Bottom Up: Immigration and the Remaking of the Working Class in the United States, 1880–1930', *The Journal of American History* 79, no. 3 (1992): 996–1020.

Bartlett, Thomas (ed.), *The Cambridge History of Ireland, vol. IV: 1880 to the Present* (Cambridge: Cambridge University Press, 2018).

Bayor, Ronald H., and Timothy J. Meagher (eds.), *The New York Irish* (Baltimore, MD: Johns Hopkins University Press, 1997).

Belchem, John, 'Nationalism, Republicanism and Exile: Irish Emigrants and the Revolutions of 1848', *Past & Present* 146 (1995): 103–135.

Belchem, John, 'Priests, Publicans and the Irish Poor: Ethnic Enterprise and Migrant Networks in Mid-Nineteenth-Century Liverpool', *Immigrants & Minorities* 23, nos. 2–3 (2005): 207–231.

Belchem, John, *Irish, Catholic and Scouse: The History of the Liverpool-Irish, 1800–1939* (Liverpool: Liverpool University Press, 2007).

Belchem, John (ed.), *Popular Politics, Riot and Labour: Essays in Liverpool History, 1790–1940* (Liverpool: Liverpool University Press, 1992).

Bell, Duncan, 'Empire and International Relations in Victorian Political Thought', *The Historical Journal* 49, no. 1 (2006): 281–298.

Bell, Duncan, *Reordering the World: Essays on Liberalism and Empire* (Princeton: Princeton University Press, 2016).

Bell, Stephen, *Rebel, Priest and Prophet: A Biography of Dr. Edward McGlynn* (New York: Devin-Adair, 1937).

Bellamy, Richard, *Liberalism and Modern Society: An Historical Argument* (Oxford: Polity Press, 1992).

Berresford Ellis, Peter, *A History of the Irish Working Class* (London: Victor Gollancz, 1972).

Betts, Jocelyn Paul, 'John Stuart Mill, Victorian Liberalism, and the Failure of Co-operative Production', *The Historical Journal* 59, no. 1 (2016): 153–174.

Bevir, Mark, *The Logic of the History of Ideas* (Cambridge: Cambridge University Press, 1999).

Bevir, Mark, 'Sidney Webb: Utilitarianism, Positivism, and Social Democracy', *Journal of Modern History* 74, no. 2 (2002): 217–252.

Bevir, Mark, and Frank Trentmann (eds.), *Critiques of Capital in Modern Britain and America: Transatlantic Exchanges 1800 to the Present Day* (Basingstoke: Palgrave Macmillan, 2002).

Bew, Paul, *Land and the National Question in Ireland, 1858–82* (Dublin: Gill and Macmillan, 1978).

Bew, Paul, *Enigma: A New Life of Charles Stewart Parnell* (Dublin: Gill and Macmillan, 2011).

Biagini, Eugenio F., *British Democracy and Irish Nationalism, 1876–1906* (Cambridge: Cambridge University Press, 2007).

Biagini, Eugenio F. (ed.), *Citizenship and Community: Liberals, Radicals and Collective Identities in the British Isles, 1865–1931* (Cambridge: Cambridge University Press, 1996).

Biagini, Eugenio F., *Liberty, Retrenchment and Reform: Popular Liberalism in the Age of Gladstone, 1860–1880* (Cambridge: Cambridge University Press, 1992).
Birnie, Arthur, *Single-Tax George* (London: Thomas Nelson, 1936).
Black, Robert Denis Collison, 'Economic Policy in Ireland and India in the Time of J. S. Mill', *The Economic History Review* 21, no. 2 (1968): 321–336.
Black, Robert Denis Collison, *Economic Thought and the Irish Question, 1817–1870* (Cambridge: Cambridge University Press, 1960).
Blackledge, Paul and Kelvin Knight (eds.), *Virtue and Politics: Alasdair MacIntyre's Revolutionary Aristotelianism* (Notre Dame, IN: University of Notre Dame Press, 2011).
Blaug, Mark (ed.), *Henry George* (Aldershot: Edward Elgar Publishing, 1992).
Boase, Paul (ed.), *The Rhetoric of Protest and Reform, 1878–1898* (Athens OH: Ohio University Press, 1980).
Bock, Kenneth E., 'Comparison of Histories: The Contribution of Henry Maine', *Comparative Studies in Society and History* 16, no. 2 (1974): 232–262.
Bock, Kenneth E., 'The Moral Philosophy of Sir Henry Sumner Maine', *Journal of the History of Ideas* 37, no. 1 (1976): 147–154.
Bogin, Ruth, 'Petitioning and the New Moral Economy of Post-Revolutionary America', *The William and Mary Quarterly* 45, no. 3 (1988): 391–425.
Bourke, Richard, 'Languages of Conflict and the Northern Irish Troubles', *Journal of Modern History* 83, no. 3 (2011): 544–578.
Bourke, Richard, 'Political and Religious Ideas during the Irish Revolution', *History of European Ideas* 46, no. 7 (2020): 997–1008.
Bourke, Richard, and Ian McBride (eds.), *The Princeton History of Modern Ireland* (Princeton: Princeton University Press, 2016).
Boyce, D. George, Robert Eccleshall, and Vincent Geoghegan (eds.), *Political Thought in Ireland since the Seventeenth Century* (London: Routledge, 1993).
Boylan, Thomas, Renee Prendergast, and John D. Turner (eds.), *A History of Irish Economic Thought* (Abingdon: Routledge, 2011).
Boylan, Thomas A., and Timothy P. Foley, *Political Economy and Colonial Ireland: The Propagation and Ideological Function of Economic Discourse in the Nineteenth Century* (London: Routledge, 1992).
Boyle, John W., *The Irish Labour Movement in the Nineteenth Century* (Washington, DC: Catholic University of America Press, 1988).
Bradley, John, 'Archbishop McGettigan, the Catholic Bishops of Ireland and the Irish Land Bill 1881', *Seanchas Ardmhacha: Journal of the Armagh Diocesan Historical Society* 17, no. 2 (1998): 121–157.
Brett, Annabel, *Liberty, Right and Nature: Individual Rights in Later Scholastic Thought* (Cambridge: Cambridge University Press, 1997).
Brett, Thomas, *Life of the Most Reverend Patrick Duggan, Bishop of Clonfert* (Dublin: W. Leckie, 1921).
Bric, Maurice J., 'The United Irishmen, International Republicanism and the Definition of the Polity in the United States of America, 1791–1800', *Proceedings of the Royal Irish Academy* 104, no. 4 (2004): 81–106.
Bristow, Edward, 'The Liberty and Property Defence League and Individualism', *The Historical Journal* 18, no. 4 (1975): 761–789.
Broadie, Alexander (ed.), *The Cambridge Companion to the Scottish Enlightenment* (Cambridge: Cambridge University Press, 2003).

Broderick, James, *The Economic Morals of the Jesuits: An Answer to Dr. H. M. Robertson* (London: Oxford University Press, 1934).

Bronner, Simon J., 'The American Concept of Tradition: Folklore in the Discourse of Traditional Values', *Western Folklore* 59, no. 2 (2000): 143–170.

Bronstein, Jaime L., *John Francis Bray: Transatlantic Radical* (Pontypool: Merlin Press, 2009).

Bronstein, Jaime L., *Land Reform and Working-Class Experience in Britain and the United States, 1800–1862* (Stanford: Stanford University Press, 1999).

Brooks, Frank (ed.), *The Individualist Anarchists: An Anthology of Liberty (1881–1908)* (New Brunswick, NJ: Transaction, 1994).

Brown, Michael, 'The Biter Bitten: Ireland and the Rude Enlightenment', *Eighteenth-Century Studies* 45, no. 3 (2012): 393–407.

Brown, Michael, *The Irish Enlightenment* (Cambridge, MA: Harvard University Press, 2016).

Brown, Thomas N., *Irish American Nationalism, 1870–1890* (Philadelphia: J. B. Lippincott, 1966).

Bruce, James P., *Ireland's Hope: The 'Peculiar Theories' of James Fintan Lalor* (Wilmington: Vernon Press, 2020).

Brundage, David, 'After the Land League: The Persistence of Irish-American Labor Radicalism in Denver, 1897–1905', *Journal of American Ethnic History* 11, no. 3 (1992): 3–26.

Brundage, David, *Irish Nationalists in America: The Politics of Exile, 1798–1998* (New York: Oxford University Press, 2016).

Brundage, David, 'Recent Directions in the History of Irish American Nationalism', *Journal of American Ethnic History* 28, no. 4 (2009): 82–89.

Bueger, Christian, 'Pathways to Practice: Praxiography and International Politics', *European Political Science Review* 6, no. 3 (2014): 383–406.

Bull, Philip, *Land, Politics and Nationalism: A Study of the Irish Land Question* (Dublin: Gill and Macmillan, 1996).

Bull, Philip, 'The Formation of the United Irish League, 1898–1900: The Dynamics of Irish Agrarian Agitation', *Irish Historical Studies* 33, no. 132 (2003): 404–423.

Butler, Leslie, *Critical Americans: Victorian Intellectuals and Transatlantic Liberal Reform* (Chapel Hill: UNC Press, 2007).

Butt, John and Ignatius Frederick Clarke (eds.), *The Victorians and Social Protest: A Symposium* (Newton Abbot: David & Charles Archon, 1973).

Buurman, Gary B., 'A Comparison of the Single Tax Proposals of Henry George and the Physiocrats', *History of Political Economy* 23, no. 3 (1991): 481–496.

Byrne, William F., 'William Graham Sumner and the Problem of Liberal Democracy', *The Review of Politics* 72, no. 4 (2010): 571–597.

Cain, Peter, 'Empire and the Languages of Character and Virtue in Later Victorian and Edwardian Britain', *Modern Intellectual History* 4, no. 2 (2007): 1–25.

Calhoun, Charles W. (ed.), *The Gilded Age: Essays on the Origins of Modern America* (Wilmington, DE: Scholarly Resources, 1996).

Cameron, Ewen A., 'Communication or Separation? Reactions to Irish Land Agitation and Legislation in the Highlands of Scotland, c.1870–1910', *English Historical Review* 120, no. 487 (2005): 633–666.

Campbell, Fergus, 'Irish Popular Politics and the Making of the Wyndham Land Act, 1901–1903', *The Historical Journal* 45, no. 4 (2002): 755–773.

Campbell, Fergus, *Land and Revolution: Nationalist Politics in the West of Ireland, 1891–1921* (Oxford: Oxford University Press, 2005).

Campbell, Fergus, and Tony Varley (eds.), *Land Questions in Modern Ireland* (Manchester: Manchester University Press, 2013).

Campbell, Malcolm, 'Ireland's Furthest Shores: Irish Immigrant Settlement in Nineteenth-Century California and Eastern Australia', *Pacific Historical Review* 71, no. 1, (2002): 59–90.

Campbell, Malcolm, 'Irish Nationalism and Immigrant Assimilation: Comparing the United States and Australia', *Australasian Journal of American Studies* 15, no. 2 (1996): 24–43.

Campbell, Patrick J. and Peter Kerr, 'Davitt in Carrickmore', *Seanchas Ardmhacha: Journal of the Armagh Diocesan Historical Society* 11, no. 2 (1985): 363–394.

Casey, Brian (ed.), *Defying the Law of the Land: Agrarian Radicals in Irish History* (Dublin: The History Press Ireland, 2013).

Casey, Brian, 'Matt Harris and the Irish land Question, 1876–1882', *Rural History* 25, no. 2 (2014): 183–201.

Caton, Hiram, 'The Preindustrial Economics of Adam Smith', *The Journal of Economic History* 45, no. 4 (1985): 833–853.

Chappey, Jean-Luc, and Julien Vincent, 'A Republican Ecology? Citizenship, Nature and the French Revolution (1795–1799), *Past & Present* 243 (2019): 109–140.

Charbonnier, Pierre, *Affluence and Freedom: An Environmental History of Political Ideas* (Cambridge: Polity Press, 2021).

Chase, Malcolm, 'From Millennium to Anniversary: The Concept of Jubilee in Late Eighteenth and Nineteenth-Century England', *Past & Present* 129 (1990): 132–147.

Chase, Malcolm, 'Out of Radicalism: The Mid-Victorian Freehold Land Movement', *English Historical Review* 106, no. 419 (1991): 319–345.

Chase, Malcolm, *The People's Farm: English Radical Agrarianism, 1775–1840* (Oxford: Oxford University Press, 1988)

Chase, Malcolm, '"Wholesome Object Lessons": The Chartist Land Plan in Retrospect', *English Historical Review* 118, no. 475 (2003): 59–85.

Claeys, Gregory, *Machinery, Money and the Millennium: From Moral Economy to Socialism, 1815–1860* (Princeton: Princeton University Press, 1987).

Claeys, Gregory, *Mill and Paternalism* (Cambridge: Cambridge University Press, 2013).

Claeys, Gregory, 'The Origins of the Rights of Labour: Republicanism, Commerce, and the Construction of Modern Social Theory in Britain, 1796–1805', *The Journal of Modern History* 66, no. 2 (1994): 249–290.

Claeys, Gregory, 'The "Survival of the Fittest" and the Origins of Social Darwinism', *Journal of the History of Ideas* 61, no. 2 (2000): 223–240.

Claeys, Gregory, *Thomas Paine: Social and Political Thought* (Abingdon: Routledge, 1989).

Clark, Constance Areson, 'Evolution for John Doe: Pictures, the Public, and the Scopes Trial Debate', *Journal of American History* 87, no. 4 (2001): 1275–1303.

Clark, Gemma, *Everyday Violence in the Irish Civil War* (Cambridge: Cambridge University Press, 2014).

Clark, Samuel, 'The Social Composition of the Land League', *Irish Historical Studies* 17, no. 68 (1971): 447–469.

Clark, Samuel, *The Social Origins of the Irish Land War* (Princeton: Princeton University Press, 1979).

Clark, Samuel, and Donnelly, James S. (eds.), *Irish Peasants: Violence and Political Unrest, 1780–1914* (Madison: University of Wisconsin Press, 2003).
Cleary, Joe, and Claire Connolly (eds.), *The Cambridge Companion to Modern Irish Culture* (Cambridge: Cambridge University Press, 2005).
Coats, Alfred William, 'The Historicist Reaction in English Political Economy, 1870–90' *Economica* 21, no. 82 (1954): 143–153.
Coats, Alfred William (ed.), *The Classical Economists and Economic Policy* (London: Methuen and Co., 1971).
Coats, Alfred William, *The Sociology and Professionalization of Economics, vol. II, British & American Essays* (London: Routledge, 2003).
Cohen, Gerald Allan, *Karl Marx's Theory of History: A Defence* (Princeton: Princeton University Press, 2000).
Cohen, Nancy, *The Reconstruction of American Liberalism, 1865–1914* (Chapel Hill: University of North Carolina Press, 2002).
Colaiaco, James A., *James Fitzjames Stephen and the Crisis of Victorian Thought* (Basingstoke: Palgrave Macmillan, 1983).
Collini, Stefan, 'Hobhouse, Bosanquet and the State: Philosophical Idealism and Political Argument in England, 1880–1918', *Past & Present* 72 (1976): 86–111.
Collini, Stefan, *Liberalism and Sociology: L. T. Hobhouse and Political Argument in England, 1880–1914* (Cambridge: Cambridge University Press, 1979).
Collini, Stefan, 'Liberalism and the Legacy of Mill', *The Historical Journal* 20, no. 1, (1977): 237–254.
Collini, Stefan, Richard Whatmore, and Brian Young (eds.), *Economy, Polity, and Society: British Intellectual History 1750–1950* (Cambridge: Cambridge University Press, 2000).
Conkin, Paul K., *Prophets of Prosperity: America's First Political Economists* (Bloomington: Indiana University Press, 1980).
Comerford, R. Vincent, *The Fenians in Context: Irish Politics and Society, 1848–82* (Dublin: Wolfhound Press, 1985).
Cord, Steven P., 'A New Look at Henry George', *American Journal of Economics and Sociology* 27, no. 4 (1968): 393–404.
Cotkin, George B., 'The Spencerian and Comtian Nexus in Gompers' Labor Philosophy: The Impact of Non-Marxian Evolutionary Thought', *Labor History* 20, no. 4 (1979): 510–523.
Cotlar, Seth, 'Radical Conceptions of Property Rights and Economic Equality in the Early American Republic: The Trans-Atlantic Dimension', *Explorations in Early American Culture* 4 (2000): 191–219.
Cragoe, Mathew, 'Conscience or Coercion? Clerical Influence at the General Election of 1868 in Wales' *Past & Present* 149 (1995): 140–169.
Cragoe, Matthew and Paul Readman (eds.), *The Land Question in Britain, 1750–1950* (Basingstoke: Palgrave Macmillan, 2010).
Cromartie, Alan, 'Harringtonian Virtue: Harrington, Machiavelli, and the Method of the Moment', *The Historical Journal* 41, no. 4 (1998): 987–1009.
Cronin, Maura, *Agrarian Protest in Ireland, 1750–1960* (Dundalk: Dundalgen Press, 2012).
Cunningham, John, *Labour in the West of Ireland: Working Life and Struggle, 1890–1914* (Belfast: Athol Books, 1995).
Cunningham, John, and Niall Ó Ciosáin (eds.), *Culture and Society in Ireland since 1750: Essays in Honour of Gearóid Ó Tuathaigh* (Dublin: The Lilliput Press, 2015).

Curran, Robert E., 'Confronting "The Social Question:" American Catholic Thought and the Socio-Economic Order in the Nineteenth Century', *U.S. Catholic Historian* 5, no. 2, (1986): 165–193.

Curran, Robert E., *Michael Augustine Corrigan and the Shaping of Conservative Catholicism in America, 1878–1902* (New York: Arno Press, 1878).

Curran, Robert E., 'Prelude to "Americanism": The New York Accademia and Clerical Radicalism in the Late Nineteenth Century', *Church History* 47, no. 1 (1978): 48–65.

Curran, Robert E., 'The McGlynn Affair and the Shaping of the New Conservatism in American Catholicism, 1886–1894', *The Catholic Historical Review* 66, no. 2 (1980): 184–204.

Currarino, Rosanne, *The Labor Question in America: Economic Democracy in the Gilded Age* (Urbana: University of Illinois Press, 2011).

Curtis, L. Perry Jr., 'Moral and Physical Force: The Language of Violence in Irish Nationalism', *Journal of British Studies* 27, no. 2 (1988): 150–189.

Dal Lago, Enrico, 'Lincoln, Cavour, and National Unification: American Republicanism and Italian Liberal Nationalism in Comparative Perspective', *The Journal of the Civil War Era* 3, no. 1 (2013): 85–113.

Davie, George Elder, *The Democratic Intellect: Scotland and Her Universities in the Nineteenth Century* (Edinburgh: Edinburgh University Press, 1961).

Davie, George Elder, 'Victor Cousin and the Scottish Philosophers', *Journal of Scottish Philosophy* 7, no. 2 (2009): 193–214.

Dawson, Hannah, 'The Normativity of Nature in Locke and Pufendorf', *Historical Journal* 63, no. 3 (2020): 528–558.

De Nie, Michael, '"A Medley Mob of Irish-American Plotters and Irish Dupes": The British Press and Transatlantic Fenianism', *Journal of British Studies* 40, no. 2 (2001): 213–240.

De Vál, Séamas S., 'Father Tom: The Land League Priest', *The Past: The Organ of the Uí Cinsealaigh Historical Society* 12 (1978): 23–30.

Deane, Seamus, 'Land & Soil: A Territorial Rhetoric', *History Ireland* 2, no. 1 (1994): 31–34.

Delaney, Enda, 'Directions in Historiography, Our Island Story? Towards a Transnational History of Late Modern Ireland', *Irish Historical Studies* 37, no. 148 (2011): 83–105.

Delaney, Enda, and Breandán Mac Suibhne (eds.), *Ireland's Great Famine and Popular Politics* (New York: Routledge, 2016).

Delaney, Enda, and Donald M. MacRaild, 'Irish Migration, Networks and Ethnic Identities since 1750: An Introduction', *Immigrants & Minorities* 23, nos. 2–3 (2005): 127–142.

DeLeon, David, *The American as Anarchist: Reflections on Indigenous Radicalism* (Baltimore, MD: Johns Hopkins University Press, 1978).

Den Otter, *Sandra, British Idealism and Social Explanation: A Study in late Victorian Thought* (Oxford: Oxford University Press, 1996).

Denby, David, 'Ireland, Modernization and the 'Enlightenment' Debate', *Irish Review* 31 (2004): 28–39.

Deverell, William F., 'To Loosen the Safety Value: Eastern Workers and Western Lands', *Western Historical Quarterly* 19, no. 3 (1988): 269–285.

Devine, T. M. (ed.), *Irish Immigrants and Scottish Society in the Nineteenth and Twentieth Centuries* (Edinburgh: John Donald, 1991).

Dewey, Clive, 'Celtic Agrarian Legislation and the Celtic Revival: Historicist Implications of Gladstone's Irish and Scottish Land Acts, 1870–1886', *Past & Present* 64 (1974): 30–70.

Dewey, Clive, 'The Rehabilitation of the Peasant Proprietor in Nineteenth Century Economic Thought', *History of Political Economy* 6, no. 1 (1974): 17–47.

Diamond, Alan (ed.), *The Victorian Achievement of Sir Henry Maine: A Centennial Reappraisal* (Cambridge: Cambridge University Press, 1991).

Dillon, Paul, 'James Connolly and the Kerry Famine of 1898', *Saothar: Journal of Irish Labour History* 25 (1998): 29–42.

Dolan, Jay P., *The Immigrant Church: New York's Irish and German Catholics, 1815–1865* (Baltimore, MD: Johns Hopkins University Press, 1975).

Dolan, Thomas, 'Imprisonment, Islands, Imperialism: Patrician Dimensions of the Irish Imagination' *History of European Ideas* 46, no. 7 (2020): 1027–1046.

Donnelly, James S., *The Land and People of Nineteenth-Century Cork: The Rural Economy and the Land Question* (London: Routledge, 1975).

Dooley, Terence, 'Land and Politics in Independent Ireland, 1923–48: The Case for Reappraisal' *Irish Historical Studies* 34, no. 134 (2004): 175–197.

Doyle, David N., 'Irish Elites in North America and Liberal Democracy, 1820–1920', *Radharc* 3, (2002): 29–53.

Doyle, David N., 'The Irish and American Labour, 1880–1920', *Saothar: Journal of Irish Labour History* 1 (1975): 42–53.

Doyle, David N., 'The Irish in Chicago', *Irish Historical Studies* 26, no. 103 (1989): 293–303.

Doyle, David N., and Owen Dudley Edwards (eds.), *America and Ireland, 1776–1976: The American Identity and the Irish Connection* (Westport, CT: Greenwood Press, 1976).

Doyle, Patrick, 'The Clergy, Economic Democracy, and the Co-operative Movement in Ireland, 1880–1932' *History of European Ideas* 46, no. 7 (2020): 982–996.

Drudy, Patrick J. (ed.), *Ireland: Land, Politics and People* (Cambridge: Cambridge University Press, 1982).

Drudy, Patrick J. (ed.), *The Irish in America: Emigration, Assimilation and Impact* (Cambridge: Cambridge University Press, 1985).

Dubofsky, Melvyn, *When Workers Organize: New York City in the Progressive Era* (Amherst: University of Massachusetts Press, 1968).

Dubofsky, Melvyn, and Warren Van Tine (eds.), *Labor Leaders in America* (Urbana: University of Illinois Press, 1987).

Dunbabin, J. P. D., 'The "Revolt of the Field": The Agricultural Labourers' Movement in the 1870s', *Past & Present* 26 (1963): 68–97.

Dunleavy, John, 'Michael Davitt's Lancashire Apprenticeship', *Journal of the Galway Archaeological and Historical Society* 59 (2007): 109–121.

Durey, Michael, 'The Dublin Society of United Irishmen and the Politics of the Carey-Drennan Dispute, 1792–4', *The Historical Journal* 37, no. 1 (1994): 89–111.

Durey, Michael, 'Thomas Paine's Apostles: Radical Emigres and the Triumph of Jeffersonian Republicanism', *William and Mary Quarterly* 44, no. 4 (1987): 661–688.

Durey, Michael, *Trans-Atlantic Radicals in the Early American Republic* (Lawrence: University of Kansas Press, 1997).
Dwan, David, *The Great Community: Culture and Nationalism in Ireland* (Dublin: Field Day, 2008).
Eagleton, Terry, *After Theory* (London: Penguin, 2004).
Eagleton, Terry, 'God, the Universe, Art, and Communism', *New Literary History* 32, no. 1 (2001): 23–32.
Eagleton, Terry, *Materialism* (New Haven: Yale University Press, 2016).
Eagleton, Terry, *Saints and Scholars* (London: Verso, 1987).
Eagleton, Terry, 'The Radicalism of William Thompson', *The Irish Review* 26 (2000): 80–88.
Eagleton, Terry, Frederic Jameson and Edward W. Said, *Nationalism, Colonialism and Literature* (Minneapolis: University of Minnesota Press, 1990).
Ehrlich, Richard L. (ed.), *Immigrants in Industrial America, 1850–1920* (Charlottesville: University Press of Virginia, 1977).
Ellis, Richard J., 'Radical Lockeanism in American Political Culture', *The Western Political Quarterly* 45, no. 4 (1992): 825–849.
Eltis, Walter, 'The Contrasting Theories of Industrialization of François Quesnay and Adam Smith', *Oxford Economic Papers* 40, no. 2 (1988): 269–288.
Emmons, David M., *Beyond the Pale: The Irish in the West, 1845–1910* (Norman: University of Oklahoma Press, 2010).
Emmons, David M., 'Exiles, 'Evangelizers,' and Anti-imperialists: Ireland's Disputed American 'Empire'', *American Journal of Irish Studies* 9 (2012): 53–78.
Emmons, David M., *The Butte Irish: Class and Ethnicity in an American Mining Town, 1875–1925* (Urbana: University of Illinois Press, 1990).
English, Richard, 'Directions in Historiography: History and Irish Nationalism', *Irish Historical Studies* 37, no. 147 (2011): 447–460.
Epstein, James A., 'The Constitutional Idiom: Radical Reasoning, Rhetoric and Action in Early Nineteenth-Century England', *Journal of Social History* 23, no. 3 (1990): 553–574.
Erie, Steven P., 'Politics, the Public Sector and Irish Social Mobility: San Francisco, 1870–1900', *The Western Political Quarterly* 31, no. 2 (1978): 274–289.
Erie, Steven P., *Rainbow's End: Irish-Americans and the Dilemmas of Urban Machine Politics, 1840–1985* (Berkeley: University of California Press, 1988).
Faherty, William Barnaby, 'The Clergyman and Labor Progress: Cornelius O'Leary and the Knights of Labor', *Labor History* 11, no. 2 (1970): 175–189.
Fanning, Charles, 'Robert Emmet and Nineteenth-Century America', *New Hibernia Review* 8, no. 4 (2004): 53–83.
Fatovic, Clement, 'The Anti-Catholic Roots of Liberal and Republican Conceptions of Freedom in English Political Thought', *Journal of the History of Ideas* 66, no. 1 (2005): 37–58.
Fenton, Elizabeth, *Religious Liberties: Anti-Catholicism and Liberal Democracy in Nineteenth-Century U.S. Literature and Culture* (New York: Oxford University Press, 2011).
Feuer, Lewis S., 'The North American Origin of Marx's Socialism', *The Western Political Quarterly* 16, no. 1 (1963): 53–67.
Fink, Leon, *The Long Gilded Age: American Capitalism and the Lessons of a New World Order* (Philadelphia: University of Pennsylvania Press, 2015).
Fink, Leon, *Workingmen's Democracy: The Knights of Labor and American Politics* (Urbana: University of Illinois Press, 1983).

Fitzpatrick, David, 'The Disappearance of the Irish Agricultural Labourer, 1841–1912', *Irish Economic and Social History* 7 (1980): 66–92.

Fletcher, Roger, 'British Radicalism and German Revisionism: The Case of Eduard Bernstein', *The International History Review* 4, no. 3 (1982): 339–370.

Fogarty, Lillian, *James Fintan Lalor: Patriot & Political Essasyist, 1807–1849* (Dublin: The Talbot Press, 1919).

Foner, Eric, *Free Soil, Free Labor, Free Men: The Ideology of the Republican Party before the Civil War* (New York: Oxford University Press, 1970).

Foner, Eric, *Politics and Ideology in the Age of the Civil War* (New York: Oxford University Press, 1981).

Foner, Eric, *Reconstruction: America's Unfinished Revolution*, rev. ed. [1988], (New York: Harper Collins, 2015).

Foner, Eric, 'Why Is There No Socialism in the United States?', *History Workshop* 17 (1984): 57–80.

Foote, Lorien, *Seeking the One Great Remedy: Francis George Shaw and Nineteenth Century Reform* (Athens, OH: Ohio University Press, 2003).

Forkosch, Morris D., 'Henry George: The Economist as Moralist', *American Journal of Economics and Sociology* 38, no. 4 (1979): 357–369.

Foster, Roy F., *Luck and the Irish: A Brief History of Change, 1970–2000* (London: Allen Lane, 2007).

Freeden, Michael, 'J. A. Hobson as a New Liberal Theorist: Some Aspects of his Social Thought until 1914', *Journal of the History of Ideas* 34, no. 3 (1973): 421–433.

Freeden, Michael (ed.), *Reappraising J. A. Hobson: Humanism and Welfare* (London: Unwin Hyman, 1990).

Freeden, Michael, *The New Liberalism: An Ideology of Social Reform* (Oxford: Oxford University Press, 1978).

Frye, Jerry K., 'Rhetorical Strategies Employed by Henry George and His Followers', *American Journal of Economics and Sociology* 32, no. 4 (1973): 405–419.

Gabaccia, Donna R., 'Is Everywhere Nowhere? Nomads, Nations and the Immigrant Paradigm of United States History', *The Journal of American History* 86, no. 3 (1999): 1115–1134.

Garvin, James Louis, *The Life of Joseph Chamberlain, vol. I, Chamberlain and Democracy* (London: Macmillan, 1932).

Garvin, Tom, 'Defenders, Ribbonmen and Others: Underground Political Networks in Pre-Famine Ireland', *Past & Present* 96 (1982): 133–155.

Garvin, Tom, 'Republicanism and Democracy in Ireland', *Studies: An Irish Quarterly Review* 102, no. 406 (2013): 181–189.

Gates, Paul W., 'Pre-Henry George Land Warfare in California', *California Historical Society Quarterly* 46, no. 2 (1967): 121–148.

Geiger, George Raymond, *The Philosophy of Henry George* (New York: Macmillan, 1933).

Genovese, Eugene. D., *Roll, Jordan, Roll: The World the Slaves Made* [1972], (New York: Vintage Books, 1976).

Genovese, Eugene. D and Elizabeth Fox-Genovese., 'The Political Crisis of Social History: A Marxian Perspective', *Social History* 10, no. 2 (1976): 205–220.

George, Charles H., 'English Calvinist Opinion on Usury, 1600–1640', *Journal of the History of Ideas* 18, no. 4 (1957): 455–474.

George de Mille, Anna, 'Henry George: Edward McGlynn', *The American Journal of Economics and Sociology* 5, no. 3 (1946): 403–410.

George de Mille, Anna, 'Henry George: The English Land Reform Campaign', *The American Journal of Economics and Sociology* 4, no. 3 (1945): 395–405.

George de Mille, Anna, 'Henry George: The Fight for Irish Freedom', *The American Journal of Economics and Sociology* 3, no. 2 (1944): 251–272.

George de Mille, Anna, 'Henry George: The 'Progress and Poverty' Period', *The American Journal of Economics and Sociology* 2, no. 4 (1943): 543–555.

Gerstle, Gary, *American Crucible: Race and Nation in the Twentieth Century* (Princeton: Princeton University Press, 2001).

Gerstle, Gary, 'The Protean Character of American Liberalism', *The American Historical Review* 99, no. 4 (1994): 1043–1073.

Gilbert, Alan, 'An Ambiguity in Marx's and Engel's Account of Justice and Equality', *American Political Science Review* 76, no. 2 (1982): 328–346.

Glazer, Nathan, and Daniel Patrick Moynihan, *Beyond the Melting Pot: The Negroes, Puerto Ricans, Jews, Italians, and Irish of New York City* (Cambridge, MA: MIT and Harvard University Press, 1963).

Gleason, Philip, 'The Melting Pot: Symbol of Fusion or Confusion', *American Quarterly* 16, no. 1 (1964): 20–46.

Gledhill, John, 'Agrarian Social Movements and Forms of Consciousness', *Bulletin of Latin American Research* 7, no. 2 (1988): 257–276.

Gleeson, David T., 'Smaller Differences: "Scotch Irish" and "Real Irish" in the Nineteenth-Century American South', *New Hibernia Review* 10, no. 2 (2006): 68–91.

Gleeson, David T. (ed.), *The Irish in the Atlantic World* (Columbia, SC: University of South Carolina Press, 2010).

Gleeson, Philip, 'An Immigrant Group's Interest in Progressive Reform: The Case of the German-American Catholics', *The American Historical Review* 73, no. 2 (1967): 367–379.

Glickman, Lawrence A., *A Living Wage: American Workers and the Making of Consumer Society* (Ithaca, NY: Cornell University Press, 1997).

Goldberg, Harvey (ed.), *American Radicals: Some Problems and Personalities* (New York: Monthly Review Press, 1957).

Goldie, Mark, and Robert Wolker (eds.), *The Cambridge History of Eighteenth-Century Political Thought* (Cambridge: Cambridge University Press, 2006).

Goldman, Lawrence (ed.), *The Blind Victorian: Henry Fawcett and British Liberalism* (Cambridge: Cambridge University Press, 1989).

Goldwater, Barry, *The Conscience of a Conservative* (Shepherdsville, KY: Victor Publishing, 1960).

Golway, Terry (ed.), *Catholics in New York: Society, Culture, and Politics, 1808–1946* (New York: Fordham University Press, 2008).

Gordon, Michael A., 'The Labor Boycott in New York City, 1880–1886', *Labor History* 16, no. 2 (1975): 184–229.

Gourevitch, Alex, *From Slavery to the Cooperative Commonwealth: Labor and Republican Liberty in the Nineteenth Century* (Cambridge: Cambridge University Press, 2015).

Grant, Susan-Mary, and Peter J. Parish (eds.), *Legacy of Disunion: The Enduring Significance of the American Civil War* (Baton Rouge: Louisiana State University Press, 2003).

Gray, John, 'After the New Liberalism', *Social Research* 61, no. 3 (1994): 719–735.

Gray, Peter, 'Famine and Land in Ireland and India, 1845–1880: James Caird and the Political Economy of Hunger', *The Historical Journal* 49, no. 1 (2006): 193–215.

Gray, Peter, *Famine, Land and Politics: British Government and Irish Society, 1843–1850* (Dublin: Irish Academic Press, 1999).

Gray, Peter, 'Irish Social Thought and the Relief of Poverty, 1847–80', *Transactions of the Royal Historical Society* 20 (2010): 1–23.

Gray, Peter (ed.), *Victoria's Ireland: Irishness and Britishness, 1837–1901* (Dublin: Four Courts Press, 2003).

Green, James J., 'American Catholics and the Irish Land League, 1879–1882', *The Catholic Historical Review* 35, no. 1 (1949): 19–42.

Guinnane, Timothy W. and Ronald I. Miller, 'Bonds without Bondsmen: Tenant-Right in Nineteenth-Century Ireland', *The Journal of Economic History* 56, no. 1 (1996): 113–142.

Guinnane, Timothy W. and Ronald I. Miller, 'The Limits to Land Reform: The Land Acts in Ireland, 1870–1909', *Economic Development and Cultural Change* 45, no. 3 (1997): 591–612.

Guldi, Jo, 'Global Questions about Rent and the Longue Durée of Urban Power, 1848 to the Present', *Southern Methodist University History Faculty Publications* 13 (2018): 1–27.

Guldi, Jo, *The Long Land War: The Global Struggle for Occupancy Rights* (New Haven, CT: Yale University Press, 2022).

Gutman, Herbert G., 'Work, Culture, and Society in Industrializing America, 1815–1919', *The American Historical Review* 78, no. 3 (1973): 531–588.

Habermas, Jurgen, *The Philosophical Discourses of Modernity* (Cambridge: Polity Press, 1987).

Habermas, Jurgen, *The Structural Transformation of the Public Sphere: An Inquiry into a Category of Bourgeois Society* [1962], (Cambridge: Polity Press, 1989).

Hahn, Frank, and Martin Hollis (eds.), *Philosophy and Economic Theory* (New York: Oxford University Press, 1979).

Halpern, Rick, and Jonathan Morris (eds.), *American Exceptionalism? US Working-Class Formation in an International Context* (London: Macmillan, 1997).

Hamati-Ataya, Inanna, 'The Sociology of Knowledge as Postphilosophical Epistemology: Out of IR's "Socially Constructed" Idealism', *International Studies Review* 20, no. 1 (2018): 3–29.

Hamowy, Ronald, 'Jefferson and the Scottish Enlightenment: A Critique of Garry Wills' *Inventing America: Jefferson's Declaration of Independence*', *The William and Mary Quarterly* 36, no. 4 (1979): 503–523.

Harris, Jose, 'Enterprise and Welfare States: A Comparative Perspective', *Transactions of the Royal Historical Society* 40 (1990): 175–195.

Harrison, Royden, 'The Land and Labour League', *Bulletin of the International Institute of Social History* 8, no. 3 (1953): 169–195.

Harpham, Edward J., 'Liberalism, Civic Humanism, and the Case of Adam Smith', *The American Political Science Review* 78, no. 3 (1984): 764–774.

Hawkins, Richard, 'Liberals, Land and Coercion in the Summer of 1880: The Influence of the Carraroe Ejectments', *Journal of the Galway Archaeological and Historical Society* 34 (1975): 40–57.

Hazelkorn, Ellen, 'Why Is There No Socialism in Ireland? Theoretical Problems of Irish Marxism', *Science and Society* 53, no. 2 (1989): 136–164.

Heath, Andrew, '"The Producers on the One Side, and the Capitalists on the Other": Labor Reform, Slavery, and the Career of a Transatlantic Radical', *American Nineteenth Century History* 13, no. 2 (2012): 199–227.

Heavy, Jerome F., 'Henry George, Émile de Laveleye, and the Issue of Peasant Proprietorship', *The American Journal of Economics and Sociology* 67, no. 1 (2008): 47–60.

Hellman, Rhoda, *Henry George Reconsidered* (New York: Carlton Press, 1987).

Hickman, Mary, J., 'Diaspora Space and National (Re)Formations', *Éire-Ireland* 47, nos. 1–2 (2012): 19–44.

Hilton, Boyd, *The Age of Atonement: The Influence of Evangelicalism on Social and Economic Thought, 1785–1865* (Oxford: Oxford University Press, 1986).

Himmelfarb, Gertrude, 'The Idea of Compassion: The British vs. the French Enlightenment', *The Public Interest* 145 (2001): 3–24.

Himmelfarb, Gertrude, *The New History and the Old* (Cambridge, MA: Belknap Harvard, 1987).

Hobsbawm, Eric J., 'Peasant Land Occupations', *Past & Present* 62 (1974): 120–152.

Hobsbawm, Eric J. (ed.), *Peasants in History: Essays in Honour of Daniel Thorner* (Calcutta: Oxford University Press, 1980).

Hobsbawm, Eric J., *Primitive Rebels: Studies in Archaic Forms of Social Movement in the Nineteenth and Twentieth Centuries* (Manchester: Manchester University Press, 1959).

Hobsbawm, Eric J., *Worlds of Labour: Further Studies in the History of Labour* (London: Weidenfeld and Nicolson, 1984).

Hoerder, Dirk (ed.), *American Labor and Immigration History, 1877–1920s: Recent European Research* (Urbana: University of Illinois Press, 1983).

Hoffman, Tobias, Jörn Müller, and Matthias Perkams (eds.), *Aquinas and the Nicomachean Ethics* (Cambridge: Cambridge University Press, 2013).

Hofstadter, Richard, 'William Graham Sumner, Social Darwinist', *The New England Quarterly* 14, no. 3 (1941): 457–477.

Hollis, Martin, 'Economic Man and Original Sin', *Political Studies* 29, no. 2 (1981): 167–180.

Honohan, Iseult (ed.), *Republicanism in Ireland: Confronting Theories and Traditions* (Manchester: Manchester University Press, 2008).

Hont, Istvan, *Jealousy of Trade: International Competition and the Nation-State in Historical Perspective* (Cambridge, MA: Harvard University Press, 2005).

Hont, Istvan, and Michael Ignatieff (eds.), *Wealth and Virtue: The Shaping of Political Economy in the Scottish Enlightenment* (Cambridge: Cambridge University Press, 1983).

Hook, Sidney, *Reason, Social Myths and Democracy* (New York: John Day, 1940).

Hook, Sidney, 'The Enlightenment and Marxism', *Journal of the History of Ideas* 29, no. 1 (1968): 93–108.

Horn, Pamela L. R., 'The National Agricultural Labourers' Union in Ireland, 1873–9', *Irish Historical Studies* 17, no. 67 (1971): 340–352.

Howe, Anthony, *Free Trade and Liberal England, 1846–1946* (Oxford: Oxford University Press, 1998).

Howell, David, *Land and People in Nineteenth Century Wales* (London: Routledge and Kegan Paul, 1977).

Howell, David, 'The Land Question in Nineteenth-Century Wales, Ireland and Scotland: A Comparative Perspective', *Agricultural History Review* 61, no. 1 (2013): 83–110.

Howkins, Alun, 'From Diggers to Dongas: The Land in English Radicalism, 1649–2000', *History Workshop Journal* 54 (2002): 1–23.

Hudson, Michael, 'Henry George's Political Critics', *American Journal of Economics and Sociology* 67, no. 1 (2008): 1–46.

Hunter, James, 'The Gaelic Connection: The Highlands, Ireland and Nationalism, 1873–1922', *The Scottish Historical Review* 54, no. 158 (1975): 178–204.

Hunter, James, 'The Politics of Highland Land Reform, 1873–1895', *The Scottish Historical Review* 53, no. 155 (1974): 45–68.

Hurvitz, Haggai, 'American Labor Law and the Doctrine of Entrepreneurial Property Rights: Boycotts, Courts, and the Juridical Reorientation of 1886–1895', *Industrial Relations Law Journal* 8, no. 3 (1986): 307–361.

Huston, James L., 'The American Revolutionaries, the Political Economy of Aristocracy, and the American Concept of the Distribution of Wealth, 1765–1900', *The American Historical Review* 98, no. 4 (1993): 1079–1105.

Huston, Reeve, *Land and Freedom: Rural Society, Popular Protest, and Party Politics in Antebellum New York* (New York: Oxford University Press, 2000).

Huston, Reeve, 'The Parties and "The People": The New York Anti-Rent Wars and the Contours of Jacksonian Politics', *Journal of the Early Republic* 20, no. 2 (2000): 241–271.

Iggers, George G., 'Historicism: The History and Meaning of the Term', *Journal of the History of Ideas* 56, no. 1 (1995): 129–152.

Jacob, Margaret, and James Jacob (eds.), *The Origins of Anglo-American Radicalism* (London: George Allen & Unwin, 1984).

Jacobson, Matthew Frye, *Special Sorrows: The Diasporic Imagination of Irish, Polish, and Jewish Immigrants in the United States* (Berkeley: University of California Press, 2002).

Janis, Ely M., *A Greater Ireland: The Land League and Transatlantic Nationalism in Gilded Age America* (Madison: University of Wisconsin Press, 2015).

Janis, Ely M., 'Petticoat Revolutionaries: Gender, Ethnic Nationalism, and the Irish Ladies' Land League in the United States', *Journal of American Ethnic History* 27, no. 2 (2008): 5–27.

Jenkins, William, 'Remapping: "Irish America": Circuits, Places, Performances', *Journal of American Ethnic History* 28, no. 4 (2009): 90–99.

Jones, Emily, 'Conservatism, Edmund Burke, and the Invention of a Political Tradition, c. 1885–1914', *The Historical Journal* 58, no. 4 (2015): 1115–1139.

Jones, David Seth, *Graziers, Land Reform and Political Conflict in Ireland* (Washington, DC: Catholic University of American Press, 1995).

Jones, David Seth, 'Land Reform Legislation and Security of Tenure in Ireland after Independence', *Eire-Ireland* 33, no. 1 (1997): 116–143.

Jones, Peter d'A., 'Henry George and British Socialism', *American Journal of Economics and Sociology* 47, no. 4 (1988): 473–491.

Jones, Peter d'A., *The Christian Socialist Revival, 1877–1914: Religion, Class, and Social Conscience in Late-Victorian England* (Princeton: Princeton University Press, 1968).

Jordan, Donald, 'John O'Connor Power, Charles Stewart Parnell and the Centralization of Popular Politics in Ireland', *Irish Historical Studies* 25, no. 97 (1986): 46–66.

Jordan, Donald, *Land and Popular Politics in Ireland: County Mayo from the Plantation to the Land War* (Cambridge: Cambridge University Press, 1994).

Jordan, Donald, 'The Irish National League and the "Unwritten Law": Rural Protest and Nation-Building in Ireland, 1882–1890', *Past & Present* 158 (1998): 146–171.

Joyce, Patrick, *Visions of the People: Industrial England and the Question of Class, 1848–1914* (Cambridge: Cambridge University Press, 1991).

Kahn, Joel S., 'Peasant Ideologies in the Third World', *Annual Review of Anthropology* 14 (1985): 49–74.

Kalyvas, Andreas and Ira Katznelson, 'The Republic of the Moderns: Paine's and Madison's Novel Liberalism', *Polity* 38, no. 4 (2006): 447–477.

Kane, Anne, '*The Fall of Feudalism in Ireland*: A Guide for Cultural Analysis of the Irish Land War', *New Hibernia Review* 5, no. 1 (2001): 136–141.

Kane, Anne, 'Theorizing Meaning Construction in Social Movements: Symbolic Structures and Interpretation during the Irish Land War, 1879–1882', *Sociological Theory* 15, no. 3 (1997): 249–276.

Kastner, Justin, *Food and Agricultural Security: An Historical, Multidisciplinary Approach* (Santa Barbara: Praeger, 2010).

Katz, Claudio J., 'Thomas Jefferson's Liberal Anticapitalism', *American Journal of Political Science* 47, no. 1 (2003): 1–17.

Katznelson, Ira, and Aristide R. Zolberg (eds.), *Working-Class Formation: Nineteenth-Century Patterns in Western Europe and the United States* (Princeton: Princeton University Press, 1986).

Katznelson, Ira and Gareth Stedman Jones (eds.), *Religion and the Political Imagination* (Cambridge: Cambridge University Press, 2010).

Kaye, Joel, *Economy and Nature in the Fourteenth Century: Money, Market Exchange, and the Emergence of Scientific Thought* (Cambridge: Cambridge University Press, 1998).

Kazin, Michael, *The Populist Persuasion: An American History,* rev. ed. [1995], (Ithaca, NY: Cornell University Press, 2017).

Kelleher, Patricia, 'Class and Catholic Irish Masculinity in Antebellum America: Young Men on the Make in Chicago', *Journal of American Ethnic History* 28, no. 4 (2009): 7–42.

Kelley, Robert, *The Transatlantic Persuasion: The Liberal-Democratic Mind in the Age of Gladstone* (New York: Alfred A. Knopf, 1969).

Kelly, James, *Food Rioting in Ireland in the Eighteenth and Nineteenth Centuries: The 'Moral Economy' and the Irish Crowd* (Dublin: Four Courts Press, 2017).

Kelly, Matthew, 'Irish Nationalist Opinion and the British Empire in the 1850s and 1860s', *Past & Present* 204 (2009): 127–154.

Kelly, Matthew, 'Languages of Radicalism, Race, and Religion in Irish Nationalism: The French Affinity, 1848–1871', *Journal of British Studies* 49, no. 4 (2010): 801–825.

Kelly, Matthew, *The Fenian Ideal and Irish Nationalism, 1882–1916* (Woodbridge: Boydell and Brewer, 2006).

Kenny, Kevin, *Making Sense of the Molly Maguires* (New York: Oxford University Press, 1998).

Kenny, Kevin, *The American Irish: A History* (Harlow: Pearson, 2000).

Kenny, Kevin, 'Twenty Years of Irish American Historiography', *Journal of American Ethnic History* 28, no. 4 (2009): 67–75.

Kerrigan, Colm, 'Irish Temperance and US Anti-Slavery: Father Mathew and the Abolitionists', *History Workshop* 31 (1991): 105–119.

Kibler, Alison, 'The Stage Irishwoman', *Journal of American Ethnic History* 24, no. 3 (2005): 5–30.

Kidd, Colin, 'Gaelic Antiquity and National Identity in Enlightenment Ireland and Scotland', *English Historical Review* 109, no. 434 (1994): 1197–1214.

King, Carla (ed.), *Famine, Land and Culture in Ireland* (Dublin: University College Dublin Press, 2000).

King, Carla, *Michael Davitt* (Dublin: University College Dublin Press, 2009).

Kinzer, Bruce L., 'J. S. Mill and Irish Land: A Reassessment', *The Historical Journal* 27, no. 1 (1984): 111–127.

Kloppenberg, James T., 'The Virtues of Liberalism: Christianity, Republicanism, and Ethics in Early American Political Discourse', *The Journal of American History* 74, no. 1 (1987): 9–33.

Knott, John William, 'Land, Kinship and Identity: The Cultural Roots of Agrarian Agitation in Eighteenth- and Nineteenth-Century Ireland', *Journal of Peasant Studies* 12, no. 1 (1984): 93–108.

Knox, Thomas R., 'Thomas Spence: The Trumpet of Jubilee', *Past & Present* 76 (1977): 75–98.

Knox, William W., 'Religion and the Scottish Labour Movement c.1900–39', *Journal of Contemporary History* 23, no. 4 (1988): 609–630.

Koch, Adrienne, and William Peden (eds.), *The Life and Selected Writings of Thomas Jefferson* (New York: Random House, 1944).

Kolko, Gabriel, 'Intelligence and the Myth of Capitalist Rationality in the United States', *Science and Society* 44, no. 2 (1980): 130–154.

Kolko, Gabriel, *The Triumph of Conservatism: A Reinterpretation of American History, 1900–1916* (New York: The Free Press, 1963).

Koselleck, Reinhart, 'Social History and Conceptual History', *Politics, Culture, and Society* 2, no. 3 (1989): 308–325.

Krall, Lisi, 'Thomas Jefferson's Agrarian Vision and the Changing Nature of Property', *Journal of Economic Issues* 36, no. 1 (2002): 131–150.

Krantz, Frederick (ed.), *History from Below: Studies in Popular Protest and Popular Ideology in Honour of George Rudé* (Montréal: Concordia University Press, 1985).

Lacey, Michael J., and Mary O. Furner (eds.), *The state and social investigation in Britain and the United States* (Cambridge: Cambridge University Press, 1993).

Lamb, Robert, 'Liberty, Equality, and the Boundaries of Ownership: Thomas Paine's Theory of Property Rights', *The Review of Politics* 72, no. 3 (2010): 438–511.

Lane, Fintan, 'P. F. Johnson, Nationalism, and Irish Rural Labourers, 1869–82', *Irish Historical Studies* 33, no. 130 (2002): 191–208.

Lane, Fintan, *The Origins of Modern Irish Socialism, 1881–1896* (Cork: Cork University Press, 1997).

Lane, Fintan, 'William Thompson, Bankruptcy and the West Cork Estate, 1808–34', *Irish Historical Studies* 38, no. 153 (2014): 24–39.

Lane, Fintan, and Andrew G. Newby (eds.), *Michael Davitt: New Perspectives* (Dublin: Irish Academic Press, 2009).

Lane, Fintan, and Donal O'Drisceoil (eds.), *Politics and the Irish Working Class, 1830–1945* (Basingstoke: Palgrave Macmillan, 2005).

Lane, Pádraig G., 'Agricultural Labourers and Rural Violence, 1850–1914', *Studia Hibernica* 27 (1993): 77–87.

Lane, Pádraig G., 'The Irish Agricultural Labourer in Folklore and Fiction', *Saothar: Journal of Irish Labour History* 28 (2003): 79–89.

Lane, Roger, 'James Jeffrey Roche and the Boston Pilot', *The New England Quarterly* 33, no. 3 (1960): 341–363.

Larkin, Emmet, 'Socialism and Catholicism in Ireland', *Studies: An Irish Quarterly Review* 74, no. 293 (1985): 66–92.

Larkin, Emmet, *The Roman Catholic Church and the Creation of the Modern Irish State 1878–1886* (Philadelphia: American Philosophical Society, 1975).

Laslett, John H. M., 'Haymarket, Henry George, and the Labor Upsurge in Britain and America during the Late 1880s', *International Labor and Working Class History* 29 (1986): 68–82.

Laslett, Peter and James Fishkin (eds.), *Philosophy, Politics and Society* (Oxford: Oxford University Press, 1979).

Lause, Mark A., *Free Labor: The Civil War and the Making of an American Working Class* (Urbana: University of Illinois Press, 2015).

Lawrence, Elwood P., *Henry George in the British Isles* (East Lansing: Michigan State University Press, 1957).

Lawrence, Elwood P., 'Henry George's Analysis of British Social Conditions', *American Journal of Economics and Sociology* 12, no. 3 (1953): 267–287.

Lawrence, Elwood P., 'Henry George's Oxford Speech', *California Historical Society Quarterly* 30, no. 2 (1951): 117–123.

Lawrence, Jon, 'Popular Radicalism and the Socialist Revival in Britain', *Journal of British Studies* 31, no. 2 (1992): 163–186.

Lee, Joseph J., *The Modernisation of Irish Society, 1848–1918* (Dublin: Gill and Macmillan, 1973).

Lindsay, Peter, 'The 'Disembodied Self' in Political Theory: The Communitarians, Macpherson and Marx', *Philosophy and Social Criticism* 28, no. 2 (2002): 191–211.

Lipkes, Jeff, *Politics, Religion and Classical Political Economy in Britain: John Stuart Mill and His Followers* (Basingstoke: Palgrave, 1999).

Lloyd, David, 'The Clachan and the Chartists: Irish Models for Fergus O'Connor's Land Plan', *Irish Review* 47 (2013): 28–43.

Lobban, Michael, 'Blackstone and the Science of Law', *The Historical Journal* 30, no. 2 (1987): 311–335.

Lough, Alex Wagner, 'Henry George, Frederick Jackson Turner, and the "Closing" of the American Frontier', *California History* 89, no. 2 (2012): 4–23.

Lucey, Donnacha Seán, *Land, Popular Politics and Agrarian Violence in Ireland: The Case of County Kerry, 1872–86* (Dublin: University College Dublin Press, 2011).

Luminiello, Rose, 'Ireland Is Not Going to Take Her Orders from Rome': Leo XIII, Thomism, and the Irish Political Imagination', *History of European Ideas* 46, no. 7 (2020): 964–981.

Lustig, B. Andrew, 'Natural Law, Property, and Justice: The General Justification of Property in John Locke', *The Journal of Religious Ethics* 19, no. 1 (1991): 119–149.

Lutz, Donald S., 'The Relative Influence of European Writers on Late Eighteenth-Century American Political Thought', *The American Political Science Review* 78, no. 1 (1984): 189–197.

Lynch, Niamh, 'Defining Irish Nationalist Anti-Imperialism: Thomas Davis and John Mitchel', *Éire-Ireland* 42, nos. 1–2 (2007): 82–107.

Lynch, Timothy G., '"A Kindred and Congenial Element": Irish-American Nationalism's Embrace of Republican Rhetoric', *New Hibernia Review* 13, no. 2 (2009): 77–91.

Lyons, Francis S. L., *Charles Stewart Parnell* (Dublin: Gill and Macmillan, 1977).

MacColl, Allan W., *Land, Faith and the Crofting Community: Christianity and Social Criticism in the Highlands of Scotland, 1843–93* (Edinburgh: Edinburgh University Press, 2006).

MacDonagh, Oliver, *States of Mind: Two Centuries of Anglo-Irish Conflict, 1780–1980* (London: Pimlico, 1983).

MacDowell, Michael A., 'Malthus and George on the Irish Question: The Single Tax, Empiricism and Other Positions Shared by the 19th Century Economists', *The American Journal of Economics and Sociology* 36, no. 4 (1977): 401–416.

MacIntyre, Alasdair, *After Virtue: A Study in Moral Theory* (London: Duckworth, 1981).

MacIntyre, Alasdair, *Dependent Rational Animals* (London: Duckworth, 1999).

MacIntyre, Alasdair, *The Tasks of Philosophy: Selected Essays*, vol. 1 (Cambridge: Cambridge University Press, 2006).

MacMahon, Joseph A., 'The Catholic Clergy and the Social Question in Ireland, 1891–1916', *Studies: An Irish Quarterly Review* 70, no. 280 (1981): 263–288.

Madden, Edward H., 'Victor Cousin and the Commonsense Tradition', *History of Philosophy Quarterly* 1, no. 1 (1984): 93–109.

Mailer, Gideon, 'Nehemias (Scotus) Americanus: Enlightenment and Religion between Scotland and America', *The Historical Journal* 54, no. 1 (2011): 241–264.

Maloney, John, *Marshall, Orthodoxy and the Professionalisation of Economics* (Cambridge: Cambridge University Press, 1985).

Marley, Laurence, *Michael Davitt: Freelance Radical and Frondeur* (Dublin: Four Courts Press, 2007).

Marsh, Jan, *Back to the Land: The Pastoral Impulse in Victorian England from 1880–1914* (London: Quarter Books, 1982).

Martin, Ged, 'Parnell at Cambridge: The Education of an Irish Nationalist', *Irish Historical Studies* 19, no. 73 (1974): 72–82.

Mason, John W., 'Political Economy and the Response to Socialism in Britain, 1870–1914', *The Historical Journal* 23, no. 3 (1980): 565–587.

Mason, John W., 'The Duke of Argyll and the Land Question in Late Nineteenth-Century Britain', *Victorian Studies* 21, no. 2 (1978): 149–170.

Maurer, Sara L., *The Dispossessed State: Narratives of Ownership in 19th Century Britain and Ireland* (Baltimore, MD: Johns Hopkins University Press, 2012).

Merrill, Michael, 'Cash Is Good to Eat: Self-Sufficiency and Exchange in the Rural Economy of the United States', *Radical History Review* 16 (1977): 42–71.

McAleer, Margaret H., 'In Defense of Civil Society: Irish Radicals in Philadelphia during the 1790s', *Early American Studies: An Interdisciplinary Journal* 1, no. 1 (2003): 176–197.

McBride, Ian (ed.), *History and Memory in Modern Ireland* (Cambridge: Cambridge University Press, 2001).

McBride, Ian, 'The Edge of Enlightenment: Ireland and Scotland in the Eighteenth Century', *Modern Intellectual History* 10, no. 1 (2013): 135–151.

McBride, Lawrence W., 'Nation and Narration in Michael Davitt's The Fall of Feudalism in Ireland', *New Hibernia Review* 5, no. 1 (2001): 131–135.

McBride, Terence, 'John Ferguson, Michael Davitt and Henry George – Land for the People', *Irish Studies Review* 14, no. 4 (2006): 421–430.

McBride, Terence, 'The Secular and the Radical in Irish Associational Culture of Mid-Victorian Glasgow', *Immigrants & Minorities* 28, no. 1 (2010): 31–41.

McCaffrey, Lawrence, 'Ireland and Irish-America: Connections and Disconnections', *U.S. Catholic Historian* 22, no. 3 (2004): 1–18.

McCaffrey, Lawrence, 'Irish Nationalism and Irish Catholicism: A Study in Cultural Identity', *Church History* 42, no. 4 (1973): 524–534.

McCaffrey, Lawrence, 'Irish Textures in American Catholicism', *The Catholic Historical Review* 78, no. 1 (1992): 1–18.

McCaffrey, Peter, *When Bosses Ruled Philadelphia: The Emergence of the Republican Machine, 1867–1933* (University Park: Pennsylvania State University Press, 1993).

McCarthy, Conor, 'Edward Said and Irish Criticism', *Éire-Ireland* 42, nos. 1–2 (2007): 311–335.

McConville, Sean, *Irish Political Prisoners, 1848–1922: Theatres of War* (London: Routledge, 2003).

McFarland, Elaine W., *John Ferguson, 1836–1906: Irish Issues in Scottish Politics* (East Linton: Tuckwell Press, 2003).

McGarry, Feargal and James McConnel (eds.), *The Black Hand of Republicanism: Fenianism in Modern Ireland* (Dublin: Irish Academic Press, 2008).

McGovern, Bryan, 'John Mitchel: Ecumenical Nationalist in the Old South', *New Hibernia Review* 5, no. 2 (2001): 99–110.

McGreevy, John T., *Catholicism and American Freedom: A History* (New York: Norton, 2003).

McMahon, Cian T., 'Caricaturing Race and Nation in the Irish American Press, 1870–1880: A Transnational Perspective', *Journal of American Ethnic History* 33, no. 2 (2014): 33–56.

McQuillan, Peter, *Native and Natural: Aspects of the Concepts of 'Right' and 'Freedom' in Irish* (Cork: Cork University Press, 2004).

Meagher, Timothy J., 'From the World to the Village and the Beginning to the End and After: Research Opportunities in Irish American History', *Journal of American Ethnic History* 28, no. 4 (2009): 118–135.

Meagher, Timothy J., *Inventing Irish America: Generation, Class, and Ethnic Identity in a New England City, 1880–1928* (Notre Dame, IN: University of Notre Dame Press, 2001).

Mehta, Uday Singh, *Liberalism and Empire: A Study in Nineteenth-Century British Liberal Thought* (Chicago: University of Chicago Press, 1999).

Meiksins Wood, Ellen, *Peasant, Citizen & Slave: The Foundations of Athenian Democracy* (London: Verso, 1988).

Miller, Edward H., 'They Vote Only for the Spoils: Massachusetts Reformers, Suffrage Restriction, and the 1884 Civil Service Law', *The Journal of the Gilded Age and Progressive Era* 8, no. 3 (2009): 341–363.

Miller, Fred D., *Nature, Justice, and Rights in Aristotle's Politics* (Oxford: Clarendon Press, 1995).

Miller, James J., 'Legal and Economic History of the Secondary Boycott' *Labor Law Journal* 12, no. 8 (1961): 751–59.

Miller, Kerby, *Emigrants and Exiles: Ireland and the Irish Exodus to North America* (New York: Oxford University Press, 1985).

Miller, Kerby, *Ireland and Irish America: Culture, Class, and Transatlantic Migration* (Dublin: Field Day, 2008).

Mirowski, Philip, 'Macroeconomic Instability and the "Natural" Processes in Early Neoclassical Economics', *Journal of Economic History* 44, no. 2 (1984).

Mirowski, Philip, 'Physics and the "Marginalist Revolution"', *Cambridge Journal of Economics* 8, no. 4 (1984): 361–379.

Mishra, Kaushal Kishore, 'Problem of Sovereignty in Gandhian Thought', *The Indian Journal of Political Science* 66, no. 3 (2005): 515–530.

Mitchell, Martin J. (ed.), *New Perspectives on the Irish in Scotland* (Edinburgh: John Donald, 2008).

Moloney, Deirdre M., 'Land League Activism in Transnational Perspective', *U.S. Catholic Historian* 22, no. 3 (2004): 61–74.

Moloney, Deirdre M., 'Who's Irish? Ethnic Identity and Recent Trends in Irish American History', *Journal of American Ethnic History* 28, no. 4 (2009): 100–109.

Montgomery, David, *Beyond Equality: Labor and the Radical Republicans, 1862–1872* (Urbana: University of Illinois Press, 1981).

Montgomery, David, *Citizen Worker: The Experience of Workers in the United States with Democracy and the Free Market during the Nineteenth Century* (Cambridge: Cambridge University Press, 1993).

Moody, Theodore W., *Davitt and Irish Revolution, 1846–82* (Oxford: Oxford University Press, 1982).

Moody, Theodore W., 'Michael Davitt and the British Labour Movement, 1882–1906', *Transactions of the Royal Historical Society* 3 (1953): 53–7.

Moran, Gerard, *A Radical Priest in Mayo: Fr. Patrick Lavelle: The Rise and Fall of an Irish Nationalist, 1825–1886* (Dublin: Four Courts Press, 1994).

Moran, Gerard, 'James Daly and the Rise and Fall of the Land League in the West of Ireland, 1879–82', *Irish Historical Studies* 29, no. 114 (1994): 189–207.

Moran, Gerard, '"Near Famine": The Roman Catholic Church and the Subsistence Crisis of 1879–82', *Studia Hibernica* 32 (2002): 155–77.

Moran, Gerard, 'The Land War, Urban Destitution and Town Tenant Protest, 1879–1882', *Saothar: Journal of Irish Labour Studies* 20 (1995): 17–30.

Moran, Gerard, 'The Origins and Development of Boycotting', *Journal of the Galway Archaeological Society* 40 (1985/1986): 49–64.

Morris, A. J. Anthony (ed.), *Edwardian Radicalism, 1900–1914: Some Aspects of British Radicalism* (London: Routledge, 1974).

Moss, Bernard H., 'Republican Socialism and the Making of the Working Class in Britain, France, and the United States: A Critique of Thompsonian Culturalism', *Comparative Studies in Society and History* 35, no. 2 (1993): 390–413.

Moyn, Samuel, *Not Enough – Human Rights in an Unequal World* (Cambridge, MA: Harvard University Press, 2018).

Moyn, Samuel, and Darrin M. McMahon (eds.), *Rethinking Modern European Intellectual History* (New York: Oxford University Press, 2014).

Murray, A. C., 'Agrarian Violence and Nationalism in Nineteenth-Century Ireland: The Myth of Ribbonism', *Irish Economic and Social History* 13 (1986): 56–73.

Muthu, Sankar (ed.), *Empire and Modern Political Thought* (Cambridge: Cambridge University Press, 2012).

Nadon, Christopher, 'Aristotle and the Republican Paradigm: A Reconsideration of Pocock's "Machiavellian Moment"', *The Review of Politics* 58, no. 4 (1996): 677–698.

Newby, Andrew G., 'Edward McHugh, the National Land League of Great Britain and the "Crofters' War", 1879–1882', *Scottish Historical Review* 82, no. 213 (2003): 74–91.

Newby, Andrew G., *Ireland, Radicalism and the Scottish Highlands, c. 1870–1912* (Edinburgh: Edinburgh University Press, 2007).

Newby, Andrew G., '"Scotia Major and Scotia Minor": Ireland and the Birth of the Scottish Land Agitation, 1878–82', *Irish Economic and Social History* 31 (2004): 23–40.

Newton, Bernard, 'Henry George and Henry M. Hyndman: The Forging of an Untenable Alliance', *American Journal of Economics and Sociology* 35, no. 3 (1976): 311–323.

Ní Chuanchâin, Deirdre, *Utopianism in Eighteenth-Century Ireland* (Cork: Cork University Press, 2016).

Nicklason, Fred, 'Henry George: Social Gospeller', *American Quarterly* 22, no. 3 (1970): 649–664.

Nuesse, C. Joseph, 'Henry George and "Rerum Novarum": Evidence Is Scant that American Economist Was a Target of Leo XIII's Classic Encyclical', *American Journal of Economics and Sociology* 44, no. 2 (1985): 241–254.

Nussbaum, Martha, 'Human Functioning and Social Justice: In Defence of Aristotelian Essentialism', *Political Theory* 20, no. 2 (1992): 202–246.

O'Brien, William, and Desmond Ryan (eds.), *Devoy's Post Bag, 1871–1928*, vol. II (Dublin: Fallon, 1948).

O'Callaghan, Margaret, *British High Politics and a Nationalist Ireland: Criminality, Land and the Law under Forster and Balfour* (Cork: Cork University Press, 1994).

Ó Catháin, Máirtín, *Irish Republicanism in Scotland, 1858–1916: Fenians in Exile* (Dublin: Irish Academic Press, 2007).

Ó Catháin, Máirtín, 'Michael Davitt in Scotland', *Saothar: Journal of Irish Labour Studies* 25 (2000): 19–26.

O'Connor, Emmet, *A Labour History of Ireland, 1824–2000* (Dublin: University College Dublin Press, 2011).

O'Connor, Thomas, *The Boston Irish: A Political History* (Boston: Back Bay Books, 1995).

O'Day, Alan, 'Imagined Irish Communities: Networks of Social Communication of the Irish Diaspora in the United States and Britain in the Late Nineteenth and Early Twentieth Centuries', *Immigrants & Minorities* 23, nos. 2–3 (2005): 399–424.

O'Donnell, Edward T., *Henry George and the Crisis of Inequality: Progress and Poverty in the Gilded Age* (New York: Columbia University Press, 2015).

O'Donnell, Edward T., '"Though Not an Irishman": Henry George and the American Irish', *American Journal of Economics and Sociology* 56, no. 4 (1997): 407–419.

Offer, Avery, *Property and Politics, 1870–1914: Landowners, Law, Ideology and Urban Development in England* (Cambridge: Cambridge University Press, 1981).

O'Farrell, Patrick, *England and Ireland since 1800* (Oxford: Oxford University Press, 1975).

O'Neill, Thomas P., 'From Famine to Near Famine, 1845–1879', *Studia Hibernica* 1 (1961): 161–171.

O'Neill, Thomas P., 'The Irish Land Question, 1830–1850', *Studies: An Irish Quarterly Review* 44, no. 175 (1955): 325–336.

Oestreicher, Richard, 'Urban Working-Class Political Behaviour and Theories of American Electoral Politics, 1870–1940', *Journal of American History* 74, no. 4 (1988): 1257–1286.

Orren, Karen, *Belated Feudalism: Labor, the Law, and Liberal Development in the United States* (Cambridge: Cambridge University Press, 1991).

Orridge, Andrew W., 'Who Supported the Land War: An Aggregate Data Analysis of Irish Discontent, 1879–82', *Economic and Social Review* 12, no. 3 (1981): 214–215.

Ó. Síocháin, Séamas. (ed.), *Social Thought on Ireland in the Nineteenth Century* (Dublin: University College Dublin Press, 2009).

Osofsky, Gilbert, 'Abolitionists, Irish Immigrants, and the Dilemmas of Romantic Nationalism', *The American Historical Review* 80, no. 4 (1975): 889–912.

Packer, Ian, *Lloyd George, Liberalism and the Land: The Land Issue and Party Politics in England, 1906–1914* (Woodbridge: Boydell and Brewer, 2001).

Pagden, Anthony (ed.), *Languages of Political Theory in Early Modern Europe* (Cambridge: Cambridge University Press, 1987).

Palen, Marc-William, *The 'Conspiracy' of Free Trade: The Anglo-American Struggle over Empire and Economic Globalisation, 1846–1896* (Cambridge: Cambridge University Press, 2016).

Palmer, Norman Dunbar, *The Irish Land League Crisis* (New Haven: Yale University Press, 1940).

Parel, Anthony, and Thomas Flanagan (eds.), *Theories of Property: Aristotle to the Present* (Waterloo: Wilfred Laurier Press, 1979).

Parfitt, Richard, *Musical Culture and the Spirit of Irish Nationalism, 1848–1972* (London: Routledge, 2020).

Parssinen, Terry Mitchell., 'Thomas Spence and the Origins of English Land Nationalization', *Journal of the History of Ideas* 34, no. 1 (1973): 135–141.

Peatling, Gary K., 'Who Fears to Speak of Politics? John Kells Ingram and Hypothetical Nationalism', *Irish Historical Studies* 31, no. 122 (1998): 202–221.

Pelling, Henry, 'The Knights of Labor in Britain, 1880–1901', *The Economic History Review* 9, no. 2 (1956): 313–331.

Pessen, Edward, *Most Uncommon Jacksonians: The Radical Leaders of the Early Labor Movement* (Albany: State University of New York Press, 1967).

Pessen, Edward, 'Thomas Skidmore, Agrarian Reformer in the Early American Labor Movement', *New York History* 35, no. 3 (1954): 280–296.

Pessen, Edward, 'We Are All Jeffersonians, We Are All Jacksonians: or a Pox on Stultifying Periodizations', *Journal of the Early Republic* 1, no. 1 (1981): 1–26.

Pettit, Philip, 'The Tree of Liberty: Republicanism: American, French, and Irish', *Field Day Review* 1 (2005): 29–42.

Phillips-Fein, Kim, *Invisible Hands: The Making of the Conservative Movement from the New Deal to Reagan* (New York: W. W. Norton, 2009).

Philpin, Charles H. E., *Nationalism and Popular Protest in Ireland* (Cambridge: Cambridge University Press, 1987).

Pitts, Jennifer, *A Turn to Empire: The Rise of Imperial Liberalism in Britain and France* (Princeton: Princeton University Press, 2005).

Plowright, John, 'Political Economy and Christian Polity: The Influence of Henry George in England Reassessed', *Victorian Studies* 30, no. 2 (1987): 235–252.

Pocock, John G. A., 'Between Gog and Magog: The Republican Thesis and the *Ideologia Americana*', *Journal of the History of Ideas* 48, no. 2 (1987): 325–346.

Pocock, John G. A., 'Historiography and Enlightenment: A View of Their History', *Modern Intellectual History* 5, no. 1 (2008): 83–96.

Pocock, John G. A., *Political Thought and History: Essays on Theory and Method* (Cambridge: Cambridge University Press, 2009).

Pocock, John G. A., *The Machiavellian Moment: Florentine Political Thought and the Atlantic Republican Tradition* (Princeton: Princeton University Press, 1975).

Pocock, John G. A., 'The Reconstruction of Discourse: Towards the Historiography of Political Thought', *Modern Language Notes* 96, no. 5 (1981): 959–980.

Polanyi, Karl, *The Great Transformation: The Political and Economic Origins of Our Time* [1944], (Boston: Beacon Press, 1957).

Pole, Adam, 'Sheriffs' Sales during the Land War, 1879–82', *Irish Historical Studies* 34, no. 136 (2005): 386–402.

Post, David M., 'Jeffersonian Revisions of Locke, Education, Property-Rights, and Liberty', *Journal of the History of Ideas* 47, no. 1 (1986): 147–157.

Purdy, Jedediah, *After Nature: A Politics for the Anthropocene* (Cambridge, MA: Harvard University Press, 2015).

Quinn, James, 'Southern Citizen: John Mitchel, the Confederacy and Slavery', *History Ireland* 15, no. 3 (2007): 30–35.

Rafferty, Oliver, 'Fenianism in North America in the 1860s: The Problems for Church and State', *History* 84, no. 274 (1999): 257–277.

Readman, Paul, *Land and Nation in England: Patriotism, National Identity, and the Politics of Land, 1880–1914* (Woodbridge: The Boydell Press, 2008).

Reid, Colin, 'Democracy, Sovereignty and Unionist Political Thought during the Revolutionary Period in Ireland, c. 1912–22', *Transactions of the Royal Historical Society* 27 (2017): 211–232.

Ricci, David M., 'Fabian Socialism: A Theory of Rent as Exploitation', *Journal of British Studies* 9, no. 1 (1969): 105–121.

Rich, Paul B., 'Social Darwinism, Anthropology and English Perspectives of the Irish, 1867–1900', *History of European Ideas* 19, nos. 4–6 (1994): 777–785.

Robertson, John, 'The Enlightenment above National Context: Political Economy in Eighteenth-Century Scotland and Naples', *The Historical Journal* 40, no. 3 (1997): 667–697.

Robertson, John, *The Enlightenment, the Public Sphere and Political Economy, C. Th. Dimaras Annual Lecture, 2010* (Athens: National Hellenic Research Foundation, 2011).

Rodechko, James P., 'An Irish-American Journalist and Catholicism: Patrick Ford of the Irish World', *Church History* 39, no. 4 (1970): 524–540.

Rodechko, James P., *Patrick Ford and His Search for America: A Case Study of Irish-American Journalism, 1870–1913* [1968], (New York: Arno Press, 1976).

Rodden, John, '"The Lever Must Be Applied in Ireland": Marx, Engels, and the Irish Question', *The Review of Politics* 70, no. 4 (2008): 609–640.

Rodgers, Daniel T., *Age of Fracture* (Cambridge, MA: Harvard University Press, 2011).

Rodgers, Daniel T., *Atlantic Crossings: Social Politics in a Progressive Age* (Cambridge, MA: Harvard University Press, 1998).

Rodgers, Daniel T., *Contested Truths: Keywords in American Politics since Independence* (Cambridge, MA: Harvard University Press, 1987).

Rodgers, Daniel T., 'Republicanism: The Career of a Concept', *The Journal of American History* 79, no. 1 (1992): 11–38.

Rogan, Tim, *The Moral Economists: R. H. Tawney, Karl Polanyi, E. P. Thompson, and the Critique of Capitalism* (Princeton: Princeton University Press, 2017).

Ross, Dorothy, 'Historical Consciousness in Nineteenth-Century America', *The American Historical Review* 89, no. 4 (1984): 909–928.

Ross, Dorothy, 'Socialism and American Liberalism: Academic Social Thought in the 1880s', *Perspectives in American History* 11 (1978): 7–79.

Ross, Dorothy, 'The Many Lives of Institutionalism in American Social Science', *Polity* 28, no. 1 (1995): 117–123.

Ross, Steven J., 'The Culture of Political Economy: Henry George and the American Working Class', *Southern California Quarterly* 65, no. 2 (1983): 145–166.

Rothschild, Emma, 'Adam Smith and Conservative Economics', *The Economic History Review* 45, no. 1 (1992): 74–96.

Rothschild, Emma, *Economic Sentiments: Adam Smith, Condorcet, and the Enlightenment* (Cambridge, MA: Harvard University Press, 2002).

Rowe, Adam, 'The New Creed of the Nation: Charles Eliot Norton, E. L. Godkin, and the Meaning of Freedom in the Civil War Era', *Journal of American Studies* 54, no. 4 (2020): 671–705.

Runciman, David, *Political Hypocrisy: The Mask of Power, from Hobbes to Orwell and Beyond* (Princeton: Princeton University Press, 2008).

Sabine, George H., *A History of Political Theory*, 4th ed. [1937], (London: Harcourt Brace, 1973).

Samuel, Raphael (ed.), *People's History and Socialist Theory* (London: Routledge and Kegan Paul, 1981).

Sandel, Michael J., *Liberalism and the Limits of Justice,* 2nd ed. [1982], (Cambridge: Cambridge University Press, 1998).

Saxton, Alexander, *The Rise and Fall of the White Republic: Class Politics and Mass Culture in Nineteenth-Century America* (London: Verso, 1990).

Schatzki, Theodore R., Karin Knorr Cetina, and Eike von Savigny (eds.), *The Practice Turn in Contemporary Theory* (London: Routledge, 2000).

Schiffrin, Harold, and Pow-Key Sohn, 'Henry George on Two Continents: A Comparative Study in the Diffusion of Ideas', *Comparative Studies in Society and History* 2, no. 1 (1959): 85–109.

Schmidt, James, 'What Enlightenment Was, What It Still Might Be, and Why Kant May Have Been Right after All', *American Behavioural Scientist* 49, no. 5 (2006): 647–663.

Schneirov, Richard, 'Thoughts on Periodizing the Gilded Age: Capital Accumulation, Society, and Politics, 1873–1898', *The Journal of the Gilded Age and Progressive Era* 5, no. 3 (2006): 189–224.

Schneirov, Richard, Shelton Stromquist, and Nick Salvatore (eds.), *The Pullman Strike and the Crisis of the 1890s* (Urbana: University of Illinois Press, 1999).

Schrover, Marlou and Eileen Yeo (eds.), *Gender, Migration and the Public Sphere, 1850–2005* (New York: Taylor and Francis, 2010).

Scott, James C., *The Moral Economy of the Peasant: Peasant Rebellion and Subsistence in Southeast Asia* (New Haven: Yale University Press, 1975).

Scott, James C., *Weapons of the Weak: Everyday Forms of Peasant Resistance* (New Haven: Yale University Press, 1986).

Seretan, Glen L., 'Daniel De Leon as American', *The Wisconsin Magazine of History* 61, no. 3 (1978): 210–223.

Sewell, Mike J., 'Rebels or Revolutionaries? Irish-American Nationalism and American Diplomacy, 1865–1885', *The Historical Journal* 29, no. 3 (1986): 723–733.

Shelly, Thomas. J., 'Catholic Greenwich Village: Ethnic Geography and Religious Identity in New York City, 1880–1930', *The Catholic Historical Review* 89, no. 1 (2003): 60–84.

Sheps, Arthur, 'The American Revolution and the Transformation of English Republicanism', *Historical Reflections* 2, no. 1 (1975): 3–28.

Sigmund, Paul, *Natural Law in Political Thought* (Cambridge, MA: Winthrop, 1971).

Sigmund, Paul, 'The Catholic Tradition and Modern Democracy', *The Review of Politics* 49, no. 4 (1987): 530–548.

Silagi, Michael, 'Henry George and Europe: As Dissident Economist and Path-Breaking Philosopher, He Was a Catalyst for British Social Reform', *American Journal of Economics and Sociology* 48, no. 1 (1989): 113–122.

Silagi, Michael, 'Henry George and Europe: Ireland, the First Target of His Efforts to Spread His Doctrines Internationally, Disappointed Him', *American Journal of Economics and Sociology* 46, no. 4 (1987): 495–501.

Silverman, Marilyn, *An Irish Working Class: Explorations in Political Economy and Hegemony, 1800–1950* (Toronto: University of Toronto Press, 2001).

Sim, David, *A Union Forever: The Irish Question and U.S. Foreign Relations in the Victorian Age* (Ithaca, NY: Cornell University Press, 2013).

Skinner, Andrew S., 'Pufendorf, Hutcheson and Adam Smith: Some Principles of Political Economy', *Scottish Journal of Political Economy* 42, no. 2 (1995): 165–182.

Skinner, Quentin, *Liberty before Liberalism* (Cambridge: Cambridge University Press, 1998).

Skinner, Quentin, *The Foundations of Modern Political Thought: Volume II, The Age of Reformation* (Cambridge: Cambridge University Press, 1979).

Skinner, Quentin, *Visions of Politics: Volume 1, Regarding Method* (Cambridge: Cambridge University Press, 2002).

Sklansky, Jeffrey, *The Soul's Economy: Market Society and Selfhood in American Thought, 1820–1920* (Chapel Hill: University of North Carolina Press, 2002).

Skok, Deborah S., 'Organized Almsgiving: Scientific Charity and the Society of St. Vincent de Paul in Chicago, 1871–1918', *U.S. Catholic Historian* 16, no. 4 (1998): 19–35.

Small, Stephen, *Political Thought in Ireland 1776–1798: Republicanism, Patriotism, and Radicalism* (Oxford: Oxford University Press, 2002).

Smith, Craig Bruce, 'Claiming the Centennial: The American Revolution's Blood and Spirit in Boston, 1870–1876', *Massachusetts Historical Review* 15 (2013): 7–53.

Smyth, Jim, 'Robert Emmet's Copy of John Locke's "Two Treatises of Government"', *History Ireland* 11, no. 3 (2003): 26–28.

Smyth, Jim, 'Wolfe Tone's Library: The United Irishmen and "Enlightenment"', *Eighteenth-Century Studies* 45, no. 3 (2012): 423–435.

Snay, Mitchell, *Fenians, Freedmen, and Southern Whites: Race and Nationality in the Era of Reconstruction* (Baton Rouge: Louisiana State University Press, 2007).

Solow, Barbara L., *The Land Question and the Irish Economy, 1870–1903* (Cambridge, MA: Harvard University Press, 1971).

Soper, Kate, 'The Dialectics of Progress: Irish "Belatedness" and the Politics of Prosperity', *Ephemera: Theory and Politics in Organization* 13, no. 2 (2013): 249–267.

Sowell, Thomas, *Classical Economics Reconsidered* (Princeton: Princeton University Press, 1974).

Sproat, John G., *"The Best Men": Liberal Reformers in the Gilded Age* (New York: Oxford University Press, 1968).

Stabile, Donald R., 'Adam Smith and the Natural Wage: Sympathy, Subsistence and Social Distance' *Review of Social Economy* 55, no. 3 (1997): 292–311.

Stack, David, 'The Death of John Stuart Mill', *The Historical Journal* 54, no. 1 (2011): 167–190.

Steele, E. David, *Irish Land and British Politics: Tenant-Right and Nationality, 1865–1870* (Cambridge: Cambridge University Press, 1974).

Steele, E. David, 'J.S. Mill and the Irish Question: The Principles of Political Economy, 1848–1865', *The Historical Journal* 13, no. 2 (1970): 216–236.

Stedman Jones, Gareth, *An End to Poverty? A Historical Debate* (London: Profile Books, 2004).

Stedman Jones, Gareth, *Languages of Class: Studies in English Working Class History, 1832–1982* (Cambridge: Cambridge University Press, 1983).

Stedman Jones, Gareth, and Gregory Claeys (eds.), *The Cambridge History of Nineteenth-Century Political Thought* (Cambridge: Cambridge University Press, 2011).

Steinfels, Peter, 'From Adam Smith to the American Catholic Bishops: Debating Visions of Economic Life', *Journal of Business Ethics* 7, no. 6 (1988): 405–411.

Stone, Lawrence (ed.), *The University in Society, volume II: Europe, Scotland, and the United States from the 16th to the 20th Century* (Princeton: Princeton University Press, 1974).

Stuart, Robert, '"Jesus the *Sans-Culotte*": Marxism and Religion during the French *Fin de Siecle*', *The Historical Journal* 42, no. 3 (1999): 705–727.

Swift, Roger, 'Thomas Carlyle, "Chartism", and the Irish in Early Victorian England', *Victorian Literature and Culture* 29, no. 1 (2001): 67–83.

Taylor, Anthony, '"The Old Chartist": Radical Veterans on the Late Nineteenth- and Early Twentieth-Century Political Platform', *History* 95, no. 4 (2010): 458–476.

Taylor, Leonard Francis, *Catholic Cosmopolitanism and Human Rights* (Cambridge: Cambridge University Press, 2020).

Taylor, Michael, *Community, Anarchy and Liberty* (Cambridge: Cambridge University Press, 1982).

Taylor, Michael, *Herbert Spencer and the Limits of the State: The Late Nineteenth-Century Debate between Individualism and Collectivism* (Bristol: Thoemmes Press, 1996).

TeBrake, Janet K., 'Irish Peasant Women in Revolt: The Land League Years', *Irish Historical Studies* 28, no. 109 (1992): 63–80.

Teichgraeber, Richard F., *'Free Trade' and Moral Philosophy: Rethinking the Sources of Adam Smith's Wealth of Nations* (Durham, NC: Duke University Press, 1986).

Teichgraeber, Richard F., *Sublime Thoughts/Penny Wisdom: Situating Emerson and Thoreau in the American Market* (Baltimore, MD: Johns Hopkins University Press, 1995).

Thomas, John L., *Alternative America: Henry George, Edward Bellamy, Henry Demarest Lloyd and the Adversary Tradition* (Cambridge, MA: Harvard University Press, 1983).

Thompson, Edward P., *Customs in Common: Studies in Traditional Popular Culture* (Pontypool: The Merlin Press, 1991).

Thompson, Edward P., 'Rough Music Reconsidered', *Folklore* 103, no. 1 (1992): 3–26.

Thompson, Edward P., *The Making of the English Working Class* [1963], (London: Penguin, 1981).

Thompson, Edward P., *The Poverty of Theory and Other Essays* (London: Merlin Press, 1978).

Tierney, Brian, 'Natural Law and Natural Rights: Old Problems and Recent Approaches', *The Review of Politics* 64, no. 3 (2002): 389–406.

Tierney, Brian, 'Permissive Natural Law and Property: Gratian to Kant', *Journal of the History of Ideas* 62, no. 3 (2001): 381–399.

Tierney, Brian, *The Idea of Natural Rights* (Grand Rapids, MI: William B. Eerdmans, 1997).

Townend, Paul A., 'Between Two Worlds: Irish Nationalists and Imperial Crisis, 1878–1880', *Past & Present* 194 (2007): 139–174.

Trachtenberg, Alan, *The Incorporation of America: Culture and Society in the Gilded Age* (New York: Hill and Wang, 1982).

Travers, Pauric, 'Reading between the Lines: The Political Speeches of Charles Stewart Parnell', *Studia Hibernica* 31 (2000): 243–256.

Trentmann, Frank, 'Wealth versus Welfare: The British Left between Free Trade and National Political Economy before the First World War', *Historical Research* 70, no. 171 (1997): 70–98.

Tuck, Richard, *Natural Rights Theories: Their Origin and Development* (Cambridge: Cambridge University Press, 1979).

Tully, James, *A Discourse on Property: John Locke and His Adversaries* (Cambridge: Cambridge University Press, 1980).

Turner, Michael, 'Output and Productivity in Irish Agriculture from the Famine to the Great War', *Irish Economic and Social History* 17 (1990): 62–78.

Twomey, Richard, *Jacobins and Jeffersonians: Anglo-American Radicalism in the United States, 1790–1820* (New York: Garland Publishing, 1989).

van Voss, Lex Heerma and Marcel van der Linden (eds.), *Class and Other Identities: Gender, Religion and Ethnicity in the Writing of European Labour History* (New York: Berghahn Books, 2002).

Varley, Tony, 'A Region of Sturdy Smallholders? Western Nationalist and Agrarian Politics during the First World War', *Journal of the Galway Archaeological and Historical Society* 55 (2003): 127–150.

Vaughan, William Edward (ed.), *A New History of Ireland, Volume V: Ireland under the Union, 1801–70* (Oxford: Oxford University Press, 1989).

Vaughan, William Edward (ed.), *A New History of Ireland, Volume VI: Ireland under the Union, 1870–1921* (Oxford: Oxford University Press, 1989).

Vaughan, William Edward, *Landlords and Tenants in Mid-Victorian Ireland* (Oxford: Oxford University Press, 1994).

Vincent, K. Steven, *Pierre-Joseph Proudhon and the Rise of French Republican Socialism* (New York: Oxford University Press, 1984).

Viner, Jacob, *Religious Thought and Economic Society: Four Chapters of an Unfinished Work,* Jacques Melitz, and Donald Winch (eds.), (Durham, NC: Duke University Press, 1978).

Vogel, Ursula, 'The Land-Question: A Liberal Theory of Communal Property', *History Workshop* 27 (1989): 106–135.

Voss, Kim, *The Making of American Exceptionalism: The Knights of Labor and Class Formation in the Nineteenth Century* (Ithaca, NY: Cornell University Press, 1993).
Walker, William M., 'Irish Immigrants in Scotland: Their Priests, Politics and Parochial Life', *The Historical Journal* 15, no. 4 (1972): 649–667.
Walsh, Victor A., 'A Fanatic Heart: The Cause of Irish American Nationalism in Pittsburgh during the Gilded Age', *Journal of Social History* 15, no. 2 (1981): 187–204.
Watt, Lewis, 'Henry George and the Ownership of Land', *Studies: An Irish Quarterly Review* 26, no. 101 (1937): 107–122.
Wei, Ian P., *Intellectual Culture in Medieval Paris: Theologians and the University c. 1100–1330* (Cambridge: Cambridge University Press, 2012).
Weir, Robert E., 'A Fragile Alliance: Henry George and the Knights of Labor', *American Journal of Economics and Sociology* 56, no. 4 (1997): 421–439.
Wenzer, Kenneth C. (ed.), *Henry George, the Transatlantic Irish, and Their Times* (Bingley: Emerald Group Publishing, 2009).
Wenzer, Kenneth C., 'Tolstoy's Georgist Spiritual Political Economy (1897–1910): Anarchism and Land Reform', *American Journal of Economics and Sociology* 56, no. 4 (1997): 639–667.
West, Edwin G., and Rik W. Hafer, 'J. S. Mill, Unions, and the Wage Fund Recantation: A Reinterpretation', *The Quarterly Journal of Economics* 92, no. 4 (1978): 603–619.
Whatmore, Richard, and Brian Young (ed.), *A Companion to Intellectual History* (Newark: Wiley, 2015).
Whelan, Kevin, *The Tree of Liberty: Radicalism, Catholicism and the Construction of Irish Identity, 1760–1830* (Cork: Cork University Press, 1996).
Whelehan, Niall, *Changing Land: Diaspora Activism and the Irish Land War* (New York: NYU Press, 2021).
Whelehan, Niall, 'Skirmishing, The Irish World, and Empire, 1876–86', *Éire-Ireland* 42, nos. 1–2 (2007): 180–200.
Whelehan, Niall, *The Dynamiters: Irish Nationalism and Political Violence in the Wider World, 1867–1900* (Cambridge: Cambridge University Press, 2012).
Widerquist, Karl and Grant S. McCall, *Prehistoric Myths in Modern Political Philosophy* (Edinburgh: Edinburgh University Press, 2017).
Wiebe, Robert H., *The Search for Order, 1877–1920* (New York: Hill and Wang, 1967).
Wightman, Andy, *The Poor Had No Lawyers: Who Owns Scotland (and How They Got It)* (Edinburgh: Birlinn, 2010).
Wilentz, Sean, 'Against Exceptionalism: Class Consciousness and the American Labor Movement, 1790–1920', *International Labor and Working-Class History* 26 (1984): 1–24.
Wilentz, Sean, *Chants Democratic: New York City & the Rise of the American Working Class, 1788–1850* (New York: Oxford University Press, 1984).
Wilentz, Sean, 'Industrializing America and the Irish: Towards the New Departure', *Labor History* 29, no. 4 (1979): 579–595.
Willems, Emilio, 'Peasantry and City: Cultural Persistence and Change in Historical Perspective, a European Case', *American Anthropologist* 72, no. 3 (1970): 528–544.
Williams, Raymond, *Culture and Materialism: Selected Essays* (London: Verso, 1980).
Williams, Raymond, *Keywords: A Vocabulary of Culture and Society* (London: Fourth Estate, 1976).
Williams, Raymond, *The Country and the City* [1973], (Nottingham: Spokesman, 2011).

Wilson, David A., *United Irishmen, United States: Immigrant Radicals in the Early American Republic* (Ithaca, NY: Cornell University Press, 1998).
Winch, Donald, 'Adam Smith: Scottish Moral Philosopher as Political Economist', *The Historical Journal* 35, no. 1 (1992): 91–113.
Winch, Donald, 'Darwin Fallen among Political Economists', *Proceedings of the American Philosophical Society* 145, no. 4 (2001): 415–437.
Winch, Donald, 'Economic Liberalism as Ideology: The Appleby Version', *The Economic History Review* 38, no. 2 (1985): 287–297.
Winch, Donald, *Riches and Poverty: An Intellectual History of Political Economy in Britain, 1750–1834* (Cambridge: Cambridge University Press, 1996).
Winch, Donald, and Patrick O'Brien (ed.), *The Political Economy of British Historical Experience, 1688–1914* (Oxford: Oxford University Press, 2002).
Wolfe, Willard, *From Radicalism to Socialism: Men and Ideas in the Formation of Fabian Socialist Doctrines, 1881–1889* (New Haven: Yale University Press, 1975).
Wolff, Jonathan, 'Libertarianism, Utility, and Economic Competition', *Virginia Law Review* 92, no. 7 (2006): 1605–1623.
Wood, Ian S., 'Irish Nationalism and Radical Politics in Scotland, 1880–1906', *Journal of the Scottish Labour History Society* 9 (1975): 21–38.
Wood, John D., 'Transatlantic Land Reform: America and the Crofters' Revolt, 1878–1888', *The Scottish Historical Review* 63, no. 175 (1984): 79–104.
Woods, Christopher J., 'The Politics of Cardinal McCabe, Archbishop of Dublin, 1879–85', *Dublin Historical Record* 26, no. 3 (1973): 101–110.
Yellen, Samuel, *American Labor Struggles* (New York: S. A. Russell, 1936).
Young, James D., 'The Irish Immigrants' Contribution to Scottish Socialism, 1880–1926', *Saothar: Journal of Irish Labour Studies* 13 (1988): 89–98.
Zastoupil, Lynn, 'Moral Government: J. S. Mill on Ireland', *The Historical Journal* 26, no. 3 (1983): 707–717.
Zinn, Howard, and Anthony Arnove (eds.), *Voices of a People's History of the United States* (New York: Seven Stories, 2004).
Zuckert, Michael P., *Natural Rights and the New Republicanism* (Princeton: Princeton University Press, 1994).

Unpublished Dissertations

Cunningham, Miriam Ann, 'A Thomistic Appraisal of the Philosophy of Henry George' (MA diss., Catholic University of America, 1950).
Donnelly, James F., 'Catholic New Yorkers and New York Socialists, 1870–1920' (PhD diss., New York University, 1982).
Frame, John R., 'America and the Scottish Left: The Impact of American Ideas on the Scottish Labour Movement from the American Civil War to the end of World War One' (PhD diss., University of Aberdeen, 1998).
Gordon, Michael A., 'Studies in Irish and Irish American Thought and Behaviour in Gilded Age New York City' (PhD diss., University of Rochester, 1977).
Green, James J., 'The Impact of Henry George's Theories on American Catholics' (PhD diss., University of Notre Dame, 1956).
O'Donnell, Edward T., '"Henry George and the New Political Forces": Ethnic Nationalism, Labor Radicalism and Politics in Gilded Age New York City' (PhD diss., Columbia University, 1995).

Index

Printed by Printforce, United Kingdom